Designing Successful Transitions:

A Guide for Orienting Students to College

3rd Edition

Jeanine A. Ward-Roof, Editor

NODA
National Orientation Directors Association

National Resource Center for
The First-Year Experience®
& Students in Transition
UNIVERSITY OF SOUTH CAROLINA
2010

Cite as:

Ward-Roof, J. A. (2010). *Designing successful transitions: A guide for orienting students to college* (Monograph No. 13, 3rd ed.). Columbia, SC: University of South Carolina, National Resource Center for The First-Year Experience and Students in Transition.

Sample chapter citation:

Rode, D. L., & Cawthon, T. W. (2010). Theoretical perspectives on orientation. In J. A. Ward-Roof (Ed.), *Designing successful transitions: A guide for orienting students to college* (Monograph No. 13, 3rd ed., pp. 11-28). Columbia, SC: University of South Carolina, National Resource Center for The First-Year Experience and Students in Transition.

ISBN 978-1-889-27169-9

The First-Year Experience® is a service mark of the University of South Carolina. A license may be granted upon written request to use the term "The First-Year Experience." This license is not transferable without written approval of the University of South Carolina.

Production Staff for the National Resource Center:

Project Manager	Tracy L. Skipper, Assistant Director for Publications
Project Editor	Dottie Weigel, Editor
Design and Production	Shana Bertetto, Graphic Artist

Additional copies of this monograph may be obtained from the National Resource Center for The First-Year Experience and Students in Transition, University of South Carolina, 1728 College Street, Columbia, SC 29208. Telephone (803) 777-6229. Fax (803) 777-4699.

Library of Congress Cataloging-in-Publication Data

Designing successful transitions : A guide for orienting students to college/ Jeanine A. Ward-Roof, editor. -- 3rd ed.
    p. cm. -- (The first-year experience monograph series ; no. 13)
  Includes bibliographical references.
  ISBN 978-1-889271-69-9
  1. College student orientation--United States. 2. College freshmen--United States. I. Ward-Roof, Jeanine A. II. National Resource Center for the First-Year Experience & Students in Transition (University of South Carolina)
  LB2343.32.D47 2010
  378.1'98--dc22
                    2010032083

Contents

Part I: Establishing the Rationale for Orientation Programs

Chapter 1

Chapter 2

Chapter 3

Part II: Organizing Orientation Programs

Part III: Serving the Needs of All Students in Orientation

Chapter 13

Part IV: Institutionalizing and Sustaining Orientation Programs

Chapter 14

Chapter 15

Chapter 16

Tables and Figures

Preface

Orientation means finding your place and knowing the direction you want to move in as you face a new situation, environment, or experience. I once belonged to a volunteer organization that did not have a formal or informal orientation program for new members. My first year with the group was frustrating for I did not know and understand the folkways and mores of the organization. Through observation and discussions with more experienced members, I finally learned my way within the organization; but it was a frustrating process for me and I am sure it also was for other more experienced members of the organization. That experience reinforced a valuable lesson for me. Taking time to orient new members of the community is time well spent.

For students contemplating entering institutions of higher education, orientation programs are designed to provide sufficient information and support so that each person can make the appropriate choices to meet his or her needs and goals. Yet, orientation programs are unique because, in contrast to most programs and services in higher education, they focus primarily on those who are not yet enrolled in the institution sponsoring the program. To be sure, there are extended orientation programs, first-year seminars and the like, but they are all built on the foundation of orientation programs for admitted, but not yet enrolled students and their families. For some of these prospective students, involvement in an orientation program cements the commitment they have made to enter higher education. For others, participation in orientation and transition programs helps ease the anxiety of entering a new learning environment. For still others, it is a means to ensure that they will complete the necessary hurdles for course selection and registration for the new academic term. An individual chooses to participate in orientation programs for many reasons, but the central goal is to help him or her transition from being a high school student, a community college student, a person who has been involved in the world of work, or a person with a specific educational need to a student at an institution of higher education. That transition is not always easy or without challenges for the individual involved, yet orientation programs help ease the process, building bridges from one life stage to another.

The prospective students that orientation programs serve are changing in important and significant ways, and orientation programs must accommodate those changes. Veterans, for example, are returning from combat zones to the classroom in ever-increasing numbers and orientation and transition programs need to be prepared to deal with these new learners who have already faced so much in their lives. The economy has also brought a new wave of potential learners to higher education—those seeking job-related certification or skills for career advancement or career change. These new learners will pose significant challenges as orientation and transition programs attempt to develop and market programs to students who may feel they already know what the collegiate experience is all about. But as all of us associated with higher education know, institutions as well as individuals change and transform over time and even returning students with knowledge of higher education can benefit from an orientation program designed to help them be successful in this new environment.

Orientation programs also are unique within higher education because these programs serve individuals who have no intention of enrolling in the institution—that is, the family members of prospective students. For traditionally aged students, orientation programs focus on parents or guardians. For nontraditional students, there is a growing emphasis on outreach to other family members who will be affected by the enrollment of the prospective student in higher education, such as spouses, partners, and children. For families, college enrollment brings change, and assistance is sometimes needed to help all family members cope with the challenges that may come with that change.

Providing quality orientation programs seems deceptively simple. All the orientation professional has to do is identify the essential information prospective students need and provide an easy and useful way for students to access and absorb the information. For those professionals involved in orientation, however, the process is far from simple and the choices of how to best provide assistance to prospective students and their families are many. For example, orientation and retention programs present and explain the values, expectations, and purpose of the institution to prospective students. Anyone involved in orientation programs knows first-hand that the number of requests from departments, programs, and people to present their program, service, or expectation to new students grows each year. Thus, an essential responsibility of orientation professionals is sorting out which of these messages are critical to hear prior to enrollment and which might be better received during the first term on campus.

Investment in quality orientation programs is money well spent by an institution of higher education. However, convictions must be supported by data. Assessment, evaluation, research, and outcome measures are essential components of orientation, and financial and human resources must be sufficiently allocated to support these components. Assessment data are invaluable in identifying the changing needs of students and in adapting programs and services to better meet those needs. Such data will also be critical in securing and maintaining resources to support orientation and transition programs and activities. Thus, high-quality assessment is another challenge facing orientation professionals.

As a student affairs professional, I have always found that I learn a great deal from the wisdom and experience of other professionals. This monograph, written by professionals for professionals, is designed to help student affairs administrators navigate the challenges in providing high-quality orientation and transition initiatives. I am confident that you will find it helpful to you as you examine your own orientation and transition programs to ensure that they continue to meet the needs of prospective students and their families.

Although the content of your programs and the participants they serve may change and evolve over time, your essential goal of helping prospective students make a successful transition into an institution of higher education remains the same. Make good use of this monograph. Write to the authors and let them know whether you agree with what they have said. For it is through such dialogue that our shared profession continues to grow and flourish.

I wish all of you the best as you help students make this important journey.

Margaret J. Barr
Professor Emeritus
School of Education and Social Policy
Retired, Vice President for Student Affairs
Northwestern University

Foreword

We are pleased to introduce the third edition of *Designing Successful Transitions: A Guide for Orienting Students to College*. The original edition of this monograph was published in 1993 as a partnership between the National Orientation Directors Association (NODA) and the National Resource Center for The Freshman Year Experience (now the National Resource Center for The First-Year Experience and Students in Transition). Given the similarity of our organizations' values and core commitments, the collaboration on that volume was a wonderful complement of ideas and charting of a vision for orientation programs, success in the first year of college, and higher education at large. The second edition, published in 2003, allowed our respective organizations to work together again to consider how orientation and the field of higher education had evolved and changed.

We are delighted to collaborate on another edition of this monograph, which once again affords us the opportunity to reflect on what has changed in higher education, especially in the 17 years since the original edition of this monograph was published. As predicted by M. Lee Upcraft in his prologue to the second edition of this monograph, titled "Reflections on the Future of Orientation," the passage of time has also brought about new opportunities and concerns in our field as well as new tools and resources to address them. To that end, the 2010 edition addresses many topics (e.g., administration of orientation programs, family involvement, student characteristics and needs, assessment, and orientation for specific student populations and institutional types) that were included in previous editions but approaches them with new information, updated data, and current theory. However, this edition also takes up new topics in response to the "opportunities and concerns" facing orientation, transition, and retention professionals such as collaborations among campus units in the development and delivery of orientation, the increase in nontraditional student populations, the need for effective crisis planning and management in orientation programs, new technologies, and even the challenge of making the case for orientation in an era of diminishing resources. The authors have carefully penned chapters incorporating contemporary information, ideas, and concepts while being reflective of traditional practices. Whether you are new to the field or have years of experience, this monograph should serve as a valuable, professional resource.

As with any publication of this magnitude, there are numerous individuals who worked to produce the final product. We are grateful to each author who dedicated the time, energy, and passion to the success of this publication, to Jeanine Ward-Roof for serving as the editor, and to Tracy Skipper with the National Resource Center for her management of the project. We are confident that you will enjoy and benefit from this valuable resource and use the content contained herein to help shape the next era of research, policy, and practice on student orientation to colleges and universities.

For more than 20 years, NODA and the National Resource Center have worked together to provide resources about the orientation, transition, and retention of college and university students. As we reflect on our ongoing collaboration, we are also excited about what lies ahead for our field and look forward to your contributions to the future of orientation and first-year programming.

Jennifer R. Keup, Director
National Resource Center for The First-Year Experience and Students in Transition

Craig E. Mack, President
National Orientation Directors Association

Notes on the Third Edition

The third edition of *Designing Successful Transitions: A Guide for Orienting Students to College* continues a successful collaboration between the National Orientation Directors Association and the National Resource Center for The First-Year Experience and Students in Transition. Once again, the work of many individuals resulted in the creation of a valuable resource for orientation, transition, and retention professionals.

The first and second editions of the monograph were created to close the gap in the literature and to offer orientation, transition, and retention professionals support, guidance, and resources for their work. The third edition of *Designing Successful Transitions* updates and expands the treatment of issues addressed in earlier editions while offering insights into student populations, university and college environments, and expectations for the orientation process. This edition also introduces three new chapters including one on planning for and managing crises; a second on making the case for orientation; and a third on collaboration in orientation programs with a special focus on campus culture, politics, and power. New and experienced professionals alike will find this monograph to be a comprehensive resource for orientation program development on college and university campuses.

Orientation, transition, and retention professionals are faced with managing the trends and issues that shape the development and implementation of transition programs for new students and their families. These trends include increasing levels of student and parent consumerism, rising expectations for accountability, increasing diversity of students, a growing need for all levels of crisis management, increasing demands for the use and availability of technology, and expanding parental involvement. At the same time, orientation professionals must meet these challenges amid decreasing levels of financial and human resources. The authors of this monograph offer insights on how orientation professionals can effectively address and, in some cases, assume leadership for responding to these issues. Many of the authors are current practitioners and NODA members who encounter the same challenges as readers of this monograph; therefore, their insights are especially applicable. Coupled with this relevant information, the authors also share their thoughts on current practice and resources in each chapter gained through their involvement in NODA and other professional experiences.

Throughout this publication, professionals will find helpful examples of orientation and transition services from a wide range of institution types. The chapters also draw heavily on the literature that supports orientation programs, describes current student populations, and identifies current trends. Additionally, the themes and concepts presented in the chapters are supported by student development theory, current research on students and transition issues, and national standards for practice.

To help the reader digest the information presented, the monograph is divided into four sections. Part I establishes the rationale for orientation programs. Craig Mack authored the first chapter, which offers an overview of the history, purpose, and goals orientation and transition programs. In chapter 2, Denise Rode and Tony Cawthon highlight theories relevant to orientation and offer a comprehensive discussion of how the theories can be applied in practice. The third chapter includes an analysis by Bonita Jacobs focusing on the necessity of and means to make a case for orientation on campuses across North America.

Part II focuses on the organization of orientation programs. In chapter 4, April Mann, Charlie Andrews, and Norma Rodenburg describe best practices for administering and implementing programs and discuss a variety of considerations including the timing of programs, fees, and staffing. In chapter 5, Cathy Cuevas and Christine Timmerman compile a plethora of resources on community college practices for assessing institution environments and building programming. I joined colleagues Laura Page and Ryan Lombardi in chapter 6 to discuss how to best meet the needs of parents and family members in an orientation program as well as how to channel parental influences toward a shared goal of student success. Chapter 7 by Tracy Skipper, Jennifer Latino, Blaire Moody Rideout, and Dorothy Weigel offers readers an exploration of extending the benefits of orientation through outdoor experience programs, community service, common reading initiatives, and first-year seminars. In chapter 8, J.J. Brown and Cynthia Hernandez add an overview of the impact of technology on orientation programs and best practices for implementation. In the conclusion to this section, Dian Squire, Victor Wilson, Joe Ritchie, and Abbey Wolfman offer their insights on how to manage crises in orientation.

Part III of the monograph focuses on the needs of and best practices for serving specific student populations. Chapter 10, written by Maureen Wilson and Michael Dannells, anchors this section by providing an analysis of today's college students while, in chapter 11, Archie Cubarrubia and Jennifer Schoen offer insight into the needs of diverse student populations along with a developmental framework for serving these students. Shandol Hoover reviews the needs and best practice associated with transfer populations in chapter 12, and Michael Knox and Brittany Henderson offer their insights about working with nontraditional students in chapter 13.

The last section (Part IV) of the monograph addresses strategies for institutionalizing orientation. Beth Lingren Clark and Matthew Weigand lead this section in chapter 14, offering readers a better understanding of collaboration in orientation by focusing on culture, politics, and power. Robert Schwartz and Dennis Wiese outline the importance of evaluation and assessment in implementing successful orientation programs and offer the readers a process for completing such activities in chapter 15. Chapter 16, written by me and Kathy Guthrie, shares the sagacity of nine seasoned professionals' reflection on the topics of how orientation and students have changed during their careers, predictions for the future of orientation, and advice for professionals.

I am grateful for the contributions the authors; editors; reviewers; NODA Board members; and National Resource Center staff, especially Tracy Skipper, made to this publication. Thanks to each of you for the time, energy, and patience you committed to this project. Due to all of these efforts, I believe orientation professionals will find this edition of the monograph to be an incredible resource for their work.

Jeanine A. Ward-Roof
Florida State University
March 2010

PART I:

Establishing the Rationale for Orientation Programs

Chapter 1

A Brief Overview of the Orientation, Transition, and Retention Field

Craig E. Mack

First-year students, many being of traditional age (18 - 22 years old), are at developmental crossroads in their lives and need a relevant, academic introduction to their college experience (Pascarella & Terenzini, 1991). An orientation program can provide such an introduction for new students and contribute positively to their transition. Because orientation and new student programs provide students with an opportunity to determine institutional fit (Rentz & Saddlemire, 1988), it may also serve as the signal event where new students finalize their decisions about enrollment. This chapter sets the groundwork for the remaining chapters in the monograph by providing a brief history of orientation, exploring the purpose and goals of orientation programs, and discussing benchmarking and data trends.

Brief History of Orientation

Higher education in the United States has evolved from a single private institution in 1636 (i.e., Harvard College) to more than 4,500 public, private, and proprietary institutions nearly four centuries later. During this time, efforts to welcome new students and help them make the transition to higher education have become an important part of the mission of postsecondary institutions. As with much of the profession of student affairs, orientation and new student programs have been influenced by the ever-changing landscape of higher education (Komives, Woodard, & Associates, 2003).

Orientation, as a function, has a rich history in American higher education. Boston University is credited with organizing the first orientation program in 1888 to acquaint new students with college life, and the University of Maine is credited with hosting the first freshman week in 1923 (Packwood, 1977). These introductory programs come from a need for faculty to help students understand the role of a student at a particular institution. Documentation about the evolution of orientation in the early part of the 20th century is limited. Prior to the 1920s, faculty members assumed responsibility for welcoming students with informal gatherings on campus. These small gatherings of new students often occurred within smaller areas, often residential settings, across the campus. These forums were used to indoctrinate new students into the college and to conduct basic transactions that needed to occur prior to the start of classes, such as, helping new students get settled in their residences, signing up for classes, and learning about institutional traditions and faculty roles. Upperclass students were also a part of these efforts for new students. Convocation programs served as an opportunity to bring all new students together at one time to offer an official welcome and set the tone for new students becoming full members of the scholarly community.

Between 1920 and 1940, more than 100 institutions were coordinating orientation-related efforts. This era marked the beginning of more formal orientation programs managed by institutional administration. Because few professionals at institutions were solely concerned with student affairs practice prior to the 1950s (Komives et al., 2003), student services were largely handled by faculty or other academic professionals. However, as orientation programs emerged, the responsibility for coordinating such programs shifted to student affairs personnel allowing faculty members the opportunity to focus on the classroom and course content. Thus, orientation planning was often coordinated by the dean of men. As an administrator, the dean of men, operating *in loco parentis,* was also responsible for student discipline. Throughout the 1960s and 1970s, orientation programs became a college-wide effort as the material covered spanned services and resources from across the institution. Orientation, transition, and retention-related efforts became an integral part of higher education administration (Tinto, 1993).

A quality orientation program considers students' development and delivers information, content, and challenges for students accordingly. For example, student affairs professionals often design new student programs to serve as an introduction to distinct community values and to set high expectations of students during their tenure at the institution (Kuh, Schuh, Whitt, & Associates, 1991). Cubarrubia, a senior analyst at the U. S. Department of Education, asserts,

> [O]rientation is an intentional set of developmentally appropriate programs delivered in a systematic timeline and designed to integrate students into the academic and social fabric of the campus community; as gatekeepers to institutional culture and context, orientation programs promote student success and development. (personal communication, October 30, 2008)

As such, stakeholders from all areas of the campus soon realized that they also had a vested interest in ensuring that new students learned about their resources during orientation. Hence, orientation programs designed with the purposes of addressing students' successful transition and retention have become increasingly important to the entire institution.

Realizing the importance of new students' transition, orientation slowly became what might be considered a movement in higher education. Coordinators and directors of orientation programs first met in 1948 in Columbus, Ohio. At this initial gathering of what would become the National Orientation Directors Association (NODA), participants discussed shared experiences and best practices about orientation and new student programs. This meeting of professionals proved helpful in spreading effective practices to support students' successful transition to college. However, little comprehensive research was being conducted on orientation-specific efforts and their benefits.

To address the lack of research on orientation efforts, NODA chartered the *Databank* in 1979 to help professionals compare their institutions' programs with those at other institutions and to consider changes in the field. This publication proved valuable in lending credence to professional work related to the areas of orientation and student transition. Data are gathered, compiled, and published every three to five years by the professional association. The information has proven useful for determining best practices; it has also allowed professionals to gauge their institution's growth and the impact of their work in orientation and transition, as well as retention. In fact, it is through the gathering of these data that NODA professionals expanded their work to include more transition and retention-related initiatives.

In 1979, NODA became a charter member of the Council for the Advancement of Standards in Higher Education (CAS, 2003). CAS provides a forum for the student affairs profession to establish standards of practice similar to those that accrediting bodies and disciplinary associations have established for academic programs. Orientation standards were developed to provide a comprehensive set of criteria for institutions to create, or modify, and evaluate their orientation programs (CAS). The standards and guidelines have utility for institutions of all types and sizes and include resources on assessment, student development, and learning outcomes. CAS also developed *Self-Assessment Guides* for institutions to evaluate their programs. Chapter 4 provides further discussion on the Council for the Advancement of Standards as well as information on orientation goals and how these goals add structure to the programs accordingly. NODA's *Databank* and CAS' orientation standards certainly lent more credence to orientation, transition, and retention as a profession and provided a foundation for future research endeavors.

Purpose, Goals, and Outcomes of Orientation

Orientation programs help new students get acquainted with their learning community and educate them about college resources to ensure their academic and social success. As the orientation movement evolved, professionals asked, what makes an orientation an orientation? It is not just the transactions before classes, but also the coordinated efforts to introduce students to their new environment in a way that is seamless and meaningful to them. This requires careful planning and implementation while considering the nuances of an institution. Orientation professionals create an intentional experience that demonstrates to a new student the interrelationship among the college's various departments and how he or she fits in. College orientation programs encapsulate the essence of their institutions by introducing new students to the academic life, culture, traditions, history, people, and surrounding communities. The goal is to provide individuals with a holistic view of the new college experience. At the same time, it sets expectations for students' responsibilities in their academic career. A positive experience during orientation helps prospective students make that conclusive determination about their college choice. In the 1980s and 1990s as orientation was tied more to retention efforts at colleges and universities, these programs were described as the need to create a staying environment for students (Noel, Levitz, Saluri, & Associates, 1986; Tinto, 1993). Orientation as a college-wide endeavor was becoming a more refined process for administrators. Institutional administrators quickly realized the value of an orientation program. The upfront investment to retain students was more than worth the cost of replacing a student lost through attrition.

While offering a formal introduction to the institution, the primary objective of an orientation program is to familiarize students to academic and behavioral expectations, education programs, and the student life of the institution. Seminal researchers Noel et al. (1986) suggest orientation programs are necessary to offer assistance to new students during the initial adjustment period. Yet, determining students' needs and delivering an orientation program to meet those needs is a complex endeavor. Originally, orientation programs were designed to meet students' needs as perceived by institutions rather than as identified by students (MacKinnon, 2004). However, it was not long before administrators realized that it was vital to take an inventory of students' needs from the students themselves. Covering basic preparatory items was not enough for new students. They wanted to know where to meet with their friends, how to use academic support resources such as the library, and where to eat and socialize. Administrators learned that it was important to create integrated student learning experiences (MacKinnon). They also realized that students would leave the institution if they were not happy or if they felt that they did not fit in, whether or not they were succeeding academically. Therefore, it was imperative that institutions develop opportunities for student adjustment and involvement through educational and social programs

(Kuh et al., 1991). Thus, identifying goals that facilitate students' transitions and delivering a program that tends to students' general needs and expectations are vital aspects of an orientation program. It is important to note that this type of program also creates a foundation for students' further development as they progress through their academic career. It is unrealistic to anticipate the perceptions and expectations of every new student, yet each institution has an obligation to provide a general overview of the educational environment students might expect to experience during their tenure.

The adjustment period may be the first week of classes or continue through the first semester. Therefore, orientation has become a critical part of institutions' enrollment management and retention plans. Professional literature and organizations continue to identify the value of orientation programs as the key to accountability for both the institution and the student. The Association of American Colleges and Universities (AAC&U, 2008) notes, "Orientation should be provided for the student during the first year about the institution's expectations for important learning outcomes, benchmark assessments of each student's demonstrated accomplishment, and expected further progress in relation to these outcomes should be made" (p. 8). See chapter 15 for information on assessment and learning outcomes of orientation.

A student's integration into a college or university can be multi-faceted with a successful orientation program breaking the institution down into manageable parts and helping students navigate their new community in a way that also supports their personal and academic development.

Trends in Orientation Programs

As noted earlier, the NODA *Databank* serves as a repository for the collection and comparison of orientation-related data from participating institutions, which has proven to be useful as a research tool and a practical aid in program planning and improvement. Each version of the *Databank* consists of data compiled through a series of approximately 40 questions organized in categories that reflect the various aspects of planning, implementation, and outcomes of orientation programs. The categories include: institutional characteristics; coordination of orientation programs; staffing structure; orientation program type; parent involvement; fees and funding; introductory courses; special programs; and a miscellaneous category that allows for new initiatives such as technology, common book, faculty participation, and assessment tools. Practitioners using information from the *Databank* can identify changes and new initiatives in the field.

While the *Databank* categories have remained fairly stable through the years, questions have been added or modified as changes in orientation programs were noted by participants. For example, technology, orientation program type, parent participation, and funding were all questions in the *Databank*; however, additional questions have been added that allowed the *Databank* user to better understand how these areas impact program planning. For example, the use of audiovisuals now relates to various uses of multimedia, and orientation program type now has many different options, from a single day or multiple days in the summer to a program that is offered immediately prior to the start of classes. Data were originally gathered via mailed questionnaires, but more recently the *Databank* has moved to an online survey for NODA member institutions. The information below provides data at a glance as well as a brief narrative of some of the variety and innovation in programs over the past 28 years.

Table 1.1 provides an overview of participating institutions since the 1979-1980 administration. Over a span of 28 years, 21 institutions—18 public, four-year institutions and three private, four-year institutions—participated in the *Databank* series, allowing for the documentation of possible trends in the field. These institutions are fairly representative of the general NODA membership. For convenience, this group of institutions will be referred to as the longitudinal data set in the discussion below.

Table 1.1

Overview of Databank Participation

Year	Number of Participating Institutions			
	Total	Small (5,000 or less)	Medium (5,000 - 15,000)	Large (15,000+)
1979-1980	282	163	89	50
1986-1987	272	149	94	29
1990-1991	352	179	112	61
1995-1997	461	245	140	76
2000-2001	278	128	83	48
2007-2008	314	88	110	116

Mandatory vs. Volunteer Participation

The 1979-1980 version of the *Databank* did not ask whether orientation was voluntary or mandatory. In 1986-1987, more than one third of the institutions declared that participation in the institution's orientation was mandatory. In 2007-2008, almost three fourths of the institutions required participation in orientation for their students. This is consistent with a trend in the longitudinal data set. In the 1980s, 30% of these institutions indicated that their orientation programs were mandatory compared to 60% in the 2000s. Thus, it appears that institutions may be moving toward mandatory orientations.

Participation Rates

Small institutions (5,000 or less) experienced the biggest increase in orientation attendance. In 1979-1980, approximately 60% of students attended an orientation program; in 2007-2008, approximately 90% of students participated in an orientation program. Medium institutions (5,000-15,000) and large institutions (15,000+) experienced a moderate increase from 78% and 88%, respectively, to 90% attendance. Within the longitudinal data set, 18 institutions reported that their attendance rates at orientation increased during this same time period. Three institutions reported that their attendance decreased; participation in orientation was voluntary for students at two of these institutions. Thus, increasing participation in orientation may be partly a function of the trend toward mandatory programs.

Transfer Students

Transfer students accounted for less than half the participation in orientation for all types of institutions in 1979-1980. In 2007-2008, nearly all participating institutions had approximately 70% of their transfer students attending an orientation program. Chapter 12 includes further information on transfer students and transfer orientation programs.

Orientation Program Type

In 1979-1980, approximately one third of all institutions, regardless of size, offered orientation programs during the summer; more than 70% of the institutions offered summer orientation programs in 2007-2008. Other institutions offered single-day and/or multi-day orientation programs that occurred immediately preceding the fall semester. Whether or not an institution offered an orientation program during the summer, many institutions offered a welcome week activity for their students as an additional experience. This is consistent with the trend identified by the longitudinal data set. In the 1980s, the primary delivery mode for an orientation was a single-day orientation program scheduled immediately prior to the beginning of classes. Twenty institutions now offer a multi-day orientation program during the summer and the fall.

Professional Staff

Consistently, individual staff members at smaller institutions handle orientation in addition to other duties or functions. Meanwhile, at medium and large institutions, the role for coordinating orientation programs was identified as a staff member's primary responsibility.

Faculty Participation in Orientation

In 1979-1980, fewer than half of institutions reported that faculty members were involved in orientation programs. According to 2007-2008 data, 95% of institutions reported having faculty involvement; 53% indicated that faculty members were "very involved" to "somewhat involved." This is consistent with the trend identified by the longitudinal data set, which clearly indicated an increase in faculty involvement in orientation over the past three decades. Faculty involvement in orientation was noted in a number of ways (e.g., academic advising, presenting academic curricula, and participating in parent orientation).

Introductory/First-Year Course

Consistently, there has been an increase in the number of institutions that offer a first-year seminar course for credit; approximately 35% of institutions in 1979-1980 and more than 70% of institutions in 2000 offered this type of course. This is borne out by information from the longitudinal data set. None of the institutions reported offering a seminar course in the 1979-1980 edition of the *Databank*, while 60% reported offering a seminar course in the 2000-2001. Chapter 7 offers further information on extended orientation and first-year programs.

Common Reading Program

A new inquiry was introduced in the mid-1990s, exploring whether institutions offered a common reading program or book initiative for their new students. In 1995-1997, fewer than one fourth of institutions offered this type of program. In 2007-2008, nearly 37% of all institutions offered a common reading program as part of their orientation-related activities. Common reading initiatives are discussed in greater depth in chapter 7.

Parent Programs

Opportunities for parents to participate in orientation have been prevalent for some time as noted in the 1979-1980 *Databank*; more than 50% of the institutions participating noted that they offered some type of parent orientation program. In 2007-2008, 96% of institutions reported offering a parent orientation program. Responses from the longitudinal data set seem to confirm this trend. All but four institutions offered a parent orientation program in the 1980s; by 1995, all 21 institutions offered a parent orientation program. Thus, parent programs appear to have been an important component of orientation for the past three decades. Chapter 6 provides further information on parent orientation programs.

Other Programs

Additional innovations mentioned over the past 28 years have evolved into larger program components for many institutions. These included specialized orientation programs for international students, younger siblings, transfer students, and commuter students. Some institutions have created affinity groups developed around students' hobbies, interests, or identity. Other institutions have developed learning communities around similar themes.

Orientation and transition programs have consistently used technology as a dynamic medium to engage students. However, multimedia and technology use in 1979-1980 meant using 8mm film and slide projectors. In 2007-2008, technology and multimedia were incorporated into many facets of programs whereby students could be fully engaged in orientation, whether they participated online or in person. Many institutions now offer online orientation programs for new students blending the latest developments in interactive and social networking technologies. This concept will continue to impact the delivery of orientation and transition programs and services to new students.

Conclusion

Orientation programs have made important gains in the last century. Orientation research and best practices have made an impact in higher education by shifting orientation from an informal welcome program for new students to an organized profession. Colleges and universities serve as independent agents and stewards for education and civic and community engagement allowing students growth opportunities contributing to their own success. Increasingly, regional accrediting agencies have identified the value of orientation and transition programs, cautioning those institutions without structured programs and celebrating those with well-developed ones. As orientation programs have been linked to student retention, it has been increasingly important for them to be a part of the accreditation process. Meanwhile, orientation is often the catalyst for institutional accountability concerning compliance. Consequently, precautionary information such as student responsibilities, crime statistics, and safety are incorporated into new student programs.

An orientation program generally involves the efforts of many departments (e.g., academic, including faculty members; business; and student affairs) and their corresponding staff members. Many academic support and engagement departments use orientation as a venue to market their services to students. This allows students to see presentations, receive brochures, and tour various campus buildings that house these resources.

It is imperative to find the delicate balance between students' transitional needs, institutional responsibility, and appropriate accountability by providing a thorough orientation program to allow for students' successful transitions during their first year of college. The profession will continue to grow and contribute to student success and assist institutions in providing appropriate transition services to the ever-changing college student population. In order to appropriately document the contributions and impact of these programs, evaluation, assessment, and scholarly work must be a vital part of practitioners' professional work in orientation, retention, and transition.

References

Association of American Colleges and Universities (AAC&U). (2008). *Our students' best work: A framework for accountability worthy of our mission* (2nd ed.). Washington, DC: Author.

Council for the Advancement of Standards in Higher Education (CAS). (2003). *The CAS book of professional standards for higher education*. Washington, DC: Author.

Komives, S. R., Woodard, D. B., & Associates. (2003). *Student services: A handbook for the profession*. San Francisco: Jossey-Bass.

Kuh, G. D., Schuh, J. H., Whitt, E. J., & Associates. (1991). *Involving colleges: Successful approaches to fostering student learning and development outside the classroom*. San Francisco: Jossey-Bass.

MacKinnon, F. J. D. (Ed.). (2004). *Rentz's student affairs practice in higher education* (3rd ed.). Springfield, IL: Charles C. Thomas.

Noel, L., Levitz, R., Saluri, D., & Associates. (1986). *Increasing student retention*. San Francisco: Jossey-Bass.

Packwood, W. T. (1977). *College student personnel services*. Springfield, IL: Charles C. Thomas.

Pascarella, E. T., & Terenzini, P. T. (1991). *How college affects students*. San Francisco: Jossey-Bass.

Rentz, A. L., & Saddlemire, G. L. (1988). *Student affairs functions in higher education*. Springfield, IL: Charles C. Thomas.

Tinto, V. (1993). *Leaving college: Rethinking the causes and cures of student attrition* (2nd ed.). Chicago: University of Chicago Press.

Chapter 2

Theoretical Perspectives on Orientation

Denise L. Rode and Tony W. Cawthon

Nevitt Sanford (1967), one of the earliest writers to examine how students change in college, described development as "the organization of increasing complexity" (p. 47). Similarly, Miller and Prince (1976) defined student development as "the application of human development concepts in postsecondary settings so that everyone involved can master increasingly complex developmental tasks, achieve self-direction, and become interdependent" (p. 3). More recently, Evans, Forney, Guido, Patton, and Renn (2010) defined development as a "positive growth process in which the individual becomes increasingly able to integrate and act on many different experiences and influences" (p. 6). While developmental theories provide insight into this increasing complexity, Knefelkamp, Widick, and Parker (1978) also noted that theories offer educators "ways of organizing our thinking about students, suggestions for areas for exploration, and keys to insights about possible courses of action" (p. xiv).

The Council for the Advancement of Standards in Higher Education (2006) calls for the inclusion student learning and development in the missions of orientation programs. At the heart of this emphasis on learning and development is a concern for the whole student, encompassing intellectual, physical, interpersonal, social, and spiritual dimensions. Having a foundational understanding of student development theories, models, and concepts—and knowledge of how to apply them—is essential to good practice in orientation. Further, the application of student development theories to orientation and transition programs must reflect this holistic emphasis.

Both informal and formal theories guide practice in orientation. Orientation professionals use practical experience, assumptions, presumptions, and biases—informal theories—to guide their work with numerous new students and their families. Yet, informal theories have their limitations. For example, informal theory is not self-correcting (Parker, 1977), and practitioners may not be able to claim more than anecdotal evidence to explain student behavior.

Formal theories, on the other hand, have been validated by quantitative, qualitative, or mixed-methods research and provide a framework for explaining relationships among variables and for empirically testing hypotheses. DiCaprio (1975) stated that formal theory is used to describe, explain, predict, and control student growth or experiences. McEwen (2003a) added two more uses of theory: (a) the generation of new knowledge and (b) the research and assessment of practice. While Parker (1979) acknowledged the tension between the use of formal and informal theories, he suggested that both are ultimately necessary for effective practice:

Formal theory building and testing is the means of increasing our knowledge of student development in general.... However, just as it is formal theory that advances the body of knowledge for a professional field, it is the informal theories which each person constructs that make it possible to practice. (p. 421)

This chapter is designed to help orientation professionals examine both theory and practice and begins with a general overview of formal theories of student development, emphasizing those most widely used in orientation and transition programs. It also examines campus environment and typological models that may be useful to the orientation professional. We conclude with a theory-to-practice model to demonstrate how theoretical knowledge informs actual orientation practice.

Categories of Student Development Theories

This chapter explores four general categories of student development theories and models: (a) psychosocial, (b) cognitive structural, (c) typology models, and (d) person-environment interaction models. Each family of theories represents a unique perspective on student experience, sharing basic assumptions and using similar constructs to describe that experience. The clusters often complement each other in their view of development, providing a rich picture of student growth and learning.

The focus on college student development emerged during the 1960s and 1970s, and several of the theories described in this chapter date from this period. As noted by Dannells and Wilson (2003), these theorists sought to answer such questions as: How do college students grow and change? What factors most influence those processes? How do college environments affect students and their development? In the 1980s, theorists shifted their attention toward challenging and filling in the "theoretical gaps" of earlier theories that did not address the development process of subpopulations, including women; international students; students from various racial and ethnic groups; older students; and gay, lesbian, bisexual, transgendered, questioning (GLBTQ) students.

In using theory in our work with students, we realize that no single theory or model is adequate. Effective professionals should be knowledgeable about both early foundational theories and emerging theories to understand the influences of gender, race, culture, ethnicity, sexual orientation, age, and other factors on students' development. Pope, Reynolds, and Mueller (2004) concluded that multiculturally sensitive professionals must:

◇ Commit themselves to deep study of theory, learning enough about them to "wrestle with their underlying meaning and values"
◇ Stay current with student affairs literature and attempt to fill gaps in their knowledge base
◇ See the "complexity of growth and change as an ongoing process rather than as a destination." (pp. 43-44)

Readers are encouraged to keep these recommendations in mind as they review the theories presented in this chapter and consider how they might shape their work with students in transition.

Psychosocial Theories

Sanford (1967) noted that psychosocial theories and "identity development models describe a process of increasing differentiation in the sense of self and the integration of that growing complexity into a coherent whole" (as cited in Pascarella & Terenzini, 2005, p. 23). In developing psychosocial theories, many theorists built on the work of Erik Erikson (1963), arguing that an individual develops through a sequence of stages that define the life cycle. These stages, also called developmental tasks, arise when students' biological and psychological maturation converge with societal expectations. For example, it is a cultural norm to question high school seniors about their college plans and prospective majors. Physical and intellectual maturation, combined with social expectations surrounding the impending graduation date, challenge students to navigate these decisions at approximately the age of 18. The result of this convergence is a qualitative change in how the individual thinks, feels, behaves, values, and relates to the self and others. Sanford's (1962) balance of support and challenge; Chickering's (1969; Chickering & Reisser, 1993) Theory of Identity Development; and Schlossberg, Waters, and Goodman's (1995) transition theory are the most applicable to orientation practice. In addition to these theories, a growing body of work focuses on social identity development, examining the role that race/ethnicity, sexual orientation, ability/disability status, gender, and other factors play in defining the self. Readers are encouraged to expand their study of the diverse range of psychosocial theories by exploring the work of individual theorists discussed in this chapter.

Sanford's balance of support and challenge. Sanford was one of the first scholars to address the relationship between college environments and the transition from late adolescence to young adulthood. He added two foundational concepts to our understanding of development: (a) cycles of differentiation and integration and (b) balancing support and challenge. According to Sanford (1962), individual development is characterized by the process of differentiation and integration. Chickering and Reisser (1993) suggest increasing differentiation occurs as we become more complex human beings and is accompanied by increasing integration, in which relationships among parts are constructed into more meaningful wholes. Orientation often begins a new student's journey into the cycle of differentiation and integration that is higher education.

Sanford (1966) believed that college should be a developmental community and asserted that optimal development occurs when students are presented with a balance of challenge and support in the college environment. Knefelkamp et al. (1978) noted that "development involves an upending which brings about new, more differentiated responses" (p. ix), but the college environment must also provide adequate support so that challenges do not become overwhelming. Sanford recognized that if challenge or disequilibrium were too great, individuals would retreat. Conversely, if supports were too protective, individuals would fail to develop.

The challenge and support model has many implications for orientation practice and should be considered when making programmatic decisions related to the format, timing, and staffing of orientation, among others. Exposure to a new environment, institutional policies, academic advising, and course selection are a few challenges awaiting new students at orientation. The widespread use of student orientation leaders is one example of how many institutions help first-year students manage these new challenges.

Chickering's theory of identity development. Chickering (1969) provided an overview of the developmental tasks encountered by college students and examined the environmental conditions that impact development. The establishment of identity is the central developmental issue facing students during the college years. He argued that "significant human development occurs through cycles of challenge and response, differentiation and integration, and disequilibrium and regained equilibrium" (Chickering & Reisser, 1993, p. 476). An individual's culture, environment, and other factors influence the timing and ways in which tasks are addressed. Chickering believed that successful resolution of the many facets of identity led to the ability to address later life issues. He identified seven vectors or developmental tasks that contribute to identity formation during the college years. The term "vector" was intentionally chosen to convey a sense of development as having both direction and magnitude. Chickering and Reisser described vectors as "maps to help us determine where students are and which way they are headed. Movement along any one can occur at different rates and can interact with movement along others" (p. 34).

Chickering (1969; Chickering & Reisser, 1993) allowed for the possibility that students could recycle through vectors previously experienced. He postulated that the vectors built on each other, leading to greater complexity, stability, and integration as issues within each vector were addressed. Chickering envisioned a spiral or helix as the prototype for psychosocial growth, recognizing that student development does not necessarily proceed in a linear fashion.

Although some vectors will be more prominent than others in orientation, most institutions—whether consciously or not—include elements of Chickering's (1969; Chickering & Reisser, 1993) theory in their work with entering students and their parents. The seven vectors of the revised model (Chickering & Reisser) along with implications for orientation programming are presented below.

1. *Developing competence* (intellectual competence, physical and manual skills, and interpersonal competence). The task to be resolved in this vector is achieving a strong sense of competence along these three dimensions. Through their orientation and first-year programs, institutions assist students in identifying and developing the competencies they need for academic, social, and interpersonal success through study skills workshops, social activities, and sessions on communicating with roommates, among others.

2. *Managing emotions* (allowing emotions into awareness, acknowledging them as signals, and developing flexible control). The task to be resolved is appropriate expression of emotions and an ability to feel, accept, and integrate a range of emotions (e.g., excitement, depression, anxiety, frustration, aggression). Education about alcohol use, sexual assault prevention, personal safety, and body image are among the topics often treated during orientation and first-year programs that support students' development along this vector. Orientation programs also introduce new students to resources for managing emotions, including counseling centers, residence hall staff, and other student affairs professionals.

3. *Moving through autonomy toward interdependence* (requires both emotional and instrumental independence, and later recognition and acceptance of interdependence). The goal of this vector is achieving freedom from the need for continual reassurance from others and discovering an inner sense of control and direction. Related to the development of autonomy and interdependence, orientation sessions, new student convocations, and extended orientation programs set out for students the academic and behavioral expectations the college or university holds for them, as well as the importance of balancing freedom and responsibility as new members of the community. The goal of staying connected with family and friends while becoming independent is also a frequent subject of discussion in both new student and parent orientation.

4. *Developing mature interpersonal relationships* (involves tolerance and appreciation of differences and the capacity for intimacy and empathy). The task is to develop relationships built on openness, endurance, and concern for others. Orientation programs foster the development of mature interpersonal relationships when they incorporate components on understanding and appreciating differences and when they help students build skills for living in a diverse community. Service-learning opportunities, which are growing in

popularity as part of orientation activities on many campuses, are also helpful in this respect. Such opportunities may also encourage the development of purpose (vector 6) and integrity (vector 7).

5. *Establishing identity* (a solid sense of self). Success in this vector, which Chickering and Reisser believed followed successful resolution of the first four vectors, is a comfort with all facets of the self and a resulting increased self-esteem. Helping students achieve a positive identity often begins at orientation and continues through the undergraduate experience. An orientation program that acknowledges the importance of intellectual, social, physical, spiritual, interpersonal, and cultural identity sets the stage for healthy identity development throughout college.

6. *Developing purpose* (formulating vocational plans and aspirations, personal interests, and interpersonal and family commitments). The task in this vector is success in navigating where one is headed and where one wants to go. Almost all orientation programs aim to help students identify realistic academic goals and career plans by introducing them to faculty, academic advisors, and career specialists.

7. *Developing integrity* (humanizing and personalizing values, and developing congruence between personal values and socially responsible behavior). The outcome of this vector is to develop and practice values that impact and guide one's life. Particularly at private colleges and universities, development of character and moral values is addressed from the first year on, starting with orientation and continuing through first-year seminars, workshops, and courses.

Chickering and Reisser's theory is noted for its comprehensiveness and applicability to student affairs settings (Pascarella & Terenzini, 2005), including orientation. Understanding that most first- and second-year students of traditional age encounter these vectors allows orientation professionals to plan programs that address acquiring study skills; managing time, money, and other resources; meeting expectations and taking personal responsibility; managing conflict; planning for academic success; and developing new relationships while staying connected to existing ones with family and friends at home.

Social identity theories. Often considered as a subset of psychosocial theories, social identity theories merit discussion as a unique entity. These theories address the ways in which individuals construct aspects of their identities, such as race, ethnicity, gender, ability/disability status, and sexual orientation (McEwen, 2003a). They emerge "from the sociohistorical and sociopolitical climate of the United States, in which social groups that are not White, heterosexual, male, able-bodied, and of the privileged class have been oppressed" (McEwen, 2003b, p. 205). Development in the social identity theories moves from conformity toward an awareness and abandonment of internalized racism, heterosexism, and sexism (McEwen, 2003b). One theme that underlies social identities is that the movement away from internalized prejudices is valued as a goal for college students. Among the prominent social identity theories are:

◇ Racial and Ethnic Identity Development
  ◇ Helms' (1995) Model of People of Color or ALANA (African, Latino, Asian, and Native American) racial identity development
  ◇ Helms' Model of White Identity Development (1990; 1992; 1994; Helms & Cook, 1999)
  ◇ Cross and Fhaghen-Smith's Model of Black Identity Development (2001)
  ◇ Rowe, Bennett, and Atkinson's White Racial Consciousness Model (1994)
  ◇ Ferdman and Gallegos' Model of Latino Identity Development (2001)

- ◇ Kim's Asian Identity Development Model (2001)
- ◇ Horse's Perspective on American Indian Identity Development (2001)
- ◇ Phinney's Model of Ethnic Identity Development (1990)
- ◇ Biracial and Multiracial Identity Development (Kerwin & Ponterotto, 1995; Kich, 1992; Poston, 1990; Root, 1990; 1992; 1996; Wijeyesinghe, 2001)
  - ◇ Sexual Identity Development
- ◇ Homosexual Identity Formation (Cass, 1979)
- ◇ Fassinger's Model of Gay and Lesbian and Gay Identity Formation (McCarn & Fassinger, 1996)
- ◇ D'Augelli's Life-span Model of Lesbian-Gay-Bisexual Development (1994)
  - ◇ Gender and Gender Identity Development
- ◇ Feminist Identity for Women (Downing & Roush, 1985)
- ◇ Womanist Identity Development (Ossana, Helms, & Leonard, 1992)
- ◇ Bilodeau's adaption of D'Augelli for transgender students (2005)

McEwen (2003b) also discussed dimensions of identity that have emerged as important considerations in serving new students, including ability and disability, social class, religious identity, geographic region, first-generation status, and multiple identities. During orientation, specific services and resources that support the development of students who identify with these subpopulations should be prominently featured.

The social identity theories illustrate the complexity of identity development during the college years. In addition to the expected psychosocial developmental tasks and the anticipated cognitive-structural maturation of the college years, many students are also working through identity dimensions viewed through the social constructions of race, gender, sexual orientation, social class, ability/disability status, and other factors.

Transition theory. Schlossberg, Waters, and Goodman (1995) defined a transition as "any event, or non-event, that results in changed relationships, routines, assumptions, and roles" (p. 27). Transitions may be anticipated, unanticipated, or non-events (i.e., expected events that did not occur). Non-events may be personal (a change in "individual aspirations," such as not being admitted to a first-choice college), ripple ("unfulfilled expectations," such as an illness or lay-off of a parent, which makes it necessary for a student to commute rather than live on campus as planned), resultant ("an event that leads to a non-event," such as a car accident that prevents a student from starting college classes on schedule), or delayed (such as being wait-listed for admission to a prestigious school). The impact of a transition is determined by the degree to which it alters one's daily life. Both positive and negative transitions cause stress. The role of perceptions in transitions is also important; significance must be attached by the individual experiencing the change for it to be considered a transition. According to Evans et al. (2010), "transitions provide opportunities for growth and development, but a positive outcome ... cannot be assumed" (p. 213). Students' effectiveness in coping with transition depends on their assets and liabilities. The ratio of assets to liabilities explains why people respond differently to similar transitions.

Schlossberg et al. (1995) identified four "S's" (situation, self, support, and strategies) that influence how an individual copes with transitions. Thus, to assess the meaning of a transition and a student's ability to navigate it, we might pose a series of questions (Schlossberg et al., 1995):

- ◇ *Situation:* What triggered the transition? Is this a good or bad time for the transition? Does the individual feel that the transition is under his or her control? If a role change is involved, is it a gain or a loss? Are there other sources of stress present in the student's life? Who or what is responsible for the transition? Has the student experienced similar transitions in the past, and how did he or she handle it?

◇ *Self:* What personal and demographic characteristics describe the student (e.g., socioeconomic status, gender, age, stage of life, state of health, ethnicity)? What psychological resources does the student possess (e.g., ego development, self-efficacy, outlook, commitment, values)?

◇ *Support:* Schlossberg et al. (1995) postulated four types of social support (intimate relationships; family units; networks of friends; and institutions and communities, such as clubs, religious organizations, and neighborhoods). What kinds of social supports does the student have on the campus and external to the campus?

◇ *Strategies:* Does the student seem to favor a particular response, or does he or she seem to use a wide range of coping responses? How effective are the student's current coping strategies?

Orientation programs are an appropriate venue to practice transition theory. Goodman, Schlossberg, and Anderson (2006) referred to the transition process as "moving in, moving through, and moving out" (p. 50). Orientation participants are at the "moving in" stage in their college transition. Understanding the value of support in the campus environment allows practitioners to design orientation materials (e.g., handbooks, web sites) and program components (e.g., resource fairs, organizational expos) to make students aware of specific institutional supports (e.g., counseling centers, academic advising, tutoring opportunities, and faculty office hours). Specific strategies (e.g., small-group networks, peer leaders, first-year experience courses, and opportunities to connect with student organizations) are tangible ways to provide support for students experiencing transition.

Often applied to transfer, adult, and nontraditional students (Goodman et al., 2006), transition theory is also effective for parent and family orientation programs. Coburn and Treeger (2003) noted that both students and their parents are likely to experience "some feelings of dislocation and loss" (p. 9) in the transition to college. A growing number of colleges and universities have created units for parent services that provide communication, resources, and support for the parents and families of their students during and after orientation. Savage and Hippert (2008) found that family members who participated in parent orientation and parents weekend, who made use of communication tools such as online video and audio workshops, and who read the biweekly parents' e-mails were likely to feel strongly connected to the campus community during the transition process.

Cognitive-Structural Theories

In contrast to psychosocial theories that are concerned with *what* students think, cognitive-structural theories consider *how* students think, reason, and make meaning of their experiences in the college years. Building on the work of Piaget (1952), cognitive-structural theorists view development as "a progression along a hierarchical continuum, which is divided into a sequence of stages, with each stage representing a qualitatively different way of thinking" (King, 1978, p. 36).

Cognitive development occurs as a result of assimilation and accommodation (Piaget, 1952). During assimilation, new information is integrated into the current reasoning structure. Accommodation is the process of modifying current structures or creating new ones to adjust or adapt. A balance between assimilation and accommodation is needed for the individual to interact in the environment. Disequilibrium (cognitive conflict) occurs when expectations are different from experience. When conflict occurs, individuals must assimilate the new information or experience into the existing reasoning structure. If that is not possible, individuals must accommodate (i.e., create or adopt new structures) to achieve equilibrium. Piaget also recognized that development proceeded through two growth stages: (a) a readiness phase, in which the individual acquires the prerequisites for the next stage, and (b) an attainment stage, in which the individual can demonstrate skills in using the new stage. Cognitive development is uneven, and, during transitions between stages, individuals may be limited in their capacity to use a higher reasoning structure in all situations.

Perry's theory of intellectual and ethical development. William Perry (1970; 1999) developed a theory of intellectual and ethical development, tracing students' movement from a simplistic, categorical view of the world to a more relativistic, committed perspective. In Perry's scheme, students began with an unquestioning, dualistic reasoning structure (right/wrong, good/bad) and gradually accepted that knowledge, values, and truth were qualitative and contextual. As students moved through the stages of development as a result of their college experiences, they integrated their intellects and identity and found personal meaning in the world through an affirmation of their own commitments (Moore & Upcraft, 1990). Perry's (1970) nine positions represent changes in intellectual and ethical development and are described as the concepts of dualism, multiplicity, relativism, and commitment to relativism.

Dualism (Positions 1-2): Students in dualism view people, knowledge, and values dichotomously—in absolute, discrete, and concrete ways. "Right answers" are determined by established authorities, and students learn these truths without substantiation and without question (Perry, 1999). "Authorities" possess the right answers, and the student's job is to receive those answers. Alternative perspectives or multiple points of view are confusing and thus not acknowledged. Students using a dualistic reasoning pattern come to orientation expecting their academic advisor to identify majors and select courses for them. Failure to do so by the advisor frustrates these students.

Multiplicity (Positions 3-4): In multiplicity, students acknowledge uncertainty and multiple perspectives, but they feel that questions ultimately have an answer. Perry (1981) characterized multiplicity as honoring diverse views when the right answers are not yet known. In areas of uncertainty, everyone has a right to their own opinion. All points of view are equally valid and not subject to judgment; fairness may emerge as an issue.

Students moving through multiplicity shift their perception of the purpose of higher education from learning how to learn and working hard to learning how to think more independently and analytically. In later multiplicity, students begin to distinguish between an unconsidered belief (knowledge or values taught by an authority) and a considered judgment (thinking independently using supportive evidence) (Perry, 1999). Authorities (e.g., faculty, academic advisors) may be defied or resisted in Position 4, and peers become legitimate sources of knowledge.

Some first-year and transfer students come to orientation as multiplistic learners. Students early in multiplicity might attend an advising session unsure of a major but confident that the right major exists for them, believing that the advisor will help them discover the process for finding it. In the latter stages of multiplicity, these students may be interested in exploring many academic and extracurricular options as they open up to possibilities for their future. They also may be particularly interested in the perspectives of their peers, especially those of orientation leaders.

Relativism (Positions 5-6): The transition to relativism begins with recognizing the need to support opinions. Knowledge is viewed more qualitatively based on context, evidence, and supporting arguments. Multiple points of view are now seen as pieces that fit together into a "big picture." Students are able to evaluate their own and other's ideas. Authorities are now valued for their expertise, not their infallibility.

Commitment in Relativism (Positions 7-9): Movement beyond Position 5 does not involve changes in cognitive structure but rather represents qualitatively different ways of thinking. These "post-contextual positions are more likely to be reflected in value questions and decision dilemmas than in a particular approach to learning" (Knefelkamp, 1999, p. xx). Perry (1999) defined commitment as "an act, or ongoing activity relating a person as agent and chooser to aspects of his life in which he invests his energies, his care, and his identity" (pp. 149-150). Perry's commitment process involves choices, decisions, and affirmations that are made from a relativistic perspective. These commitments are characterized by area (i.e., social commitments, such as decisions about career, religion, friendships, and politics) and style, which involves balancing external (e.g., narrowness vs. breadth, number vs. intensity) with subjective (e.g., action vs. contemplation, stability vs. flexibility) considerations (Perry, 1999). These last three positions, rarely seen in first-year students, chart the evolution of commitments in an individual's life, beginning with initial commitment (Position 7). In this way, the latter Perry positions parallel Chickering's (1969; Chickering & Reisser, 1993) last two vectors, Developing Purpose and Developing Integrity.

Orientation coordinators may work with advanced student leaders, graduate students, professional staff, and nontraditional students who are in positions 7-9. Professional staff members working with or supervising these groups will find a general knowledge of the full theory beneficial in providing appropriate cognitive dissonance (i.e., challenges and supports) for continued student development. Staff members who are reasoning at relativistic stages or above (positions 5-9) may find that a basic understanding of student development theory can guide their interactions with students and families at an appropriate level.

Typology Theories

Typology theories are explanatory and descriptive, and they look at individual differences in how people view and relate to the world. They are typically referred to as "models" because they do not consist of stages through which students progress. Typologies help us understand how students take in and process information, how they learn best, what types of activities interest them, and how they prefer to spend their time. Different types are not seen as "good" or "bad" as each type makes unique and positive contributions to a work environment, the classroom, or an organization.

According to Evans, Forney, and Guido-DiBrito (1998), typologies provide "a framework within which psychosocial and cognitive-structural development takes place" (p. 204), adding another dimension to our understanding of college student development. These models also suggest sources of challenge and support for students with differing personality characteristics. Typologies can assist in designing orientation program components and training sessions, and they help explain group and interpersonal interactions to maximize staff assignments and performance.

The most widely used typologies are Kolb's Theory of Experiential Learning (1984), Holland's Theory of Vocational Personalities and Environments (1985; 1992), and the Myers-Briggs Adaptation of Jung's Theory of Personality Type (1923; 1971). The models and their corresponding instruments are often used as tools for staff development, strengthening awareness of the complementary nature of personality differences, making work assignments, and building skills in interpersonal communication.

There are numerous opportunities in orientation to apply typologies. Through the use of Kolb's Learning Style Inventory (1976; 1985), workshops on learning styles can help new students understand their preferred methods of understanding knowledge in the classroom and forming effective study habits. Career development and academic advising components of orientation can employ Holland's Self-Directed Search (1994) to assist students in exploring potential major and career options. The Myers-Briggs Type Indicator (Myers & McCaulley, 1985) can be used in staff orientation training programs to build awareness and appreciation of personality differences, and it can help new students understand the dynamics of interpersonal relationships, especially in residential living. Because orientation practitioners often are familiar with the major typology theories, this chapter does not detail their constructs. (A full treatment of typology theories is provided by Evans et al. [2010] and Evans [2003].)

Campus Environments

Established by Lewin (1936), person-environment theories assume that behavior is a function of the interaction between the person and the environment, illustrated by $B = f(P \times E)$ (Lewin, 1951). Building on this idea, Strange and Banning (2001) stated that "[t]he degree of person-environment congruence is predictive of an individual's attraction to and satisfaction or stability within an environment" (p. 52). Individuals who have much in common with an environment are expected to be attracted to that environment. They are likely to be encouraged in the behaviors, values, attitudes, and expectations that attracted them initially. Strange and Banning predicted that the likelihood of a person remaining in that environment is high. On the other hand, students in an incompatible environment may experience a lack of fit, increasing the likelihood of leaving that environment. Smart, Feldman, and Ethington (2000) asserted that a high degree of person-environment congruence is usually evident in greater satisfaction, a desire to persist, and higher retention.

Strange and Banning (2001) pointed out four key components in all human environments: (a) physical condition, design, and layout; (b) characteristics of the people inhabiting the environment; (c) organizational structures related to their purposes and goals; and (d) inhabitants' collective perceptions or constructions of the context and culture of their setting. These four environmental variables—and the dynamics among them—comprise the sources of influence on human behavior. In addition to influencing decisions about persistence, Chickering (1969) and Chickering and Reisser (1993) underscored the importance of the college environment in facilitating student development.

The environment created at orientation sets the stage for students' entry into the academic community. Orientation coordinators must consider the four key components of environmental factors when designing their programs. For some students and family members, orientation may provide the first impression of the campus. Both the human or social aspects and the physical components matter in creating a welcoming environment. For example, orientation parking areas should be as close as possible to the program's starting location, and signage should be clear and plentiful. Students and family members should be welcomed by friendly and enthusiastic staff members. A level of comfort will be achieved by guiding newcomers through orientation with practical, accurate publications and by personable student leaders and professional staff members. Campus tours should feature well-tended grounds and buildings and incorporate elements of the campus culture through artifacts and symbols as well as through stories of the institution's history and traditions. The culture, expectations, and values of a college or university are communicated through a well-designed campus tour led by knowledgeable and enthusiastic student leaders. Helping incoming students find their way around campus and conveying a sense of community where all new students are welcome is accomplished by attention to the environment.

New students must quickly find people, activities, and environments that fit with their characteristics. Making those connections early eases students' transitions and promotes their satisfaction and retention. In particular, it is valuable for students to be introduced to the climate of their academic program through group meetings and contact with faculty and their academic advisor during orientation.

Making connections to the campus culture may be particularly difficult for students from underserved populations attending a majority institution. Rendón (1994), in her work with nontraditional students, found that active intervention in the form of validation was needed to encourage these students to become involved in campus life and to enhance their self-esteem. She defined validation "as an enabling, confirming, and supportive process initiated by in- and out-of-class agents that foster academic and interpersonal development" (p. 46). Validation can occur in many settings, including the classroom, student organizations, and the community. "Validating agents" can be faculty, peers, campus employees, student affairs staff, and others who are significant to the student. Evans et al. (2010) concluded that validation is most effective and powerful during the early stages of a student's college career and may especially be important for students whose diverse racial, ethnic, and cultural backgrounds may predispose them to doubts about their abilities. Validation of new students should begin with orientation. Every person the student encounters— from orientation leaders to food service workers to academic advisors to testing staff—can convey that the new student is valued by the institution.

Closely related to validation are the concepts of mattering and marginality. Schlossberg (1989) defined mattering as "our belief, whether right or wrong, that we matter to someone else" (as cited in Evans et al., 2010, p. 32). The five aspects of mattering are:

◇ Attention (the feeling that one is being noticed)
◇ Importance (the belief that one is cared about)
◇ Ego extension (the sense that someone else will be proud of one's accomplishments or will sympathize with one's failures)
◇ Dependence (the feeling of being needed)
◇ Appreciation (the sense that one's efforts are appreciated by others)

Schlossberg (1989) postulated that feeling that one matters is an important "precursor to students' involvement in activities and academic programs designed to facilitate development and learning" (as cited in Evans et al., p. 32). Again, personal interactions—whether with student leaders, academic advisors, or peers—at orientation can help new students feel that they matter and belong to the institution.

Marginality is defined as not fitting in, and it occurs when a person takes on a new role, especially when there is uncertainty about what the role entails. Such feelings can lead to negative emotions and impede a student's transition to the new academic institution. Orientation is the first place to create conditions in which students feel they matter, not that they are marginalized.

Theory to Practice in Orientation

Orientation provides a rich environment for linking theory to practice, but many professionals struggle to make the connection between learning student development theory and implementing it in their daily work. Theoretical models have emerged in recent decades to help student affairs practitioners operationalize the expanding body of theories available. In distinguishing between theories and models, Evans et al. (2010) stated, "Models do not define phenomena or explain relationships; they provide guidance in using theory" (p. 349).

Two types of models have been identified by Evans et al. (2010) as a "developmental bridge" (p. 349) between theory and practice: (a) process models and (b) procedural models. Process models, such as those of Knefelkamp, Golec, and Wells (The Practice-to-Theory-to-Practice Model, 1985) and Rodgers and Widick (The Grounded Formal Theory Model, 1980), consist of "cognitive maps" (Blocher, 1987, p. 299), or action steps, to blend theory with practice. Procedural models, represented by Morrill, Oetting, and Hurst's Cube (1974) and Evans' Developmental Intervention

Model (1987), offer ways to develop programs creatively, think purposefully in designing theoretical approaches, and evaluate the effectiveness of programs and interventions.

A thorough treatment of process and procedural models is beyond the scope of this chapter, but one model developed by Strange and King (1990) can be useful. The Strange and King model provides five areas for explanation when attempting to apply theory to practical problem. Strange and King call the process of translating explanations of student behavior "the art of student development" (p. 12). The case study below is an example of this model in use and demonstrates how an observation made by a single unit can lead to collaborative partnerships and systemic institutional changes.

Case Study: Choosing an Academic Major at Orientation

For several years, the orientation program at a fictitious, large, public institution located in the Midwest has seen an increase in the number of first-year students who change their majors on site at the orientation program. An initial declaration of major is made on the application for admission to the university, which is then transferred to the student's orientation reservation information. Students have the option of changing the major when making an online or mail-in reservation. After students are confirmed for an orientation session, they receive a postcard that provides the procedure for making a major change online. Finally, an e-mail reminder is sent three days before each orientation session, which again allows students to make major changes so that academic records are available for advising during the program.

Despite these opportunities, the office and professional staff at this university have noticed that 20% or more of first-year students are changing majors when they arrive at orientation, a percentage that is increasing every year. This phenomenon results in a flurry of paperwork and record changes that must be made before students see their advisors, increasing the workload for both the orientation staff and the advising offices. Without academic records from students' high schools and their entrance exam scores, it is difficult to provide accurate and appropriate advising for these students. In the case of some students, multiple major changes occur at orientation (the current record stands at four), compounding the concern. The testing office is also affected by the number of first-year students who must complete placement exams for their new majors at orientation.

Before the next new student orientation cycle begins, there is a desire to develop an intervention to help students make and communicate informed major decisions and to manage the situation as smoothly as possible when the student arrives for orientation. A series of meetings is planned in which the professional staff of the orientation program will collaborate with representatives from admissions, academic advising, testing, and other stakeholders to consider ways to address the problem. The orientation director, who has initiated the major declaration conversation, uses Strange and King's (1990) model in formulating an approach to the problem.

Formulating a Theory

From a theoretical standpoint, there may be several reasons for the increasing numbers of major changes at orientation:

◇ Using the psychosocial theory of Chickering (1969; Chickering & Reisser, 1993), the group might postulate that entering first-year students are more occupied with the early developmental tasks of developing competence (intellectual, physical, and interpersonal) and managing emotions than with the later task of developing purpose, which would include making academic plans and setting career goals. In other words, many first-year students may not demonstrate readiness (Sanford, 1962; 1966) for making a firm decision about a major.

◇ Perry's Scheme of Intellectual and Ethical Development (1970) may also shed light on why students may have difficulty committing firmly to a major. For some students who are reasoning at a dualistic level, an initial major declaration may be affected or determined by external agents (e.g., parents, guidance counselors, high school teachers). As the student is exposed to greater complexity in reasoning structures, thoughts about majors may change. Students using early multiplistic thinking may perceive many available choices but may not yet be at a point of evaluating the merits of one option over another.

◇ Major and career choice go hand-in-hand so theories and models from academic advising and career development may enhance understanding of the increasing number of changes at orientation. Super's developmental approach (Super, 1969; Super, Crites, Hummel, Moser, Overstreet, & Warnath, 1957; Super, Starishevsky, Matlin, & Jordaan, 1963) informs us that students between ages 18 and 21 are in the "exploration" stage of career development and, specifically, are crystallizing vocational preferences while attempting to implement a self-concept (Super, p. 125). As a major task of psychosocial development is resolving issues of identity, it may be counterproductive to expect students to have a clear major and/or career in mind at the start of college.

From the inventory of theories above, the orientation team at our fictitious university, in conjunction with partners from admissions, academic advising, and testing, has concluded that the majority of major declarations made prior to orientation should be considered tentative and subject to change. Approximately 40% of the first-year students at this university are first-generation, and one third comes from single-parent families—factors that may partially explain why students have not yet fully explored their major options. Indeed, orientation may be the "trigger event" that causes entering students to first think seriously about their academic path. The team has also concluded that any interventions implemented should allow for parental involvement and should be provided at times convenient for student access.

Exploring the Available Research

This part of the model encourages the investigation of existing literature. The orientation professional should investigate the growing body of literature available on first-generation students and on major declaration, including research published in the major student affairs and higher education journals and other human development journals in psychology and sociology. In addition, the professional should examine the numerous print resources, listservs, benchmarking and best practices, and web information written on this topic to assist with exploration of options for addressing the problem of first-year student needs and change of major.

Designing a Practice

Based on their understanding of the demographics of entering first-year students at the fictitious university and a review of literature and research on the topic of major choice, the team designs a multifaceted intervention to assist students in exploring potential majors and understanding their own values, interests, and abilities, and how they combine to influence decisions about majors. The plan includes:

◇ Print and web-based materials delivered through the admissions portal (orientation, testing, and academic advising units are also connected) that provide an overview of the major decision-making process and an "it's okay to be undecided (or undeclared)" campaign. Current students are featured on the site, sharing their experiences about how they arrived at their major choice(s) and highlighting university resources available to assist in this process. These resources are well-designed and heavily promoted at open houses, special programs for targeted populations (e.g., prospective honors students, athletes, students of color), campus tours, high school visits, and orientation sessions for students and their families. A link to the portal is prominently featured on the university's home page.

◇ Phone calls made by trained, current students encourage their newly admitted peers to think through their major options or to declare themselves as "undecided" before orientation. The callers suggest that prospective students talk with their families and their high school guidance counselors to explore their interests through instruments such as the Strong Vocational Interest Inventory and the Myers-Briggs Type Indicator.

◇ A special section of the web site is created for parents and family members, providing resources for talking with their students (e.g., "Ten Tips for Talking With Your Student About Declaring a Major," "testimonials" from parents of currently enrolled students). It will assist new parents in supporting their students in making decisions about a major.

◇ Enrollment in the university's career planning course is promoted during orientation.

Long-term, systemic approaches may also come about as a result of the focus on major decision-making. These may include:

◇ Increasing the number of sections of the career planning course and heavily promoting it at orientation

◇ Changing the mindset of faculty, administrators, and staff on campus in regard to major declaration so that first-year students are encouraged to intentionally explore their interests, values, and skills in preparation for declaring a major

◇ Considering the implementation of a general college model for most first-year students, resulting in a major decision by the time students register for sophomore-year courses

Obviously, changes of this magnitude involve shifting resources and reconceptualizing the major declaration and career decision-making process. Additionally, strong support from the university's leadership team is needed to make a "culture shift" in the delivery of academic advising and other services for first-year students.

Evaluating the Outcomes

Several assessment methods are planned for these initiatives:

◇ In terms of quantitative measures, the percentage of major changes made at orientation before and after the interventions will be compared. These results will be analyzed by gender, race/ethnicity, first-generation status, and other variables.

◇ An online follow-up survey will be administered to first-year students to determine achievement of pre-determined learning objectives and to explore students' perceptions and satisfaction with the process of major declaration.

◇ A series of focus groups will be held with academic advisors, first-year students, and, if possible, parents of first-year students to supplement the quantitative data above. The focus groups will also yield suggestions for enhancing the major declaration process for the future.

Summary

This chapter has defined the concept of student development and has provided an overview of several prominent theories that provide a foundation for practice in orientation programs and services. The chapter also explored a model of applying theory to practice. Essential for successful practice as an orientation professional is understanding how students develop as they enter a new higher education environment. Creating a climate conducive for maximizing student development and learning should be an aim of every orientation practitioner.

Authors' Note

The authors would like to thank Samvedna Dean for her invaluable assistance in developing this chapter.

References

Bilodeau, B. L. (2005). Beyond the gender binary: A case study of two transgender students at a midwestern university. *Journal of Gay and Lesbian Issues in Education, 3*(1), 29-46.

Blocher, D. H. (1987). On the uses and misuses of the term theory. *Journal of College Student Development, 66*, 67-68.

Cass, V. C. (1979). Homosexual identity formation: A theoretical model. *Journal of Homosexuality, 4*, 219-235.

Chickering, A. W. (1969). *Education and identity.* San Francisco: Jossey-Bass.

Chickering, A. W., & Reisser, L. (1993). *Education and identity* (2nd ed.). San Francisco: Jossey-Bass.

Coburn, K. L., & Treeger, M. L. (2003). *Letting go: A parents' guide to understanding the college years* (4th ed.). New York: HarperCollins.

Council for the Advancement of Standards in Higher Education. (2006). *CAS professional standards for higher education* (6th ed.). Washington, DC: Author.

Cross, W. E., Jr., & Fhagen-Smith, P. (2001). Patterns in African American identity development: A life span perspective. In C. L. Wijeyesinghe & B. W. Jackson, III (Eds.), *New perspectives on racial identity development: A theoretical and practical anthology* (pp. 243-270). New York: New York University Press.

Dannells, M., & Wilson M. E. (2003). Theoretical perspectives on orientation. In *Designing successful transitions: A guide for orienting students to college* (2nd ed., Monograph No. 13; pp. 15-30). Columbia, SC: University of South Carolina, National Resource Center for The First-Year Experience and Students in Transition.

D'Augelli, A. R. (1994). Identity development and sexual orientation: Toward a model of lesbian, gay, and bisexual development. In E. J. Trickett, R. J. Watts, & D. Birman (Eds.), *Human diversity: Perspectives on people in context* (pp. 312-333). San Francisco: Jossey-Bass.

DiCaprio, N. S. (1975). *Personality theories: Guides to living.* Philadelphia: Saunders.

Downing, N. E., & Roush, K. L. (1985). From passive acceptance to active commitment: A model of feminist identity development for women. *Counseling Psychologist, 13*, 695-709.

Erikson, E. H. (1963). *Childhood and society* (2nd ed.). New York: Norton.

Evans, N. J. (1987). A framework for assisting student affairs staff in fostering moral development. *Journal of Counseling and Development, 66*, 191-194.

Evans, N. J. (2003). Psychosocial, cognitive, and typological perspectives on student development. In S. R. Komives, D. B. Woodard, Jr., & Associates, *Student services: A handbook for the profession* (pp. 179-202). San Francisco: Jossey-Bass.

Evans, N. J., Forney, D. S., & Guido-DiBrito, F. (1998). *Student development in college: Theory, research, and practice*. San Francisco: Jossey-Bass.

Evans, N. J., Forney, D. S., Guido, F. M., Patton, L. D., & Renn, K. W. (2010). *Student development in college: Theory, research and practice* (2nd ed.). San Francisco: Jossey-Bass.

Ferdman, B. M., & Gallegos, P. I. (2001). Racial identity development and Latinos in the United States. In C. L. Wijeyesinghe & B. W. Jackson, III (Eds.), *New perspectives on racial identity development: A theoretical and practical anthology* (pp. 32-66). New York: New York University Press.

Goodman, J., Schlossberg, N. K., & Anderson, M. L. (2006). *Counseling adults in transition: Linking practice to theory* (3rd ed.). New York: Springer.

Helms, J. E. (1990). Toward a model of White racial identity development. In J. E. Helms (Ed.), *Black and White racial identity: Theory, research, and practice* (pp. 49-66). New York: Greenwood Press.

Helms, J. E. (1992). *A race is a nice thing to have: A guide to being a White person, or understanding the White persons in your life*. Topeka, KS: Content Communications.

Helms, J. E. (1994). The conceptualization of racial identity and other "racial" constructs. In E. J. Trickett, R. J. Watts, & D. Birman (Eds.), *Human diversity: Perspectives on people in context* (pp. 285-311). San Francisco: Jossey-Bass.

Helms, J. E. (1995). An update of Helms's White and People of Color racial identity models. In J. G. Ponterotto, J. M. Casas, L. A. Suzuki, & C. M. Alexander (Eds.), *Handbook of multicultural counseling* (pp. 181-198). Thousand Oaks, CA: Sage.

Helms, J. E., & Cook, D. A. (1999). *Using race and culture in counseling and psychotherapy: Theory and process*. Boston: Allyn & Bacon.

Holland, J. L. (1985). *Making vocational choices: A theory of vocational personalities and work environments*. Englewood Cliffs, NJ: Prentice Hall.

Holland, J. L. (1992). *Making vocational choices: A theory of vocational personalities and work environments* (2nd ed.). Odessa, FL: Psychological Assessment Resources.

Holland, J. L. (1994). *The Self-Directed Search (SDS)*. Odessa, FL: Psychological Assessment Resources.

Horse, P. G. (2001). Reflections on American Indian identity. In. C. L. Wijeyesinghe & B. W. Jackson, III (Eds.), *New perspectives on racial identity development: A theoretical and practical anthology* (pp. 91-207). New York: New York University Press.

Jung, C. G. (1923). *Psychological types*. New York: Harcourt, Brace.

Jung, C. G. (1971). *Psychological types*. Bollingen Series 20. The Collected Works of C. G. Jung, vol. 6. Princeton, NJ: Princeton University Press.

Kerwin, C., & Ponterotto, J. G. (1995). Biracial identity development: Theory and research. In J. G. Ponterotto, J. M. Casas, L. A. Suzuki, & C. M. Alexander (Eds.), *Handbook of multicultural counseling* (pp. 199-217). Thousand Oaks, CA: Sage.

Kich, G. K. (1992). The developmental process of asserting a biracial, bicultural identity. In M. P. P. Root (Ed.), *Racially mixed people in America* (pp. 304-317). Newbury Park, CA: Sage.

Kim, J. (2001). Asian American identity development theory. In. C. L. Wijeyesinghe & B. W. Jackson, III (Eds.), *New perspectives on racial identity development: A theoretical and practical anthology* (pp. 67-90). New York: New York University Press.

King, P. M. (1978). William Perry's theory of intellectual and ethical development. In L. L. Knefelkamp, C. Widick, & C. A. Parker (Eds.), *Applying new developmental findings* (New Directions for Student Services, No. 4, pp. 35-51). San Francisco: Jossey-Bass.

Knefelkamp, L. L (1999). Introduction. In W. G. Perry, Jr., *Forms of ethical and intellectual development in the college years: A scheme* (pp. xi-xxxviii). San Francisco: Jossey-Bass.

Knefelkamp, L. L., Golec, R. R., & Wells, E. A. (1985). *The practice-to-theory-to-practice model.* Unpublished manuscript, University of Maryland, College Park.

Knefelkamp, L. L., Widick, C., & Parker, C. A. (1978). Editors' notes: Why bother with theory? In L. Knefelkamp, C. Widick, & C. A. Parker (Eds.), *Applying new developmental findings* (New Directions for Student Services No. 4, pp. vii-xvi). San Francisco: Jossey-Bass.

Kolb, D. A. (1976). *Learning styles inventory technical manual.* Boston: McBer.

Kolb, D. A. (1984). *Experiential learning: Experience as the source of learning and development.* Englewood Cliffs, NJ: Prentice Hall.

Kolb, D. A. (1985). *The Learning Style Inventory.* Boston: McBer.

Lewin, K. (1936). *Principles of topological psychology.* New York: McGraw-Hill.

Lewin, K. (1951). *Field theory in social science: Selected theoretical papers by Kurt Lewin.* London: Tavistock.

McCarn, S. R., & Fassinger, R. E. (1996). Revisioning sexual minority identity formation: A new model of lesbian identity and its implications for counseling and research. *The Counseling Psychologist, 24,* 508-534.

McEwen, M. K. (2003a). The nature and uses of theory. In S. R. Komives & D. B. Woodard, Jr. (Eds.), *Student services: A handbook for the profession* (4th ed., pp. 153-178). San Francisco: Jossey-Bass.

McEwen, M. K. (2003b). New perspectives on identity development. In S. R. Komives & D. B. Woodard, Jr. (Eds.), *Student services: A handbook for the profession* (4th ed., pp. 203-233). San Francisco: Jossey-Bass.

Miller, T. K., & Prince, J. S. (1976). *The future of student affairs.* San Francisco: Jossey-Bass.

Moore, L. V., & Upcraft, M. L. (1990). Theory in student affairs: Emerging perspectives. In L. V. Moore (Ed.), *Evolving theoretical perspectives on students* (New Directions for Student Services No. 51, pp. 3-23). San Francisco: Jossey-Bass.

Morrill, W. H., Oetting, E. R., & Hurst, J. C. (1974). Dimensions of counselor functioning. *Personnel and Guidance Journal, 52,* 354-359.

Myers, I. B., & McCaulley, M. H. (1985). *Manual: A guide to the development and use of the Myers-Briggs Type Indicator.* Palo Alto, CA: Consulting Psychologists Press.

Ossana, S. M., Helms, J. E., & Leonard, M. M. (1992). Do "womanist" identity attitudes influence college women's self-esteem and perceptions of environmental bias? *Journal of Counseling and Development, 70,* 402-408.

Parker, C. A. (1977). On modeling reality. *Journal of College Student Personnel, 18*(5), 419-425.

Pascarella, E. T., & Terenzini, P. T. (2005). *How college affects students: A third decade of research* (Vol. 2). San Francisco: Jossey-Bass.

Perry, W. G., Jr. (1970). *Forms of intellectual and ethical development in the college years: A scheme.* New York: Holt, Rinehart and Winston.

Perry, W. G., Jr. (1981). Cognitive and ethical growth: The making of meaning. In A. W. Chickering & Associates, *The modern American college* (pp. 76-116). San Francisco: Jossey-Bass.

Perry, W. G., Jr. (1999). *Forms of intellectual and ethical development in the college years: A scheme.* New York: Holt, Rinehart and Winston.

Phinney, J. S. (1990). Ethnic identity in adolescents and adults: Review of research. *Psychological Bulletin, 108,* 499-514.

Piaget, J. (1952). *The origins of intelligence in children.* New York: International University Press.

Pope, R. L., Reynolds, A. L., & Mueller, J. A. (2004). *Multicultural competence in student affairs.* San Francisco: Jossey-Bass.

Poston, W. S. C. (1990). The biracial identity development model: A needed addition. *Journal of Counseling and Development, 69,* 152-155.

Rendón, L. I. (1994). Validating culturally diverse students: Toward a new model of learning and student development. *Innovative Higher Education, 19,* 33-51.

Rodgers, R. F., & Widick, C. (1980). Theory to practice: Using concepts, logic and creativity. In F. B. Newton & K. L. Ender (Eds.), *Student development practice: Strategies for making a difference* (pp. 5-25). Springfield, IL: Thomas.

Root, M. P. P. (1990). Resolving "other" status: Identity development of biracial individuals. In L. S. Brown & M. P. P. Root (Eds.), *Complexity and diversity in feminist theory and therapy* (pp. 185-205). New York: Haworth.

Root, M. P. P. (Ed.). (1992). *Racially mixed people in America.* Newbury Park, CA: Sage.

Root, M. P. P. (Ed.). (1996). *The multiracial experience: Racial borders as the new frontier.* Thousand Oaks, CA: Sage.

Rowe, W., Bennett, S. K., & Atkinson, D. R. (1994). White racial identity models: A critique and alternative proposal. *Counseling Psychologist, 22,* 129-146.

Sanford, N. (1962). *The American college.* New York: Wiley.

Sanford, N. (1966). *Self and society.* New York: Atherton Press.

Sanford, N. (1967). *Where colleges fail: A study of the student as a person.* San Francisco: Jossey-Bass

Savage, M., & Hippert, B. (2008). Parent Survey 2008. Retrieved from http://www.parent.umn.edu/ParentSurvey08.pdf

Schlossberg, N. K., Waters, E. B., & Goodman, J. (1995). *Counseling adults in transition* (2nd ed.). New York: Springer.

Smart, J. C., Feldman, K. A., & Ethington, C. A. (2000). *Academic disciplines: Holland's theory and the study of college students and faculty.* Nashville, TN: Vanderbilt University Press.

Strange, C. C., & Banning, J. H. (2001). *Educating by design: Creating campus learning environments that work.* San Francisco: Jossey-Bass.

Strange, C. C., & King, P. M. (1990). The professional practice of student development. In D. G. Creamer & Associates, *College student development: Theory and practice for the 1990s* (Media Publication No. 49). Alexandria, VA: American College Personnel Association.

Super, D. E. (1969). Vocational development theory: Persons, positions, and processes. *The Counseling Psychologist, 1,* 2-9.

Super, D. E., Crites, J. O., Hummel, R. C., Moser, H. P., Overstreet, P. L., & Warnath, C. F. (1957). *Vocational development: A framework for research.* New York: Teachers College, Columbia University.

Super, D. E., Starishevsky, R., Matlin, N., & Jordaan, J. P. (1963). *Career development: Self-concept theory.* New York: College Entrance Examination Board.

Wijeyesinghe, C. L. (2001). Racial identity in multiracial people: An alternative paradigm. In C. L. Wijeyesinghe & B. W. Jackson, III (Eds.), *New perspectives on racial identity development: A theoretical and practical anthology* (pp. 129-152). New York: New York University Press.

Chapter 3

Making the Case for Orientation: Is It Worth It?

Bonita C. Jacobs

According to Alexander (2007), principal themes facing higher education include greater societal expectations, rising college costs, increased accountability, and identification of alternative revenue streams. While these are not new issues or unique to orientation, orientation is nonetheless profoundly affected by them. As the cost of higher education continues to increase in record amounts, policy makers, students, parents, and the public are requesting that colleges and universities carefully weigh the cost of attendance and, especially, to review the cost of special program fees, including new student orientation. At the same time, institutions may be struggling to pay for critical first-year programs, including orientation, during a time of diminishing financial resources. Orientation, if funded as an auxiliary, can become an identifiable revenue stream for other uses. In some cases, parent associations, wilderness camps, and other programs may fill the funding gap for the operation of various first-year student programs. Whatever the budgetary situation, administrators will be expected to demonstrate program effectiveness and focus on improving programs through enhanced assessment efforts.

Beyond addressing funding issues, orientation directors must also promote the importance of orientation to campus constituents. Helping the campus understand the value of orientation can position the program for priority scheduling of facilities, increased participation by faculty and staff, additional funding if needed, and cooperative relationships with offices such as the registrar, academic advising, and academic deans.

While most administrators understand that there is a need for new student orientation, at times there is a lack of understanding about its full range of contributions and importance to the campus community. As recently as the early 1980s, "orientation was still [seen as] little more than academic counseling, registration, and showing students to dorms" (Clayton, 1998, p. B1). As a result, orientation programs may receive less than impressive facility assignments, be forced to compete for resources, and receive little recognition. Interestingly, while the importance of providing the physical and budgetary needs of orientation may be low, it is not uncommon for a campus to believe that orientation can be the panacea to aid retention, student engagement, and the development of campus community. Neither extreme is accurate, and orientation staff must make the case that orientation is a priority event for the campus, while setting realistic expectations about its contributions to student engagement and retention. In order to do this, orientation professionals must, themselves, understand the salient issues and trends affecting higher education and why it is crucial that the university make orientation an institutional priority. They must also articulate the importance of orientation in student persistence and graduation. This chapter will address orientation's role in disseminating information, facilitating academic services such as advising and registration, framing a support for academic success, building community, and affecting campus culture. It will further suggest the value of these functions and how an orientation director might make the case that orientation serves an important campus need.

The Changing Higher Education Landscape

Institutions increasingly struggle to retain students and respond to the ever-increasing need to educate a growing percentage of the populace. "Getting people into college and helping them stay through graduation is essential to our collective well-being" (Merisotis, 2008). It is not surprising that the Association of Governing Boards of Universities and Colleges names student access and success as one of their top 10 policy issues (AGB, 2007).

Higher education continues to report sweeping changes in the demographics of college students. In 1976, only 15.4% of college students identified themselves as belonging to a minority group compared to 3 out of 10 students enrolled today. Likewise, there has been a major shift in the gender balance of college students. Between 1998 and 2008, the enrollment of females increased by 34% while the enrollment of males increased 29%. During that same period, the number of full-time students rose by 37% compared to an increase of only 24% for part-time students (National Center for Educational Statistics, 2009). Predictions indicate that colleges and universities will continue to see changes in the diversity of students, a fact that orientation directors must understand if they are to effectively articulate the value of new student orientation.

Further, record numbers of transfer students are entering universities, primarily from community colleges. The growth of the community college system is at an all-time high with students choosing to stay closer to home for reasons as varied as finances, a desire for additional academic preparation, transportation issues, family obligations and background. Four-year institutions are struggling with how best to help students make the transition from two-year institutions and are implementing, in addition to transfer-specific orientation, parent programs for transfer students and year-long transfer orientations (Ward-Roof & Cawthon, 2004; Ward-Roof, Kashner, & Hodge, 2003). Two-year schools are developing orientation programs specific to students who plan to transfer and are emphasizing the importance of initiating a path to successful transfer early in the students' academic careers (Pope, 2004; Swanson & Jones-Johnson, 2004).

Growing public pressure for accountability and institutional effectiveness also contribute to changes in higher education. Institutions increasingly find that they must be responsive to public needs. An understanding of the mission and core values of the institution is necessary for orientation programs to be effective in a changing institutional environment.

The Value of Orientation

In order to make the case that the cost of orientation is warranted and, further, that the cost to produce a quality program is imperative, orientation directors must first grasp the purposes and benefits of orientation. Included in these purposes are: (a) disseminating information, (b) reducing costly errors, (c) building a framework for academic success, (d) building community, and (e) defining campus culture.

Disseminating Information

Administrators typically realize the importance of disseminating information for orientation; however, they do not always understand the critical nature of providing information that "leads students to establish personal contacts with the individuals and offices which are responsible for providing advising and counseling services and/or which can provide the types of informal information new students require" (Tinto, 1994, p. 159). Providing the information that students need to be successful as well as providing a mechanism for students to establish personal connections to others on campus can have a powerful impact on student acculturation.

Written materials can also underscore the value of orientation in achieving a successful transition. It is important to note that the selection of written materials should be carefully vetted to be certain that they address student success issues as well as concerns students or their parents (or other family members) are likely to have. The "many eyes approach" to materials review can yield valuable results in terms of clarifying the message a campus sends to its newest members. After all, new student orientation is a window to the institution and a responsibility of the entire campus community.

Including multiple individuals to select the information that should be part of the orientation program can be quite helpful to the orientation director. This is important for two reasons. First, the various perspectives and input will be invaluable, and second, a wide range of individuals will be capable of articulating the value and successes of the program. Thus, these individuals can make the program stronger and, in turn, can more capably articulate the goals of the program. For example, the Orientation Committee at the University of North Texas is composed of individuals from a wide range of programs and departments. The Committee determined that, given the financial struggles of students, an educational program on financial management was an important component of orientation. The sessions were expanded to include information about the services of the Student Money Management Center. The input from the committee identified the need for financial literacy education, and the evaluations by participants and the campus community, substantiated in a dramatic way the effect that an active committee can have on identifying programmatic issues.

It should be noted that orientation's importance in the dissemination of information goes beyond providing interesting handouts, flyers, skits, panel discussions, and familiarization of the campus buildings. It is a methodology to shape students' important first impressions of the campus and should help students learn more about the institution, develop friendships and connections, realize the importance of resources available to them, and learn about strategies for achieving academic success.

Reducing Costly Errors

An effective orientation program can help students avoid missing deadlines, registering for unnecessary classes, and demonstrating poor academic performance, thus promoting student retention and the enrollment well-being of the campus. Furthermore, as retention and graduation rates are increasingly cited as benchmarks of institutional effectiveness, orientation takes on an increased importance as a vital campus intervention.

It should be noted that, whereas orientation was once a mechanism to register the masses with little thought given to the registration procedure, orientations today must be concerned with a sophisticated, integrated process. Through the use of technology, professional advisors, and extensive training, the registration process no longer resembles the early days of orientation programs where advisement was almost non-existent and registration was frequently a cumbersome, multi-day process. These changes in technology and the professionalization of advisement and registration have decreased the likelihood of errors in course selection and created a more streamlined process. It remains a fact, however, that advisement and registration are the impetus that draw students initially to orientation and, depending on the strength of the process, can be highly instrumental in setting the tone for a successful first year. Advisors play an important role in integrating students into the academic fabric of the institution (McGillin, 2000) and contribute greatly to the value of new student orientation and to the reduction of student error.

Orientation can also help institutions avoid costly errors. The summer registration process—typically a summer orientation program or a registration process for the fall term—provides important information for departmental planning (i.e., potential class sizes, residential housing needs). It also assists the campus in determining the need for adjunct faculty members or additional personnel in housing and dining.

There is a direct relationship between enrollment and institutional finances—when enrollments decrease, financial resources typically decline. By providing a comprehensive orientation program with effective advisement and efficient registration, administrators see accepted students matriculating and can begin to lay the ground work for those students to be retained beyond the first year.

Building a Framework for Academic Success

The most significant goal of orientation is to accentuate an environment where students are encouraged to succeed academically. No matter how well-orchestrated the program or how efficient the process, orientation has not completed its job unless students are actually more prepared to face the challenges of academe. The transition from high school to college is a difficult one. Social adjustments, career choices, and academic expectations leave first-year students with multiple choices to make. Students who attend orientation and make connections, both academic and social, persist at a higher rate than those who do not (Busby, Gammel, & Jeffcoat, 2002; Jacobs, Busby, & Leath, 1992; Mullendore, 1998). Orientation can, and must, set the academic tone of the collegiate experience and establish a comprehensive approach to student academic success. "Orientation can be the defining moment in the transition to college for the student—a time in which basic habits are formed that influence students academic success and personal growth—and marks the beginning of a new educational experience" (Mullendore & Banahan, 2005, p. 391).

Ensuring that students have opportunities to learn about the institutional expectations and resources available to them is a critical part of the orientation process (Jacobs, 2003; Rode, 2004). Faculty interaction can greatly impact a student's college experience (Cotton & Wilson, 2006), and orientation directors are wise to promote faculty involvement whenever possible. Depending on the campus, faculty support may include advisement, panel discussions, luncheon discussions, social events, small-group discussions, and large-group addresses. Learning communities and one book, one community programs have also provided opportunities for faculty involvement in orientation. Whether orientation is in academic affairs or student affairs, the partnership between faculty and student affairs is crucial (Kramer, 2003).

Building Community

No matter the type of institution, it is important for students to feel they belong to a community. Research has shown that building community has a strong positive impact on student persistence (Forrest, 1985; Pascarella, Terenzini, & Wolfle, 1986). Learning communities and residential programs have advanced the community-building agenda. Orientation programs typically include in their mission (often institutionally mandated) a responsibility to develop a sense of community. Numerous techniques are designed to build community. Trained peer orientation leaders are particularly effective as are programs and activities structured to acculturate students to campus. Nonetheless, extended orientation programs that go beyond the first two semesters (Tinto, 1994; Tobolowsky & Cox, 2007; Troxel & Cutright, 2008), first-year seminars (Barefoot, Warnock, Dickinson, Richardson, & Roberts, 1998; Fidler & Moore, 1996), and service-learning projects (Skipper, 2005; Vogelgesang, Ikeda, Gilmartin, & Keup, 2002) have a strong effect on the creation of positive campus identification and should be used in addition to the traditional orientation programs.

The National Survey of Student Engagement (NSSE) indicates that students who are engaged in their academic careers are more likely to persist and graduate. There are five benchmarks for student engagement: (a) academic challenge, (b) student-faculty interaction, (c) active collaborative learning, (d) supportive campus environment, and (e) enriched educational experiences. Each of these avenues for student engagement creates opportunities for students to become involved in the campus community. The two primary reasons students persist, according to Tinto (1994), are academic integration and social integration. Thus, creating opportunities during orientation for students to engage academically and socially, with particular attention to student engagement benchmarks as defined by NSSE, is beneficial to the student, the campus, and the orientation program.

Defining Campus Culture

Many view orientation as an opportunity to set the tone for a student's academic career and to change campus culture. It provides the first impression of college for a student and can have a great impact on the entering class. In effect, an orientation program defines the institutional expectations for students and identifies the campus culture. If orientation is silent about expectations, it has by default sent a message to students that expectations are low. Likewise, if it is silent about student behavior, traditions, honor codes, pride, and student responsibilities, they have negated the importance of those issues.

The Documenting Effective Educational Practice (DEEP) project (Kuh, Kinzie, Schuh, Whitt, & Associates, 2005) from the Center for Postsecondary Research at Indiana University, Bloomington, studied institutions that produced higher-than-predicted student engagement and graduation. They reviewed a wide range of sizes and types of institutions and found that they each shared commonalities in their cultures that contributed to the success of their students.

> [The DEEP schools] teach students what the institution values, what successful students do in their context, and how to take advantage of institutional resources for their learning. We refer to this as acculturation. Second, they make available what students need when they need it, and have responsive systems in place to support teaching, learning, and student success. We call this alignment—making certain that resources match the institution's mission and educational purposes and students' abilities and needs. (Kuh et al., p. 110)

Orientation can be an effective tool for both acculturation and alignment. It can define the culture and values of the institution for the students and provide students information about the resources they need for a successful transition.

Orientation programs may also be an efficient way to alter a campus culture and enhance campus identity and pride. New students have no institutional history, and a view of the campus culture emerges as expectations, values, and traditions are laid out during orientation. To be impactful, orientation programs must give students a clear view of the campus, including how to fit in and find a niche. There is an opportunity for the orientation director to emphasize the institution's core values and to focus on the behaviors that support those values. The determination of the institutional messaging for orientation participants should be developed through organizational linkages.

Troxel and Cutright (2008) cited examples of successful culture-changing initiatives in the first college year and noted five commonalities among them. First, programs were not isolated "silver bullets" but were, rather, integrated in a larger institutional strategy. Second, the campus clearly determined measurable goals from the initiation of the highlighted programs. Third, each created a campus-wide approach that was a "blending of strengths and perspectives from faculty, staff, and administrators" (p. viii). Fourth, evaluation was an ongoing commitment and not a final conclusion. Finally, the programs had strong administrative support.

Making Your Case for Orientation

Even when orientation directors understand the importance of orientation, the value may not be realized by the campus community unless efforts are made to map the success of the program. For an orientation staff to clearly convey the value of the program, they must have knowledge about national and local trends, be able to build strong, effective alliances, and systematically accumulate data to support the arguments. To be successful, orientation directors need to supervise a department and manage a program while also focusing on the various stakeholders, including new students and their families, faculty, staff, administrators, high school counselors, and even the surrounding community. To make the case that a campus needs a strong orientation program, orientation personnel should keep in mind that there are several rudimentary premises for a successful program. These include: staying abreast of changes in the field and in the institution, knowing your students, creating a sense of urgency, being aware of competing interests, understanding the campus climate, building allies, and assessing the program.

Staying Abreast of Changes in the Field and the Institution

It is dangerous for an orientation director to be unaware of the traits and attributes of incoming students, what behaviors seem to be positively affecting student success, or general information about the institution. Orientation professionals must understand developmental theory, best practices for orientation and the first-year experience, changes in enrollment management goals, and the institutional mission and vision. Professional development, both on campus and beyond, is important to maintain the level of understanding needed for continued program quality. Further, student staff, as well as professional staff, must have a wide range of knowledge and receive quality training.

Orientation trends and best practices change more frequently than do many other parts of the campus because incoming students bring a different set of life experiences to campus each year. Many orientation programs today address issues such as social networking, sustainability issues, binge drinking, and campus violence in a much different way than in years past, provided they were addressed at all. Thus, the orientation staff needs to be actively involved in professional associations such as the National Orientation Directors Association (NODA), and they need to be current in professional literature about students and orientation.

Knowing the Students Admitted to the Institution—All of Them!

In order to effectively orient students to campus, the staff must be able to respond to the challenges of serving various student cohorts (Jacobs & Bowman, 2003). The needs are different for a part-time student versus a full-time student, or for a transfer versus one coming directly from high school or someone entering college after time spent in the workforce. Additionally, there will invariably be groups of students who will need more individualized attention in orientation programming. Depending on the campus, some of the smaller, and often overlooked, groups may include students with children, veterans, students with disabilities, victims of violence, divorced students, transgendered students, commuters, and many others. While there may not be a need for a separate orientation for different cohorts of students, there may be a real need to provide an opportunity for these students to make specific connections with each other and to learn about services designed to support them during the orientation process. For example, on some campuses, out-of-state students are a small minority, and they face transition issues that are different from in-state students. Alerting them to campus resources specifically designed to support out-of-state students may prove to be highly beneficial to their transition.

Creating a Sense of Urgency

Successful orientation programs create a sense of urgency for the campus. In order to determine orientation objectives, set schedules, secure facility priorities, create a program, implement data-based changes, and meet publication guidelines, orientation staff and the campus orientation advisory board must help the campus understand the importance of orientation and the urgency of its mission.

Kotter (2008) describes how to create a sense of urgency "that is as high as possible, among as many people as possible" (p. 13). He states that this sense of urgency "is the first step in a series of actions needed to succeed in a changing world" (p. 13) and outlines eight components of an effective group that negotiates change.

- ◇ *Critical mass.* A sufficient number of people must feel a sense of urgency.
- ◇ *A guiding team.* With a strong sense of urgency, even overworked individuals will identify critical issues and guide ambitious change.
- ◇ *Visions and strategies.* Committed teams will find smart visions and strategies
- ◇ *Communication.* High-urgency teams will inherently feel a need to relentlessly communicate the visions and strategies.
- ◇ *Empowerment.* Those with a true sense of urgency will empower others to make the vision a reality.
- ◇ *Short-term wins.* High-urgency teams guide empowered people to achieve short-term wins.
- ◇ *Persistence.* Groups with a true sense of urgency never let up until a vision is a reality.
- ◇ *Changes that stick.* Effective high-urgency organizations find ways to make sure their changes become institutionalized into the culture.

The orientation director must be a master at building a team and empowering them to determine desired outcomes and to put necessary changes in place. An effective cross-divisional team is invaluable for orientation program success and a sense of urgency will provide much needed results.

Being Aware of Competing Interests

The fact is that there will probably never be enough resources or recognition to satisfy those with a craving for each. However, it is wise to understand the various competing interests of an institution and to be able to make the case for a fair share.

Campuses are increasingly faced with having to make difficult funding decisions among such diverse needs as faculty and staff salaries, research investments, student scholarships, fundraising, and marketing materials. There are also competing issues with maintaining a reasonable fee for orientation versus assessing a fee that will enhance the quality of the program.

Thus, an understanding of the campus budgeting process will help the orientation director most effectively articulate the need for a fair share of resources. A realization of how space is assigned and used is helpful to negotiate appropriate facilities for the orientation program. An understanding of how students perceive the orientation leader positions will help build a strong orientation staff. Budget, space, and staff are all key components of an effective orientation program, and understanding the processes and perceptions will help the director make the case for the needs of orientation.

Building Allies

In her book *How to Zing! Your Life & Leadership*, Denney (2004) provides 21 insights into maximizing one's influence. She calls this capability "Zing," which, she states, is "the ability to override competing forces to positively influence others towards a greater social good" (p. xi). Among the 21 insights are key elements in building allies: the magnetism of praise, the rules of respect, the necessity of nourishment, the art of interpersonal communication, the attraction of listening, the building of relationships, the appeal of playfulness, and the hand of humility. By building allies, the orientation director also builds a cadre of individuals who will be able to communicate the value of orientation to the campus. A successful orientation director will find a way to praise those who do well, respect those who agree and those who disagree, nurture a wide range of individuals, communicate well, listen well, build relationships, keep a sense of humor, and remain appreciative.

Orientation will never be able to function successfully within a vacuum, and it is important to build a sense of community among campus professionals who contribute to the orientation endeavor. Open communication is necessary, and a sense of collaboration, flexibility, mutual understanding, and respect are crucial and well worth the effort. Chapter 14 provides a more in-depth discussion of how to build allies.

Assessing the Program

A thorough, ongoing assessment of orientation is necessary for the program to verify its effectiveness and to target areas for improvement (Mullendore, Biller, & Busby, 2003; Wiese, 2004). Assessment must go beyond end-of-program satisfaction and document the effectiveness of the overall program, including its effect on student behaviors and outcomes. Troxel and Cutright (2008) noted that outstanding first-year programs not only measure retention but also include "documentation on student learning, positive changes in students' attitudes and behaviors, increased levels of meaningful interaction with faculty and other students, and improved academic skills" (p. v). Orientation program assessment might include such varied assessments as a programmatic review, participant evaluations, focus groups, faculty and staff surveys, administrative interviews, orientation leader debriefings, parent surveys, and benchmark data. The assessment should also include data on student matriculation after orientation, persistence and graduation rates, and students' levels of participation in campus resources. It would be important to know the difference in perceptions of parents who attended orientation and those who did not. Pre- and post-orientation attitudes of students can also provide helpful information.

It is good practice for orientation programs to have a five-year plan for assessment. Some reviews should be done each year—most notably, the end-of-program evaluation—while others, such as a complete program review, may be conducted only periodically. There should be enough flexibility in the long-range plan to allow for new assessment goals as the need arises.

There are numerous ways to receive assistance with assessment. The Institutional Research Office will be invaluable, and there are typically faculty members who will help develop a comprehensive program, supervise a class project, or suggest an intern. The orientation review committee and student leaders can assist in determining what questions need to be answered. The Council for the Advancement of Standards in Higher Education (CAS, 2003) is a good resource for programs and publications on assessment of orientation. Chapter 15 offers a more detailed treatment of program assessment.

Conclusion

Some of the most impressive transition programs will specify goals for various functional areas and ask for specific activities to achieve those goals. For example, during orientation, an academic dean may reinforce the importance of out-of-class student/faculty interactions and a program that supports the goal of encouraging student engagement, while the learning center may discuss study habits.

While orientation can never function well without strong leadership, neither can it function alone. A strong orientation program includes components as diverse as course selections, parking and housing information, articulation of the keys to academic success, community building, and programs on responsible choices. It is important that those who work with the various areas have an opportunity to claim a shared ownership of the orientation process. It is then incumbent upon the orientation director to articulate the benefits of orientation to the campus community and to make the case that human and financial resources provided for orientation are resources well spent.

The value of orientation is manifested in a variety of ways, and none more powerful than the effect it can have on student persistence and graduation:

> New Student Orientation Programs ... make a substantial impact on welcoming and connecting students as they transition to a college or university. More importantly, these orientations introduce students to the individuals and resources they will need when they are in personal or academic jeopardy—resources that many students overlook or forget are available to assist with their success in college. Ultimately, orientation programs are the bridge, the linchpin, between the last stages of recruitment and the first stages of retention. (Shupp, 2006)

References

Alexander, F. K. (2007). Balancing the challenges of today with the promise of tomorrow: A presidential perspective. In M. B. d'Ambrosio & R. G. Ehrenberg (Eds.), *Transformational change in higher education: Positioning colleges and universities for future success* (pp. 16-29). Northhampton, MA: Edward Elgar Publishing.

Association of Governing Boards of Universities and Colleges (AGB). (2007). *Top ten policy issues for higher education 2007-08.* Washington, DC: Author.

Barefoot, B. O., Warnock, C. L., Dickinson, M. P., Richardson, S. E., & Roberts, M. R. (Eds.). (1998). *Exploring the evidence: Reporting the outcomes of first-year seminars, Vol. II* (Monograph No. 25). Columbia, SC: University of South Carolina, National Resource Center for The First-Year Experience & Students in Transition.

Busby, R. R., Gammel, H. L., & Jeffcoat, N. K. (2002). Grades, graduation, and orientation: A longitudinal study of how new student programs relate to grade point averages and graduation. *Journal of College Orientation and Transition, 10*(1), 45-50.

Clayton, M. (1998, September 1). Getting to know you. *Christian Science Monitor, 90*(195), B1-B5.

Cotton, S. R., & Wilson, B. (2006). Student-faculty interactions: Dynamics and determinants. *Higher Education, 51,* 487-519.

Council for the Advancement of Standards in Higher Education (CAS). (2003). *The CAS book of professional standards for higher education.* Washington, DC: Author.

Denney, N. H. (2004). *How to zing! your life & leadership: 21 insights on maximizing your influence.* St. Louis, MO: Viaticum Press.

Fidler, P. P., & Moore, P. S. (1996). A comparison of effects of campus residence and freshman seminar attendance on freshman dropout rates. *Journal of The Freshman Year Experience & Students in Transition. 8*(2), 7-16.

Forrest, A. (1985). Creating conditions for student and institutional success. In L. Noel, D. Leviz, & D. Saluri (Eds.), *Increasing student retention: Effective programs and practices for reducing the dropout rate* (pp. 62-77). San Francisco: Jossey-Bass.

Jacobs, B. C. (2003). New student orientation in the twenty-first century: Individualized, dynamic, and diverse. In G. L. Kramer & Associates (Eds.), *Student academic services* (pp. 127-146). San Francisco: Jossey-Bass.

Jacobs, B. C., & Bowman, B. S. (2003). Methods for orienting diverse populations. In J. A. Ward-Roof & C. Hatch (Eds.), *Designing successful transitions: A guide for orienting students to college* (Monograph No. 13, 2nd ed., pp. 83-95). Columbia, SC: University of South Carolina, National Resource Center for The First-Year Experience and Students in Transition.

Jacobs, B. C., Busby, R., & Leath, R. (1992). Assessing the orientation needs of transfer students. *The College Student Affairs Journal, 12*(1), 91-98.

Kotter, J. P. (2008). *A sense of urgency.* Boston: Harvard Business Press.

Kramer, G. L. (2003). Preface. In G. L. Kramer & Associates (Eds.), *Student academic services* (pp. xi-xxiii). San Francisco: Jossey-Bass.

Kuh, G. D., Kinzie, J., Schuh, J. H., Whitt, E. J., & Associates. (2005). *Student success in college: Creating conditions that matter.* San Francisco: Jossey-Bass.

McGillin, V. A. (2000). Current issues in advising research. In V. N. Gordon, W. H. Habley, & Associates (Eds.), *Academic advising: A comprehensive handbook* (pp. 365-380). San Francisco: Jossey-Bass.

Merisotis, J. (2008, July 18). *Investing in lasting change: Productivity and U.S. higher education.* Address presented at the SHEEO Annual Meeting, Boston.

Mullendore, R. H. (1998). Orientation as a component of institutional retention efforts. In R. H. Mullendore (Ed.), *Orientation planning manual* (pp. 1-7). Bloomington, IN: National Orientation Directors Association.

Mullendore, R. H., & Banahan, L. A. (2005). Designing orientation programs. In M. L. Upcraft, J. N. Gardner, & B. O. Barefoot (Eds.), *Challenging and supporting the first-year student: A handbook for improving the first year of college* (pp. 391-409). San Francisco: Jossey-Bass.

Mullendore, R. H., Biller, G., & Busby, R. (2003). Evaluating and assessing orientation programs. In J. A. Ward-Roof & C. Hatch (Eds.), *Designing successful transitions: A guide for orienting students to college* (Monograph No. 13, 2nd ed., pp. 83-95). Columbia, SC: University of South Carolina, National Resource Center for The First-Year Experience and Students in Transition.

National Center for Educational Statistics. (2009). *Digest of education statistics: 2009.* Retrieved from http://nces.ed.gov/programs/digest/d09/

Pascarella, E. T., Terenzini, P. T., & Wolfle, L. M. (1986). Orientation to college and freshman year persistence/withdrawal decisions. *Journal of Higher Education, 57*(2), 155-175.

Pope, M. L. (2004). Preparing transfer students to succeed: Strategies and best practices. In B. C. Jacobs (Ed.), *The college transfer student in America: The forgotten student* (pp. 143-159). Washington, DC: AACRAO Publishing.

Rode, D. (2004). The role of orientation in institutional retention. In M. B. Fabich (Ed.), *Orientation planning manual* (pp. 1-7). Pullman, WA: National Orientation Directors Association.

Shupp, M. (2006). *Rethinking new student orientation.* Retrieved from http://www.newfoundations.com/orgtheory/schupp721sp06.htm

Skipper, T. L. (2005). *Student development in the first college year: A primer for college educators.* Columbia, SC: University of South Carolina, National Resource Center for The First-Year Experience and Students in Transition.

Swanson, K., & Jones-Johnson, N. (2004). Preparing community college students to transfer. In B. C. Jacobs (Ed.), *The college transfer student in America: The forgotten student* (pp. 131-142). Washington, DC: AACRAO Publishing.

Tinto, V. (1994). *Leaving college: Rethinking the causes and cures of student attrition* (2nd ed.). Chicago: The University of Chicago Press.

Tobolowsky, B. F., & Cox, B. E. (Eds.). (2007). *Shedding light on sophomores: An exploration of the second college year* (Monograph No. 47). Columbia, SC: University of South Carolina, National Resource Center for The First-Year Experience and Students in Transition.

Troxel, W. G., & Cutright, M. (Eds.). (2008). *Exploring the evidence: Initiatives in the first college year* (Monograph No. 49). Columbia, SC: University of South Carolina, National Resource Center for The First-Year Experience and Students in Transition.

Vogelgesang, L. J., Ikeda, E. K., Gilmartin, S. K., & Keup, J. R. (2002). Service-learning and the first-year experience: Learning from the research. In E. Zlotkowski (Ed.), *Service-learning and the first-year experience: Preparing students for personal success and civic responsibility* (Monograph No. 34, pp. 15-26). Columbia, SC: University of South Carolina, National Resource Center for The First-Year Experience and Students in Transition.

Ward-Roof, J., & Cawthon, T. W. (2004). Strategies for successful transfer orientation programs. In B. C. Jacobs (Ed.), *The college transfer student in America: The forgotten student* (pp. 47-67). Washington, DC: AACRAO Publishing.

Ward-Roof, J. A., Kashner, P. A., & Hodge, V. M. (2003). Orienting transfer students. In J. A. Ward-Roof & C. Hatch (Eds.), *Designing successful transitions: A guide for orienting students to college* (Monograph No. 13, 2nd ed., pp. 97-107). Columbia, SC: University of South Carolina, National Resource Center for The First-Year Experience and Students in Transition.

Wiese, D. (2004). The assessment and evaluation of orientation programs: A practical approach. In M. B. Fabich (Ed.), *Orientation planning manual* (pp. 52-58). Pullman, WA: National Orientation Directors Association.

PART II:

Organizing Orientation Programs

Chapter 4

Administration of a Comprehensive Orientation Program

April Mann, Charlie Andrews, and Norma Rodenburg

Transition is a prevailing component of our efforts to address the success, retention, and persistence of today's college students. As highlighted in previous chapters, research supports the notion that a college or university's new student orientation program plays a pivotal role in supporting that transition process. According to a 2004 ACT Policy Report on college retention (Lotkowski, Robbins, & Noeth), student integration into the campus community increases the chance of student academic success. Orientation programs have the ability to initiate student integration and have been credited in several sources as an effective means for increasing student persistence, creating an inclusive and supportive environment, and facilitating the development of social and learning communities (Mangold, Bean, Adams, Schwab, & Lynch, 2003; Tinto, 1993). Furthermore, an orientation program provides the college or university with one of its first opportunities to introduce new students to both the academic and social climate of the campus and reinforce that students will be supported.

The first consideration when designing a comprehensive orientation program that assists students with making a smooth transition into their academic environment is to determine the specific program components that will be covered. This chapter will describe key program components and offer guidelines for the effective implementation of an orientation program. Specific programming components will vary from campus to campus. Orientation programs on large, commuter campuses may look different than those programs on small, residential campuses. Not only will the program components differ from campus to campus; so too will the staffing models, reporting structure, budgets, and levels of institutional support. As such, this chapter offers general guidelines with the understanding that individual campuses must take their unique contexts and missions into account when planning and implementing orientation and transition programs.

Program Components

No matter the delivery format for orientation programs, there are certain components that should be included to provide a strong foundational support for students and to assist them with their transition into a college environment. According to Mullendore and Banahan (2005), four important goals of orientation include: (a) helping students succeed academically; (b) assisting students in their adjustment to and involvement with the college; (c) helping families understand the complexity, demands, and services of the collegiate environment; and (d) providing the institution an opportunity to learn more about incoming students through formal and informal means. To provide students with a successful transition and integration into the campus community, orientation professionals should draw upon appropriate theorists to inform their student programming. For the purposes of this chapter, Maslow's (1970) theory of human motivation will be used as a framework for understanding and responding to students' needs during orientation and throughout their college experience.

The primary focus of any orientation program should be students' integration into the academic environment. With that said, consideration also needs to be given to viewing the student as a whole person and addressing the diverse needs and concerns of each individual in the appropriate order. In his hierarchy of needs, Maslow (1970) suggested that people must have their basic physiological needs met before they can focus on psychological needs such as identity and purpose. Maslow's hierarchy of needs is often depicted as a five-level pyramid divided into the following categories: (a) physiological needs, (b) safety needs, (c) love/belongingness needs, (d) esteem, and (e) self-actualization (Table 4.1). Using Maslow's theory of motivation as a contextual framework, the primary components of orientation can be categorized according to the needs they are most likely to address.

Table 4.1

Maslow's Hierarchy of Needs

Need	Examples
Physiological	Air, food, water, sex, sleep, homeostasis, excretion
Safety	Security of body, employment, resources, morality, the family, health, property
Love/belonging	Friendship, family, sexual intimacy
Esteem	Self-esteem, confidence, achievement, respect of others, respect by others
Self-actualization	Morality, creativity, spontaneity, problem solving, lack of prejudice, acceptance of facts

I. Physiological

Physiological needs encompass what humans need for survival (e.g., food, shelter). For new students and their families, these are the base needs with which they are concerned because the campus will be a new, unfamiliar environment. Physiological needs may be addressed by including information and/or a tour of on- and off-campus housing facilities. Also, presentations and/or information about dining options and costs as well as campus health services (e.g., emergency care, health insurance) are particularly helpful. The orientation experience may include an opportunity to eat in a dining facility or meet a medical staff member to address these concerns. Students may also be eager to address other needs such as obtaining a student identification card, acquiring a parking permit, registering for classes, and purchasing related materials (e.g., books, laptops)—academic survival needs. Until these basic needs are satisfied, it will be challenging to engage students and families in additional matters relating to the college experience. It is also important to note that while physiological needs are important for all students, these needs may be perceived to be of lesser importance to commuter students who do not live in campus housing. For example, a student living off campus will not need an in-depth tour or information session about on-campus housing amenities, but they might need to know where to eat on campus and the services that are available to them. As such, orientation programs should address these diverse needs in the context of their student population.

II. Safety

With a desire for a routine and orderly world, safety needs materialize in the want for the security of the body, of financial resources, and of employment (Maslow, 1970). First, given increased awareness about campus violence, student safety is being addressed more frequently during orientation. Students need to be aware of the services available to support their safety on campus, as well as understand the personal responsibility they have in keeping the campus safe for everyone. Families will want to know what the institution does to keep students safe and what happens in the event of an emergency. This program component could be addressed by multiple campus constituents including campus police, housing, and/or the dean of students.

Though not physical in nature, an important component of personal safety that also needs to be addressed relates to one's personal financial security. Students and families need to be oriented to an institution's financial resources including financial aid and billing processes. While financial matters can be both a sensitive and challenging topic to address, it is valuable for students and families to become aware of their options. In addition to university finances, they may need additional resources regarding personal finances, such as local banks and their services, monthly allowances, and budgeting. Finally, students and families want to feel secure in knowing that student employment will be available. For some students, employment is a necessity and contributes to their educational endeavors. Offering information about on- and off-campus options as well as work-study positions provides students with the ability to better address their financial needs. Again, an understanding of the institution's student population is necessary to gauge this need. Providing financial education through orientation programming will better prepare students and families to address the financial aspects of the college experience.

III. Love/Belonging

People desire to feel accepted and belong to a group or groups. This social need is fulfilled by friendship, romantic relationships, and a supportive family. In the context of orientation, students may feel more connected to the institution if they experience orientation in a smaller peer group, allowing them to make a social connection with other students. These small groups are typically led by peer leaders who assist students with the various aspects of their orientation experience. Peer leaders enhance the "academic experience of ... students by serving as academic peer advisors, supplemental instruction leaders, and mentors" (Clason & Beck, 2001, p. 53). Similarly, family members may feel a greater sense of belonging if they also connect with other family members during orientation.

In addition to peer connections, it is also important for students to link with faculty and staff as mentors and advisors. According to Kuh, Kinzie, Schuh, and Whitt (2005), "meaningful, substantive interactions between students and their teachers are essential to high-quality learning experiences" (p. 51). This type of introduction to faculty is a very important aspect of orientation because it can "ensure that students have the confidence to approach their faculty once the semester begins" (Abel, Bice, & Cox, 2007, p. 26). Also, Pascarella and Terenzini (1991) indicate that "student involvement will be greatest if new students can be immediately linked with people who are already invested in the institution, whether faculty members or other students" (p. 650). Thus, orientation can be one of the most valuable ways in which colleges influence new students' perceptions of and connection to faculty members (Abel et al.). In addition to instilling confidence in new students, involving faculty in orientation programming helps to promote an environment where students want to belong and contribute (Smith & Brackin, 2003). Figure 4.1 depicts the amount of time faculty members spend with new students during their orientation programs. Typically, faculty/student interaction is limited to one or two hours. Transfer students are more than twice as likely as new first-year students to have no contact with faculty during orientation (Figure 4.2). This number seems surprisingly low considering the potential benefits of student and faculty interaction. To reinforce these benefits, student and faculty interaction should be encouraged and scheduled during the orientation process.

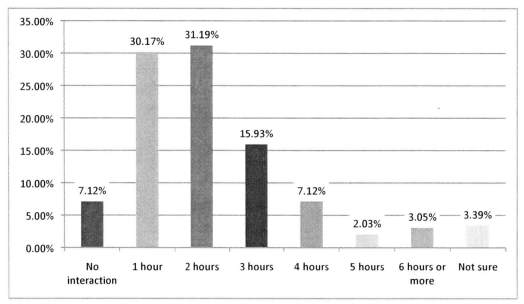

Figure 4.1. Number of hours new first-year students spend interacting with faculty during orientation (*N* = 295).

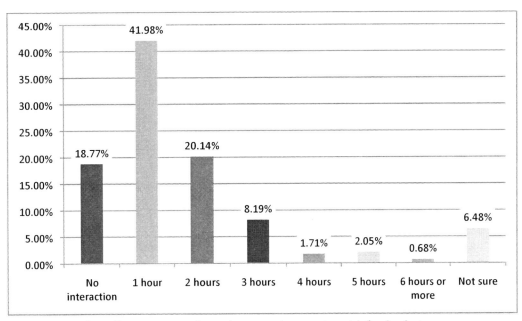

Figure 4.2. Number of hours new transfer students spend interacting with faculty during orientation (*N* = 293).

Finally, one of the most challenging aspects of belonging relates to family changes. No matter whether a student is a commuter or residential student, he or she will have to negotiate changing family dynamics. Just as students evolve throughout their college experience, so too will their families. College and university administrators are

> encouraging this generation of involved parents to be a sounding board for their son or daughter, to ask open-ended questions rather than provide simple answers, and to know the resources on campus and coach their kid to use them instead of jumping in and trying to solve dilemmas for him or her. (Coburn, 2006, p. 12)

Therefore, it is important to address relational development with both students and families.

IV. Esteem

Once a feeling of belonging is established, people want to gain recognition, to engage in activities that give a sense of contribution, and to find self-value in a profession or hobby (Maslow, 1970). For the purpose of orientation programming, students can gain feelings of achievement via academic planning, leadership activities, career self-assessment, and by participating in live or simulated classes. Additionally, students can begin to learn about future engagement opportunities, including research with a faculty member, studying abroad, and serving as a student leader. Students can also learn about support skills such as study techniques, time management, and other academic resources. Finally, esteem comes in the form of self-respect and respect for others. It is important for students to feel valued for who they are in their new community, and it is equally important for all students to respect the diverse population of their student peers. Respect for self and community values is reflected in the overt and covert messages that are conveyed to students and families throughout the orientation program.

Another critical aspect related to esteem and achievement, and one of the primary program components of a successful orientation program is academic content. First, academic advising during orientation allows new students to clarify their educational goals and provides an educational opportunity for students to interact with faculty and staff advisors. According to the 2007-2008 NODA *Databank*, nearly 68% of the institutions that responded provided advising for first-year students as a part of their orientation programs, while 55% provided advising for transfer students, suggesting that many institutions recognize the value of this. In addition to advising, more than two thirds of institutions incorporated a common reading experience for new students to build community and introduce students to college intellectual engagement (Figure 4.3). These reading programs convey diverse viewpoints, "give students an early taste of academic life, and set the tone for the first year of college" (Ferguson, 2006, p. 9). Common reading programs are discussed in more depth in chapter 7.

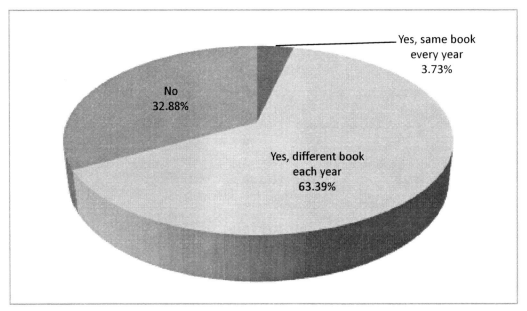

Figure 4.3. Percentage of institutions offering a common reading program as part of new student orientation (*N* = 295).

Another opportunity for students to become integrated into a community of scholars is via convocation, which allows the college community to formally welcome its newest members, celebrate their entry into higher education, officially induct students into college, articulate the university's mission and expectations, and build a group identity among the class (Cuseo, 2003). According to the 2000 Survey of First-Year Co-Curricular Experiences, the number of four-year institutions that offer convocation as a part of orientation ranged from 39% at research-intensive universities to 75% at liberal arts institutions (Barefoot, 2001).

V. Self-Actualization

The final level of need in Maslow's hierarchy is self-actualization, in which people are focused on their maximum potential and possibilities. As such, people seek to solve problems, think creatively, and feel a moral responsibility. This final level can be demonstrated through service to the community, discussions about global needs and citizenship, and spiritual awareness. While students may not be developmentally prepared to engage on this level at orientation, an introduction to such broader topics is important because it conveys institutional values and expectations to incoming students. Chapter 7, for example, offers a discussion of institutional efforts to introduce students to service during new student orientation.

Table 4.2 outlines the results of a survey question on the 2007-2008 NODA *Databank* related to the program components of orientation programs across the United States and Canada. These program components are shown in relation to the need that they meet according to Maslow's Hierarchy.

Table 4.2

Orientation Program Components Organized by Maslow's Hierarchy (N = 303)

Maslow's need	Program component	Percentage of programs that offer this component
Physiological	Living on campus	88
	Commuter issues	66
	Overnight stay	76
	Campus tour	94
Safety	Safety	87
	Financial information	90
	Alcohol awareness	79
	Date rape/sexual assault	69
	Campus policies/community standards	92
Love/belonging	Diversity	74
	Campus activities	97
	Icebreakers with other students	97
Esteem	Academic resources	97
	Academic integrity	75
	Academic requirements	96
	Study skills	65
	Interaction with faculty	80
	Academic advising	96
	Course registration	91
Self-actualization	Live/simulated class	29
	Service component	40
	Career planning information	69

Programming Models

Once the key elements of the orientation program are established, the implementation phase can begin. Orientation programs across the US and Canada use different approaches for delivering orientation to new students. Various models emerge based on program length, point in the matriculation process students attend, and availability of specific orientation programs for certain populations of new students (e.g., international students, transfer students, student athletes). This section offers a general description of the most popular program models and a summary of information taken from the 2007-2008 NODA *Databank*. These data were collected via surveys from orientation professionals at more than 300 institutions across the US and Canada.

Timing of Program Delivery

Orientation programs occur throughout the year, with the highest percentage of programs taking place during the summer months (Table 4.3).

Table 4.3

Timing of Orientation Programs ($N = 303$)

Timing of program	Percentage
Summer (June – August)	85.8
Fall (September – November)	46.2
Winter (December – February)	68.3
Spring (March – May)	22.8

Note. Respondents were able to select multiple options.

Summer programs. One popular model for delivering orientation to incoming students is to bring them to campus in the summer prior to their matriculation. This model can be administered in a one- to three-day format. During these programs, new students are exposed to various aspects of the institution's academic and social climates. This is the first opportunity to inform students of the institution's expectations and introduce them to the resources and systems available to assist them. While the specifics of these programs vary from campus to campus, they are typically linked to the course selection and registration for new students. In many cases, such as at the University of Michigan, new students are not eligible to enroll until they attend one of these summer orientation sessions.

Fall programs. Another model for orientation programs involves bringing students together during the days right before their first semester/term. These fall programs last anywhere from one day to an entire week. According to the NODA *Databank*, this model is more popular at smaller, private institutions (e.g., Washington University in St. Louis) and is particularly prevalent at Canadian institutions (e.g., University of Alberta). Due to the timing, fall programs are not usually linked to course registration. Once again, the particular components will vary, but they often continue until the first days of classes and include opportunities for students to interact with their new community (both on campus and the surrounding area).

Programs offered at multiple times. At some institutions, orientation is delivered in a fashion that is a hybrid of summer and fall models. In this model, colleges and universities may bring students to campus during the summer and focus mainly on getting the students registered for courses. To supplement that, they develop programming related to several aspects of college life and deliver them during the days immediately prior to the start of the term/semester. It is interesting to note that about one third of institutions (30%) using the summer program model supplement their efforts through Welcome Week programming that takes place immediately prior to or during the first week of classes. For example, the University of Minnesota and Appalachian State University implement this two-prong orientation model by planning complementary programming for summer and fall.

Location of Programs

Off-campus programs. As a way to meet the needs of out-of-state students and students at area schools, some institutions offer students the option of attending an orientation program in their geographical region or in their local community college or high school. This opportunity demonstrates concern for out-of-state students, in particular, by saving them money on travel costs and for students with job and family commitments who may need more flexible program options. For example, because of the distance between Corvallis, Oregon, and the hometowns of many incoming students, the orientation staff at Oregon State University travel to other states to orient incoming students and their families.

Online orientation. A relatively new approach to orientation has emerged with the development of online orientation programs, which are more thoroughly explored in chapter 8. While most institutions do not offer online orientation programs, those that do more commonly offer them to incoming transfer students (Table 4.4). These online versions of orientation programs can be developed for transfer students, nontraditional students, or students who will be attending classes solely online. For example, to better serve the needs of its student population, Tallahassee Community College provides an online orientation program. Additionally, the University of Central Florida offers a solely online orientation for students attending its satellite campuses and offers a hybrid model (a portion of the program online) to students who attend the main campus. Though the delivery mode differs from the face-to-face models, online orientation should still include the same foundational components and an assessment plan.

Table 4.4

Availability of Online Orientation Programs (N = 303)

Availability of online option	Percentage
Yes, for first-year students	9.6
Yes, for transfer students	14.2
No	81.9

Populations Served

Many institutions have begun to develop separate orientation programs for special populations of students. In most cases, the length and timing of delivery are consistent with orientation programs that have been developed for the general student population. These special populations may include student athletes, international students, honors students, and students participating in special programs or pursuing specific degrees. During these programs, students receive the same information as those who attend traditional summer or fall programs, but the delivery of the information is tailored to address the needs of the particular student population and is supplemented with specific information about resources available to assist with their unique transitions. This approach can also be a combined method, allowing special populations of students to attend orientation with the general student population while receiving additional information during a program or session tailored specifically for them.

Transfer Students

At some colleges and universities, students transferring from another institution receive their orientation separately from students attending college for the first time. The orientation program often focuses on introducing transfer students to important policies and structures that may be very different from those at their former institutions and is often shorter than the orientation programs offered for first-year students (Table 4.5). An important component of transfer orientation is to help students identify how their previous coursework fits into their current degree requirements. It often includes some of the same institutional information as the programs for first-year students, but the information is tailored to the transfer perspective. While programs for first-year students are often mandatory, transfer programs are more likely to be optional (Table 4.6). Chapter 12 provides a more detailed discussion of orientation programs for transfer students.

Table 4.5

Length of Orientation Program by Student Type (N = 336)

	First-year students (n = 300)	Transfer students (n = 279)
Half day	7.3%	30.5%
One day	24.7%	45.5%
One and a half days	19.0%	4.3%
Two days	24.7%	8.2%
Two and a half days	7.0%	---
Three or more days	24.0%	---
Other	---	14.0%

Table 4.6

Orientation Requirement for New Students $(N = 336)$

Requirement	First-year students	Transfer students
Yes	66.4%	43.8%
No	33.6%	56.2%

Parent programs. Parents have become increasingly involved in the lives of their students, and it is having an impact on the delivery of orientation programs. Based on the NODA *Databank*, more than 95% of responding institutions offer orientation programming for parents/family members of first-year students, while over 57% of respondents offer such programming to the parents/families of transfer students. Many campuses offer a parent orientation program either in conjunction with the student orientation program or held on a separate date. For more information on parent orientation, please refer to chapter 6.

There are many factors to take into consideration when designing an orientation program. It is important that each program be tailored specifically to the unique student demographics at each institution. As orientation professionals design their own models, they should consider the following:

◇ What are the student demographics of the institution?
  ◇ Are the students primarily living on campus, or are they commuting?
  ◇ What is the average age of the incoming class?
  ◇ From which counties, states, regions, or provinces do the majority of students come? (If travel time is considerable, this may impact the timing of the program.)
◇ What special populations exist within the student body?
◇ Is the orientation program mandatory or optional? Are there certain components of the program that are required?
◇ What kind of support does the program have from the faculty and staff of the institution?
◇ Are there major events held on campus or in the city that may restrict dates for the program?

Assessment Considerations

When designing orientation programs, it is critical to develop a comprehensive plan for assessment. The most common aspect of such a plan typically involves providing orientation participants with satisfaction surveys to gather information on the impact and effectiveness of the program. While student satisfaction is both an important and valuable outcome, comprehensive assessment requires much more. To go beyond participant satisfaction, orientation professionals need to consider what the orientation program is trying to accomplish and what students will learn as a result of their participation. Identifying a set of desired learning outcomes not only supports the context and goals of the orientation program, but it also provides a framework for assessment and supports the notion that institutions should measure their effectiveness by examining the ways students exhibit what they have learned (Maki, 2004).

As higher education institutions place a greater emphasis on measuring effectiveness, orientation programs have a responsibility to do the same. That often involves developing a set of program goals and identifying the measurable learning outcomes, as mentioned above. It is not enough to say that orientation will provide new students with tools to ease their transition to college. Some examples of learning outcomes for orientation might include learning general academic requirements, navigating the online registration system, identifying academic support/career development resources on campus, and valuing diversity. Starting with a list of what students and guests should learn at orientation not only enables professionals to be intentional about designing the program, but it also provides direction as to how to implement each component. Consequently, the concept of developing and assessing learning outcomes is both useful and vital to designing a comprehensive program.

The final piece of program assessment involves understanding that orientation is a collaborative process and gathering feedback from others who support and participate in the implementation of the program. Every campus has its own nuances and politics, and it would be impractical to provide a specific list of whom that should include. With that in mind, some individuals to consider including are academic administrators; admissions/enrollment management administrators; faculty; students; and staff from departments such as student activities, counseling services, career planning, and alumni affairs. Generally speaking, professionals should consider which stakeholders at their institutions have the most direct impact on the orientation program and be sure to include as many of them as possible. See chapter 15 for a more detailed discussion of assessment.

Organization and Administration

The key to any successful orientation program originates with the proper administrative foundational support, which comes in the form of organizational structure, well-prepared personnel, and adequate monetary resources. These practical aspects of orientation are necessary in order to create an effective program. According to the 2006 CAS Standards, orientation programs must be structured as purposeful events that are effectively managed in order to achieve the stated goals of the orientation program. The remainder of this chapter will focus on the organizational and administrative components of an orientation program.

Administrative Home of Orientation

The orientation function is performed by a variety of campus departments including orientation offices, admissions, first-year experience departments, undergraduate education, student activities, and enrollment management offices. Based on the 2007-2008 NODA *Databank*, 61.7% of respondents indicated that their institutions have a specific office devoted to orientation programming. While there may not be a defined office that oversees orientation at every institution, it is important that each college and university have a person(s) responsible for the "coordination of the program...even though a number of offices may be involved in the delivery of the structured activities" (CAS, 2006, p. 270). Further, it is critical for college administrators to understand the size, nature, and complexity of the institution and that information should guide the administrative scope of orientation programming (CAS). If possible, it is recommended that a stand-alone orientation/new student office provide oversight and leadership for an orientation program. By making such an office well-established and visible to internal and external constituents, orientation professionals are better equipped to provide a quality program for new students and families.

Orientation professionals are also being asked to provide programs and services beyond orientation programming that take place during a short period of time. These additional responsibilities may include admissions recruitment, first-year experience programming, transfer student programming, and/or parent and family programming. Though these additional functional areas may not directly relate to orientation, professionals have an opportunity to create innovative programs that allow new students and families to experience the university in a seamless way. In thinking about what other areas are most closely associated with orientation programming, the importance of the institutional mission and learning outcomes should be considered.

Another consideration in the administration of orientation programs is the location of the orientation function in the university hierarchy. The positioning of orientation in a college or university's organizational structure varies depending upon institutional culture, needs, and politics. Oversight for orientation programs may lie in student affairs, academic affairs, admissions, or enrollment management. In some cases, orientation programs are organized by the student union. Based on data provided from the 2007-2008 NODA *Databank*, more than 75% of orientation professionals reported to a division of student affairs (Table 4.7). As such, it is important that collaborative relationships are forged with other divisions, particularly academic affairs. No matter where orientation programs are organizationally situated, working across campus departments is of critical importance. While it may be argued that orientation programs are better served in one division or another, it is most important to understand the nuances of a particular institution. Also, if the opportunity allows, orientation professionals should assess the institutional political landscape and align with the areas or divisions that will best assist orientation programs in achieving their mission of serving new students and parents.

Table 4.7

Institutional Home for Orientation Programs (N = 339)

Institutional Home	Percentage
Student affairs	73.5
Academic affairs	10.3
Enrollment management	10.3
Split between student/academic affairs	5.3
Other	0.6

Staffing

According to the NODA *Databank*, more than 62% of respondents have a director-level position associated with orientation, in addition to other possible positions (Figure 4.4). Orientation professionals, along with graduate and undergraduate students, serve as an institution's representatives to incoming students and families. They are the key customer service and front-line associates, serving as both educators and public relations agents. For this reason, it is imperative for institutions to hire appropriately educated staff members who are prepared to organize and deliver comprehensive, university-wide programming.

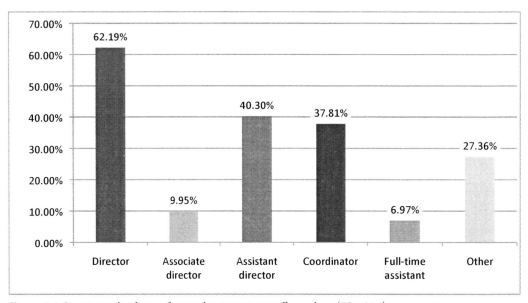

Figure 4.4. Position titles for professional orientation staff members ($N = 201$).

Professional Staff

Staffing an orientation program will vary among institutions because of differences in mission and size; however, several fundamental staffing considerations are critical for orientation programming. As indicated by the CAS Standards (2006), orientation professionals "must hold an earned graduate degree in a field relevant to the position they hold or must possess an appropriate combination of educational credentials and related work experience" (p. 270). In addition to appropriate educational levels, orientation professionals should be able to coordinate numerous program-related details, collaborate with numerous stakeholders, and be politically astute. Because of the skills required, it is not recommended that an entry-level professional serve as an orientation director. However, if an entry-level professional is given the responsibility for managing an orientation program, he/she should report to someone who can fully support the program and the new professional. This is particularly valuable in assisting the professional with institutional politics and financial management.

At some institutions, the job responsibilities of an orientation professional go beyond the scope of orientation programming, encompassing other functional area responsibilities such as admissions or student activities. If this is the case, additional skills and experience beyond those expected of the professional focused solely on orientation may be required.

Support Staff

Given the number of students and families who contact an orientation program and the numerous administrative tasks related to orientation programming, it is imperative that adequate support staff be hired. The number of support staff needed will vary from institution to institution, but they are critical to the overall program. Most likely, support staff will be the ones who provide the first impression of the institution to students and families via the telephone, e-mail, or in person. Therefore, the customer service that support staff provide is extremely valuable, and support staff should be appropriately trained in all needed skill areas. Also, it is important to involve these individuals in orientation planning, since they will be responsible for implementing administrative details and answering questions about the program.

Student Staff

The final critical staffing aspect of any orientation program is student staff—undergraduate and graduate students. Because of their role as peer leaders, student staff connect with new students in a different way than full-time staff. For institutions that may have graduate students on campus or at another nearby university, the opportunity to have them serve as program assistants, interns, and practicum students is invaluable to the program and to students who benefit educationally from such experiences. Such graduate positions may be paid or unpaid. However, when compensation is offered as salary, housing, and/or meals, it should be commensurate with the amount of work and responsibility required.

In terms of undergraduate student staff, most colleges and universities use students as peer leaders (i.e., orientation leaders, peer mentors, and student volunteers). Peer leaders are a key to a successful orientation program because of their unique position of relating to incoming students as both an employee and peer. Therefore, it is important that these student leaders reflect a cross section of the campus student demographics. By selecting a group of diverse peer leaders, incoming students can more easily identify with someone who shares similar characteristics.

Funding

In difficult economic times, when there is a decrease in funding for higher education, it is critical that orientation programs demonstrate their value to the institution by connecting the program to stated learning student outcomes. By doing so, a stronger case can be made for how orientation contributes to student retention. Also, at many institutions, budgetary procedures may be directly tied to student outcomes, increasing the importance of assessment.

Depending on the scope of an orientation program, the expenses of a program will vary. However, it is important to consider the following areas for expenses:

◇ Staff salaries
◇ Office operating expenses
◇ Professional development and training
◇ Facility usage fees
◇ Orientation program supplies
◇ Marketing and printed materials
◇ Online resources such as web sites and databases

The CAS Standards (2006) recommend that budget priorities "be determined in the context of the stated mission, goals, objectives, and comprehensive analysis" (p. 271) of what students need and the availability of resources. Additionally, CAS notes that orientation programs must have suitably located facilities, sufficient technology, and equipment to support its mission—all of which relate directly to appropriate funding.

In terms of funding resources, there are a variety of ways in which orientation can be financially supported. While it is often assumed that orientation programs are funded primarily via institutional funds, this is often not the case. A number of sources can be used to support orientation programming, including institutional general funds, student/guest participation fees, enrollment/matriculation fees, internal donations, external donations/sponsorship, fundraising, and grants. Orientation professionals should be able to make sound financial decisions, weighing the needs of students and families with program costs.

Summary

This chapter has provided insight regarding orientation program components as well as guidelines for the effective implementation of an orientation program. While programming components will vary from campus to campus, all orientation programs are designed to assist students and their families with the transition into the college environment. In addition to program components, this chapter provided insight into the staffing models, reporting structures, budgets, and levels of institutional support for orientation programs. Regardless of the differences between institutions, it is important that all orientation programs focus on meeting the needs of their participants so that new students and their families will benefit from efforts to ease their transition to their new institutional homes.

References

Abel, M. J., Bice, A., & Cox, B. E. (2007). Importance of faculty involvement in orientation. *Journal of College Orientation and Transition, 14*(2), 25-31.

Barefoot, B. (2001). *National survey of first-year co-curricular practices.* Brevard, NC: Policy Center on the First-Year of College. Retrieved January 24, 2010, from http://www.jngi.org/uploads/File/00co-curricularsurveyresponses_all.pdf

Clason, M., & Beck, J. (2001). Creative peer leadership: Beyond the classroom. In S. L. Hamid (Ed.), *Peer leadership: A primer on program essentials* (Monograph No. 32, pp. 53-62). Columbia, SC: University of South Carolina, National Resource Center for The First-Year Experience and Students in Transition.

Coburn, K. L. (2006). Organizing a ground crew for today's helicopter parents. *About Campus, 11*(3), 9-16.

Council for the Advancement of Standards (CAS) in Higher Education. (2006). *CAS student orientation standards and guidelines self-assessment guide.* Washington, DC: Author.

Cuseo, J. (2003). The big picture: Key causes of student attrition & key components of a comprehensive student retention plan. Retrieved March 2, 2009, from http://www.qep.eku.edu/course/articles/total-package.doc

Ferguson, M. (2006). Creating common ground: Common reading and the first-year of college. *Peer Review, 8*(3), 8-12.

Kuh, G. D., Kinzie, J., Schuh, J. H., & Whitt, E. J. (2005). *Assessing conditions to enhance educational effectiveness: The inventory for student engagement and success.* San Francisco: Jossey-Bass.

Lotkowski, V. A., Robbins, S. A., & Noeth, R. J. (2004). *The role of academic and non-academic factors in improving college retention, ACT Policy Report.* Iowa City: ACT, Inc.

Maki, P. (2004). *Assessing for learning: Building a sustainable commitment across the institution.* Sterling, VA: Stylus.

Mangold, W. D., Bean, L. G., Adams, D. J., Schwab, W. A., & Lynch, S. M. (2003). Who goes who stays: An assessment of the effect of a freshman mentoring and unit registration program on college persistence. *Journal of College Student Retention: Research, Theory & Practice, 4*(2), 95-122.

Maslow, A. (1970). *Motivation and personality.* New York: Harper & Row.

Mullendore, R. H., & Banahan, L. A. (2005). Designing orientation programs. In M. L. Upcraft, J. N. Gardner, & B. O. Barefoot (Eds.), *Challenging & supporting the first-year student: A handbook for improving the first year of college* (pp. 391-409). San Francisco: Jossey-Bass.

Pascarella, E. T., & Terenzini, P. T. (1991). *How college affects students: Findings and insights from twenty years of research.* San Francisco: Jossey-Bass.

Smith, B. F., & Brackin, R. (2003). Components of a comprehensive orientation program. In J. A. Ward-Roof & C. Hatch (Eds.), *Designing successful transitions: A guide for orienting students to college* (Monograph No.13, 2nd ed., pp. 39-53). Columbia, SC: University of South Carolina, National Resource Center for The First-Year Experience and Students in Transition.

Tinto, V. (1993). *Leaving college: Rethinking the cause and cures of student attrition* (2nd ed.). Chicago: University of Chicago Press.

Chapter 5

Community College Orientation and Transition Programs

Cathy J. Cuevas and Christine Timmerman

Currently, two-year institutions help close to 12 million students achieve a variety of goals, such as completing GEDs, certificates, and associate's degrees; transferring prerequisite credits to four-year institutions; acquiring job or language skills for workforce employment; and participating in self-improvement or personal enrichment courses through continuing education programs. More than 6.5 million U.S. undergraduates attend a community college, accounting for nearly half of the nation's entire undergraduate population. John Gardner, president of the John N. Gardner Institute for Excellence in Undergraduate Education (formerly the Policy Center on the First Year of College), refers to the community college as "the new American comprehensive college" (personal communication, March 14, 2009), reflecting the multiple missions of two-year colleges and a new direction for higher education. Community colleges, once referred to and viewed as junior colleges, today find themselves in the mainstream of postsecondary education (Bailey & Morest, 2006).

Community college students are diverse in their makeup, with an average age of 29. Thirty-four percent of two-year students are of minority dissent, 39% are first-generation students, 61% of students are female, and 60% are enrolled part-time (AACC, 2008). Two-year students also often have a multitude of additional commitments outside of school obligations, including work, family, and involvement in their community.

Students enrolled at community colleges often struggle to meet the financial burdens of furthering their education. According to Hermes (2008), two-year colleges have recently seen a significant increase in the number of students applying for financial aid, although annual tuition and fees at two-year public colleges are 61% less than their four-year counterparts. The number of students applying for aid at the community college increased 37.3% over a five-year period from 2001-2006, compared to increases of 7.1% and 10.5% for private and public four-year colleges, respectively (Hermes).

Open admission policies and strong articulation agreements with four-year institutions make community colleges an attractive option for students seeking to further their education in a flexible and affordable environment. While enrollment in four-year colleges has doubled since 1965, enrollment in community colleges has increased five-fold (Rosenbaum, Deil-Amen, & Person, 2006). Such rapid growth demonstrates that two-year colleges juggle not only multiple institutional missions but also the growing challenges provided by increasing enrollment.

Two-year colleges serve a distinct purpose in higher education and society, working to meet the needs of a diverse population challenged by both academic and financial barriers. Without the access and affordability offered by such institutions, many who aspire to attain a certificate or degree would be unable to do so. The Achieving the Dream (ATD) *Success is What Counts* report (2007) stated,

> If students aren't well served by their community colleges, many of them won't have other opportunities for education—and are likely to drain resources from society rather than contribute to it. However, when students do attain their educational goals (complete courses, earn certificates and earn degrees), they improve their own lives and benefit the nation. (p. 3)

Having presented an overview of two-year colleges, this chapter will further explore some of the challenges faced by community college orientation practitioners and present possible solutions. The essential elements of a community college orientation program will also be addressed, followed by suggestions for first-year programming beyond traditional orientation sessions. Examples of practice in the two-year college will be shared throughout the chapter as models of innovative approaches to traditional programming obstacles.

Challenges in Orienting Community College Students

Challenge #1: Student Retention and Success

When entering college, 71% of community college students expect to earn a bachelor's degree or higher (NCES, 2002), but only a fraction of these students actually achieve this goal. Close to one sixth of first-time college students starting out at community colleges complete no more than 10 credit hours (Bailey & Alfonso, 2005). Of those students entering two-year institutions in 2003 with plans to earn an associate's degree, only 43% had done so in four years (Berkner, He, Mason, & Wheeless, 2007).

According to McClenney and Oriano-Darnall (2008), "evidence shows that if students can successfully complete 12 to 15 credit hours (the equivalent of one semester), then they are more likely to attain further milestones and, ultimately, certificates and degrees" (p.1). Yet, findings from the 2007 Survey of Entering Student Engagement (SENSE) suggest that community colleges lose half of their students prior to the second year. Engagement for two-year colleges is not only important; it is imperative. To increase retention and student success, community colleges must focus time, energy, and critical resources on the front door experience of new students, including new student orientation programming.

While open admission policies create access for students seeking a higher education, the lack of admission requirements can make engaging students in the enrollment process a more daunting task. Challenges begin at admission. The excitement that seems built into acceptance at a selective institution is sometimes non-existent at an open-admission, two-year college. Students tend to be familiar with the institution, as a large percentage of students who enroll in a community college are typically from the local area. Encouraging students to be proactive, especially by participating in orientation, advising, and registration activities, is an uphill battle. SENSE (2007) data suggest that "one in five entering students was not aware of an orientation program on their campus" (p. 10); about one third (32%) of two-year college students did not attend orientation (CCSSE, 2007). Much of the community college struggle with orientation participation numbers is due to the large number of two-year colleges with non-mandatory programs. CCSSE's (2008) report indicates that community colleges can better serve students by "making engagement strategies and support services inescapable... making them mandatory, or otherwise bringing them to students" (p. 4).

As Kay McClenney, CCSSE director, notes, "Community college students don't do optional" (personal communication, May 26, 2009).

Solution: Critical Partnerships and Mandatory Programs

Partnerships across campus are critical in implementing orientation and other transition programs for new students. The responsibility for student engagement, retention, and success rests on the shoulders of all staff and faculty members. The college's executive leadership team must make orientation a priority, and members of both academic affairs and student affairs must work together to ensure that all entering students are served in the best way possible. Collaboration should lead to a cohesive and seamless enrollment intake process that continues through the first semester and beyond. This collaboration should reach beyond administrators traditionally involved in the enrollment process to include faculty members who play a key role in student retention. To illustrate the important role of faculty in promoting student success, Brookhaven College in Dallas, Texas, offers a workshop for faculty entitled, Preparing for the Critical First Three Weeks of Class. The workshop explores important aspects of the first few weeks of class, including course preparation, students' first-day experiences, and working with students who enroll after the first class meeting. Such workshops can help create college-wide buy-in for orientation efforts and first-year programs.

Early engagement and strong, interactive programming are critical to the success of the orientation process, but many two-year colleges struggle with low orientation attendance. Students are either unaware of orientation offerings or uninterested in participating in what seems to be an optional program. When faced with such challenges, many institutions explore making orientation mandatory. While mandatory programs provide great student and institutional benefit, the logistics of a mandatory program can create challenges for program coordinators and institutional processes. Below is a discussion of the advantages and challenges of a mandatory orientation requirement.

Advantages of a mandatory orientation program. Current community college research supports the importance of early student engagement, making a strong case for mandatory orientation programming. By ensuring that students attend orientation, the institution can begin to outline their expectations for students—challenging them to commit to the role they play in their own success while connecting them with the resources in place to support their efforts. Orientation provides the college an opportunity to set clear expectations for students related to academics, student responsibility, appropriate conduct, and the role technology will play in a student's experience (a critical topic for many low-income students who are often less technologically savvy).

The 2007 Survey of Entering Student Engagement indicates that an important role of two-year colleges is "knowing what matters and doing it for all students" (p. 14). The key is ensuring that all students have the tools they need to be successful. A mandatory orientation program establishes an institutional baseline of knowledge for entering students. The institution determines what is most important for students to learn before stepping into the classroom. Many students served by the two-year college lack the proper preparation and experience to seek out the needed information on their own and are, therefore, starting the process *below* baseline, without a formal orientation to the college (Grubb, 2006). Disadvantaged students may also benefit from what Grubb and others term "intrusive advising." Such advising includes structured meetings with advisors, mandatory activities such as academic planning (similar to those found in student success courses), and close tracking of student success. This concept supports mandatory orientation programming and emphasizes the importance of academic planning and advising as part of that process.

Challenges of a mandatory orientation program. For each institutional benefit provided by a mandatory orientation program, there is likely an equally taxing logistical challenge to be considered.

It is worth noting that most challenges can be worked through if there is a true institutional commitment to a mandatory orientation. Below are the questions that should be addressed when creating a mandatory orientation program.

1. *For whom should orientation be mandatory?* Deciding that orientation will be an institutional requirement is the first step. Two-year colleges must next identify which student populations will be required to complete orientation. Is this a requirement for all incoming students (both transfer and first-year students)? Will readmitted students also be required to complete orientation? Will high school dual-enrollment students be required to participate? Does the requirement include transient students? Is there an orientation for non-degree-seeking students?

2. *How will the mandatory requirement be enforced?* Will the consequence of missing orientation be serious enough to encourage students to participate in orientation programming? Will a registration hold be created for all students who do not complete orientation? Does the college's registration or enrollment system have the necessary technology to implement and enforce such a hold? Perhaps most importantly, is the institution prepared to support the consequence of missing orientation? (For example, if students cannot register without attending orientation, can the institution support the initial impact the policy may have on enrollment numbers?)

3. *How will the requirement be communicated to the students impacted by the policy?* It is critical that the requirement be promptly and clearly communicated to the students affected. In what format are students most likely to receive, read, and understand the message? Does the institution have ample resources to communicate this message in large numbers? Will the requirement impact postal budgets? Can the institution's infrastructure support an e-mail or electronic version of this message?

4. *Is the institution prepared to commit more staff time to planning and programming activities?* A mandatory program requirement will quickly increase the number of students served by an orientation program. The logistics of programming for larger numbers can be quite time consuming. Additionally, an increase in the number of students served will likely mean an increase in the number of orientation programs offered. This means more days away from the office and other daily activities for those involved in the program. A mandatory program often requires additional session dates. Campuses that previously limited programming to fall orientation sessions may quickly find that one week is not enough time to accommodate the large number of students served by a mandatory program. Thus, another important question related to staff time includes "Is the college prepared for a longer orientation season?"

5. *Can the college's facilities support a mandatory program?* Space is frequently a concern for two-year college orientation practitioners. Institutions must confirm that space is available to accommodate the number of students and families who will participate in a mandatory program. Will the space be available for all program dates? Is the space conducive for engaging and interactive programming?

6. *Can the college support a mandatory program with limited funding?* As mentioned previously, few community colleges have offices devoted solely to orientation programming and new student services. Many two-year programs operate on little to no money, making funding for traditional giveaways, speakers, staff shirts, and orientation packets a significant challenge. While these problems are certainly not insurmountable, they do present significant challenges for newly established mandatory programs.

7. *Is there a sincere, campus-wide commitment to instituting a mandatory orientation program?* While many of the challenges presented by a mandatory orientation program are listed here, it is impossible to predict the unique (and often unexpected) challenges that may arise on specific two-year college campuses. Most important to working through such challenges is a strong institutional commitment to mandatory new student orientation. Increased student participation in orientation programs will impact the demand for advising services, the depth of registration support provided, the number of financial aid inquiries encountered by staff, and the number of urgent requests for the processing of admissions records. It is critical that other student service areas (as well as the faculty) are on board when the orientation requirement is implemented. Perhaps most important is the role that college administration plays in supporting the requirement and unifying campus processes to support new student activities.

Valencia Community College in Orlando, Florida, offers a mandatory orientation for all degree-seeking students, including both first time in college (FTIC) and transfer students. The program was implemented as part of Valencia's Start Right initiative. Valencia offers several different modes of new student orientation, including first-year orientation for recent high school graduates, which includes sessions for parents, on-campus new student orientation for FTIC students placing into two or more developmental classes, online new student orientation for FTIC students who place into fewer than two developmental courses, transfer student orientation (which is a hybrid of online and on-campus programs) for students with previous college experience, and an orientation for English as a Second Language (ESL) students. Tallahassee Community College (TCC) in Tallahassee, Florida, also offers a mandatory orientation program for all new degree-seeking students. New students (FTIC as well as transfers) and their families take part in an on-campus program, which includes student success programming, technology sessions that familiarize students with student portal functionality, and group advising sessions that use online advising modules to encourage the development of a student educational plan.

While many community college students completing the 2008 SENSE instrument admitted not attending orientation (64%), they "consistently recommended mandatory orientation," acknowledging that a required program would be helpful (p. 9). By making orientation a requirement, community colleges can demonstrate their commitment to student success. The step is a bold one, and one that should be carefully considered.

Other alternatives. If creating a mandatory orientation program for all new students is not feasible, colleges may consider smaller steps. Is there a specific group of students the institution would like to target initially? Programming could be required for all students taking remedial courses, for instance, as a first step, with the goal of expanding the requirement in future terms. Another option is incentivizing orientation for those who choose to participate. An attractive incentive such as an early registration opportunity may attract larger numbers of students to the program.

Challenge #2: Staff and Student Leader Support

As many two-year institutions do not have an office devoted solely to new student programming, it is common for admissions or advising offices to take on orientation, juggling programming with other job responsibilities. This common reality makes staff support and involvement in orientation a significant concern. Likewise, student or peer support of new student programming is often limited. While four-year institutions pull from the upper-division student population when recruiting orientation leaders, two-year schools have no such population.

Solution: Creative Staffing Approaches

Peer leaders can often be an excellent resource for low-budget, short-staffed orientation programs. While upperclass students are not an available resource for community colleges, many two-year campuses coordinate peer leader programs, training and using returning students as orientation leaders, tour guides, or ambassadors. Some institutions seek out students already involved in other aspects of campus leadership for such positions. Other programs work with faculty and deans to identify appropriate peer leaders for new student programming. Students in the peer leader role can facilitate discussions, answer general questions, and provide guidance in class scheduling and other basic advising activities. Peer involvement permits professionals to address more challenging student needs or concerns, ensuring quality service for all orientation participants. An additional advantage of peer leader programs is the student-to-student connection that often occurs between peer leaders and new students. This connection contributes to new student engagement and can generally facilitate feelings of self-empowerment among first-time, two-year college students.

Incorporating a number of college service areas in orientation programming is another effective method for combating staffing challenges. Inviting a campus mental health counselor, for instance, to coordinate college adjustment and stress management discussions can relieve another staff member of programming duties and offer students the opportunity to interact with a staff member outside the orientation or advising office. Campus recreation or athletic offices can also provide programming support by leading activities that encourage student-to-student connections. Faculty involvement in orientation programming can provide exciting opportunities for student/faculty interaction and provide students unique insights regarding classroom expectations. While an expansion of staff and faculty participation can require relationship building throughout campus, it can also foster greater campus-wide commitment to new student orientation activities.

To facilitate a more global approach to orientation programming, many colleges create coordinating committees. Asking a number of staff and faculty from various college divisions to invest in the orientation planning process can quickly translate into campus-wide support for orientation. Coordinating committees can educate non-student service areas on the importance of new student programming and assist in building bridges with various campus constituencies. Practitioners should also note the importance of a diverse committee makeup. A diversified committee provides greater benefit to orientation programming and encourages new partnerships throughout campus.

Challenge #3: Limited Funding is a Common and Ongoing Problem for the Community

Limited funding is often due to a lack of a clearly established orientation office and/or mission. Without a formal orientation office, many campuses have little (to no) budget for orientation programming, and orientation fees for program participants are uncommon. Limited resources force programmers to put together programs that are limited in scope and often lack support and commitment from the campus community.

Solution: Creative Funding and Fiscal Responsibility

Funding for two-year college orientation programs is frequently limited and often non-existent. Creativity is the key to successful orientation programming on a shoestring programming budget. Below are some creative approaches for dealing with budget shortfalls.

1. *Instituting orientation fees.* Such fees are a logical funding solution for many four-year colleges and universities, but the financial constraints of two-year college students commonly limit additional fee assessment. Due to the financial challenges of many two-year students,

orientation programs should be careful when considering an additional orientation fee. If an orientation fee must be administered, scholarships or other subsidies should be made available for students in financial need.

2. *Seeking donations.* In-kind gifts from a campus bookstore or other appropriate vendor can allow programs to provide quality orientation materials to participants without taxing a limited budget. Many college bookstores are willing to provide folders, pens, and giveaways in exchange for an ad in a publication or recognition during orientation activities. Local vendors are also happy to work with programs as they are hoping to market their property, services, or merchandise to new students. If providing food for participants and families is a concern, programs can consider asking dining services or an on-campus food vendor for complimentary meals or discount coupons. While such partnerships can be beneficial, orientation directors should be sure to clear all sponsorships/partnerships with appropriate college administration, as many institutions have established policies for such in-kind arrangements. It is also important that practitioners consider the appropriateness of any partnership with an outside vendor and are comfortable with subsequent affiliations created by partnership agreements.

3. *Asking other campus departments to support orientation.* If a program creates orientation packets that include information about campus services and programs, service areas wishing to include information in the packets can be asked to make their own copies. If the Student Programs/Activities Office has a healthy budget, they may be willing to provide backpacks with their logo (or contact information) for new students. Foundation offices may also be willing to provide funding to support orientation activities. Orientation staff members will also want to look into campus-based grant programs focused on student success and retention. These programs often strive to have a campus-wide impact on student retention activities and may be able to provide support for new student programming.

4. *Making the most of the money spent by the program.* When a program does decide to spend money that is scarce, practitioners should be sure to spend funds wisely. Student orientation leader shirts, if printed with appropriate logos and information, can double as shirts for tour guides throughout the year. Ordering folders and brochures in large quantities can often reduce the per unit price. Programs may consider printing folders that can be used for multiple programs and activities throughout the year. Orientation materials can also be used in student success classes or workshops. Making dollars go farther is a smart way to tackle budget shortfalls.

5. *Being careful about unnecessary expenses.* Programs should consider all orientation expenses and think carefully about any possible areas of waste. Is the program mailing too many postcards and reminders to orientation participants? Can some communications be sent to new students electronically? Using student portals or e-mail systems can save money and begin to familiarize students with the technologies they will be expected to access when they become an enrolled student.

Challenge #4: Outside Commitments Faced by Many Community College Students

More than half (57%) of community college students work more than 20 hours per week (CCSSE, 2007). Nearly two thirds (60%) of community college students attend college less than full time (AACC, 2008), and "...about one third of two-year college students spend 11 hours or more per week caring for dependents" (Powers, 2008). The overwhelming list of outside student commitments can make an on-campus, daytime program challenging.

Solution: Flexible Orientation Offerings

In response, many two-year colleges offer abbreviated or evening programs to provide more options for full student schedules. Online orientation programs are also growing in popularity among two-year institutions with 2007 SENSE data indicating that 11% of new students participated in online orientation. Colleges should be careful, however, not to rely on this format as the primary method of new student orientation as there is no documented evidence of the effectiveness of the online orientation approach (Barefoot, 2008).

Essential Elements for Two-Year College Orientation Programs

Promoting Engagement Through Programming

Recognizing the importance of student engagement, two-year orientation program facilitators must be proactive when planning information sessions. Long, lecture-style meetings work against critical factors for student engagement. Sessions should be dynamic, exciting, empowering, and interactive. The need for engagement extends to all student populations, including at-risk students (e.g., part-time, first-time in college, students needing remediation). For students juggling work, family, and other commitments, engagement begins by granting easier access to programs. A variety of orientation options (including morning, evening, or weekend programs) is imperative for the diverse student population being served by two-year colleges.

To encourage immediate student engagement in orientation programming, Tallahassee Community College (Florida) facilitates a student success activity during the first 45 minutes of orientation programming. In the activity, students are invited to identify factors that impact their success. The participants then group the factors, as appropriate, into three categories: (a) factors they can control, (b) factors they can manage, and (c) factors they can adapt to. The activity is enlightening, as students soon learn how much personal impact they have on their own success.

Equally important for student engagement is the opportunity for participants to socialize and interact with other students. Peer-to-peer relationships can be a powerful method of engagement, often putting students at ease with the process and experiences ahead of them. Finding others they can relate to makes students more comfortable and helps them to feel less alone. To encourage peer-to-peer connections, many community colleges have gone beyond traditional orientation programming, offering celebratory activities and special pre-semester trips for incoming students. Butler County Community College (Kansas) offers Camp Grizzly, a five-day program the week preceding the academic term, which encourages first-time students, commuters, and on-campus residents to engage in 12 interactive events designed to assist them in making integral connections. More than 30 returning students serve as Camp Grizzly counselors working directly with groups of first-year students to facilitate interaction, share college experiences, and answer standard new student questions.

Another creative approach to interactive student programming is well modeled by Central Oregon Community College's Campus Connections program. Campus Connections offers students the opportunity to participate in one of four themed outdoor programs during their second day of orientation activities. Options for new students include: exploring an underground desert cave, hiking in Central Oregon, "Out on the Town" activities, or rafting on the Deschutes River. Another community college venturing beyond single-day programming is Southwestern Oregon Community College (SOCC) in Coos Bay, Oregon. SOCC offers a four-day new student orientation program the week prior to the fall semester. Special sessions include a tour of the surrounding community; dinner with the college president; presentations on alcohol and safe sex; and student entertainment, including bowling, open gym activities, and a hypnotist. The extended program also includes more traditional programming, such as an orientation for parents, meetings with advisors, an on-campus housing meeting, breakfasts for special student populations, and skill-building workshops. Program materials include free student planners and college sports packs. These programs illustrate creative approaches to facilitating student engagement with both peers and the campus community.

While engaging students in the orientation program is critical, practitioners must also design activities that connect students with critical support services. Programs must emphasize students' roles in their own success, challenging participants to use student support services and programs. Academic and career planning activities should also hold a prominent position on orientation program agendas.

Ninety percent of students surveyed say advising and planning (activities) are either "somewhat" or "very" important (CCSSE, 2007). Unfortunately, fewer than half of students responding to the 2007 CCSSE discussed academic plans with an advisor during the first four weeks of the academic term. This disconnect emphasizes the importance of connecting students with advisors early in the process. Orientation advising activities can ensure initial engagement in the academic planning process, but programs should be careful to emphasize planning over scheduling. Beyond merely scheduling class times, students should gain an understanding of the connection between appropriate class selection today and long-term academic success tomorrow. Programs should engage students in the planning process, emphasizing the importance of successful (and timely) class completion and clarifying the importance of planning to meet educational goals. This is particularly important for the numerous at-risk populations served by the community college who may not recognize the importance of planning beyond the next semester.

Beyond advising, social interactions, and academic resources, orientation programs should strive to prepare students for the rigors and challenges of their first academic semester. Many incoming students from at-risk populations are ill prepared for the increased academic responsibility placed on them by college instructors, as 42% of first-year community college students were required to take at least one remedial course (Parsad & Lewis, 2003). In addition to lack of preparation, lack of student engagement in the classroom can also be a barrier for ill-prepared students. Powers (2008) notes,

> Nearly a third of all faculty … said they spend more than half of class time lecturing. More than one in five spend no time on small-group activities, and the majority [of respondents] spend less than 20% of class time on such activities.

These findings demonstrate a real challenge for new students. To prepare students properly, orientation programs should encourage students to create strategies for managing lecture-based classes with an emphasis on seeking help when needed. For example, learning lab assistance can supplement classroom lectures for students who feel they need additional instruction in specific subject areas; study groups with other students can be of great assistance when preparing for exams; and workshops on learning styles, test anxiety, and study strategies can help students acquire skills in areas where they lack confidence.

Financial support is another critical issue for first-semester community college students, and both students and families should be engaged and informed regarding their financial resources. The SENSE Survey (2008) indicates that finances significantly impact two-year student drop-out rates. Successful academic planning and class registration without financial support often leaves students struggling to complete the enrollment process. Ensuring students are connected to financial aid services is a critical piece of successful and engaging orientation programming.

Promoting Student Success

In planning transitional programming for new students, it is important to first evaluate what skills students need to be successful in college. Students making the transition from high school directly to the community college must have realistic expectations about the college experience. According to Antonio, Kirst, and Venezia (2003),

> America's high school students have higher educational aspirations than ever before. Eighty-eight percent of 8th graders expect to participate in some form of postsecondary education, and approximately 70 percent of high school graduates actually do go to college within two years of graduating. These educational aspirations cut across racial and ethnic lines. (p. 6)

Orientation can help students achieve their educational goals by introducing critical student success strategies. Orientation is the first real step in the important process of engaging students early. Programs should "articulate the institution's expectations of students... and provide information that clearly identifies relevant administrative policies, procedures, and programs to enable students to make well-reasoned and well-informed choices" (Dean, 2006, p. 269). Orientation is pivotal in helping students become aware of resources, programs, and services available to them. This support can be emphasized throughout offered programming in the form of campus tours, presentations, information tables, small-group discussions, and printed materials. Orientation staff should refer to the college's web site so students know how to navigate this resource on their own when they are later looking for specific information or registering for classes online. Students and family members should also leave orientation with contact information for key offices and staff members so they have someone to turn to for guidance once they leave campus.

Orientation should also help create excitement for the students and their family members. Sharing information about the long-term benefits of attending college is always a helpful method for creating both excitement and discussion. In addition to the ability to earn a considerably higher salary, college graduates also experience better health (i.e., smoking less and exercising more), participate in more volunteer activities, are more likely to vote, have much lower rates of unemployment, and raise children who are better prepared for school and are more involved in extracurricular activities (Baum & Ma, 2007). For two-year students struggling financially and working long hours to attend college, such a discussion on the benefits of college can contribute greatly to their persistence and motivation throughout their college career.

First-Year Programming Beyond Orientation

Due to the unique challenges community colleges face regarding student success and retention, institutions would be wise to provide transitional programming beyond traditional orientation programs. A number of strategies or approaches can prove successful, but as research demonstrates, it is important that these programs are designed to be both intentional and engaging. John Gardner and Betsy Barefoot of the John N. Gardner Institute for Excellence in Undergraduate Education have highlighted the top three most effective first-year experience initiatives in colleges today—Supplemental Instruction, first-year seminars, and learning communities (Barefoot, 2008). Similarly, Muraskin, Lee, and Swail (2004) found that institutions with high graduation rates offered a variety of institutional programs and approaches that appear to have positive effects on student retention. Examples include summer bridge programs prior to the first year, first-year seminars, first-year interest groups, linked classes, learning communities, flexible academic scheduling, and other academic support programs. Unfortunately, in spite of the fact that two-year institutions enroll more at-risk students than their four-year counterparts, community colleges are much less likely to offer first-year seminars, learning communities, Supplemental Instruction, and other educational initiatives linked to retention and academic success (Barefoot, 2000).

To be an effective advocate for student success and retention, two-year colleges must embrace orientation and new student support programming beyond the traditional preterm orientation program. Successful long-term approaches include:

Supplemental Instruction (SI). Supplemental Instruction is an academic assistance program using regularly scheduled review sessions in which students compare notes, discuss readings, develop organizational tools, and predict test items. Students learn how to integrate course content and study skills, working together on problems encountered. The sessions are facilitated by SI leaders—students who have previously done well in the course and who attend all class lectures, take notes on important class topics and discussions, and act as overall model students (The International Center for Supplemental Instruction, 2008). Supplemental Instruction can be particularly helpful for new students struggling in gateway courses required for higher-level study.

First-year seminars. First-year seminars can vary in content and scope, taking the form of an extended orientation, an academic seminar with generally uniform content, an academic seminar with various topics, or a seminar related to pre-professional or discipline-specific topics. The National Resource Center for The First-Year Experience and Students in Transition web site (http://www.sc.edu/fye/) offers a searchable database of community college first-year seminar syllabi. Additional information on first-year seminars offered at two-year colleges is provided in chapter 7 of this monograph.

La Guardia Community College (New York) has developed a first-year seminar model. The La Guardia First-Year Experience (FYE) Academy creates a cohesive and comprehensive first-year experience for students, linking student development services with curricular offerings. The entire La Guardia first-year class is divided into four academies that encompass the majors offered at the college, such as a health/science academy, a technology academy, a business academy, and a liberal arts academy. Elements of the FYE Academy Model include a first-semester new student seminar; a Gateway to the Workplace program (focusing on career development) during the second semester, specialized basic skills courses (designed to introduce critical basic skills to new La Guardia students), and a year-long series of extracurricular activities and orientation events. Students in La Guardia's FYE Academy also create an electronic portfolio highlighting their experiences, including personal academic and career preparation.

Learning communities. Curricular learning communities are classes that are linked or clustered and are often related by an interdisciplinary theme. These courses enroll a common cohort of students and use a variety of approaches. Learning communities restructure student class time, credit hours, and learning experiences to build community between students, between students and faculty members, and between different faculty members of various academic disciplines (Washington Center for Improving the Quality of Undergraduate Education, n.d.). Such offerings provide an ideal opportunity for connecting new students to peer and faculty resources.

Beyond Supplemental Instruction, first-year seminars, and learning communities, a number of transition programs are in place on community college campuses throughout the country. The list below offers additional options for institutions seeking to expand their support of new students.

1. *Welcome week.* Welcome Week is a series of activities and events designed to help students acclimate to their new environment and add a sense of excitement for the beginning academic experience. Kingsborough Community College (KCC) in Brooklyn, New York, offers a comprehensive approach to first-year student support that begins with their Campusfest welcome week program. During Campusfest, the president hosts a barbeque luncheon on

the college's unique beach patio, as faculty and staff from throughout campus participate in welcoming new students to the Kingsborough campus. This week also includes campus tours, workshops, a club fair, and a department showcase.

2. *Mentor program.* New students who participate in a mentor program are assigned to peer or faculty/staff mentors. Mentors can assist students with any issues or concerns that arise during the first semester and can also serve as a valuable campus resource. Bellevue College (Washington) offers a peer-to-peer mentoring and volunteer program that connects first-year students with successful continuing students with whom they are likely to identify. Select continuing students take the lead in designing, planning, and delivering the student presence at new student orientation, in first-year experience programs, and the throughout the first three days of school. The group also welcomes new students to the school every quarter in a phone-a-thon and designs social events, including food-themed parties, hikes, and trips to the city.

3. *Student activities.* While student activities are available for all students on campus, such programming can be of particular value to new students, assisting them in making purposeful connections with other students and staff. Student activities and organizations often help students improve their leadership skills, and some activities are specifically designed to encourage first-year student engagement.

4. *Tutoring.* Many tutoring programs are peer-based programs that enlist successful, established students to provide support for students in need of academic assistance. Programs can provide one-on-one or small-group tutoring, focusing on individual student needs. Tutoring is often a free service for enrolled students.

5. *Early alert/intervention.* Half of all community colleges responding to the 2000 National Survey of First-Year Curricular Practices have an early-alert system in place (Barefoot, 2000). This is typically a cooperative and/or collaborative program between academic affairs and student services, designed to assist faculty in identifying students who are at risk of failing, dropping a course, or withdrawing from the college. This is a particularly important approach to consider in light of the challenges most community colleges face in both student success and retention.

6. *Early and consistent communication.* Many institutions are placing new emphasis on regular and consistent communication with new students. Approaches range from newsletters and e-mails to Blackboard groups and Facebook networks. Salt Lake Community College (Utah) sends out a weekly e-mail, entitled StartSmart, to new students during their first semester. StartSmart includes helpful and timely information on advising, registration, financial aid, tutoring, and other important student resources.

7. *Summer bridge programs.* Summer bridge programs offer at-risk students the opportunity to get a jump start on the fall semester. These specialized programs frequently establish learning communities that provide academic support, social connections and supplemental student support services. Scholarships for summer bridge programs are commonly available to increase student access. The Lone Star College System offers a summer bridge program targeting graduating high school seniors in need of upper-level developmental courses in reading, writing, or math. The program enables students to complete developmental courses quickly (in three- to four-week sessions) so they can begin studies in the fall semester at the college level. The accelerated program allows incoming students to effectively transition from high school to college. An added advantage is that the program also links students to faculty and/or staff who serve as student mentors. Workshops on learning styles, career planning and study skills are also provided. Grants provide textbooks free of charge for

participating students, and $100 scholarships are awarded to students who complete the program successfully.

There are also successful programs taking a more comprehensive approach. The First Generation Student Success (FGSS) Program at the Community College of Denver (Colorado) provides a model environment for first-generation students. The program enrolls participants in first-year seminars, learning community initiatives, tutoring and peer mentor programs, service-learning opportunities, and community-service activities. Two full-time FGSS educational case managers (and other faculty and staff) work closely with students to help them adapt to college life. The FGSS program has an impressive annual retention rate of 80%. Beyond Kingsborough Community College's (New York) welcome week programming, 60% of first-year students participate in learning communities during the fall semester. These communities include an English course, a student development course, and a third course from an additional content area. During the second semester of enrollment, students are assigned an academic advisor in their area of study who works with them for the remainder of their time at Kingsborough. Broward Community College (Florida) promotes a holistic approach to advising new students. The model consists of multiple advising interventions, including a formal advising and registration session, an individual advising appointment where an action plan is developed, and a meeting to begin the career planning process as a component of the student's future educational plan.

Conclusion and Recommendations

Conversations with community colleges throughout the country indicate that many institutions have taken a new approach to student retention, implementing a cluster of coordinated student success strategies. Below is a listing of some successful approaches that can make a significant impact when implemented together as one coordinated student engagement effort.

1. *Make orientation mandatory.* "Engagement matters for all students, but it matters more for some than for others" (CCSSE, 2007, p. 5). An optional orientation program leaves the decision in the hands of the student and increases the likelihood of missing students who need additional guidance and support. Orientation is a critical step toward student empowerment and engagement, and many institutions have demonstrated that mandatory orientation plays a significant role in their college-wide retention strategy. Mandatory approaches to first-year programming may also include required participation in first-semester student success classes and/or attendance at student advising workshops.

2. *Include advising and registration as part of the orientation process.* This strategy emphasizes the vital importance of timely and accurate academic advising. Students must meet with an advisor prior to registration to ensure that future academic major and career goals are considered as part of a long-term student academic plan. Such planning is essential in promoting student understanding of academic requirements and expectations. Incorporating advising and registration activities into orientation encourages proper placement, accurate advising, and informed decision making when students make class selections.

3. *Offer special orientation programs for subgroups of students.* Washtenaw Community College in Ann Arbor, Michigan, offers separate orientation programming for traditional students, nontraditional students, F1 Visa students, and ESL students. Specialized orientation sessions offer institutions the opportunity to tailor programming to meet the needs of the students being served. Special programs may also allow institutions to offer evening or Saturday

programs, which provide more opportunities for nontraditional or part-time students to attend. Additional benefits of specialized programming include increased student inter-action (with others in similar circumstances) and increased student engagement through relevant programming and information sharing.

4. *Create a college transition program.* Two-year colleges are approaching this strategy in a number of different ways. Achieving the Dream (n.d.) suggests that many institutions are creating transition programs that target students who have delayed their entry to college after high school. Many community colleges have implemented summer bridge programs for first-generation or at-risk students. Both approaches focus on acclimating students to the college environment with an emphasis on student resources and support. Students in transition programs are encouraged to seek out assistance when needed as they begin to take a more active role in their educational experience.

One final note is a recommendation that more two-year college orientation and retention staff participate in professional assessment and research activities to be sure that others in the field are aware of the unique issues related to orienting students to two-year colleges. Nearly half of all undergraduate students in the country attend two-year colleges. Yet of the 317 colleges who completed surveys for inclusion in the 2007-2008 NODA *Databank*, only 5% of respondents were employed by two-year colleges. As more two-year colleges begin focusing on the entering student experience, student service professionals must be able to more easily access research, data, and best practices in the field of orientation and transition.

In conclusion, it is critical to remember the role that every staff member, faculty member, and college representative plays in promoting students' success and engagement. Beyond a successful orientation program, the entire college must commit itself to promoting success and encouraging students at each point in a student's educational journey:

> Every college has a stated commitment to educating all students, but their actions tell us more than their mission statements. Even a casual visitor can walk onto a college campus and know, almost instantly, whether the college community *believes* that all students can learn… Institu-tions that expect students to perform well use language that communicates students' value and potential. (CCSSE, 2007, p. 11)

Such messages are the cornerstone of a successful two-year orientation program. The institution must believe in its students' ability to succeed and communicate that belief to students, parents, and family members. Programming should highlight student support mechanisms, connect students with resources before they are needed, and connect students with staff or faculty members who can serve as guides or mentors throughout the enrollment and transition process.

Resources for Practitioners

Achieving the Dream: Community Colleges Count (ATD)
www.achievingthedream.org
ATD is a multi-year national initiative to help more community college students succeed. The initiative is particularly concerned about student groups that traditionally have faced significant barriers to success, including students of color and low-income students. ATD works on multiple fronts, including efforts at community colleges and in research, public engagement, and public policy. It emphasizes the use of data to drive change.

American Association of Community Colleges (AACC)
www.aacc.nche.edu
Based in Washington, DC, AACC is the main membership organization for the nation's nearly 1,200 two-year institutions.

Community College Research Center (CCRC)
ccrc@columbia.edu
CCRC was established in 1996 by the Alfred P. Sloan Foundation and is housed at the Institute on Education and the Economy (IEE) at Teachers College, Columbia University. A national partner in Achieving the Dream, CCRC conducts research on community college issues including (a) access and equity, (b) the high school-to-college transition, (c) institutional mission and governance, (d) programs and practice, and (e) workforce education.

Community College Survey of Student Engagement (CCSSE)
www.ccsse.org
Established in 2001 as a project of the Community College Leadership Program at the University of Texas at Austin. The survey, adapted from a similar tool used on four-year campuses, assesses community colleges' effectiveness in actively engaging their students.

John N. Gardner Institute for Excellence in Undergraduate Education
www.firstyear.org
Formerly the Policy Center on the First Year of College, the Institute supports colleges and universities as they pursue the attainment of excellence in undergraduate education. By focusing its expertise on the development of assessment-based action plans with measurable outcomes, the Institute fosters institutional change by enhancing accountability, coordination, and the delivery of efforts associated with student learning, success, and retention during the undergraduate experience. While the Institute undertakes activities to strengthen all of undergraduate education, it places particular emphasis on special efforts to improve the success of beginning college students. One of the Institute's signature projects is Foundations of Excellence in the First College Year, a comprehensive, guided self-study and improvement process that enhances an institution's ability to realize its goals for student learning, success, and persistence. The Foundations project features dimensions of excellence specifically tailored to the two-year college environment.

League for Innovation in the Community College
www.league.org
Founded in 1968, this membership organization for community colleges includes more than 800 two-year institutions in 16 countries. This organization hosts conferences and institutes; develops

web resources; conducts research; produces publications; provides services and leads projects and initiatives with member colleges, corporate partners, and other agencies.

National Resource Center for The First-Year Experience and Students in Transition
www.sc.edu/fye/
The National Resource Center for The First-Year Experience and Students in Transition has as its mission to support and advance efforts to improve student learning and transitions into and through higher education. This mission is achieved by providing opportunities for the exchange of practical, theory-based information and ideas through the convening of conferences, institutes, and workshops; publishing monographs, a peer-reviewed journal, electronic newsletters, guides, and books; generating and supporting research and scholarship; hosting visiting scholars; and administering a web site and listservs. The National Resource Center provides resources for two-year college educators through its publications, conferences, and web site.

Office of Community College Research and Leadership (OCCRL)
www.occrl.edu.uiuc.edu
The Office of Community College Research and Leadership (OCCRL) was established in 1989 at the University of Illinois at Urbana-Champaign. OCCRL is affiliated with the Department of Educational Organization and Leadership of the College of Education. Their mission is to provide research, leadership, and service to community college educators and assist in improving community college education policy and practice, particularly in the Illinois community college system.

Opening Doors
www.mdrc.org/project_31_2.html
In this initiative, experts from New York-based Manpower Demonstration Research Corporation (MDRC) are working with community colleges in several states to design and implement new types of financial aid, student services, and classroom innovations to increase the success rates of low-income students.

Survey of Entering Student Engagement (SENSE) – A CCSSE Initiative
www.ccsse.org/sense/
The Survey of Entering Student Engagement (SENSE) helps community and technical colleges focus on the front door of the college experience. Grounded in research about what works in retaining and supporting entering students, SENSE collects and analyzes data about institutional practices and student behaviors in the earliest weeks of college. These data can help colleges understand students' critical early experiences and improve institutional practices that affect student success in the first college year

References

Achieving the Dream. (n.d.). *College implementation strategy overview.* Retrieved January 18, 2010, from http://www.achievingthedream.org/CAMPUSSTRATEGIES/STRATE-GIES ATACHIEVINGTHEDREAMCOLLEGES/implementationstrategyoverview.tp#studentsupportservices

Achieving the Dream. (2007, October). *Success is what counts.* Retrieved January 18, 2010, from http://www.achievingthedream.org/docs/SUCCESS-counts-FINAL-11.6.pdf

American Association of Community Colleges (AACC). (2008). *College fact sheet.* Retrieved May 28, 2008, from http://www2.aacc.nche.edu/research/index.htm

Antonio, A., Kirst, M., & Venezia, A. (2003). *Betraying the dream: How disconnected K-12 and postsecondary education systems undermine student aspirations.* Stanford University Bridge Project. Retrieved January 18, 2010, from http://www.stanford.edu/group/bridgeproject/betrayingthecollegedream.pdf

Bailey, T., & Alfonso, M. (2005). *Paths to persistence: An analysis of research on program effectiveness at community colleges.* New Agenda Series. Indianapolis: Lumina Foundation for Education.

Bailey, T., & Morest, V. S. (2006) *Defending the community college equity agenda.* Baltimore: Johns Hopkins University Press.

Barefoot, B. O. (2000). *National survey of first-year curricular practices: Summary of findings.* Brevard, NC: Policy Center on the First Year of College. Retrieved January 18, 2010, from http://www.jngi.org/uploads/File/Final_Summary_Curricular.pdf

Barefoot, B. O. (2008, March). *Foundations of excellence in the two-year college: Lessons learned for new student success.* Proceedings from Entering Student Success Institute. Santa Fe, New Mexico.

Baum, S., & Ma, J. (2007). *Education pays: The benefits of higher education for individuals and society.* The College Board Trends in Education Series. Retrieved May 30, 2009, from www.collegeboard.com/prod_downloads/about/news_info/trends/ed_pays_2007.pdf

Berkner, L, He, S., Mason, M., & Wheeless, S. (2007). *Persistence and attainment of 2003-04 beginning postsecondary students: After three years* (NCES 2007-169). Washington, DC: U.S. Department of Education, National Center for Education Statistics.

Community College Survey of Student Engagement (CCSSE). (2007). *Committing to student engagement.* Austin, TX: The University of Texas at Austin, Community College Leadership Program.

Community College Survey of Student Engagement (CCSSE). (2008). *High expectations and high support.* Austin, TX: The University of Texas at Austin, Community College Leadership Program.

Dean, L. A. (Ed.). (2006). *CAS professional standards for higher education* (6th ed.). Washington, DC: Council for the Advancement of Standards in Higher Education.

Grubb, N. (2006). Like, what do I do now? The dilemmas of guidance counseling. In T. Bailey & V. S. Morest (Eds.), *Defending the community college equity agenda* (pp. 195-222). Baltimore: Johns Hopkins University Press.

Hermes, J. J. (2008, February 21). *Federal aid applications rise sharply at community colleges.* Message posted to http://chronicle.com/article/Federal-Aid-Applications-Rise/40517

The International Center for Supplemental Instruction. (2008). *Overview—Definition, purpose, and participants.* Retrieved January 18, 2010, from http://www.umkc.edu/cad/SI/overview.shtml

McClenney, K. M., & Oriano-Darnall, A. (2008). *Talking SENSE, 1*(1). Austin, TX: The University of Texas at Austin, Community College Leadership Program.

Muraskin, L., Lee, J., & Swail, W. S. (2004). *Raising the graduation rates of low-income college students.* Washington, DC: Pell Institute for the Study of Opportunity in Higher Education.

National Center for Education Statistics (NCES). (2002). *Institutional characteristics of postsecondary institutions.* [Data file] Washington, DC: U.S. Department of Education.

Parsad, B., & Lewis, L. (2003). *Remedial education at degree-granting postsecondary institutions in fall 2000* (NCES 2004–010), Table 4. Washington, DC: U.S. Department of Education, National Center for Education Statistics.

Powers, E. (2008, February 10). Rules of (community college) engagement. *Inside Higher Ed, Daily News Update.*

Rosenbaum, J. E., Deil-Amen, R., & Person, A. E. (2006). *After admission: From college access to college success.* New York: Russell Sage Foundation.

Survey of Entering Student Engagement (SENSE). (2007). *Starting right: A first look at engaging entering students.* Austin, TX: The University of Texas at Austin Community College Leadership Program.

Survey of Entering Student Engagement (SENSE). (2008). *Imagine success: Engaging entering students.* Austin, TX: The University of Texas at Austin Community College Leadership Program.

Washington Center for Improving the Quality of Undergraduate Education. *What are learning communities?* Retrieved June 5, 2008, from www.evergreen.edu/washcenter/lcfaq.htm#21

Chapter 6

Channeling Parental Involvement to Support Student Success

Jeanine A. Ward-Roof, Laura A. Page, & Ryan Lombardi

n the mid-1980s, Cohen and Halsey (1985) suggested that the work of student affairs need not be inclusive of parents. While the advice may have been practical at the time, it no longer reflects the reality of parent/child or parent/institution relationships in higher education. Parents increasingly view college and their involvement in their child's experience as an entitlement (Henning, 2007); moreover, this sense of entitlement seems to increase exponentially with the price of tuition (Conneely, Good, & Perryman, 2001; Forbes, 2001; Johnson, 2004). While student affairs professionals may have once viewed parents, guardians, and family members as "occasional participant[s]," the parent role has since been redefined as a "key stakeholder" (Merriman, 2006, p. 12). Yet, parents are not barging uninvited onto the campus. Much of the current literature on parent and student interactions indicates many students want parents to play a significant role in their college experience. Evidence of this phenomenon is illustrated in the 2008 CIRP data report for Florida State University, with 68% of students responding that they planned to communicate with their parents two to seven times a week while in college. Merriman (2007) found similar expectations among students. Thus, as orientation, transition, and retention professionals build programs, services, and processes for new students, they are faced with the challenges and rewards of including parents, guardians, and family members in these efforts. Yet, planning for such involvement is complex given shifting parental views, changing family dynamics, legislation, and campus policies.

This chapter will review the literature on parent and family involvement in college and explore the trend toward establishing parent partnerships in order to foster student success. In particular, the chapter will offer examples of parent programs connected to the orientation, transition, and retention process. To supplement the available literature, the authors conducted an electronic survey examining parent and family members' inclusion in orientation and other transition programs. The chapter opens with a discussion of the role parents and families play in students' transition to college followed by strategies for building effective partnerships with these key constituents.

The Role of Parents and Families in the College Transition

Defining the Family

For the purpose of this chapter, the authors define a parent as a responsible adult providing guidance and emotional and/or financial support for the student. As such, this adult could be a birth, adoptive, or step-parent or a legal guardian. Family members are other people in the student's life who play or support the role of the parent and may include siblings, grandparents, aunts, uncles, and others. Traditional-aged students may define their family as grandparents or siblings while nontraditional-aged students may define their families as spouses, partners, children, or aging parents. This chapter will focus primarily on the traditional-aged student population. For more information about nontraditional students with families and children, please refer to chapter 13.

Examining Parent/Child Relationships in College

Higher educators and the popular media have been exploring the connection between parents and their college-age children with a renewed intensity since the early 1990s. Further, the highly involved parent phenomenon is not just a part of the North American culture. A 2008 BBC News report explored highly involved parents of college students in the United Kingdom. One higher education administrator noted that "students were often now tied to their parents by what is 'surely the longest umbilical cord in history'—the mobile phone" (BBC News). Hofer (2008) found communication between parents and first- and second-year students averaged 13 times a week, with cell phones being the most popular method of communication. Moreover, students and parents were generally satisfied with the level of communication, and both parties were equally likely to initiate contact.

To illustrate how current students view their parent and family involvement, the authors turned to *The American Freshmen: National Norms for Fall 2007* (Higher Education Research Institute, 2007). For the most part, students reported that they believed their parents (or legal guardians) were involved to an appropriate extent in a range of college-entry activities (Table 6.1).

Table 6.1

Students' Perceptions of Parent Involvement ($N = 272,036$)

Activity	Percentage of students who thought parents involved to an appropriate extent
Choice to attend college	84.0
College applications	74.2
Choosing the college to enroll	80.5
Dealing with college officials	77.5
Selecting courses	72.5
Selecting activities	73.7

Note. Adapted from *The American College Student: National Freshman Norms for Fall 2007* [Annual Report] by Higher Education Research Institute, 2007. Copyright 2007 by the Regents of the University of California.

Overall, the survey found that although most students of color stated their parents were not as involved as they would like in the above categories, Latino/a students were more likely to desire greater parental involvement in enrollment activities. More specifically, 20.5-33% of Black students, 33.3-39.6% of Asian/Pacific Islander students, and 32.2-43.5% of Latino students, compared to fewer than 17% of White students, indicated that their parents were not involved at the level they desired in regard to interacting with college officials or selecting courses or activities. Understanding students' expectations for parent involvement across different populations can help orientation professionals create programs and design services to meet those needs.

Yet, even as students desire parent involvement, they are experiencing psychosocial growth and development that may strain their relationships with parents. As a 2007 Association for Student Judicial Affairs (ASJA) report noted, "...many [college students] are struggling to navigate and negotiate greater (not necessarily total) freedom from parental control. College administrators are caught in the middle of this generational tangle" and have to rethink their responses (p. 3). That is, the traditional advice to parents to simply let go may no longer be applicable. Instead, Forbes (2001) suggests administrators should see themselves as facilitators, helping parents "redefine their relationships in the midst of enormous shifts" (p. 17). Providing patient facilitation as both parents and students transition may lead to reduced frustration and greater satisfaction for all concerned.

Exploring the Role of Family in College Success

Carney-Hall (2008) stated, "The overwhelming increase of parental involvement reported by today's college administrators requires a careful understanding of today's parents, their influence, and their expectations" (p. 3). In many cases, the influence has been assumed to be negative. Feaver, Wasiolek, and Crossman (2008) define over-involved parents as those who believe their student should only have to study and that it is the parents' responsibility to take care of everything else. While Feaver et al. see this level of involvement as admirable, they suggest that parents who choose to take on these responsibilities keep their students from "...learn[ing] how to manage the day-to-day distractions of life while accomplishing a greater goal" (p. 47). Pryor (2008) states, "When parents intervene in their children's college life and decision-making, students may not necessarily develop their own problem-solving skills, which may limit developmental gains in their learning experiences" (p. 2). Similarly, Mullendore, King, and Watson (2008) question the long-term effect of parent involvement on students' development. Even popular media outlets such as *Time Magazine* have made the case against what they call over-parenting. In her article, Gibbs (2009) includes pictures of children encased in bubble wrap, arguing that the current generation of parents have become over-involved and created more anxiety in their children. To combat this, Gibbs encourages parents to espouse the slow-parenting movement spearheaded by Carl Honoré (2008).

These over-involved parents have frequently been called helicopter parents, suggesting that they hover over their children. Yet, Hoover (2008) found when surveying college administrators that many believed the term helicopter parent was overused and that parent involvement on campuses was typically defined as being more helpful than harmful. Hoover's insights are supported by the 2007 National Survey of Student Engagement (NSSE) annual report, which concluded that parents who were more connected to their students and the college environment actually aided their children's success. Additionally, of the 4,518 first-year students at 24 different institutions who responded, 62% reported frequent (i.e., "very often" or "often") contact with their mother, 54% with their father, and 55% with their guardian. Of the first-year students surveyed, 34% stated their parent or guardian "frequently or often intervened on their behalf" to take care of issues or concerns. In addition, the data showed that students who did have parents or guardians intervening frequently or often reported "higher levels of engagement and more frequent use of deep learning activities, greater gains on a host of desired college outcomes, and greater satisfaction with the college experience" (p. 25). Regardless of the reported involvement, the majority of students (70%) noted that they typically followed the advice of their mother, father, or guardian when offered.

Examining Parent-Institution Relationships

During the first half of the 20th century, colleges and universities frequently assumed responsibilities similar to those of the parent, acting *in loco parentis* (Melear, 2003). As such, the relationship between parent and institution was a close one. Yet, the upheaval of the late 1960s resulted in the creation of legislation that curtailed that relationship by barring faculty and staff from freely sharing student records with parents, guardians, or family members (Melear). Keeping parents at arms' length may not always be in the best interest of students, however. Pennington (2005) notes,

> as educators, we are often at odds with parents in regards to students' actions on campus and how the college or university should respond. However, both parties typically have the student's best interests at heart. Through partnerships with parents and family members, we can create additional learning opportunities and also increase the likelihood of student success. (p. ix)

Recognizing the value of partnerships with parents has led to the current hybrid system that allows for open communication with parents especially in the case of health and safety emergencies or at the onset of self-destructive or high-risk behaviors, while still restricting access to certain educational records (Melear). Henning (2007) named this hybrid style of interaction "*in consortio cum parentibus*—in partnership with parents" (p. 539).

To support these partnerships, administrators need to develop sound listening skills, clearly outline expectations for positive parental involvement, and channel parent enthusiasm and interest into mutually beneficial programs. By relaying a message to parents that their students are part of a supportive collegiate community, parents and staff can work together to enhance the student experience. In addition, using parents as conduits to relay information to students assists staff with ensuring institutional information is being received. Henning (2007) concludes, "By including parents in the relationship, staff and faculty [have] another tool in their toolkits to foster student learning" (p. 557). The task of an administrator is not to redefine the parent/student relationship, nor to offer education on how to best parent a college-aged student. Rather, staff members must reach a balance of promoting an appropriate level of parent involvement, while also encouraging students to become independent thinkers and problem-solvers. The more parents know about university resources, the more comfortable they will feel serving as a mentor and guide to their students. In turn, students will become more confident as they learn to manage the challenges that come with adulthood.

Despite the greater openness toward parents, federal legislation in the United States and Canada still places restrictions on the nature of the parent/institution relationship. The three most prominent pieces of legislation are the Family Education Rights and Privacy Act (FERPA) and the Health Insurance Portability and Accountability Act of 1996 (HIPPA) in the United States and Freedom of Information and Protection of Privacy (FOIPP) in Canada. Both FERPA and FOIPP generally prohibit the disclosure of student information to parents, family members, or anyone without an *educational need to know*, defined as information used to support the academic progress of the student. HIPPA does not allow for any disclosure of medical records without a signed release. In most cases, this legislation does not pertain to students who are under the age of 18. FERPA, FOIPP, and HIPPA also allow for disclosure of information in the event of a health or safety emergency, and FERPA allows for disclosure when financial dependence can be established or when students are involved in illegal or high-risk alcohol use, other high-risk behaviors, or emergency situations. The orientation and transition profession should be familiar with such legislation, the information disclosure limitations of these and other state or province laws, and specific institutional policies related to their enforcement. Moreover, they should be prepared to describe these restrictions to parents and family members while equipping them to access general information for managing their role in their student's life.

Strategies for Building Effective Partnerships With Parents

Although the level of parent and family involvement has increased on college campuses, the concept of involving parents is not new to orientation, transition, and retention professionals. Nehls (2007) states, "While the primary purpose of an institution is to focus on the student, colleges and universities would be remiss not to place emphasis on the relationships that students maintain with their parents during their college career" (p. 6). In order to explore the current practices involved in delivering parent and family programs, the authors created and distributed an electronic survey via the following: National Orientation Directors Association Listserv (NODA), First-Year Experience Listserv (FYE-List), and the National Association of Student Personnel Administrations' (NASPA) Parent and Family Knowledge Community Listserv. The survey consisted of four open-ended questions and asked respondents to report on the parent/family programs and services currently in existence at the institution and those they would like to initiate. Respondents were also asked to identify programs or services currently being offered that they considered "unique or innovative practices" and to note trends they had seen in parent and family involvement in higher education over their careers. The survey respondents included 114 different individuals from institutions across the United States and Canada. Table 6.2 provides an overview of survey respondents. These responses shaped the following discussion of programs and strategies for building effective partnerships with parents. Examples of unique and innovative practices are also included.

The range of existing programs and services was fairly consistent and included parent/family weekends; electronic media such as web sites, newsletters, and listservs; and parent associations; however, parent orientation was the most commonly reported program. Based on the diversity of survey responses, the authors found evidence that parent/family programming and services offered across the US and Canada existed at various levels.

Assessing Campus Climate and Family Needs

Before determining the kinds of programs and services to offer for family members, orientation professionals need to understand both the institutional climate and the students entering the institution. For example, it is important to understand the stance a campus takes in working with parents and family members in order to ensure that parent and family programs and services align with the mission of the university. Does campus practice encourage fully incorporating parents and family members into a variety of venues, offer minimal support and opportunities for involvement, or discourage involvement, either intentionally or unintentionally? The latter is less common as most campus administrators have developed some type of outreach to parents or guardians; regardless, assessing this practice is vitally important as orientation, retention, and transition programs are developed, implemented, and evaluated to ensure their alignment with institutional mission, values, and priorities. In addition, staff members should carefully follow policies and procedures

Table 6.2

Overview of Parent and Family Programs Survey Participants (N = 114)

	Number	**Percentage**
Type of Institution		
Two-year	3	3
Four-year	111	97
Private	42	37
Public	72	63
Residential	76	67
Commuter	38	33
Geographic Location		
Northeastern US	24	21
Southeastern US	36	32
Southwestern US	6	5
Western US	16	14
Midwestern US	29	25
Canada	3	3
Student Population Size		
5,000 or less	32	28
5,001 – 10,000	23	20
10,001 – 15,000	11	10
15,001 – 20,000	14	12
20,001 – 25,000	11	10
Over 25,000	20	18
No report	3	3

and listen to student cues and directives for how to best include parents and family members. It is equally important to consider the political climate at the university, and whether an attempt to communicate with parents will be met with resistance from those who are competing for their attention (e.g., development and alumni staff). Orientation professionals are encouraged to build relationships with these colleagues proactively to understand the full scope of their shared interest in this population.

It is also important to determine who will attend the parent, guardian, and family programs and what needs they bring, especially since this population is typically large and diverse. This type of assessment of parent needs and desires can be accomplished electronically, by phone, or in person. When surveys are not practical, orientation professionals can rely on historic data on parent demographics and involvement to make programming decisions. By understanding the needs of those served, the orientation professional has a better opportunity to tailor the program to meet needs and help establish a strong foundation for the participants.

Communicating Effectively With Parents and Family Members

Determining the desired level of parental inclusion is important for establishing the tone, frequency, and type of communication with family members. As noted earlier, educators have to balance what can be communicated to parents against students' right to privacy. That said, institutional policy and practice can go a long way in helping parents feel the lines of communication are open. Orientation, transition, and retention programs staff play a key role in establishing those lines of communication and in helping parents understand the expectations and culture of campus (Keppler, Mullendore, & Carey, 2005).

Strategies for communicating with parents are varied and may include print or electronic newsletters, listservs, web sites, blogs, social networking sites, mailed information, and personal interactions. Electronic communication methods are extremely cost and time efficient and typically user-friendly ways to help parents understand events and support programming on campus, and many parents have come to expect easy-to-negotiate electronic and phone access to campus resources. Although electronic media is an easy way to communicate, not all parents will have access to technology. Similarly, even when parents do have access, they may not be proficient at using technology or may have software that is out of date. Administrators will want to ensure that web sites are accessible to users with a wide range of experience and access capabilities so that messages are not lost. Moreover, when possible, it is important to monitor blogs and social networking sites to provide accurate information when parents may be venting or sharing rumors as fact.

In addition to plans for distributing standard information about the institution, its policies, and student transition experiences, orientation, transition, and retention professionals will also want to consider how they will communicate to parents and family members during a crisis situation. The first thing to be aware of is that parents and students may define a crisis differently than a professional staff member. For example, parents may see a scheduling hold or a roommate conflict as a huge stumbling block to their students' success while professionals may view it as the result of inaction or inappropriate action on the part of the student. As noted earlier, federal laws may limit what can be communicated. Professional staff should create clear guidelines about what constitutes an emergency or crisis situation and what can be shared with parents without the student's consent during those times. In addition, when responding to parents questions and concerns, professionals should determine if the message needs to be sent only to the one parent or family member who asked or if it would be beneficial to inform the entire parent or family member population about the issue or concern. There are times when issues only affect one student, and professionals will communicate with that student and their parents, guardians, or family members directly to find a solution; other situations might involve communicating with broader constituents and require a different course of action. See chapter 9 for a more in-depth discussion of communication plans during a crisis situation.

Survey respondents described a number of ways they facilitate communication with parents and family members. Several examples are listed below:

◇ Western Washington University located in Bellingham, Washington, with a student population of 13,000, offers parents many online resources including a handbook and newsletter. These resources provide the parents and family members with a directory of campus resources and explanations of campus culture so they are able to help their son or daughter with issues they encounter.

◇ At Furman University, a small (2,650 students) private institution located in Greenville, South Carolina, the staff members call every first-year student's family once per semester to check in and see how the transition is progressing. Through this program, the staff relies on and includes the parents in helping make the student transition process successful.

◇ Georgia Southern University located in Statesboro, Georgia, with a student population of more than 16,000, offers parents a unique log-in process as a way to streamline the way their campus addresses FERPA and the release of student information to parents and family members. The student is responsible for controlling access to records for their family members.

Planning Events and Services for Parents and Family Members

Prematriculation. Administrators often interact with members of the student's family during college fairs, campus tours, and admissions interviews. During that time period, students and their families are usually focused on basic aspects of a campus environment including the admissions process and deadlines, the orientation program, academic majors, housing and food options, finances, and campus safety. If parents, guardians, or family members are alumni of the college, their involvement may be more emotionally charged. Regardless of the situation, these interactions often set the stage for how parents and family members will view subsequent interactions with the institution. The University of North Texas (UNT), located in Denton, Texas with a population of more than 34,000 students, makes a conscious effort to provide positive prematriculation experiences for students and their families. The university sponsors send-off events in the students' hometowns prior to enrollment. These activities enable the students, parents, and family members to get to know those in their community who have also chosen to attend UNT.

Orientation. Often parent orientation programs and services are the most comprehensive way to help parents understand their role in supporting their child's success. One goal of parent and family orientation should be to accomplish what Ullom and Faulkner (2005) define as foundation building or helping students build or uphold a network to help them succeed well into their future. Across the nation parent, guardian, and family member orientation programs vary based on the needs of the institution and those who attend; however, there are some common facets that comprise successful programs. Austin (2003) suggested that helping parents, guardians, and family members better understand what changes could occur at home and with their child or sibling, what their role will be in all of these changes, and expectations as well as resources available to help everyone manage all of these transitions and expectations are important topics. While college students experience a number of challenges related to the transition, issues that arise at home during the first year are likely to complicate those challenges. Common experiences might include parents' divorcing or remarrying, the serious illness or death of a family member, job changes for parents, and increased attention paid to siblings who are still living at home. As the family composition changes, relationships and expectations will change. Orientation professionals should encourage parents and families to consider how they might handle some of these non-college life events so as to minimize the impact on the college transition.

Along with the students' transition, Nehls (2007) suggests parents also go through significant transitions of their own and often struggle to cope with their changing parent role. As orientation, transition, and retention professionals are building programs, it is important to include an awareness of some of the changes parents may face in the conversations. All of these changes will most likely affect the students' and parents' relationships, as illustrated in a recent study by Johnson, Gans, Kerr, and Deegan (2008), which concluded that family cohesion levels can affect students' coping strategies at college. Ultimately helping parents understand all of the possible development issues and transitions can help students obtain better support and coping mechanisms.

Ward-Roof (2005) suggests several other topics that should be addressed in parent and family orientation programs, including:

1. A discussion of boundaries so parents complete the program aware of what information they have direct access to and what they must really communicate about with their students individually
2. Guidance on where they can find information on campus resources and how to access typical campus resources
3. A conversation about some of the more difficult issues that face students and their families during college, such as drug and/or alcohol abuse, violence, or mental health crises. Campus experts such as counselors or practitioners can describe the scope of these issues on campus and the services available for students. They can also offer strategies for setting expectations about behavior with college-age children prior to their enrollment.
4. A discussion about the whole life of the student, touching on unique institutional expectations for inside and outside the classroom

Other topics that might be included in a parent and family orientation are information about campus traditions and history, students' finding fit on a campus, campus involvement, safety, and helping their child or family member manage their new-found freedoms. Orientation should help parents, guardians, and family members develop a better understanding of their student's college environment and related expectations. Research illustrates that parents who are knowledgeable of campus resources, services, and programs are better equipped to help their child negotiate the campus environment (Mann, 1998).

The typical parent orientation program is one to two days in length and covers a variety of topics to help parents adjust to the college transition and help their student accomplish the same. In addition to the length of time, determining the format of the programs is an important consideration. Parent and family programs can run concurrent to student programs, be offered before or during the term, or provided online. The important aspect of any program is making sure it fits with the parent, guardian, and family needs as well as those of the institutions. Ward-Roof (2005) offers additional suggestions to consider when creating a parent orientation:

1. Develop an awareness and understanding of both student and parent developmental needs.
2. Enlist current members of the community (e.g., students and parents) to help explain the unique aspects of the environment and introduce incoming parents, guardians, and family members to others who have been successful.
3. Tap into the campus community to find those who are currently experiencing similar transition issues in order to help explain what could occur in the lives of those participating in orientation. This could be accomplished by seeking speakers who have recently gone through an orientation program or those who have students currently enrolled in college.
4. Give parents, guardians, and family members materials to take home (e.g., handbooks, calendars) to remind them how to use campus resources and how to best help their children

or family members. When printing those materials, remember to take into consideration the unique structures of families. Given that students may now bring more than one set of parents to orientation, it may be necessary to print multiple copies per family. For example, Pryor et al. (2008) reported that nearly one quarter of students attending baccalaureate institutions who responded to a national survey of entering college students have parents living in separate households.

5. Be sure to have the participants evaluate the sessions; these results can be used to continually improve the program.

In addition to these suggestions, a senior student affairs professional or other campus administrator should have a dedicated time with parents at orientation to have a candid and in-depth conversation about their upcoming partnership and the boundaries and limitations of that relationship.

Survey respondents offered a number of examples of unique practices that are included in parent and family orientation programs.

◇ At Purdue University (38,000 students), located in West Lafayette, Indiana, the staff performs skits for parents so they are aware of typical situations their students may experience. Meetings explaining campus resources that can help the students resolve the situations are hosted after these skits.

◇ Nebraska Methodist University, located in Omaha, Nebraska, is a private college with a population of 650. It offers parent and family members two unique programs. They host a kid camp during the orientation program where younger siblings are entertained and learn about what their brother or sister will be experiencing while in college. In addition, the family orientation features a panel with a current student, parent, and spouse or significant other and offers incoming parents and family members the opportunity to interact with them.

◇ The University of Regina is a public institution with a population of more than 12,000 students located in Regina, Saskatchewan, Canada. During their orientation program, they separate the parents into faculty groups (i.e., by college or school). Parents spend one hour in their student's faculty asking questions and meeting those who might be instructing their child.

◇ San Jose State University located in San Jose, California, with a population of 35,000 students, places parents in first-year transition guide groups. These small groups of family members are led by University staff and faculty and provide a safe environment for parents to have their questions answered.

◇ At Bradley University located in Peoria, Illinois, with a population of 5,000 students, the orientation staff members offer their parents a Reader's Theatre, that is a collection of books, poems, stories, and plays that relate to letting go and the college experience. This helps parents and family members begin to think about the letting go process and how they can help their son or daughter and themselves manage during this time.

◇ At Florida State University located in Tallahassee, Florida, with a population of 40,000 students, the orientation leaders host small groups of parents to discuss campus traditions, student life, expectations, parent involvement, as well as answer questions.

◇ The University of Minnesota, a large (50,000 students) public institution in Minneapolis, Minnesota, has developed parent outcomes in conjunction with the student learning and development outcomes to outline what parents should be learning along side their children.

When planning orientation programming, it is also helpful for orientation professionals to realize that according to Mullendore and Hatch (2000), the period of letting go never ends. Orientation professionals now find they are handing parents off to their colleagues across campus as the parents, guardians, and family members are seeking additional opportunities for involvement (Ward-Roof, 2005) through parent councils or clubs, family or parent weekend planning committees, and the like. The parent and guardian role continues to morph as they seek ways to stay highly involved in their children's college experience and as their sons and daughters' continue to request their guidance and support.

Special events for parents and families. It is also important to plan special events for parents, guardians, and family members so they know they are needed and appreciated. Although this may not be a direct responsibility of the orientation, transition, or retention staff, their involvement may ease the parents' transition to campus and help reinforce a consistent message. Parent or family weekends, special communications, and invitations to student organization inductions or campus events are truly appreciated by most parents and family members. These events are effective ways for campus administrators and students to invite parents and family members to campus and showcase a variety of events and programs to help them learn more about campus. Many weekends include some type of interaction with the campus president, vice president of student affairs/dean of students, provost, deans, faculty, and other staff. Parents have the opportunity to meet the people their children are having class with, working with, or who are just part of their daily lives. Some programs include opportunities for parents to see sporting events, enjoy special meals, the chance to visit the dining hall, attend class or a student organization event, use the recreation center, take part in a 5K run, and much more. Programs might focus on challenges students are facing, key traditions on campus, and student resources. A key ingredient to offering a successful parent or family weekend is to have something for everyone. This is another good opportunity to assess the potential audience and determine whether special events such as programs for smaller siblings need to be included or if the events need to focus specifically on parents and guardians.

Parent office. Parent offices are an ongoing resource to assist parents, guardians, and family members. Some parents, guardians, or family members do not interact with parent offices until they are intervening on behalf of their student. These interactions are typically quite emotion-laden and often times the issues being addressed are complex (e.g., illnesses, grades, roommate problems, finding fit, getting involved, or personality issues between students and classmates or professors). Parents typically contact the office staff and want whomever answers the phone or e-mail to solve their children's problems immediately, or they state they will come to campus, call the president, or various other responses. Other times, they want the problem to be solved but do not want their children to know they called. Still other parents find themselves contacting the parent office because their child has exhausted all of their options, and the situation is still not resolved. Finally, some parents might simply seek information, updates, and deadlines from staff as they try to learn more about the campus.

Ideally, a parent office should provide constant communication with parents through written, verbal, or electronic media and serve as the central source for information about the college or unique situations the college is facing. These communications should include a variety of messages such as deadlines for course registration, information about upcoming events, and institutional responses to current issues or trends.

The nature of parent, guardian, and family member interactions will vary as some may be dealing with their first child, only, or last child to leave home and they may be elated, depressed, or a mixture of both. Parent office staff can help each individual negotiate his or her own issue(s) by offering personal attention, finding a solution, or directing the person(s) to another resource. Although there are limitations to how parents, guardians, and family members can be assisted (i.e., parents do not have access to many campus resources for their personal use), these interactions will ultimately help the parents deal with their issues so they can be free to offer more support to their students.

Involving Parents and Families on Campus

Once students have matriculated, parents, guardians, and family members may also seek involvement in parent councils or similar organizations. Orientation, transition, and retention professionals are often involved with these types of organizations and challenged with how to best serve those who get involved. Successful models include a hybrid programming body that also addresses development/fundraising needs. The outcome is a parent council or organization that helps to guide parent, guardian, and family involvement in healthy and productive ways and encourages them to financially support the goals of the institution.

According to the National Survey of College and University Parent Programs (Savage, 2009), there was a large increase from 2003-2007 and then a slight decrease in 2009 in the formation of parent councils at institutions across the United States. The councils grew 28.8% between 2003 (36.6%) and 2007 (65.4%), then decreased 12.9% in 2009 (52.5%). Mullendore and Banahan (2005) state, "because many parents want to continue to be involved in the lives of their students, colleges should in an intentional, purposeful way provide structure and opportunities for involvement" (p. 35). Because orientation programs are charged to relay information, expectations, and opportunities in a relatively short period of time, organizations such as these can help professionals reinforce the message about appropriate boundaries with parents (Daniel, Evans, & Scott, 2001). As Mullendore and Banahan note, continuous communication is needed to appropriately engage parents, and this can be accomplished through parent, guardian, and family member organizations and opening lines of communication with this group.

Often housed in the orientation office, parent organizations play a vital role when used as an advisory group to university administration. A focus group that orientation, retention, and transition professionals and other administrators can quickly turn to, members provide feedback and support in an effort to enhance the programs and services provided to their students. The university staff may effectively present objectives and needs and enlist members to assist in strategic planning for new and existing initiatives.

Ultimately, institutional messages have added value when parents are involved in their creation. When parents work closely with university staff and administrators, they may be groomed into well-informed ambassadors for the university. Promoting university programs that best meet the needs of students and families, advocating on behalf of student and parent interests, and encouraging legislative support are just a few of the ways parent organizations can support their campus leadership.

These types of organizations are also an excellent way to educate parents about the needs of campus and enlist their support to seek funds for priorities or potential donors. The key to successfully enlisting parents in the development/fundraising aspect of an institution is to help them understand funding structures and the costs associated with meeting institutional goals. Lastly, an important aspect of parent associations is to have a staff person who has a significant amount of time dedicated to the needs of the organizational members. Typically parents and guardians face numerous transition issues as their child leaves their home and assimilates to the campus environment, they find comfort in the availability of a staff person to answer questions, calm fears, and provide information.

Selection of parent council members may derive from an application process, suggestions from faculty, staff or other parents, or at the invitation of university administration. Although the structure of parent organizations varies among institutions, members typically represent current undergraduate students, possibly from each class, and should also reflect the diversity of the institution (i.e., geographic, ethnic, socioeconomic, religious)

Trends in Parent and Family Programs

When asked what trends have been noted in parent/family involvement in higher education, respondents to the survey overwhelmingly stated they had seen an unparalleled increase in involvement of parents throughout all types of institutions. At the same time, many responded that although there had been an increase in the involvement of parents it seemed to be highly accepted and desired by the students. The respondents stated that institutions are responding quite well to these trends and have developed new programs and services to meet the increased needs of parents and family members.

Despite this positive institutional response, survey participants identified a number of programs and services they would like to see expanded including parent offices and stronger liaison roles. They also suggested that parent associations should broaden their scope beyond development/ fundraising efforts. Survey respondents also advocated offering more communication avenues including information hotlines for campus updates, electronic family portals, a blog site, improved web sites, family calendars and/or parent handbooks. They also wanted see greater outreach to parents by establishing regional parent clubs, offering support groups for parents, and soliciting volunteers to assist with offices across campus. Recognizing the enormity of managing increased services for parents and families, respondents also called for hiring a full-time staff person solely dedicated to parent issues and programs.

Conclusion

Including parents and family members in the orientation, transition, and retention processes is vital to the success and personal development of today's students. Moreover, students desire this increased involvement, and most expect college administrators to openly include parents and family members in their daily lives. Professionals should assess their campus culture and incoming students' perspectives to create the most effective interactions with parents and family members as possible. Programs and initiatives must be inclusive of diverse student and parent needs as they may differ from majority cultures at the institution. More specifically, professionals must outline expectations and boundaries to enable parents and family members to best understand the role they play in their son or daughter's educational environment, while helping parents and family members understand they are partners in creating a shared mission of student success. Orientation, transition, and retention professionals are poised to achieve a healthy balance between student development and the parent and family member letting go process by strategically including parents and family members in the college campus and education process.

References

Association for Student Judicial Affairs (ASJA). (2007). *ASJA law and policy report.* College Station, TX: Author.

Austin, D. (2003). The role of family influence on student success. In J. A. Ward- Roof & C. Hatch (Eds.), *Designing successful transitions: A guide for orienting students to college* (Monograph No. 13, 2nd ed., pp. 137-163). Columbia, SC: University of South Carolina, National Resource Center for The First-Year Experience and Students in Transition.

BBC News. (January 4, 2008). *The curse of the meddling parent.* Retrieved January 9, 2008, from http://news/bbc/co/uk/go/pr/fr/-/2/hi/uk_news/education/7169429.stm

Carney-Hall, K. C. (Ed.). (2008). *Managing parent partnerships: Maximizing influence, minimizing interference, and focusing on student success.* San Francisco: Jossey-Bass.

Cohen, R. D., & Halsey, M. M. (1985). Organizing the institution for parent affairs. In R. D. Cohen (Ed.), *Working with parents of college students* (New Directions for Student Services No. 32, pp. 93-104). San Francisco: Jossey-Bass.

Conneely, J. F., Good, C., & Perryman, K. (2001). Balancing the role of parents in the residential community. In B. V. Daniel & B. R. Scott (Eds.), *Consumers, adversaries, and partners: Working with the families of undergraduates* (New Directions for Student Services No. 94, pp. 51-61). San Francisco: Jossey-Bass.

Daniel, B. V., Evans, S. G., & Scott, B. R. (2001). Understanding family involvement in the college experience today. In B. V. Daniel & B. R. Scott (Eds.), *Consumers, adversaries, and partners: Working with the families of undergraduates* (pp. 3-13). San Francisco: Jossey-Bass.

Feaver, P., Wasiolek, S., & Crossman, A. (2008). *Getting the best out of college: A professor, a dean, and a student tell you how to maximize your experience.* Berkeley: Ten Speed Press.

Florida State University. (2008). CIRP Data Report. Retrieved March 31, 2009, from http://studentaffairsresearch.fsu.edu/surveyresults.htm

Forbes, K. J. (2001). Students and their parents: Where do campuses fit in? *About Campus, 6*(4), 11-17

Gibbs, N. (2009, November 30). The case against over-parenting: Why mom and dad need to cut the strings. *Time.* Retrieved January 10, 2009, from http://www.time.com/time/nation/article/0,8599,1940395,00.html

Henning, G. (2007). Is in consortio cum parentibus the new in loco parentis? *NASPA Journal, 44*(3), 538-560.

Higher Education Research Institute. (2007). *The American College Student: National Freshman Norms for Fall 2007 Annual Report.* Los Angeles: University of California, Higher Education Research Institute. Retrieved from http://www.gseis.ucla.edu/heri/

Hofer, B. K. (2008). The electronic tether: Parental regulation, self-regulation, and the role of technology in college transitions. *Journal of The First-Year Experience & Students in Transition, 20*(2), 9-24.

Honoré, C. (2008). *Under pressure: Rescuing our children from the culture of hyper-parenting.* New York: HarperOne.

Hoover, E. (2008, February 1). Survey of students challenge 'helicopter parents' stereotypes. *The Chronicle of Higher Education*, p. A22.

Johnson, H. E. (2004, January 9). Educating parents about college life. *Chronicle of Higher Education*, p. B11.

Johnson, V. K., Gans, S. E., Kerr, S., & Deegan, K. (2008). Managing the transition to college: The role of family cohesion and adolescents' emotional coping strategies. *The Journal of College Orientation and Transition, 15*(2), 29-46.

Keppler, K., Mullendore, R. H. & Carey, A. (2005). Preface. In K. Keppler, R. H. Mullendore, & A. Carey (Eds.), *Partnering with the parents of today's college students* (pp. xi-xiii). Washington, DC: National Association of College Personnel Administrators.

Mann, B. A. (1998). Retention principles for new student orientation programs. *The Journal of College Orientation and Transition, 6*(10), 15-26.

Melear, K. B. (2003). From in loco parentis to consumerism: A legal analysis of the contractual relationship between institution and student. *NASPA Journal, 40*(4), 124-148.

Merriman, L (2006). *Best practices for managing parent concerns: A mixed methods study of student affairs practice at doctoral research institutions.* (Doctoral dissertation). Retrieved from Dissertation Abstracts International (AAT 2344034).

Merriman, L. (2007). Managing parents 101: Minimizing interference and maximizing good will. *Leadership Exchange, 5*(1), 14-19.

Mullendore, R. H., & Banahan, L. A. (2005). Channeling parent energy and reaping the benefits in K. Keppler, R. H. Mullendore, & A. Carey (Eds.), *Partnering with the parents of today's college students* (pp. 35-41). Washington, DC: National Association of College Personnel Administrators.

Mullendore, R. H., & Hatch, C. (2000). *Helping your first-year college student succeed: A guide for parents.* Columbia, SC: University of South Carolina, National Resource Center for The First-Year Experience and Students in Transition.

Mullendore, R. H., King, S., & Watson, A., (2008, November 12). The impact of parental involvement on college student development: A longitudinal study. *NASPA Netresults.* Retrieved January 16, 2009 from http://www.naspa.org/membership/mem/pubs/nr/PrinterFriendly.cfm?id=1666

National Survey of Student Engagement. (2007). *Annual report.* Retrieved July 2007 from http://nsse.iub.edu/NSSE_2007_Annual_Report/docs/withhold/NSSE_2007_Annual_Report.pdf

Nehls, K. (2007). Let your fingers do the talking: An analysis of a college parent listserv. *The Journal of College Orientation and Transition, 14*(2), 6-24.

Pennington, K. L. (2005) Foreword. In K. Keppler, R. H. Mullendore, & A. Carey (Eds.), *Partnering with the parents of today's college students* (p. ix). Washington, DC: National Association of College Personnel Administrators.

Pryor, J. (2008). Students appreciate parents' involvement. *UCLA Magazine.* Retrieved March 20, 2010, from http://www.magazine.ucla.edu/exclusives/freshman-survey_parents/

Pryor, J., Hurtado, S., DeAngelo, L., Sharkness, J., Romero, L., Korn, W., & Tran, S. (2008). *The American freshmen: National norms for fall 2008.* Los Angeles, CA: University of California, Higher Education Research Institute.

Savage, M. (2009). *National Survey of College and University Parent Programs.* Retrieved from http://www.parent.umn.edu/ParentSurvey07.pdf

Ullom, C., & Faulkner, B. (2005) Understanding the new relationship. In K. Keppler, R. H. Mullendore, & A. Carey (Eds.), *Partnering with the parents of today's college students* (pp. 21-28). Washington, DC: National Association of College Personnel Administrators.

Ward-Roof, J. A. (2005). Parents orientation: Begin with the end in mind. In K. Keppler, R. H. Mullendore, & A. Carey (Eds.), *Partnering with the parents of today's college students* (pp. 29-33). Washington, DC: National Association of College Personnel Administrators.

Chapter 7

Extensions of Traditional Orientation Programs

Tracy L. Skipper, Jennifer A. Latino, Blaire Moody Rideout, and Dorothy Weigel

In *Challenging and Supporting the First-Year Student*, Upcraft, Barefoot, and Gardner (2005) present a definition of student success that encompasses a series of developmental challenges students must negotiate in college. These challenges include developing intellectual and academic competence, establishing and maintaining interpersonal relationships, exploring identity, deciding on a career, maintaining health and wellness, exploring faith and the spiritual dimensions of life, developing multicultural awareness, and developing civic responsibility. We know from research on the student experience that students will spend the bulk of their time in college negotiating and renegotiating these issues and that many of these developmental challenges will remain unresolved at graduation (Pascarella & Terenzini, 1991; 2005). Yet, the college environment supplies a series of prompts that spur significant growth along these dimensions as students encounter new people and experiences that challenge their current ways of thinking about and being in the world. When the college environment is intentionally designed to provide support in light of these challenges, students test new ways of defining themselves, their relationships to others, and their relationship to knowledge—the hallmarks of developmental change. Orientation programs are ideally positioned to provide such intentional support. In fact, the Council for the Advancement of Standards (CAS) in Higher Education (Miller, 2003) demands such a role for orientation, suggesting that

> relevant and desirable outcomes include: intellectual growth, effective communication, realistic self-appraisal, enhanced self-esteem, clarified values, career choices, leadership development, healthy behaviors, meaningful interpersonal relations, independence, collaboration, social responsibility, satisfying and productive lifestyles, appreciation of diversity, spiritual awareness, and achievement of personal and educational goals. (p. 233)

In reality, such outcomes constitute the learning and developmental content of the entire college experience. In this respect, the CAS Standards have set a particularly ambitious agenda for orientation professionals. The difficulty of helping students meet these goals is apparent when one considers the structure of many orientation programs: a two-day visit to campus during the summer (or a one-day program immediately prior to the start of the term) during which time students not only receive an orientation to campus resources, but must also take placement exams, meet with an advisor, register for classes, finalize financial aid arrangements, have an ID made, buy books, and take care of any number of other details that must be addressed prior to matriculation. A host of position papers on the promotion of learning and development during the college years (*Learning*

Reconsidered [Keeling, 2004], being among the most recent) have also made clear that no single department or unit can or should be responsible for helping students achieve these goals.

As a result, many orientation programs have expanded their offerings or aligned themselves with other offices and departments on campus that are promoting initiatives designed to help students address these learning and developmental goals. This chapter explores four of these initiatives: (a) outdoor orientation experiences, (b) service experiences, (c) common reading programs, and (c) first-year seminars. In each case, we discuss the prevalence of the initiative on American college campuses and describe its typical organization and administration. We also examine ways in which the program helps support the goals of orientation, in particular, and higher education, in general. Finally, we briefly highlight outcomes associated with these initiatives, especially as they relate to the goals we have highlighted here. An exhaustive treatment of these initiatives is beyond the scope of this chapter. In addition to the reference list, we have included a list of useful print and online resources and professional organizations as an appendix to the chapter. We conclude the chapter by highlighting some of the challenges associated with implementing these outcomes and offering some recommendations for addressing those challenges.

Outdoor Orientation Experiences

As orientation programs have expanded, one of the ways students acclimate to a college or university campus is in an outdoor setting. Wilderness/outdoor orientation programs provide a unique opportunity for students to successfully transition to college life and experience learning beyond the traditional classroom setting.

Definition and Prevalence of Outdoor Orientation Programs

There are more than 166 wilderness orientation programs currently operating across the country at accredited, residential, baccalaureate institutions of higher education (McClure, 2008). Historically, outdoor education began with a focus on camping education. Sharp (1943), one of its earliest advocates, stressed the value of learning outdoors by saying, "That which can best be taught inside the schoolrooms should there be taught, and that which can best be learned through experience dealing directly with native materials and life situations outside the school should there be learned" (p. 363). Today, one of the primary characteristics of outdoor education is that it uses "real-world experiences" to achieve learning goals (Adkins & Simmons, 2003, para. 6). The Association of Experiential Education (AEE) is an accredited organization that seeks to develop and promote experiential education including, but not limited to, outdoor and adventure programming. According to the AEE (2008), there are 12 principles related to experiential learning. Six of these principles suggest that the learner will:

◇ Take initiative, make decisions, and be accountable for results
◇ Engage in posing questions, investigating, experimenting, being curious, solving problems, assuming responsibility, being creative, and constructing meaning
◇ Experience success, failure, adventure, risk-taking and uncertainty, because the outcomes of experience cannot totally be predicted
◇ Develop and nurture relationships (learner to self, learner to others, and learner to the world at large)
◇ Explore and examine their own values
◇ Learn from natural consequences, mistakes, and successes

For years, colleges and universities have used outdoor education as a means of orienting new students to their institution. One of the earliest colleges to implement an outdoor orientation program was Dartmouth College. In 1935, members of the Outing Club at Dartmouth started the "Freshman Trips" program as a tool to recruit new members (Troop, 2003). Incoming first-year students attended a three-night trip where they took part in outdoor activities (e.g., canoeing, hiking, horseback riding, rock climbing, mountain biking, organic farming, and classes). The program has grown and expanded and now includes five-night trips in the wilderness of New Hampshire and Vermont. Nearly the entire first-year class currently participates (85-90%), and organizers and leaders make phone calls to the remaining students to encourage them to participate (Troop).

Organization and Administration of Outdoor Orientation Programs

Outdoor orientation programs are often implemented through a combined effort of the department of outdoor education, the office of orientation, faculty, and staff members. Many of the trips are co-led by volunteer upper-division students who see such leadership experiences as very desirable. At Dartmouth College in 2000, 120 students applied for 40 spots as volunteer outdoor orientation leaders (Paulson, 2000). As with other orientation programs, student leaders are trained over a period of time to lead the outdoor orientation experiences. At the University of Puget Sound, student leaders receive extensive leadership training over a three-month period (Stremba, 1991). Training for student leaders includes skill development, program procedures, group facilitation skills, promotion of diversity, conservation and environmental ethics, and first-aid and CPR. Additional training in backcountry skills is required of students who serve as backpacking leaders (Stremba).

Expanding the Goals of Traditional Orientation Programs

The goals and outcomes for outdoor orientation are very similar to those of traditional orientation programs. Research indicates that successful outdoor orientation programs contribute to lower student attrition rates, increased academic performance, and more positive attitudes toward the institution (e.g., Galloway, 2000; Gass, Garvey, & Sugerman, 2003). Many of these outcomes are also indicative of successful traditional orientation programs. However, research also focuses on the unique effects of outdoor orientation, including increased self-efficacy and emotional and social support (e.g., Bell, 2006a; 2006b; Jones & Hinton, 2007; Stremba, 1991). Rick Curtis, director of Princeton University's Outdoor Action program noted, "The same process [students] use to make decisions on the trail, they can use at a party when someone hands them a drink" (Paulson, 2000, p. 16). Assessing outdoor orientation programs is, therefore, critical because the potential effects extend beyond an acclimation to the campus community.

In a study conducted by Bell (2006a), students' responses to the Campus-Focused Social Provisions Scale (CF-SPS) were measured to determine if there were differences in reported levels of social support for students involved in different types of preorientation experiences (e.g., wilderness programs, community-service programs, preseason athletics). Participants in the wilderness and community-service orientation programs reported higher levels of social support; however, wilderness programs were the only preorientation experience that had higher levels in all six subfactors of social support: (a) attachment, (b) social integration, (c) reassurance of worth/competence, (d) reliable alliance/tangible support, (e) guidance, and (f) opportunity for nurturance (Bell, 2006a). Selection bias prevented the researcher from concluding that wilderness orientation programs were directly linked to social support; however, these programs were clearly one of the potential explanations for such a result.

Outdoor/wilderness orientation programs offer students a unique opportunity to learn outside the classroom. Furthermore, research indicates that these settings foster positive outcomes such as increased academic performance, commitment to the institution, and increased self-efficacy. As programs continue to grow and expand, it will be necessary to understand the principles that guide these programs and in what ways they support student transition and success.

Service Experiences

Current incoming students arrive on campus with greater social awareness and a stronger need for civic responsibility than previous cohorts. According to the Higher Education Research Institute (Pryor et al., 2005; Pryor et al., 2006; Pryor et al., 2008; Pryor, Hurtado, Sharkness, & Korn, 2007), there is a growing commitment to service participation, societal concerns, and civic engagement among incoming US first-year students. Today's students are discussing politics more frequently, becoming more dichotomized in their political orientation, giving more attention to the environment, and identifying helping others as an essential personal goal (Pryor et al., 2005; Pryor et al., 2006; Pryor et al., 2007; Pryor et al., 2008). Thus, this new cohort of socially active and politically involved students may also enter college with the expectation that they will continue to be engaged in civic activities.

Focus of Orientation Service Experiences

New student orientation programs are recognizing the need for social action, and some schools are implementing service activities during orientation. For example, responses to the Fall 2008 Freshman Survey (Pryor et al., 2008) suggest that students are becoming more environmentally aware, with 79% agreeing that the government is not doing enough to control environmental pollution and 74.3% agreeing that addressing global warming should be a federal priority. In response to these new student interests, the State University of New York College of Environmental Science and Forestry (SUNY ESF) has implemented a Saturday of Service, which partners with the local Parks and Recreation Department in Syracuse, NY, by providing work sites for students to engage in various clean up projects (Moody, 2007).

Politics is another area where high school seniors and incoming students have become increasingly interested and involved. According to the 2008 Fall Freshman Survey (Pryor et. al., 2008), 35.6 % of high school seniors reported discussing politics frequently, which was up 8.3% from 2004, the most recent presidential election year. The 2008 survey also revealed that students may be becoming more dichotomized in their political orientations with 31.0% identifying themselves as liberal, the highest response seen on this item since 1975. Similarly, 20.7% of respondents identified themselves as conservative, down slightly from a high of 23.9% in 2006 (Pryor et al., 2007; Pryor et al., 2008). This political awareness was also evident in the 2008 presidential election. According to the 15th Biannual Youth Survey on Politics and Public Service (Purcell et al., 2008), 79% of all 18- to 24-year-olds surveyed were registered to vote. While only 35% of college students surveyed had participated in a presidential primary or caucus, 70% definitely planned to vote in the 2008 general election for president. The survey found that while students were interested in becoming more politically active, they were often unsure how to do so, suggesting that civic engagement programs with a political focus during orientation might be a welcome opportunity for some new students. Such programs could promote responsible citizenship and civic engagement through voter registration drives or activity fairs with campus political organizations represented.

Responsible citizenship and civic engagement can also be a central element for a large service event. During an orientation service activity at Concordia College in Moorhead, MN, mayors from the local towns spoke in a send-off gathering about the value of the service the students were about to engage in and the impact the students would make on the local communities (Moody, 2007). Additionally, when the students returned, the college and student body presidents reflected on the value of service not just locally but globally (Moody). The activity not only allowed students to participate in service work, but it also encouraged them to reflect on what it means to be a responsible citizen within their university and local community, a central goal of many institutional missions.

Organization and Administration of Orientation Service Experiences

Orientation professionals know all too well that planning a strong orientation program often begins a year in advance. Therefore, incorporating another aspect can be a time-consuming process. Yet many of the resources needed to implement a service program are already in place. For example, student orientation leaders can also serve as site leaders during service initiatives. Similarly, faculty or academic advisors who are already participating in orientation might be enlisted to work with small groups of students on service projects.

Expanding existing campus relationships is important, but so is forming a new network for the actual service program. The student activities office or the office of community service/ service-learning has expertise in planning large-scale social and service events. Service offices may also have contacts for local agencies that have experience and can accommodate working with college students. Such offices are ideal partners in orientation-related service initiatives. A committee consisting of representatives from community partners, transportation services, facilities, budget managers, student activities, and the campus community service office is one way to facilitate such partnerships.

The size and scale of the program should be addressed in the early planning stages. The service experience has to fit the current orientation schedule, which may be different for summer orientation sessions versus programs that happen just before classes start. Various service sites and activities may not be feasible for orientation programs that run concurrently throughout the summer. For this reason, some orientation programs may decide to hold a large, one-time service day when all students return to campus for fall classes. If a service placement is not possible during summer orientation sessions, students might be asked to donate items, such as children's books for a local library, school supplies for a local school district, or items needed at a local shelter. This project can also be continued into an overnight social activity for the summer orientation program by having students make bookmarks or cards to include with the donations. The students can then be brought back together in the fall to deliver the items, which will introduce students to the agencies where the goods were donated. Such a program could be easily integrated into a day of service during a welcome week program by being one of the sites where students can choose to work. Figure 7.1 offers other considerations when planning a service program.

Plan ahead. Talk with agencies early, reserve transportation, and solicit faculty and staff opinions about programming and participating.

Involve key players. Involve the campus service-learning office, community partners and agencies, event services, budget managers, faculty, facilities, and transportation staff.

Budget for food and extras. Consider meals and beverages, safety equipment, and other requirements needed for the project.

Select versatile sites. Choose sites with an equal amount of indoor and outdoor locations; furthermore, prepare at least one large activity on campus for late students or as a rain location.

Choose local agencies. Work with known agencies because they will know what skill level to expect from the students. Questions to consider, "What supplies do they provide? How many students can they accommodate?"

Consider the timing. Will the service activity take place during summer orientation sessions or right before the start of classes? What time of day makes most sense for participants and for the agency involved? Most agencies will find it less of a burden to host service events during normal business hours, rather than at night or on weekends. However, for certain types of service projects non-business hours may be preferable.

Consider students with disabilities. Find out which sites might find it hard to accommodate certain student needs.

Involve faculty. Ask them to lend their tools or work supplies for the project. They might want to join the fun.

Collect medical information. It is important to know the students' allergies, medications, and emergency contacts.

Advise students on appropriate dress. During registration inform students that they may get dirty and should wear closed-toe shoes.

Allow for flexibility. You might be told about one project you will work on, but that may change if the agency had a different group complete it the day before.

Keep a record. All agency site numbers and site leader cell phone numbers should be accessible. Have at least one person at home base serving as the contact person for emergencies.

Intentionally reflect on the activity. Will your reflection be led by orientation leaders, faculty/staff, or both? Do you want the reflection to tie into the orientation theme? Train your site leaders thoroughly to facilitate this component.

Capture the fun! Have someone take pictures and post them to the office web site. Students will search for themselves while being exposed to the resources offered on the web site at the same time.

Figure 7.1. Things to consider when planning a service activity during orientation. Reprinted from "Forming Connections: Combining Orientation and Community Service" by Blaire Moody, 2007, *E-Source for College Transition,* *4*(6), p. 8. Copyright 2007 by the University of South Carolina.

Extending the Goals of Traditional Orientation Programs

With 70.6% of incoming students reporting volunteering on a weekly basis and 67.3% believing there is a very good or some chance that they will participate in volunteer or community service in college, a service experience during orientation can be a successful event (Pryor et al., 2005). Not only are students engaged in an activity they would like to continue, but a service event during orientation introduces students to responsible citizenship within the university and local communities. Students can make connections with university faculty, staff, and departments while being introduced to various local organizations where they can continue to serve. This introduction to their new local community can also enhance town-gown relationships and provide opportunities for students to reflect on their own civic awareness. Such programs do not have to be one-time events. Rather, they can be starting point for community service offices. Follow-up programs can engage students through newsletters, reunion projects at the same site, or ongoing leadership experiences.

The concept of incorporating a service experience within new student orientation is a relatively new area. Much of the assessment to date has focused on participation and student satisfaction with the service experience. There has been little qualitative or longitudinal assessment to see what students gain from the experience and whether they continue service participation. As a result, we know little about what students learned, how they were affected by their experience, or if they will continue serving their communities through campus programs in the future. Additionally, most programs do not incorporate the community they serve in this assessment. Universities should not only look at how the service experience is affecting the students but also at its impact on the agency or community served or the larger community's perception of the institution.

Common Reading Programs

Prevalence of Common Reading Programs

Common reading programs are becoming an increasingly popular initiative to introduce first-year students to the academic rigor of college-level work. These initiatives can strengthen an academic community as it invites students, faculty, staff, and administrators to participate in a unifying experience (Fidler, 1997). Based on the premise that shared experiences can help ease the transition among new peers, "campus common reading programs rest on a simple idea: that reading the same book brings people closer together as a community by creating a common ground for discussion" (Ferguson, 2006, p. 8). As such, common reading programs provide early support for developing intellectual and academic competence and establishing relationships with members of the campus community.

Institutions often introduce their common reading program within the summer orientation curricula. Students are introduced to the text by their upperclass peers (orientation leaders) or campus faculty or librarians. The common reading program is often presented as a unifying event for the first-year cohort that will set the tone for the entire college experience. Students are encouraged to read the text in preparation for a common event, usually positioned within the structure of welcome week. By including an academic component with the traditional social activities of opening week, students are oriented to the academic expectations of the university and introduced to the partnership between curricular and cocurricular learning.

The National Resource Center for The First-Year Experience and Students in Transition (2008) hosts a database of institutions that support common reading programs. More than 100 institutions have voluntarily submitted their information to this database. These institutions are broad in nature including large, four-year research institutions; private institutions; two-year institutions; technical colleges; historically Black institutions; Hispanic-serving institutions; and single-gender institutions.

Organization and Administration of Common Reading Programs

The placement of the common reading programs is as diverse as the institutions that host them. Common reading programs may be coordinated and supported by the office of orientation, an academic department, campus libraries, or the first-year experience program. The organization of the program, campus support of the initiative, and relevance to institutional mission are key components of a successful common reading program.

Collaboration is an essential element of a common reading initiative; therefore, many institutions develop planning committees to coordinate program details. Collaboration among a wide group of constituents will enhance buy-in from the campus community as well as embed the event into the campus culture. Planning teams typically involve representatives from a wide array of campus departments including faculty, academic and student affairs administrators, staff from a variety of campus departments (i.e., orientation, residence life, first-year experience, campus activities), and students. Regardless of where the coordination and funding is housed, most programs involve faculty in every aspect of the event planning. If a common reading program is used to introduce students to the academic rigor of their college experience, then the presence and involvement of faculty is critical.

The key component to any common reading program is the selected text. The text serves as a vehicle for assisting students in achieving proposed learning outcomes. Book selection should consist of a broad array of participants who are informed of program goals and are committed to student learning. Many institutions use a book selection committee. Committee membership should be diverse and include students, staff, librarians, and faculty from multiple disciplines, including but not limited to English. Faculty who serve on a book selection committee or as a discussion leader should be recognized and supported. Program coordinators can offer appreciation through letters of gratitude to faculty and their respective department chairs. These types of recognition can be included in faculty portfolios for consideration in tenure and review processes.

Many campuses select a text focused on a particular institutional value or initiative. For example, in recent years, the University of South Carolina has placed an increased focus on the value of community service. The 2006 selection for the First-Year Reading Experience, *Mountains Beyond Mountains*, by Tracy Kidder, supported this initiative. Kidder's biography introduces readers to the selfless work of Paul Farmer, a physician who is recognized internationally for his public health work in Haiti, Russia, Rwanda, and Peru and his advocacy work on behalf of the sick and the poor. Institutions with unique student populations may include criteria based on student needs. For example, LaGuardia Community College considers "what the book says about American culture and how this book will inform a largely immigrant student body about issues in American culture" (Clark, as cited in Laufgraben, 2006, p. 36). Other considerations in book selection include the cost of the book, the appeal to first-year students, interdisciplinary themes, literary value, and relevance to first-year student transition issues (Laufgraben).

A well-planned and effectively implemented common reading program goes beyond book selection. Interdisciplinary partnerships can strengthen the effectiveness of a program. For example, beginning in 2007, the department of First-Year English at the University of South Carolina used the First-Year Reading Experience text in sections of the first-year English courses. Recognizing that this was a resource that all first-year students owned, had read, and had already discussed with a faculty member and peer group, provided a reasonable rationale for incorporating the text into the existing course curricula. When Gallaudet University selected Mitch Albom's *Tuesdays With Morrie* as their common text, the department of social work hosted a viewing of the made-for-television movie based on the text and, following the film, facilitated a discussion among students and faculty (Laufgraben & Dennis, 2006). The opportunities for campus partnerships are vast and can bring added value to and increased student engagement with a common reading initiative.

Common Reading in Support of Traditional Orientation Goals

The pedagogy of a common reading experience should promote the goals of the initiative as well as the established outcomes for new student programs including, but not limited to, new student orientation. The first experience that participants share is the reading of the text. If the common reading is introduced as part of new student orientation, students read the text in anticipation of their arrival on campus. Including a reading guide for students can assist them in thinking critically about the text and identifying key themes that may be brought up in later discussions. In most cases, a common activity that allows students, faculty, and staff to share in an intellectual experience, such as a keynote address or convocation event, is the anchor of the program. Most often, a small-group discussion about the selected text is included in the program design. These discussions, led by faculty and/or staff invite students to reflect upon and express their personal beliefs and thoughts about the text through engaging in conversation with others who have had a shared reading experience.

Research supports that first-year students relate particularly well to upperclass students (Ender & Newton, 2000). Involving upperclass peers (e.g., orientation leaders) in the introduction of the text as well as the program delivery further supports the traditional orientation model of students helping students. A text that is presented in a positive light by a current student may motivate a first-year student to read it outside of a classroom assignment. Additionally, peer educators can have a particularly significant impact on first-year students' academic motivation (Hamid, 2001). By modeling the behavior of reading the selected text and engaging incoming students in conversation about the themes of the book, first-year students are further exposed to the academic rigor of college-level work.

Many institutions expand programming beyond keynote and small-group discussions. Murray State University (2008) invites first-year students to compete in an essay contest about the selected text. Essays are read and evaluated by a faculty committee. Student authors of winning essays are presented with $200 cash awards, funded by the Office of the Provost. Kalamazoo College invites the author of their selected text to deliver a keynote address to the first-year class. The author is then invited to return and deliver the commencement address for that cohort (Pixley & Suess, 2006). As part of their Freshman Connections program, Ball State University (2008) hosts an online discussion board for students to chat about the text as they are reading over the summer. Other institutions show films or offer semester- or year-long lecture series that are relevant to the themes of their selected text as part of their welcome week activities. Institutions should consider innovative activities that supplement student reading and support the learning outcomes of the common reading program.

Expanding the Goals of Traditional Orientation Programs

A common reading program is an effective way to gather the campus community for a shared intellectual experience. Ferguson (2006) reported that more than 80% of surveyed institutions cited "to model intellectual engagement" and "to develop a sense of community" as goals of their common reading program (p. 8). Laufgraben (2006) noted that effective common reading programs (a) model academic behavior, (b) set expectations for student success, (c) foster involvement, and (d) promote meaningful learning. In this way, common reading programs help institutions realize the goals of orientation as cited in the CAS Standards. Laufgraben further noted that as a result of participating in a common reading program, students are introduced to academic behaviors and are able to develop academic skills that are expected of college students including:

    ◇ Effective oral, visual, and written communication skills
    ◇ The ability to interpret and evaluate information from a variety of sources
    ◇ The ability to understand and work within complex systems and with diverse groups
    ◇ The ability to transform information into knowledge and knowledge into judgment and action. (p. 3)

Unique campus characteristics and institutional culture determine the characteristics of common reading programs; therefore, no universal set of learning outcomes can be adopted. Yet, well-developed learning outcomes will assist program coordinators with planning and implementing a successful common reading initiative. It is important that program coordinators identify and evaluate the outcomes of the common reading program and use assessment findings to guide revisions to the program (Liljequist & Stone, 2009). Additionally, measurement of these outcomes can be helpful in maintaining support and resources for this important component of new students' orientation to and transition into the college environment. Many institutions have developed clear learning outcomes for their distinctive programs and have developed programming based on these outcomes. Examples of programs with well-developed and assessed learning outcomes follow.

The Common Reading Program at the University of Florida is housed in the Dean of Students Office and is guided by outcomes that include: (a) providing a shared experience with a diverse community of learners and creating a common framework upon which to base further dialogue and discussion; (b) sharpening intellectual and interpersonal skills through interdisciplinary discussion and exposure to multiple perspectives to help students be successful learners integrating material in and out of the classroom; and (c) engaging fellow students, faculty, and staff in a collaborative learning environment that develops stronger partnerships in learning (L. Hahn, personal communication, January 28, 2008). These outcomes are shared with incoming students, and activities, including a conversation with the author of the selected text and an essay contest, are designed to guide students toward realizing them (University of Florida, 2008).

In addition to the learning outcomes that common reading programs support for student participants, such programs also benefit the larger campus community. Faculty and staff who serve as discussion leaders are given the opportunity to interact with the newest students on campus, interact with colleagues from other departments, and refine their facilitation skills (Laufgraben, 2006). These initial meetings and conversations can be meaningful for first-year students' impressions of the campus faculty, staff, and administrators. Additionally, introducing students to the intrinsic value of reading a text outside of a class assignment and engaging in conversation with peers and faculty about the reading during their orientation to the campus can help shape positive relationships between faculty and students.

Common reading programs may also provide an opportunity to bridge the gap between first-year and upperclass students. Involving upperclass students as cofacilitators for discussion groups or volunteers for check-in can increase interaction between incoming students and current students, facilitating their transition to campus. Further, involving current students in the planning and implementation of a reading experience can be a valuable learning experience. For example, students in a graphic design course at the University of South Carolina are given a copy of the selected book and asked to create a poster that portrays the essence of the story and the characters. One submission is chosen as the official poster of the First-Year Reading Experience, which is also reproduced as a postcard and mailed as a reminder during the summer to students invited to participate in the reading experience. The winning student receives a cash award, but all students in the class benefit from the opportunity to participate in a real-world design project.

Common reading initiatives support the mission and goals of new student orientation. A sustainable common reading initiative is relevant to the mission of the institution, has clearly defined outcomes, receives broad campus support, and is supported by resources dedicated to the sustainability of the program (Laufgraben, 2006). The research and literature surrounding common reading initiatives is limited. However, as institutions continue to design and refine these programs and implement innovative strategies to assist students in achieving the varied learning outcomes associated with common reading programs, educators should assess their work. In this way, they can continue to develop the body of evidence surrounding this academic orientation to the institution.

First-Year Seminars

Definition and Prevalence of First-Year Seminars

The first-year seminar dates to the late-19th century when the shift from more collegial models of higher education to the modern research university demanded that institutions be more intentional in their efforts to help students succeed. Gordon (1989) notes that 43% of institutions responding to a 1948 survey on orientation programs reported the existence of a required orientation course. Despite this long history, the University of South Carolina is often credited with launching the first-year seminar in the early 1970s. Indeed, the University 101 course at South Carolina—a course focused more on process than content and designed to engage students in the life of the university—served as a model for a number of campuses interested in implementing such a course. While the term "first-year seminar" is often taken to mean the extended orientation course similar to the one developed at South Carolina, a series of national surveys conducted by the National Resource Center for The First-Year Experience and Students in Transition demonstrate that the course is defined in a number of different ways on American college campuses and that many institutions offer more than one type of seminar.

The 2006 National Survey of First-Year Seminars defines a seminar as a course "designed to enhance the academic skills and/or social development of first-year college students" (Tobolowsky & Associates, 2008, p. 105). Survey respondents were asked to identify the type(s) of first-year seminar offered on their campuses, drawing on definitions developed by Barefoot (1992). The seminar types include:

◇ *Extended orientation seminar.* Content typically includes introduction to campus resources, time management, academic and career planning, learning strategies, and student development issues. The seminar is variously called a freshman orientation, college survival, college transition, or student success course. Of those responding to the 2006 survey, 57.9% offered an extended orientation course, and these courses were more prevalent among two-year campuses (77.1% vs. 51.5%). Extended orientation seminars were the primary seminar type on about 40% of all campuses but were the primary type on nearly 60% of the two-year campuses reporting.

◇ *Academic seminar with generally uniform content across sections.* The primary focus of this seminar is on an academic theme or discipline, but academic skills such as critical thinking and expository writing are frequently emphasized. It may also be an interdisciplinary course and is sometimes part of the general education requirement. Nearly one third (28.1%) of institutions reported offering this type of seminar, with it being more common on four-year than two-year campuses (29.9% vs. 21.8%). This is the primary seminar type on 17.4% of the responding campuses.

◇ *Academic seminar on various topics.* Like the common content sections, these seminars have an explicitly academic focus, but the specific topics vary from section to section. The variable content seminar was offered by one quarter of reporting institutions and was much more common on four-year campuses than two-year campuses (31.5% vs. 6.9%). This is the primary seminar type on 17.9% of the responding campuses, but it is the primary type on less than 2% of two-year campuses.

◇ *Pre-professional or discipline-linked seminar.* These courses are typically taught within professional schools or specific disciplines such as engineering, health sciences, business, or education and are designed to prepare students for the demands of the major/discipline and profession. Pre-professional seminars are the least common type of seminar reported, offered on slightly less than 15% of campuses. These courses were slightly (but not significantly so) less likely to be offered by four-year institutions. Fewer than 2% of respondents indicated that this was the primary seminar type on their campus.

◇ *Basic study skills seminar.* These courses are offered for academically underprepared students and focus on basic academic skills such as grammar, note taking, and reading texts. While just over 20% of respondents to the survey offered basic study skills courses, these courses were offered by 41% of two-year institutions responding to the survey. Fewer than 6% of respondents indicated that this was the primary seminar type on their campuses, though it was the primary type on 18% of the two-year campuses reporting.

◇ *Hybrid seminar.* In order to capture the evolving nature of first-year seminars on college campuses, a new category was added to the 2006 survey. The hybrid seminar was defined as having elements of two or more of the previously defined seminar types. About 20% of respondents identified their seminar as a hybrid course, and four-year institutions were more likely to define their course in this way than two-year institutions (23.1% vs. 12.8%). Hybrid seminars are the predominant seminar type on about 16% of responding campuses.

Organization and Administration

One of the hallmarks of the extended orientation seminar as conceived at the University of South Carolina was small class size that would permit a process-focused learning environment (as opposed to one focused on content acquisition) and significant bonding among students. Though seminars take a variety of different forms on American campuses, small class size appears to be common across types. More than half (55.8%) of responding institutions had classes with fewer than 20 students, and nearly 30% reported class sizes of 21 to 25 students.

Slightly less than half of respondents (46%) require all first-year students to take the seminar, with private institutions being more likely to make such a requirement than public institutions. At almost all institutions (92.2%), the seminar carries credit toward graduation, though the amount of credit offered varies. Most commonly, the seminar is offered for one credit hour (42.5%) followed by three-credit-hour courses (32.5%).

On half of the responding campuses, the administrative home for the first-year seminar is academic affairs. The seminar is much less likely to be housed within student affairs (12.9%) or in an office devoted to first-year programs (10.5%). The majority (79.8%) of seminar programs have a designated course or program director, but on more than half (62.1%) of the responding campuses, the director role is less than full-time. A variety of individuals teach first-year seminars, but faculty members are by far the most commonly reported instructors. More than 90% of respondents indicated that faculty taught the seminar, with 45% reporting that student affairs professionals taught the seminar. Fewer than 10% of institutions indicated that undergraduates (e.g., peer leaders) were involved in seminar instruction. Academic advisors are fairly regularly involved in course instruction, with about one third (31.9%) of responding institutions indicating that academic advisors taught some sections of the course. On nearly half (47.8%) of the campuses reporting, more than three quarters of students were enrolled in sections taught by their academic advisors.

Goals of First-Year Seminars

Survey respondents were asked to identify the top three goals for the first-year seminar. The most frequently reported goals included developing academic skills (64.2%), orienting students to campus resources and services (52.9%), encouraging self-exploration and personal development (36.9%), creating a common first-year experience (35.9%), and developing a support network/ friendships (32.3%). Not surprisingly, course goals vary considerably across seminars. For example, developing academic skills was much more important for academic and basic study skills seminars than extended orientation seminars. On the other hand, orientation to campus resources and self-exploration/personal development were much more important goals for basic skills and extended orientation seminars than for academic seminars (Table 7.1).

Table 7.1

Most Important Course Objectives by Seminar Type ($N = 772$)

Course objective	EO ($n = 316$)	AUC ($n = 134$)	AVC ($n = 138$)	BSS ($n = 45$)	PRE ($n = 12$)	Hybrid ($n = 125$)
Develop academic skills*	56.0%	71.6%	75.4%	82.2%	67.7%	60.0%
Orient to campus resources & services*	78.2%	29.1%	23.2%	53.3%	41.7%	48.8%
Encourage self-exploration/personal development*	46.5%	29.1%	16.7%	51.1%	41.7%	39.2%
Create a common first-year experience*	27.9%	59.7%	37.7%	22.2%	50.0%	28.0%
Develop support network/friendships*	38.9%	29.9%	21.0%	28.9%	33.3%	32.0%
Increase student/faculty interaction*	20.6%	28.4%	63.8%	15.6%	33.3%	26.4%
Improve sophomore return rates	25.6%	25.4%	26.1%	26.7%	8.3%	24.0%
Introduce a discipline*	2.9%	8.2%	15.9%	2.2%	50.0%	14.4%
Encourage arts participation	1.3%	0.8%	2.2%	0.0%	8.3%	0.8%

Note. Percentages do not equal 100%. Respondents were asked to select three most important objectives. EO = extended orientation, AUC = academic with uniform content, AVC = academic with variable content, BSS = basic study skills, PRE = pre-professional. Reprinted from *2006 National Survey of First-Year Seminars: Continuing Innovations in the Collegiate Curriculum* by B. F. Tobolowsky and Associates, 2008, p. 87. Copyright 2008 by University of South Carolina. $p < 0.05$.

Closely related to course goals is the content of the seminar. Here, survey respondents were asked to identify the five most important course topics. The most commonly reported course topics included study skills (40.8%), critical thinking (40.6%), campus resources (38.1%), and academic planning/advising (28.6%). Again, course topics varied widely by course type. For example, study skills was a much more important topic for basic skills seminars than academic seminars; however, slightly more than half of extended orientation seminars also indicated this was an important topic. Academic seminars were more likely to emphasize critical thinking and writing skills than other types of seminars. Perhaps, not surprisingly, an introduction to campus resources was the most important course topic identified by extended orientation seminars (Table 7.2).

Table 7.2

Most Important Course Topics by Seminar Type ($N = 772$)

Course topic	EO ($n = 316$)	AUC ($n = 134$)	AVC ($n = 138$)	BSS ($n = 45$)	PRE ($n = 12$)	Hybrid ($n = 125$)
Study skills*	55.1%	27.6%	18.1%	75.6%	25.0%	36.0%
Critical thinking*	15.8%	63.4%	74.6%	31.1%	50.0%	44.0%
Campus resources*	57.9%	26.1%	10.9%	35.6%	25.0%	36.8%
Academic planning/ advising*	48.1%	26.1%	19.6%	40.0%	41.7%	32.8%
Time management*	40.5%	16.4%	7.3%	57.8%	16.7%	24.8%
Writing skills*	5.1%	37.3%	56.5%	8.9%	8.3%	16.0%
Career exploration/ preparation	21.2%	16.4%	3.6%	33.3%	50.0%	18.4%
Specific disciplinary topic*	1.9%	12.7%	50.7%	4.4%	41.7%	17.6%
College policies & procedures*	22.5%	12.7%	2.9%	8.9%	25.0%	8.8%
Relationship issues*	21.2%	12.7%	2.9%	8.9%	8.3%	9.6%
Diversity issues*	5.4%	22.4%	6.5%	2.2%	8.3%	8.8%

Note. Percentages do not equal 100%. Respondents were asked to select three most important objectives. EO = extended orientation, AUC = academic with uniform content, AVC = academic with variable content, BSS = basic study skills, PRE = pre-professional. Reprinted from *2006 National Survey of First-Year Seminars: Continuing Innovations in the Collegiate Curriculum* by B. F. Tobolowsky and Associates, 2008, p. 53. Copyright 2008 by University of South Carolina. $p < 0.05$.

The first-year seminar, then, is an important vehicle for achieving the learning and developmental objectives of the orientation program. The emphasis on academic skills, critical thinking, and writing support students' continued intellectual growth. As noted earlier, academic advisors serve as seminar instructors on many campuses. This, combined with the emphasis on advising in seminar content, suggests that seminars may provide support for major and career decision making. Developing social networks and friendships is an important goal for many seminars, and the small class size supports the development of meaningful relationships even when this is not an explicit goal. More than one third of survey respondents (35.3%) reported that the seminar is embedded within a learning community, a structure proven to support both academic and social integration. The seminar also supports the development of social responsibility; 40% of respondents indicated that the course includes a service-learning component. The nature of this component varied widely, but a number of respondents indicated that these were half-day or one-day events taking place before or near the beginning of the fall semester. Finally, while not explicitly reflected in the course content (as reported by survey respondents), first-year seminars—especially extended orientation seminars—would seem to support values clarification, self-knowledge, and setting and achieving personal goals—all desired outcomes for the orientation program.

Outcomes

While there is a fairly extensive literature base describing outcomes related to first-year seminars, the bulk of this research has examined the impact of the course on retention, persistence to graduation, and academic performance (i.e., grade point average). Pascarella and Terenzini (2005) comment,

> …the weight of evidence indicates that FYS [first-year seminar] participation has statistically significant and substantial, positive effects on a student's successful transition to college and the likelihood of persistence into the second year as well as on academic performance while in college. (p. 403)

More recent research (Lang, 2007; Miller, Janz, & Chen; 2007; Tobolowsky, Cox, & Wagner, 2005) continues to bear this out. Other outcomes related to the seminar are less commonly reported in the literature. A collection of campus-based research reports on first-year seminars (Tobolowsky et al., 2005) highlighted some of the following outcomes, though they were far from common:

◇ Increased career/life planning (Appalachian State University, SUNY Brockport)
◇ Increased instrumental autonomy (Appalachian State University)
◇ Improved writing ability (Cardinal Stritch University, Endicott College)
◇ Improved argumentation skills (Cardinal Stritch University)
◇ Improved critical/reflective thinking skills (Cardinal Stritch University, Endicott College, Kalamazoo College, Rollins College)
◇ Improved academic and cognitive skills (Gallaudet University)
◇ Increased knowledge of wellness (Gallaudet University)
◇ Increased commitment to a major (Ithaca College)

Using data from the 2001 administration of the Your First College Year (YFCY) survey, Keup and Barefoot (2005) found that students who were enrolled in first-year seminars were more likely to report that they developed close friendships with other students and that they had established a network of friends on campus. However, the seminar's emphasis on building relationships may not always be perceived as positive: Students enrolled in the seminar were also more likely to report that they often felt forced to interact with students they disliked. First-year seminar participants were also more likely to engage in a range of behaviors that were likely to contribute to their academic success, such as attending class, interacting with faculty, participating in class discussions, and engaging in academic collaborations with other students.

Extending the Benefits of Orientation

As noted earlier, traditional orientation programs may be hard pressed to help students realize the learning and developmental outcomes such programs and their institutions value through summer and preterm orientation sessions alone. While the programs described above, when coupled with more traditional orientation programs, can help students achieve these outcomes, they are not without their own challenges. In this last section, we highlight some of the challenges inherit in implementing these initiatives and offer strategies for overcoming these challenges.

Challenges in Implementing Extended Orientation Programs

◇ The first-year seminar is not typically housed in a student affairs division. Faculty and academic affairs administrators may resist or be unaware of the benefits of what they may refer to as "student success" content. Yet many of the goals identified as important for orientation might be as easily achieved through course structure and pedagogy as through specific content. When the seminar is housed outside student affairs and is an academic seminar, orientation professionals may find it difficult to find a seat at the table and to promote these important learning and developmental goals. Orientation staff may experience similar challenges when common reading programs are housed within academic affairs units.

◇ Funding for extended orientation programs can be a particular challenge, especially since the initiatives described here may not have a centralized institutional home and may draw funding from a number of sources. Costs associated with outdoor orientation programs may include transportation, equipment needs, staff training and certification, and insurance (Curtis, 1994). Similar costs may be associated with service programs. Furthermore, liability can be costly for an institution when staff responsible for outdoor orientation and service experiences are not properly trained in safety management skills. Costs associated with common reading programs include the price of the text for discussion leaders and for students (if they are not required to buy their own) and ancillary programming costs (e.g., speaker fees and travel, food, set-up charges, printing, and mailing). The single largest cost associated with first-year seminars is instructor pay.

◇ With the exception of first-year seminars, the assessment of extended orientation initiatives is limited and frequently focuses on student satisfaction with the program rather than learning or developmental outcomes. While seminar assessment is more common, the variables of interest have most frequently been academic success (as measured by grade point average) and retention.

◇ Another challenge related to assessment is the lack of longitudinal data related to these initiatives. Current studies on outdoor orientation programs, for example, point to short-term effects of the programs on students and their institutions; however, effects on life post-college are still being explored. Similarly, the long-term effects of participation in orientation-related service experiences and common reading programs have not been studied in any systematic way. While a number of longitudinal studies have explored first-year seminar outcomes, these have focused on retention and academic performance almost exclusively. Thus, little is known about the lasting impact of the seminar on specific learning outcomes associated with the course.

◇ Encouraging student participation in these orientation initiatives is also a challenge. While the seminar is sometimes required, participation in all of these initiatives is typically voluntary—though it may be strongly encouraged. Since there is rarely a grade attached to the common reading, service, or outdoor experience, students may not be as motivated to attend. With outdoor orientation programs, additional fees may mean that students who would otherwise like to attend feel that the program is out of their reach financially.

◇ Encouraging faculty participation in common reading programs and first-year seminars can also be challenging. Since many common reading events take place before the start of fall classes, faculty may not have returned to campus from summer appointments or may be occupied with fall course preparation and resistant to participating in an event that is outside their regular teaching duties. Similarly, teaching the first-year seminar is not typically part of faculty's regular course load. Even with additional compensation and/or a course release, faculty may be reluctant to teach the course if it takes time away from research and publication in their discipline.

Recommendations for Overcoming These Challenges

◇ *Set clear expectations for student learning and involvement.* Using terminology such as "it is an expectation that all students attend" and highlighting the tradition and purpose of the program can encourage student participation in extended orientation activities. Institutions may also send reminders to the students' permanent addresses over the summer. This way, family members will know about the events and encourage their student to participate. When events require additional fees, programs should provide need-based scholarships so that all students who would like to participate have the opportunity to do so.

◇ *Encourage full campus participation and support.* Faculty will be more likely to support common reading and other orientation events if they feel that the institution values it. Having a letter of support and encouragement to volunteer sent to all faculty and staff, on behalf of the chief academic officer or president is an effective way to gain campus-wide support. Additionally, if the institution limits other activities during that time, all university personnel will recognize the importance of the event. Where feasible, making first-year seminar instruction part of the regular teaching load also communicates its value as a primary responsibility of faculty.

◇ *Build assessment into program design.* The most effective assessment is incorporated into initial program design, rather than as an afterthought. As coordinators are planning events and considering innovative methods for reaching the goals of orientation programs and events, they must consider how they will measure not only the need for but also the effectiveness and impact of these activities. Clearly stated learning outcomes should be coupled with assessment of each outcome and recognition of any opportunities for growth. The experience of all constituents (e.g., student participants, faculty/staff, peer leaders, community members involved in service or common reading initiatives) should be captured in some way, especially if different learning or developmental goals have been identified for different constituent groups.

◇ *Build reflection components into short-term orientation experiences (i.e., outdoor experiences, service programs, and common reading initiatives) to maximize their impact on student learning and development.* One of the hallmarks of service-learning as compared to community service is a significant reflection component, whether this is a written reflection or a group-processing activity. Such reflections help students connect the initiative to their previous experiences. While some reflection activities might be part of or immediately follow the initiative, it might also be useful to ask students to reflect on the experience at later points in the first semester or the first year. These later reflections will help students see things about themselves or their experiences that might not have been immediately apparent to them. When used as part of a program assessment, such reflections may provide valuable information about the long-range impact of these initiatives.

◇ *Be creative with funding.* Orientation professionals should find both internal and external partners to fund orientation initiatives. If the college or university has a fund set aside for invited lecturers, might some of this money be tapped to support an author visit in conjunction with a common reading initiative? Are there student organizations that might be willing to provide monetary and volunteer support as a way to make themselves known to potential new members? Are there local or national corporations that might provide funding support? For example, Target Corporation sponsors local store grants for educational programs. State Campus Compact organizations or the Campus Outreach Opportunity League (C.O.O.L.) run through idealist.org are good resources for information about grant funding opportunities for service initiatives.

Conclusion

In order to help students meet the learning and developmental outcomes laid out in the CAS standards, orientation professionals must intentionally design programs that challenge students intellectually; provide them with opportunities to clarify their personal, academic, and vocational values; offer opportunities to work independently as well as part of a team; and help students enhance their feelings of self-worth while learning to value diverse others. Transition programs, like the ones describe here, extend the traditional programming window for orientation and increase the likelihood that orientation programs help students achieve these goals.

References

Adkins, C., & Simmons, B. (2003). Outdoor, experiential, and environmental education: Converging or diverging approaches? *ERIC Digest.* Retrieved May 2, 2008, from http://www.ericdigests.org/2003-2/outdoor.html

Association for Experiential Education (AEE). (2008). *What is experiential education?* Retrieved May 2, 2008, from http://www.aee.org/customer/pages.php?pageid=47

Ball State University. (2008). Freshman connections. Retrieved May 4, 2008, from http://www.bsu.edu/freshmanconnections/

Barefoot, B. O. (1992). *Helping first-year college students climb the academic ladder: Report of a national survey of freshman seminar programming in American higher education.* Unpublished dissertation. College of William and Mary, Williamsburg, Virginia.

Bell, B. J. (2006a). Wilderness orientation: Exploring the relationship between college preorientation programs and social support. *Journal of Experiential Education, 29*(2), 145-167.

Bell, B. J. (2006b). Social support development and wilderness pre-orientation experiences. *Journal of Experiential Education, 28*(3), 248-249.

Curtis, R. (1994). Running a frosh wilderness orientation program. Paper presented at the Annual International Conference of the Association for Experiential Education, Austin, TX. (ERIC Document No. ED377010)

Ender S., & Newton, F. (2000). *Students helping students.* San Francisco: Jossey-Bass.

Evans, N. J., Forney, D. S., & Guido-DiBrito, F. (1998). *Student development in college: Theory, research, and practice.* San Francisco: Jossey-Bass.

Ferguson, M. (2006, Summer). Creating common ground: Common reading and the first year of college. *Peer Review*, 8-10.

Fidler, D. S. (1997). Getting students involved from the get-go: Summer reading programs across the country. *About Campus, 2*(5), 32.

Galloway, S. P. (2000). Assessment in wilderness orientation programs: Efforts to improve college student retention. *Journal of Experiential Education, 23*(2), 75-84.

Gass, M. A., Garvey, D. E., & Sugerman, D. A. (2003). The long-term effects of a first-year student wilderness orientation program. *The Journal of Experiential Education, 26*(1), 34-40.

Gordon, V. (1989). Origins and purposes of the freshman seminar. In M. L. Upcraft & J. N. Gardner (Eds.), *The freshman year experience: Helping students survive and succeed in college* (pp. 183-198). San Francisco: Jossey-Bass.

Hamid, S. L. (Ed.). (2001). *Peer leadership: A primer on program essentials* (Monograph No. 32). Columbia, SC: University of South Carolina, National Resource Center for The First-Year Experience and Students in Transition.

Jones, J. J., & Hinton, J. L. (2007). Study of self-efficacy in a freshman wilderness experience program: Measuring general versus specific gains. *Journal of Experiential Education, 29*(3), 382-385.

Keeling, R. (Ed.). (2004). *Learning reconsidered: A campus-wide focus on the student experience.* Washington, DC: American College Personnel Association, National Association of Student Personnel Administrators.

Keup, J. R., & Barefoot, B. O. (2005). Learning how to be a successful student: Exploring the impact of first-year seminars on student outcomes. *Journal of The First-Year Experience & Students in Transition, 17*(1), 11-47.

Lang, D. J. (2007). The impact of a first-year experience course on the academic performance, persistence, and graduation rates of first-semester college students at a public research university. *Journal of The First-Year Experience & Students in Transition, 19*(1), 9-25.

Laufgraben, J. L. (2006). *Common reading programs: Going beyond the book* (Monograph No. 44). Columbia, SC: University of South Carolina, National Resource Center for The First-Year Experience and Students in Transition.

Laufgraben, J. L., & Dennis, C. (2006). Planning events and activities for common reading programs. In. J. L. Laufgraben, *Common reading programs: Going beyond the book* (Monograph No. 44, pp. 45-64). Columbia, SC: University of South Carolina, National Resource Center for The First-Year Experience and Students in Transition.

Liljequist, L. & Stone, S. (2009). Measuring the success of a summer reading program: A five-year study. *Journal of The First-Year Experience & Students in Transition, 21*(2), 87-106.

McClure, A. (2008). Orientation rites seal the deal: Creative approaches to the classic summer rite of passage help acclimate students and ensure they arrive in the fall. *University Business, 11*(2), 36-40.

Miller, T. K. (Ed.). (2003). *The book of professional standards for higher education* (3rd ed.). Washington, DC: Council for the Advancement of Standards in Higher Education.

Miller, J. W., Janz, J. C., & Chen, C. (2007). The retention impact of a first-year seminar on students with varying pre-college academic performance. *Journal of The First-Year Experience & Students in Transition, 19*(1), 9-25.

Moody, B. L. (2007). Forming connections: Combining orientation and community service. *E-Source for College Transitions*, 4(6), 7-9.

Murray State University. (2008). *Freshman reading experience*. Retrieved April 24, 2008, from http://www.murraystate.edu/fre/program.htm

National Resource Center for The First-Year Experience and Students in Transition. (2008). *Institutions reporting first-year summer reading programs*. Retrieved May 4, 2008, from http://nrc.fye.sc.edu/resources/reading/read01.php

Pascarella, E. T., & Terenzini, P. T. (1991). *How college affects students: Findings from twenty years of research*. San Francisco: Jossey-Bass.

Pascarella, E. T., & Terenzini, P. T. (2005). *How college affects students, Vol. 2: A third decade of research*. San Francisco: Jossey-Bass.

Paulson, A. (2000, September 19). Welcome to college: Now take a hike. *Christian Science Monitor*. Retrieved from http://www.csmonitor.com/2000/0919/p16s1.html

Pixley, Z., & Seuss, D. (2006). Engaging the campus, Kalamazoo College. In J. L. Laufgraben (Ed.), *Common Reading Programs: Going beyond the book* (Monograph No. 44, p.17). Columbia, SC: University of South Carolina, National Resource Center for The First-Year Experience and Students in Transition.

Pryor, J. H., Hurtado, S., DeAngelo, L., Sharkness, J., Romero, L.C., Korn, W. S., & Tran, S. (2008). *The American freshman: National norms for fall 2008*. Los Angeles: University of California-Los Angeles, Higher Education Research Institute.

Pryor, J. H., Hurtado, S., Saenz, V. B., Korn, J. S., Santos, J. L., & Korn, W. S. (2006). *The American freshman: National norms for fall 2006 HERI research brief*. Los Angeles: University of California-Los Angeles, Higher Education Research Institute.

Pryor, J. H., Hurtado, S., Saenz, V. B., Lindholm, J. A., Korn, W. S., & Mahoney, K.M. (2005). *The American freshman: National norms for fall 2005*. Los Angeles: University of California-Los Angeles, Higher Education Research Institute.

Pryor, J. H., Hurtado, S., Sharkness, J., & Korn, W.S. (2007) *The American freshman: National norms for fall 2007 HERI research brief*. Los Angeles: University of California-Los Angeles, Higher Education Research Institute.

Purcell, B., McLaughlin, C., Volpe, J. D., Perez, E., Simolaris, L., & Chavez, J. (2008). *Executive summary: The 15th Biannual Youth Survey on Politics and Public Service*. Harvard University Institute of Politics. Retrieved July 15, 2009, from http://www.iop.harvard.edu/Research-Publications/Polling/Fall-2008-Survey/Executive-Summary

Sharp, L. B. (1943). Outside the classroom. *The Educational Forum*, 7(4), 361-368.

Stremba, B. (1991). A wilderness and community building new student orientation program. *Proceedings of the International and Workshop Summaries Book of the International Association for Experiential Education*, Lake Junaluska, NC. (ERIC Document No. ED342596)

Tobolowsky, B. F., & Associates. (2008). *The 2006 national survey of first-year seminars: Continuing innovations in the collegiate curriculum* (Monograph No. 51). Columbia, SC: University of South Carolina, National Resource Center for The First-Year Experience and Students in Transition.

Tobolowsky, B. F., Cox, B. E., & Wagner, M. T. (2005). *Exploring the evidence, Vol. III: Reporting research on first-year seminars*. (Monograph No. 42). Columbia, SC: University of South Carolina, National Resource Center for The First-Year Experience and Students in Transition.

Troop, D. (2003, August 15). Into the wild. *The Chronicle of Higher Education*, p. A6.

University of Florida. (2008). Dean of students. Retrieved May 4, 2008, from http://www.dso.ufl.edu/nsp/firstyearexperience/commonread/

Upcraft, M. L., Gardner, J. N., & Barefoot, B. O. (Eds.). (2005). *Challenging and supporting the first-year student: A handbook for improving the first year of college.* San Francisco: Jossey-Bass.

Appendix

Print and Online Resources

Laufgraben, J. L. (2006). *Common reading programs: Going beyond the book* (Monograph No. 44). Columbia, SC: University of South Carolina, National Resource Center for The First-Year Experience and Students in Transition.

Summer Reading Program Database, Program List, Book List, Summer Reading Listserv
http://sc.edu/fye/resources/fyr/index.html

First-Year Seminar Searchable Database of Syllabi, Research, Textbooks, Instructor Training
http://sc.edu/fye/resources/fyr/index.html

National Service-Learning Clearinghouse
http://www.servicelearning.org/

Professional Associations and Meetings

Association of Experiential Education (AAE). A nonprofit, professional membership association dedicated to experiential education and the students, educators and practitioners who utilize its philosophy.
3775 Iris Avenue, Suite #4
Boulder, CO 80301-2043 USA
Phone: 303-440-8844
Fax: 303-440-9581
Web site: www.aee.org

Campus Compact. A national nonprofit organization dedicated to promoting community service, civic engagement, and service-learning in higher education.
Campus Compact
PO Box 1975
Brown University
Providence, RI 02912
Phone: 401-867-3950
Fax: 401-867-3925
Web site: www.compact.org

Chapter 8

Technology in Orientation

J.J. Brown and Cynthia L. Hernandez

Adoption of technological applications allow for the optimization of business practices and processes with the goal of producing efficient, cost-effective, customer-service-based programs. As higher education faces increasing demands to provide high-quality, efficient, and cost-effective learning experiences, technological advances will continue to be pervasive. Entering students' heightened use of technology also increases expectations of incorporating these technologies into orientation programming. As a result orientation program administrators must be familiar with new technologies, how to implement them, and strategies for assessing their usefulness.

It is impossible to ignore the impact that current and emerging technologies have had on the administration and delivery of orientation programs for new students. In the second edition of this monograph, Kramer (2003) explored emerging web technology and how that technology could be used to further enhance the information, services and programs for new students. Since that time, the technology available to supplement and enhance programming for new students has expanded beyond the Web. During the last decade, educational sessions focused on technology have increased at the National Orientation Directors Association (NODA) annual conferences. Initially these sessions centered on the growing use of CD-ROMS, web pages, and other forms of multimedia in orientation programs, now these sessions address social networking sites, wikis, text messaging, and blogs. The discourse surrounding the incorporation of technology into first-year programming continues to remain relevant as technologies, students, and their expectations change. This chapter focuses on the way orientation professionals can use different technological media to improve the administration, delivery, and communication of programs for new students. It concludes with considerations and recommendations when implementing new technology.

The Net Generation

Born around the time the personal computer (PC) was introduced, the current generation of college students has grown up with technology and has never known a world without the Internet. Oblinger and Oblinger (2005) refer to this generation of students as the "Net Generation." To the Net Gen students entering our campuses today, PCs, portable media devices, and cell phones are part of their daily routines. They are wired for instant communication and access to information. As a result, they have come to expect immediate access to services and have developed finely tuned skills that allow them to multitask among competing technologies. Though home access to the Internet and other technologies may vary by race and socioeconomic status, all students consider such access important (Oblinger & Oblinger). The intersection of technology and education begins long before students step on to a college campus. School districts loan laptops, preloaded with required textbooks, to all middle school children with the expectation that the students use the laptops to turn in homework assignments. Internet research for high school term papers is commonplace, if not expected. As such, rising college students expect to continue using technology as they transition to higher education and consequently, they expect higher education to support this use.

According to Oblinger and Oblinger (2005), "the activity enabled is more important to the Net Gen than the technology behind it" (p. 2.10). For instance, a new smartphone is neat technology, but more important is what it provides access to: e-mail, text messages, and the Internet. Activities such as instant messaging, text messaging, and constant access to information via the Internet has created a culture of immediacy. Technologies have allowed this generation to experience immediate gratification in relation to accessing friends, services, and responses to inquiries. This pattern of information consumption may provide insight into what students are seeking from their college experience and our orientation programs.

The Use of Technology in the Administration of Orientation Programs

New technologies are changing the way higher education professionals conduct business. Web-based admission applications, tuition payments, course registration, graduation applications, and audits have all become standards in higher education (Miller & Pope, 2003). College admissions and orientation offices are among the leaders in incorporating new technologies to attract, transition, and matriculate prospective students (Moneta, 2005).

The administration of orientation programs encompasses many processes and procedures that can be enhanced by the application of new technologies. From the way we communicate information to new students about orientation to managing orientation registration, intentional analysis of these processes may result in adoption of new technological tools that can assist in providing quality, student-centered services.

Marketing and Communication

According to the NODA *Databank*, more than 66% of orientation programs are mandatory for new first-year students; thus, thousands of college students and their families will be seeking information about their orientation program (Debellis, 2007). Even though many orientation offices still produce printed orientation materials, virtually all orientation programs use a web site to interface with new students. During a review of orientation web sites, Rielley (2000) identified three overarching categories: (a) basic, (b) enhanced, and, as will be described in detail later in this chapter, (c) online orientations.

Basic web sites contain static pages designed primarily to deliver information to the user. These web pages are online versions of the orientation program's mail-out brochure. They provide basic details about the university, the orientation program, and at times the orientation staff.

Building on the foundation of basic web pages, enhanced pages go beyond providing passive information and allow the user to interact with the site through a series of links and multimedia features, which may include video podcasts, interactive maps, and virtual campus tours. Improved features on a new generation of web sites move users from passive to active participants. Chats, blogs, wikis, and other applications allow users to engage, in a reciprocal manner, with orientation staff and other new students prior to and after coming to orientation. Many universities have partnered with companies such as Apple and YouTube.Com to produce multimedia sites where new students can learn about what institutions have to offer. Duke University, for example, developed a site under iTunesU where new students can download audio and video podcasts about university resources including orientation, student health services, and residence life. In addition, a new student can browse through different student organizations and a sample of an actual course lecture. Through programs of this nature, students can explore the institution at anytime and anywhere from their iPhone or iTouch. In addition to corporate partnerships, collaboration with other campus units such as admissions and the visitor's center can result in cost sharing and efficiency when developing multimedia features such as online tours, chats with current students, and sample video lectures.

Online Orientations

Online orientation has emerged as an alternative to traditional campus-based programs. The main goal of these programs was to provide a cost-efficient method, both to the institution and the new student, to orient students to campus. The production and use of online orientation programs has evolved over the years. In the early 1990s, the University of Utah was cutting edge, offering one of the first virtual orientation programs. In an attempt to help transfer students, who were not required to attend the campus orientation, the University mailed out a VHS tape filled with interviews about campus services and a walking tour of campus to this newly admitted population. Since then, the method of delivery has changed from VHS tapes, to CD-ROMs, to web-based interfaces—all attempting to introduce students to campus.

While virtual delivery of orientation has evolved, online orientations still account for a relatively small percentage of orientation programs. According to the NODA *Databank*, approximately 10% of respondents indicated they offered an online orientation program for new first-year students and 14% offered one for new transfer students (DeBellis, 2007). Online programs have traditionally been geared towards transfer students; students over the traditional age; and students who are unable to attend an on-campus orientation session due to cost, location, or conflict of dates. Depending on the institution, some online orientation programs can be used to fulfill the entire orientation requirement or replace portions of an on-campus program with students still attending a face-to-face advising appointment. In some cases, online orientation sessions may be the only option for an orientation program if an on-campus program is not offered.

In response to new transfer students' low participation rate in their traditional on-campus orientation, Arizona State University (ASU) created an online orientation program for this unique population. In addition to standard elements such as course registration, textbook purchase, parking permit purchase, and tuition payment (Rielley, 2000), ASU customized their program according to the student's semester of admission, academic college, and time of entry. For example, depending on the semester of entry, personalized lists of activities and deadlines for that semester are prominently displayed during the online orientation, thus alerting students to complete university business in a timely manner (Gladney, Mason, Enloe, & Burtnett, 2004).

At Governors State University, an upper-division university in the Midwest, new undergraduate students are required to complete an online orientation program. This program is unique in that not only does it allow students the opportunity to learn about services, policies, colleges, and key departments of the university, but it also allows for directed self-placement for math and writing. This portion of the online orientation assists students in assessing their level of ability in math and writing. Students will then self-select supplemental review or coursework based on this assessment (McCarthy, 2003). In an attempt to reach and prepare new students prior to an orientation program, some institutions are using the Web to deliver supplemental pre-orientation activities. These pre-orientations consist of activities that students are asked to complete prior to attending a campus-based program, such as an introduction to the university catalog, college/ major requirements, placement exams, and course selection.

Platforms used to deliver online pre-orientation and orientation programs vary by institution. Most programs have a login system enabling orientation professionals to track when new students have started and completed the program. Some institutions use online course management systems such as WebCT or Blackboard as a platform for delivery. These programs enable orientation professionals to develop quizzes to be taken after every module and create communities where college-specific information (i.e., academic policies, deadlines, and advising processes) can be delivered to new students. An advantage to using the university's course management system is that it allows students the opportunity to become familiar with the system prior to use for classroom purposes.

Although many of these course management systems allow for online discussion, many online orientation programs remain passive in nature. Text-heavy sites attempt to involve the user through quizzes; however, these sites still place the student in a passive learning environment with little personal contact with university faculty, staff, and other students. Campus-based orientation, transition, and retention programs tend to involve multiple avenues for direct interpersonal contact. A successful online orientation program finds the balance in using technology and providing an active learning environment that allows students to truly connect with the campus culture.

Reservation Processing and Data Sharing

In addition to the use of orientation web sites for marketing and communicating with new students, the next largest infusion of technology is in the process of reserving spaces in orientation programs online and sharing data captured during this process with campus constituents. Institutions are now on their second or third generation of enterprise application systems, robust systems for managing student records and handling the administrative and data-dependent functions of the university. Many of these new systems have the capability to add software modules that can assist orientation professionals in the administrative processes of orientation. One aspect of orientation that has been most impacted by these systems is the process of reserving a space in an orientation session. A user-friendly, web-based front-end interface, coupled with the enterprise system's powerful data management backend, produces an online orientation reservation system that allows participants real-time, 24-hour, seven-day-a-week access and management of their orientation reservation and payment. Since 2000, the University of San Diego (USD), a private institution in Southern California, has had an exclusively online orientation reservation system. In addition, USD is paper-free, delivering all their orientation program materials and confirmation materials electronically. Although there is hesitancy on behalf of institutions to go totally paperless (92% of institutions still send orientation information to new students through regular mail), 84% of institutions use the web for reserving a space in orientation. In addition, 65% of institutions also e-mail student materials about orientation prior to their orientation session (DeBellis, 2007).

Online orientation reservation systems allow student data to be captured and reported in a variety of ways that benefit many campus constituencies. These systems, whether locally produced or purchased through an external vendor, have the ability to capture and post data in easily accessible and downloadable web-based reports. At Colorado State University, academic advisors have the ability to see pertinent student information (i.e., SAT scores, placement scores, declared major) during the orientation program, allowing them to prepare personalized materials for each student attending orientation.

Integrated orientation fee payment modules can assist with complex accounting and refund processes. Many institutions work with their bursar's office to connect this fee payment process to the university's e-payment system. Automatic bank drafts and instant credit card verifications can minimize refund and collection processing. In addition to creating efficiencies, the automation of the orientation reservation and fee payment processes has enabled orientation staff to focus less on these administrative details and more on the content and quality of programming.

The Use of Technology in the Delivery of Orientation Programs

As noted previously, multitasking, constant connectivity, and engagement with multimedia are some of the characteristics of the Net Generation. For these students, technology must be relevant and interactive. One of the greatest challenges for orientation, transition, and retention professionals is to determine what technological elements can be added to aid in the delivery of orientation programs while on campus. When used correctly, orientation professionals can use technology to help students engage with their institutions, enhance learning, and improve their academic and social experiences (Junco & Cole-Avent, 2008).

Multimedia

Multimedia is a term that has vastly changed over the last 10 to 15 years. Approximately 15 years ago, a multimedia presentation may have involved a picture slide show or an overhead projector. Now institutions are using a variety of multimedia technologies including high definition video recorders, enhanced PowerPoint presentations, amateur and professionally edited videos, and "clicker" response systems to enhance sessions during orientation. Taking a page from news networks, orientation professionals are providing multiple messages in various formats during one presentation. Orientation presentations no longer consist solely of a talking head behind a podium; technology supplements the speaker's message and delivers a more appealing, engaging presentation. Partnering with other campus constituencies can be beneficial when producing multimedia for orientation programs. Texas A&M University partnered with the Screenwriting, Acting, and Movie Production (SWAMP) student organization to produce social issue videos used during their campus life session during orientation.

Audience Response Systems

The audience response system (ARS), more commonly known as "clickers," is a technology that has truly evolved since its early use to evaluate films prior to their release (Bugeja, 2008). Currently, universities are using this technology in new student orientation programs and in the classroom environment. At the University of Tennessee, an ARS is used to gauge student response with regards to alcohol in a discussion about safety and in a session discussing academic expectations. Responses of new students are compared to institutional data regarding academic preparedness. Using ARSs allows for the instant engagement of students, which will ultimately enhance their experience.

During new student orientation, Texas A&M University uses an ARS in a program entitled Aggieland: A Community of Respect. Students are able to answer questions related to diversity issues/scenarios anonymously, meaning students can answer truthfully with low risk. Facilitators use these responses to have intentional conversations surrounding sensitive topics. Some universities have employed an ARS for classes. In these instances, early exposure to these systems benefits new students by allowing them an opportunity to use the system prior to finding themselves in a classroom situation. If not individually purchased by the student, investing in an ARS can be a costly endeavor for the university. However, new developments in ARS technologies allow individuals to use their personal cell phones and smartphones as response devices allowing them to respond in real-time to interactive polling questions

Cell Phones and Text Messaging

College students tend to be early adopters of technology when compared to their non-college peers. For example, smartphones, cell phones with web browsing, applications, and e-mail capability, are likely to increase in popularity particularly among college students. Ball State University reported that 27% of students surveyed owned a smart phone as opposed to 19% of working adults (Ransford, 2009). In a 2007 study funded by the EDUCAUSE Center for Applied Research, Caruso and Salaway found that 86.1% of college students owned a simple cell phone while 12% owned a Smartphone. The ability to purchase reasonably priced phone plans that include unlimited data and text messaging makes this a cost-efficient method of communication employed by college students. In order to capitalize on this preferred communication method, the Massachusetts Institute of Technology (MIT) has developed a version of their web site for smart phones (Young, 2008). This quick-loading site enables students to view course syllabi and check the campus shuttle schedule from their hand-held devices. Similarly, Abilene Christian University, which provided either an iPhone or iPod Touch to incoming first-year students in 2008, developed a mobile version of its web site to help connect to students through news and calendars, course documents, in-class surveys, and polls.

Institutions of higher education have capitalized on student cell phone ownership by using Short Message Service (SMS), also known as text messaging, to deliver important notifications. Junco and Cole-Avent (2008) state that college students prefer to communicate by text messaging rather than by e-mail. In addition, another study found that 57.4% of students reported they text message at least once a day (Junco & Mastrodicasa, 2007). Universities quickly realized the benefits of using text messaging, and student affairs professionals have begun to embrace this new form of communication to enhance programming. The University of Florida and University of Texas have partnered with a third party vendor allowing student organizations to organize and send messages associated with their groups.

Orientation professionals are developing new and unique ways to use text messaging to reach new students. For example, one of the most frequently stated learning outcomes of orientation programs is for students to develop a familiarity with the physical surroundings of the campus. Several institutions are using SMS technology to transform the traditional scavenger hunt. Harvard University and Berklee College of Music connected with SCVNGR, a third party vendor, to set up a campus-wide clue hunt during welcome week to assist new students in learning the campus environment. The high-tech feature in this program is the delivery of the clues. SCVNGR works with its clients to build the hunt and deliver the clues by SMS messaging to the group leader's mobile device. In addition, the web-based software allows the coordinators of the program to monitor how each group is performing and gives extra clues to those teams needing more assistance. Some institutions have created traditions-based hunts that expose new students to the campus lore, while others have used clues to take students to buildings that house important campus services for new students (e.g., the student counseling center, the health center, and the library). In addition to using this on campus, some urban institutions are using the SMS-based hunt as a means to acquaint new students with off-campus communities by directing them to museums and other places of interests in the local area.

Reaching Family Members

Orientation, transition, and retention professionals have long recognized the need to enlist parents as partners to assist in the successful transition of new students. Junco and Mastrodicasa (2007) recommend involving parents and family members in the orientation process so they may in turn be resources for their students. More than 90% of institutions participating in the collection of information for the NODA *Databank* indicated that they offer an on-campus parent and family orientation program that runs concurrently with the new student orientation program. Unfortunately, barriers such as inability to miss work; obligations to care for younger children; and costs associated with transportation, lodging, and meals may prevent some family members from attending on-campus programs. Recognizing that not all family members have the opportunity to attend, Nehls (2007) emphasizes the growing popularity, among colleges and universities, of communicating with family members online.

Arizona State University's (ASU) has developed ASU Connect to reach out to family members of new students. ASU Connect features online parent chats, which allows family members to chat with ASU Transition and Parent Program Staff, members of the ASU Parent Association, and other new ASU parents. Every scheduled chat has a theme and a guest moderator to help answer specific questions about ASU and common transition concerns family members or new students may experience. After new student orientation, the ASU staff offers Post Orientation Parent (POP) Chats, which review information highlighted at orientation and answer any lingering questions. Another example of using the web to connect with parents is Whitman College's Parents Core, where family members gather online to read and discuss the common reading book for the entering class.

Family involvement in programs allows students to have an additional reference point during their first year of college. Parents of Net Generation students have been involved in their students' lives since elementary school, sending requests for progress reports and receiving responses from classroom teachers via e-mail were common occurrences. Parents are just as eager to stay connected to their students' higher education experience. For this reason, many orientation offices set up parent listservs to which family members can subscribe to receive frequent updates, reminders about upcoming events, and emergency notifications from the university.

Using Technology to Integrate New Students

Successful orientation programs allow students an opportunity to integrate socially and academically into the university environment (Tinto, 1987; Upcraft & Farnsworth, 1984). In this section, we focus on how to use technology to fulfill the goal of assisting students with their academic and personal adjustment to college. Orientation professionals have been deliberate in creating specialized programming to allow for academic and social connections to occur. New technology has provided colleges and universities with new methods that enable connections to and between students prior to, during, and following traditional campus-based orientation programs.

Academic Integration

Colleges recognize the importance helping students forge connections to the social and academic systems of an institution early in their college careers. Integration into one aspect at the expense of the other may lead to drop out (Tinto, 1975). For this reason, institutions may put a great deal of emphasis on providing a positive introduction to academic life once a student has been admitted. Orientation programs frequently play a key role in these early academic experiences, which include academic advising, placement testing, and course registration. All of these activities have been affected by technological advances.

Academic advising is a key component in the academic integration of a first-year student. In an address to the National Academic Advising Association (NACADA), Tinto (1975) noted that

> students are more likely to persist and graduate in settings that take advising seriously; that provide clear, consistent, and easily accessible information about institutional requirements; that help students understand the roadmap to completion and help them understand how they use that roadmap to decide upon and achieve personal goals. (p. 6)

According to the NODA *Databank* (DeBellis, 2007), 92% of respondents indicated that academic advising is included in their on-campus orientation program. A common challenge is allowing adequate time for academic advisors to meet with new students during orientation programs. As part of their First-Year Testing, Consulting, and Advising Program (FTCAP), Pennsylvania State University uses a series of online exercises to prepare students for their academic advising appointments at orientation. The exercises include homework assignments, which students print out and bring to their appointments. In addition, The University of Tennessee recently established a pre-orientation that shares information on general education requirements and advising preparation. Students at the University of Tennessee are also asked to bring this information with them to orientation. Both of these programs enable connections between academic advising units and new students prior to orientation.

Placement testing for new students during orientation has always presented a challenge for orientation directors in terms of finding time in an already saturated schedule. Traditionally, students are asked to arrive the day prior to their orientation session or on a scheduled day apart from their orientation for testing, which results in additional time and expense for new students and their family members. Advancing technologies have transformed this practice on many campuses. Initially, the shift was from a pencil and paper exam to computer labs on campus set up for this purpose. This allowed for efficiency in scoring and expedited the results to academic units. Now, the adoption of web-based exams is gaining popularity. Texas Tech University now administers placement tests through a secure web site. New students are informed of the placement tests required and of the process to complete these tests prior to orientation. Students have the ability to take these tests online at their own convenience without the expense of traveling to campus. Advances in offering these placement tests on the Web prior to orientation have enabled professionals to free up time for additional programming or, in some cases, allowed for the reduction in the length of the orientation session. Should a student not be able to access these online exams, some institutions have scheduled testing days where a student may take this exam in an on-campus computer lab prior to or during orientation.

Registering for classes used to be an all day affair at most institutions. Many times students stood in line for hours moving from table to table in the university's field house to register for classes. With advances in telecommunications, phone registration became the new mode of registering for classes. Students now have the ability to register for courses at the click of button through online course registration systems. In the new age of mobile devices, innovative applications are being developed to allow students more access to university services. Stanford and Duke University are collaborating with external vendors to develop applications for the iPhone that will allow students to register for classes, pay their tuition bills, and pull up a campus map all in the palm of their hand. The development and use of these systems have allowed orientation directors more time in their on-campus programs for advising or educational experiences. It has also brought a shift in necessary resources by employing the use of computer labs across campus during new student orientation.

Social Integration

Entering college can be an overwhelming experience for new students. When students are able to connect socially to their environment, they are more likely to persist and attain their educational goals (Tinto, 1987; Upcraft & Farnsworth, 1984). With the advent of social networking sites, student affairs professionals expressed concern that the amount of time spent in online, virtual communities would deter students from engaging with the "real" campus community. However research by Ellison, Steinfield, and Lampe (2007) found just the opposite: Students are using these sites to maintain relationships on and away from campus. The maintaining of these relationships allows new students to call on these friends in times of need and support. Heiberger and Harper (2008) examined how social networking sites and other technologies provide new opportunities for peer group interactions and social integrations. Their findings suggest that students today network with each other using technology as much as, if not more than, face-to-face communication. College administrators must not only recognize this phenomenon, but learn to use the variety of electronic media available in positive ways: to stay connected to college social networks, promote relevant events, and help students feel safe and at home on campus.

Orientation offices are creatively using social networking sites to provide opportunities for new students to interact before and after orientation. Tulane University uses Facebook to create an online group for new students to join as soon as they are admitted to the university. The group's site offers a variety of links where a new student can download university videos, explore involvement opportunities, and receive notifications of events for first-year students. The page includes a feature that allows new students to post comments and questions, in an effort for university administrators to understand and learn about students' interests and concerns. Though some institutions create groups on third-party software such as Facebook, some private institutions prefer to set up these groups on their own sites to control content.

Web logs, more commonly known as blogs, are also gaining popularity with new students. In a 2009 study commissioned by the National Association for College Admission Counseling, Barnes found that 33% of the colleges and universities used blogs in their efforts to recruit new students. The University of Texas at Austin has incorporated current student blogs on their admissions web site that allow new and prospective students an opportunity to begin to understand life as a college student on their campus. In *Connecting to the Net.Generation*, Junco and Mastrodicasa (2007) found that blogging increased from 11% to 27% within a 20-month period in 2003-2004 among college students. In addition, they found that more than 63% of college students read blogs (Junco & Mastrodicasa).

Considerations and Recommendations

As technological systems continue to evolve and the technological proficiency of our students increases, Moneta (2005) offers several considerations for student affairs professionals as we attempt to understand the value of technology in enhancing our practice and engaging students.

Access

New technologies emerge daily. As professionals we have an obligation to be prudent in our choices of implementing new technologies and consideration must be shown to populations whose access to information about our programs may be impacted. The U.S. Department of Commerce's National Telecommunications and Information Administration (NTIA) found that "people with lower incomes have lower rates of Internet use and broadband access" (qtd. in Junco & Mastrodicasa,

2007, pp. 45-46). In addition, the report concluded that access to the Internet is directly related to level of education attained. Prior to eliminating paper versions of orientation materials, careful review of the university's student population must occur. One indicator of accessibility to the Internet can be derived from reviewing the percentages of students who submitted their admissions applications online versus traditional mail.

In addition, consideration must be given to the accessibility of new technologies for students with disabilities. Inaccessible designs of web sites put students with disabilities at a disadvantage in terms of accessing information. Poorly designed web sites can affect the ability of assistive technologies such as screen reader and screen magnification software to accurately convey the content being presented. Video and audio content (e.g., podcasts and voiced-over PowerPoints) should also be properly captioned or include written transcripts for the hearing impaired. Web forms and downloadable documents should be properly tagged so that they are readable by assistive technology.

Orientation professionals should consult and partner with information technology (IT) and disability services staff to create accessible web sites for this important population. There are a number of resources available to assist web site authors in developing accessible web content such as WebAIM (http://webaim.org) and the Web Accessibility Initiative through the World Wide Web (W3C) Consortium (http://www.w3.org/WAI).

Staffing

Moneta (2005) and Blimling and Whitt (1999) emphasize that professionals working with students must acquire and maintain the technical skills relevant to their roles and responsibilities, understand the milieu of available product and technology solutions applicable to their work, and balance this technical competency on a solid conceptual foundation of knowledge about students. Moneta also suggests the primary competency needed by practitioners is "mastering the skills necessary to analyze student affairs needs and work processes along with increased education to understand better how students perceive and use technology" (p. 5). When considering the implementation of new technologies, orientation practitioners should be able to identify current challenges in the administration and delivery of programs For example, the creation of online orientation reservation systems arose out of the identification of a workflow issue that could be resolved by automating various processes.

Once a need has been established, staff should consult with IT professionals to recommend the best technology to respond to that need. The necessity of employing or forming strong partnerships with staff who have the technological expertise is critical. Working closely with IT staff from the point of conception can streamline processes for determining which technologies to employ. In addition, these professionals may assist in the application development or identification of off-the-shelf applications best suited for the institution's budget and current IT environment. Information technology staff members are essential as the need for web applications continues to expand. The University of Minnesota employs a part-time IT staff member to develop and maintain technological systems to support first-year programs. Whether housed in the orientation office or contracted through the university's information technology department, these members are important in advancing the mission of the orientation office.

Budget

Organizational alignment and funding for orientation and first-year offices vary from institution to institution. Some offices are stand-alone departments with large staffs within a larger division of student affairs or enrollment management while others are smaller program areas with minimal staff, housed within another office. While most programs are fee-based, some programs receive additional revenue from other sources such as student services fees, tuition revenue, or development monies. In any case, the decision to use funds on new technology should be conducted in a prudent manner. Many new technologies are very expensive and extremely complicated; therefore, thorough assessment of the need for the technology will prevent wasteful spending on unneeded applications.

Several items should be considered in terms of how the new technology will affect the institution's budget. First, what are the identified costs? What are the application and hardware costs right out of the box? Second, what are the unidentified costs with the system? Will new hardware such as servers, laptops, and video cameras need to be purchased? Many times companies that provide support for off-the-shelf applications charge a yearly maintenance fee. Online payment for services using a credit card can lead to an increase in credit card fees. Lastly, the question of personnel costs must be explored. Will the program have to employ more undergraduate, graduate, or professional staff to assist with the new technology? For example, will the new blog and chat feature on the orientation web site require employing an individual to conduct the chats and keep the blogs current?

Appropriate Uses

As new ways to use technology to improve services, instruction, and programs in higher education have been identified, a new struggle has emerged—determining the appropriate level of incorporation and application of technology. Kramer (2003) comments that "technology becomes effective only as it is integrated into, supports, and humanizes the service environments for providers and students" (p. 174) That is, technology implementation should focus "on high touch as much if not more than high tech and high effect" (Kramer, p. 174). To this end, Kramer suggests creating and continuing discourse among campus faculty, staff, and administrators pertaining to using technology in humanized ways to provide a seamless learning environment.

The Net Generation of college students are highly connected to each other and the institution using technology; however, research supports that when it comes to learning students still value face-to-face interactions. An EDUCAUSE study revealed mixed responses when it asked students about their preferences regarding technology. Ninety-five percent of respondents preferred traditional face-to-face classes that were supplemented with technology, 2% preferred courses without technology, and only 3% preferred entirely online classes (Caruso & Salaway, 2007). Similarly, Fresno City Community College found that most students preferred traditional face-to-face academic advising to their online academic advising option (Kostin & Unruh, 2005). Students at the community college viewed the online option as a good way to supplement the traditional face-to-face meetings but did not like an entirely online orientation process. Orientation professionals, through meaningful assessment, must determine what new students and related constituents are seeking in terms of information and methods of delivery.

Recommendations

The challenge of where to begin will be specific to the institution, mission, campus culture, and students. Whether a technology staff person is in place, campus technology professionals are used, or services are outsourced, here are some recommendations:

1. *Assess what the department can support.* Orientation professionals should engage in discussions with key individuals to develop a technology plan that includes strategies to connect

to students. This may include web sites, instant messaging, online orientation, cell phones or smartphones, Facebook, clicker systems, or other multimedia options.

2. *Determine a plan for staffing.* As resources are limited within higher education, the question of managing these initiatives is an important one. When determining a staffing plan for these technologies, program leaders should think long term. While there may be students (graduate or undergraduate) involved in technology initiatives, they will eventually graduate. For this reason, partnering with on-campus IT or a third-party vendor to provide support may be a more effective long-term solution.

3. *Assessing students' needs and access.* When developing a technology plan, orientation professionals should consider how to assess the student need. Perhaps the creation of a student technology advisory group within the department will assist staying on the cutting edge in meeting the needs of students. A yearly study involving focus groups of students who were previously involved in programs can also help refine the plan to effectively meet their needs.

Access to technology is still a challenge for many students and their families. Determining level(s) of access is extremely important. As referenced earlier, many students and families may not have access to broadband Internet service. Some of the students or family members accessing the web site may have a disability. The use of various scripts and images on a web site can impact students' or families' use of technology. Institutional research may be an additional resource to assist in determining level(s) of access for the student population.

Summary

Technology, and the way students use it, is changing at a rapid pace. Colleges and universities across the country are experimenting with how to best incorporate these technologies (e.g., online orientation, Facebook, smartphones, text messaging) to assist in the orientation, transition, and retention of new students. Capitalizing on the ever-increasing accessibility of the Web, many programs are using web-based services to streamline outdated processes. For example, many programs are uploading materials to the Internet rather than printing and mailing materials to their families. Beyond streamlining administrative processes, orientation professionals are investing human and financial resources to incorporate new technology into programming aimed at enhancing the academic and social connectivity of new students to the institution. This investment can be costly; therefore, more assessment should be conducted to examine the effectiveness of these new technologies and advocate for their use in orientation programming.

References

Barnes, N. G. (2009). *Reaching the wired generation: How social media is changing college admissions.* Arlington, VA: National Association for College Admissions Counseling.

Blimling, G. S., & Whitt, E. J. (1999). *Good practice in student affairs: Principles to foster student learning.* San Francisco: Jossey-Bass.

Bugeja, M. (2008). *Classroom clickers and the cost of technology.* Retrieved April 5, 2009, from http://chronicle.com/article/Classroom-Clickersthe-/6009/

Caruso, J. B., & Salaway, G. (2007). *The ECAR study of undergraduate students and information technology.* Boulder, CO: EDUCAUSE.

DeBellis, R. F. (2007). *NODA Databank*. Minneapolis, MN: National Orientation Directors Association. Retrieved on March 10, 2009, from http://www.nodaweb.org

Ellison, N. B., Steinfield, C., & Lampe, C. (2007). The benefits of facebook friends: Social capital and college students' use of online social network sites. *Journal of Computer-Mediated Communication, 12*(4). Retrieved from http://jcmc.indiana.edu/vol12/issue4/ellison.html

Gladney, L. B., Mason, M. C., Enloe, M., & Burtnett, J. (2004). Developing an online orientation program for transfer students to Arizona State University. *The Journal of College Orientation and Transition, 12*(1), 57-60.

Heiberger, G., & Harper, R. (2008) Have you facebooked Astin lately? Using technology to increase student involvement. In R. Junco & D. M. Trimm (Eds.), *Using emerging technologies to enhance student engagement* (New Directions for Student Services No. 124, pp. 19-35). San Francisco: Jossey-Bass.

Junco, R., & Cole-Avent, G. (2008). An introduction to technologies commonly used by college students. In R. Junco & D. M. Trimm (Eds.), *Using emerging technologies to enhance student engagement* (New Directions for Student Services No. 124, pp. 3-17). San Francisco: Jossey-Bass.

Junco, R., & Mastrodicasa, J. (2007). *Connecting to the net.generation*. Washington, DC: National Association of Student Personnel Administrators.

Kostin, Y., & Unruh, R. (2005). Virtual counseling: An examination of academic advising via the Internet. *The Journal of College Orientation and Transition, 12*(2), 28-39.

Kramer, G. L. (2003). 10 Years later: The web phenomenon and new student orientation. In J. A. Ward-Roof & C. Hatch (Eds.), *Designing successful transitions: A guide for orienting students to college* (Monograph No. 13, 2nd ed., pp. 165-176). Columbia, SC: University of South Carolina. National Resource Center for The First-Year Experience and Students in Transition.

McCarthy, K. (2003). Innovative collaboration: Transforming a university's orientation program. *The Journal of College Orientation and Transition, 11*(1), 60-63.

Miller, M. T., & Pope, M. L. (2003). Integrating technology into new student orientation programs at community colleges. *Community College Journal of Research and Practice, 27*, 15-23.

Moneta, L. (2005). Technology and student affairs: Redux. In K. Kruger (Ed.), *Technology in student affairs: Supporting student learning and services* (New Direction for Student Services No. 112, pp. 3-14). San Francisco: Jossey-Bass.

Nehls, K. (2007). Let your fingers do the talking: An analysis of college parent listserv. *The Journal of College Orientation and Transition, 14*(20), 6-24.

Oblinger, D., & J. L. Oblinger (2005). Is it age or IT: First steps toward understanding the net generation. In D. Oblinger & J. L. Oblinger (Eds.), *Educating the net generation* (pp. 2.2-2.20). Boulder, CO: EDUCAUSE.

Ransford, M. (2009). Survey finds smart phones transforming mobile lifestyles of college students. Retrieved on March 10, 2009, from http://www.bsu.edu/news/article/0,1370,-1019-61565,00.html

Rielley, D. F. (2000). The growing trends of orientation web pages. *The Journal of College Orientation and Transition, 7*(2), 41-42.

Tinto, V. (1975). Dropout from higher education: A theoretical synthesis of recent research. *Review of Educational Research, 45*(1), 89-125.

Tinto, V. (1987). *Leaving college: Rethinking the causes and cures of student attrition.* Chicago: University of Chicago Press.

Upcraft, M. L., & Farnsworth, W. E. (1984). Orientation programs and activities. In M. L. Upcraft (Ed.), *Orienting students to college* (New Directions for Student Services No. 25, pp. 27-37). San Francisco: Jossey-Bass.

Young, J. (2008). *MIT creates version of its web site for smartphones (and plans to share code).* Retrieved March 10, 2009, from http://chronicle.com/wiredcampus/article/?id=3486

Chapter 9

Incorporating Crisis Planning and Management Into Orientation Programs

Dian Squire, Victor Wilson, Joe Ritchie, and Abbey Wolfman

On April 16, 2007, at 6:47 a.m., Seung-Hui Cho stood outside West Ambler Johnston residence hall. Approximately 30 minutes later Cho shot and killed Emily Hischler and a resident assistant, Ryan Christopher Clark. By 7:30 a.m., a "person of interest" had been identified, and the University's Policy Group called a meeting. Within an hour of the incident, the chief of police provided information to the Policy Group; requested the Virginia Tech Police Department Emergency Response Team arrive at the scene; and the Policy Group discussed how to notify the community of the homicides. Meanwhile, Cho chained three doors inside Norris Hall and began shooting at 9:40 a.m., entering classrooms and firing on students and instructors. The police attempted to enter the building but were stopped by the chains holding the doors shut. At 9:50 a.m., e-mails and messages over loud speakers warned students to remain inside their buildings because a gunman was loose on campus. At 9:51 a.m., Cho shot himself in the head. In all, 174 rounds were fired. Cho killed 30 people in Norris Hall and wounded 17 more (Virginia Tech Review Panel, 2007).

In the aftermath of the tragedy at Virginia Tech, many asked how the killings could have been prevented. Others began to examine how university officials responded to the crisis and its aftermath. As a result, many campuses examined and revised or instituted crisis management plans. This chapter offers an overview of crisis management planning paying particular attention to orientation programs. The chapter opens by defining the kinds of crises educators might expect to encounter on campus and outlines strategies for developing, implementing, and assessing crisis management plans. The chapter concludes with case studies of crisis responses in the orientation setting.

What Is a Crisis?

On college and university campuses, crises can take many different forms. They include major weather-related crises like Hurricane Katrina (2005) or violence on campus like the shootings at Virginia Tech (2007) and Northern Illinois University (2008). They may also include smaller scale crises such as dealing with irate parents, misbehaving students, missing presenters, or dismissed staff members. Rollo and Zdziarski (2007) suggest that crises have five distinct components. First, crises have the perception of being a negative event or having a negative outcome. Individuals perceive that the event "exceeds the resources and coping mechanisms" currently available (Gilliland & James, 1993, p. 3). As such, crises often pose a threat to stability. Second, crises have an element of surprise.

While some crises are predictable (like a hurricane), others are not, and it is this unpredictable nature, paired with a belief that they cannot or will not happen, that make them an issue. Third, crises provide a limited time for action, requiring quick decision making and allocation of resources for responding to them. Fourth, there is an interruption or disruption of normal patterns of operation. Last, there is a threat to the safety and well-being of certain members of a community.

Sherwood and McKelfresh (2007) offer a slightly different definition of crisis, identifying three different origins: (a) environmental, or those originating from nature; (b) human, or those relating to a person and facility; and (c) those originating from inside a man-made structure (e.g., fire, internal flood, power outages). Within each type, different levels of crises are seen. The levels are defined below and examples of crises associated with these levels are found in Table 9.1.

◇ *Level 1. Minor crisis* describes those incidents that do not affect outside constituents; however, these may cause a sudden change in normal procedure. Most of these problems can be solved by a student paraprofessional, but some of them will require the action of a professional staff member.

◇ *Level 2. Moderate crisis* involves issues with a bit more severity or those that may affect outside constituents (e.g., parents/students/visitors to campus for an orientation program) but do not cause harm to these constituents. A student coordinator, graduate assistant, or professional staff member usually handles these problems. Actions may also require assistance from outside offices such as campus safety or residence life.

◇ *Level 3. Major crisis* affects outside constituents and may cause disruption to scheduled events. They may also result in minor injuries to participants.

◇ *Level 4. Severe crisis* may involve injuries requiring hospitalization or death. Such crises typically require a widespread response from multiple units within the organization.

Even though major and severe crises are low-probability events (i.e., they do not happen often or have a very slight chance of happening), an effective crisis management plan is essential for every orientation program. Crises require the ordinary practitioner to be creative, flexible, organized, energized, relaxed, and poised in the face of uncertainty, chaos, anxiety, and possible loss. They also require contingency planning and "integration and synergy across institutional networks" (McConnell & Drennan, 2006, p. 59). Because major and severe crises have the potential for the greatest disruption to campus systems and the lives of those connected to the campus community, they are the primary focus of this chapter.

Preparing for Crises in Orientation

Higher education professionals must have crisis management plans in place so that when a crisis occurs personnel can react quickly and appropriately. Events that have no immediate response protocol can cause chaos, confusion, and feelings of insecurity. Orientation staff members need guidance, guests need answers, and problems need quick solutions. As numerous schools throughout the Gulf Coast affected by Hurricane Katrina can attest, natural catastrophes have the potential to wreak havoc on campus facilities and place students, employees, and visitors in physical danger. As much as orientation professionals would rather not deal with these unwelcome situations, crises are a part of what they are charged with when handling the day-to-day care of campus guests.

According to McConnell and Drennan, a "crisis is [not] amenable to being packaged into neat scenarios" (p. 64). There is no single set of rules or strategies that can solve every problem, but developing a "broad, movable and often abstract set of principles which then need to be translated

Table 9.1

Strategies for Managing Different Levels of Crises

	Examples of crises	Planning for Crisis	Addressing the Crisis	After Crisis Tasks
Level 1. Minor crisis	◊ Firing a worker ◊ Technology problems ◊ Parking issues ◊ Presenter absence ◊ Staff member illness or tardiness ◊ Other problem not affecting outside constituents	◊ Develop basic written protocol or make staff aware of informal protocols ◊ Examine all aspects of program and discuss contingencies with appropriate coordinating partners or staff ◊ Train staff to perform multiple roles (presenting or job duties) ◊ Keep paper backup copies of all technology-based presentations	◊ Address problem immediately using protocol ◊ Replace staff member with another student worker or student coordinator ◊ Use allied office's resources ◊ Return to non-technology-based teaching if possible	◊ Address situation with staff member ◊ Contact appropriate maintenance personnel ◊ Revisit and assess crisis plan ◊ Make changes to crisis plan for future and retrain staff if necessary
Level 2. Moderate crisis	◊ Poorly behaved students ◊ Party in residence halls ◊ Disrespect toward a staff member to the extent that staff member does not feel comfortable in group ◊ FERPA-related issues ◊ Other problem that does not physically harm but may affect the integrity of the program	◊ Identify professional staff member who will handle these types of situations ◊ Coordinate with partners (residence halls/campus safety/academic colleges), including notification program dates, participants, and activities ◊ Determine who will handle reporting of crisis ◊ Train staff to identify problem issues and how to deal with non-escalated situations and role model correct behaviors	◊ Remove problem student from situation and discuss solutions. Make decisions based on best judgment. ◊ Address problems logically using evidence-based arguments (e.g., FERPA language, evidence of poor behavior, residence hall policy)	◊ Inform proper contacts about actions taken if you remove student from program (e.g., colleges, residence halls) ◊ Notify guardians of action taken (if necessary) ◊ Assess the messages being sent to guests and how they can be improved (e.g., FERPA, overnight stay rules) ◊ Revisit and assess crisis plan ◊ Make changes to crisis plan for future and retrain staff if necessary

Table 9.1 continued p. 134

Table 9.1 continued

	Examples of crises	Planning for Crisis	Addressing the Crisis	After Crisis Tasks
Level 3. **Major crisis**	◊ Weather related (non-large scale, e.g., rain, lightning, snow, ice) ◊ Injury to person (non-hospitalization)	◊ Identify professional staff member who will handle these types of situations ◊ Coordinate with partners (residence halls/campus safety/academic colleges), including notification program dates, participants, and activities ◊ Determine who will handle reporting of crisis ◊ Develop contingency plan for large-scale and small-scale programming ◊ Ensure that all staff members are signed up for campus alerts on their cell phones and e-mails	◊ Immediately move guest(s) to a safe location ◊ Assess situation and make evidence-based decision ◊ Keep a staff member with injured guest at all times ◊ Use phone tree or other communication system to inform all staff in danger of situation and actions to take ◊ Formally document all incidences and actions taken ◊ Assess student safety concerns and either implement alternative programming plan (if weather related) or continue with program	◊ Inform proper contacts about actions taken, especially if you remove student from program (e.g., legal, parents, colleges, residence halls) ◊ Make proper accommodations for injured guest for the rest of the program ◊ Revisit and assess crisis plan ◊ Make changes to crisis plan for future and retrain staff if necessary

Table 9.1 continued

	Examples of crises	Planning for Crisis	Addressing the Crisis	After Crisis Tasks
Level 4. Severe crisis	◇ Active shooter ◇ Large-scale natural disasters ◇ Injury to person (causing death or requiring hospitalization)	◇ Coordinate emergency protocol with appropriate campus constituents (e.g., safety, health center, legal, student/ academic affairs, residence life) ◇ Identify professional staff member who will handle initial procedure in these types of situations (should be highest level official in office) ◇ Keep track of weather-related events continuously until threat subsides ◇ Determine who will handle reporting of crisis ◇ Develop contingency plan for large-scale and small-scale programming ◇ Determine procedure/ technology systems needed for notifying family ◇ Ensure that all staff members are signed up for campus alerts on their cell phones and e-mails	◇ Immediately notify all staff of crisis and inform them to remain in a safe, locked location ◇ Notify all appropriate parties (e.g., police, fire, emergency, central administration) ◇ Remain calm and gather as much evidence as possible regarding situation ◇ Do not try and address the conflict yourself. Allow professionals to handle situation ◇ With serious injury or death, ensure that there is no danger for others in the area, suspend programming if needed, and notify proper channels ◇ For large-scale natural disasters, suspend programming until the threat is over ◇ Provide the basic needs (e.g., food, shelter, safety) ◇ Manage volunteers	◇ Contact campus counseling center to update on situation and provide services, if needed ◇ Ensure that targeted groups (if any) are safe and attended to (e.g., Muslim students after 9/11) ◇ Complete documentation of incident ◇ Follow-up with appropriate contacts to ensure consistent messages and information are being disseminated ◇ Provide as much information as possible without releasing sensitive information. ◇ Make proper accommodations for injured guest for the rest of the program ◇ Revisit and assess crisis plan ◇ Make changes to crisis plan for future and retrain staff if necessary

into 'good practice'" may be the next best thing (McConnell & Drennan, 2006, p. 60). In other words, orientation, transition, and retention professionals should prepare a flexible crisis management plan, train orientation staff members in best practices, and spend a significant amount of time analyzing program protocol and schedules to forecast possible issues. In short, a crisis plan should include six components:

1. A definition of the crisis
2. Clear objectives of the crisis plan
3. Detailed crisis alert procedures
4. External communication protocols
5. A game plan that includes evaluation and action
6. Tactical operations or public statements and press releases (Sherwood & McKelfresh, 2007).

By looking at the four-level crisis spectrum introduced in Table 9.1, orientation professionals can begin to discuss how to address different crises that might occur during an orientation program. The table outlines the four levels of crises as well as tips for planning for, addressing, and following up after the crisis has taken place. Table 9.1 offers few direct solutions to crisis response; rather, it provides a framework and suggested actions that may be taken in these types of situations. Because all campus organizational structures are situated differently, crisis plans should be developed around those structures. This leveled system offers orientation professionals a basis for their program's crisis management plan.

Similarly, Zdziarski, Rollo, & Dunkel's (2007) Crisis Management Cycle provides orientation professionals with an organizational structure for developing a crisis management plan. The cycle involves five stages or steps: (a) planning for the crisis, (b) preventing the crisis, (c) responding to the crisis, (d) recovering from the impact of the crisis, and (e) learning from the crisis what can be done better next time. These stages, in turn, might represent the logical sections of a written plan.

Yet, simply creating a written plan for dealing with crises is not sufficient. Rather, Perry and Lindell (2003) argued that "it is important to avoid confusing planning with a written plan...the plan itself represents a snapshot of that process at a specific point in time...preparedness is dynamic and contingent upon ongoing processes" (p. 338). In essence, creating a written plan is only the first step in a multi-step process to ensure readiness or emergency preparedness, which involves analyzing and creating a set of principles that are translated into good practice by examining possible threats, surveying human and material resources, and organizational structures and policies (McConnell & Drennan, 2006). More simply put, preparedness requires an orientation professional to examine every aspect of a program and identify possible threats as well as likely responses. It also requires ongoing training to ensure feasibility.

Perry and Lindell (2003) provide 10 guidelines for creating an emergency preparedness plan. When applied to their own work, orientation professionals can feel more assured that crises can be averted and/or handled successfully.

1. *Base processes on likely threats and likely human responses*. This is called a vulnerability assessment. After identifying possible threats (e.g., institutions located in earthquake prone areas, near nuclear power plants), orientation professionals should discuss how these threats can be reduced and, when they cannot be prevented, the resources available to those who must take action. This also allows professionals to identify areas where they have little expertise so that they can learn more about appropriate responses. Once a list of deficient resources

or response options has been identified, orientation professionals should identify a plan for addressing these deficiencies.

2. *Encourage appropriate actions by leadership.* Leaders must know how to accurately assess a crisis and the range of available response options. Orientation professionals must remember that while in the midst of a crisis, they must remain calm and collect all relevant information so that an appropriate decision can be made. The appropriate response is much more important than the speed with which a response is made. Research shows that people are less likely to panic if they receive complete and clear messages (Archer, 1992; Perry & Lindell, 2003). Making decisions based on incorrect information can cause more confusion or inappropriate actions.

3. *Encourage response flexibility.* Plans should focus on "principles of response" (Perry & Lindell, 2003, p. 342) rather than specific processes, especially since orientation professionals cannot determine all possible contingencies. Furthermore, complex plans are difficult to remember, and some aspects of those plans can become quickly outdated. Instead, orientation professionals should ensure that staff members are thoughtful, creative, and professional. Staff members should be able to take the framework of a crisis plan and apply their own good judgment in addressing the problem.

4. *Encourage interdepartmental coordination.* Stein, Vickio, Fogo, and Abraham (2007) discussed a "network approach" (p. 332) to campus coordination in university disaster preparedness. Their research showed that network creation and "boundary spanning" (p. 333) ensured that networks existed when disasters occurred, reinforced that creating these networks is not difficult, and also showed that there were not enough network connections present on university campuses especially among academic and mental health units. To ensure that a networking approach is implemented properly, a list of relevant campus offices/services must be generated and included in disaster planning meetings. It is also important to include front-line staff in the creation of crisis plans since they often bring a different perspective to crisis situations.

5. *Integrate emergency plans from all coordinating offices.* Those charged with developing a crisis plan should scrutinize individual office plans and meet with related offices and organizations to ensure that all bases are covered and to avoid duplication of efforts. Where appropriate, certain offices should be designated to lead the particular aspects of the crisis response.

6. *Provide training programs for managers.* Many schools have emergency plans, but lack a training component. Training components provide an opportunity for those charged with acting to become familiar with the plan. Training is "an integral part of the disaster planning process, and when carefully attended to, so likely to yield high dividends in terms of effectiveness of emergency response" (Perry & Lindell, 2003, p. 346).

7. *Perform testing and drills of emergency procedures.* Continuing with the training process, plans need to be tested. Testing may take the form of asking orientation leaders to respond to hypothetical crisis situations during training week. It may also include practice using a phone tree or other communication system. Schinke, Smith, Myers, and Altman (1979) found that paraprofessionals who were trained in crisis intervention and response techniques provided better service, recalled detailed information more accurately, and were more competent overall.

8. *Review and update emergency plans regularly.* Emergency plans continually evolve as new situations or conditions present themselves. If a service is no longer available, responses to incidents need to change to reflect that loss of service. Written documents should be regularly updated to reflect changes in the emergency plan.

9. *Realize that planning sometimes occurs in the face of resistance.* While campus officials are less likely to question the need for emergency response systems now than in the past, it may be necessary to stress to coordinating offices the importance of having a plan in case these highly improbable incidents take place. Stressing the importance of this sort of program to other offices may require some political maneuvering by an orientation office, which may have to prepare the plan and present it for the office instead of creating it in a collaborative manner. This does not assume that an orientation office should be responsible for creating an entire campus plan, only that it should play some role since orientation programs involve large-scale coordination of groups of people.

10. *Recognize the difference between emergency planning and emergency management.* Planning concerns all matters prior to an actual incident. Management refers to "meeting the emergency demands by implementing the assessment, corrective, protective and coordinating actions identified in the planning stage" (Perry & Lindell, 2003, p. 347). Once again, orientation professionals cannot simply create a written plan. Being prepared to implement and assess crisis management are equally important steps in the process.

While smaller organizations often rely on informal communications and personal connections to make decisions (Perry & Lindell, 2003), some formal structures for crisis management should exist. These structures are likely to become more formal as institutional size increases. A lack of preparation causes "delays, cacophony, divisions, ineptness to handle the multidimensional nature of the crisis. . . [and the] inability to form cooperative links with other external units" (Boin & Lagadec, 2000, p. 187).

Responding to Crises in Orientation

Dealing with post-crisis responses is not always the responsibility of the orientation professional, but if a crisis occurs to a student during a program, or if an orientation staff member is called on to be part of a response team, it is important to discuss some issues related to crisis response. Additionally, orientation professionals are occasionally tasked with disseminating information to various constituent groups (e.g., students, parents, local media outlets, and the general campus population). This section describes some of the issues that come with information dissemination and how to cope with those issues. Providing clear, specific information as often as possible is the best way to reduce chaos and confusion among the public.

Basic Communication Strategies

Communication is one of the most important tools that an orientation professional can use during a crisis. Effective communication can get people to safety, calm nerves, and prevent further complications. Poor communication can cause chaos, anxiety, confusion, and promote additional disruptions. First, a crisis communications team should be developed prior to implementing the first orientation program. Who will collect, compile, and disseminate information to the proper authorities? Part of the plan should include providing front-line staff members (e.g., administrative assistants, student workers) with the names and phone numbers of the university officials to whom media inquiries should be referred. Second, orientation professionals should determine what modes of communication are the most effective in different situations. In the case of natural disasters, where there may be time to make arrangements, updated school and office web sites and automated voice messages on office phones may suffice. For more immediate actions, updating a web site may not provide the necessary information in a timely way. Delegating phone call duties to other professional staff members followed by e-mails may be a more appropriate response.

When an emergency originates within the orientation program, campus police should be notified to determine whether an emergency alert alarm or text-message to the campus community may be appropriate. Communication with all appropriate staff (including student workers) is also necessary and a phone tree or texting service should be used to disseminate appropriate information to staff in affected areas.

As a part of preparing for a campus crisis, it is imperative that campus officials put forth a plan that will outline what information will be shared, who can share information, and with whom. Two federal laws—FERPA, the Family Educational Rights and Privacy Act, and HIPPA, the Health Insurance Portability and Accountability Act—place restrictions on the kinds of student information administrators can share with family members, external law enforcement officials, the media, and others on campus. While FERPA allows for information to be shared to "appropriate parties" in emergencies that involve the health and safety of students, universities are sometimes reluctant to share such information for fear of being sued (Roan, 2007). For this reason, orientation professionals and others engaged in the development of a crisis management plan should consult with institutional legal counsel to gain a better understanding of the parameters of these laws and what can be shared with whom during a crisis.

During an emergent crisis, campus officials may not be aware of all the facts and may have little information to share. Members of the campus may become very agitated if they feel administrators are withholding information. If local media outlets pick up on these tensions and report them, it can exacerbate the crisis for campus officials. To help avoid such a scenario, a designated spokesperson should address the campus community as soon as possible, providing as much detail about the nature of the crisis and the institution's response as can be reasonably shared at that time. Regular updates should continue during the resolution of the crisis.

What is important to remember is that communication during a crisis is not solely one person's task. Communicating to various publics is a team effort. As long as consistent messages are shared, a communication plan is followed, and information is disseminated quickly and accurately, communication can be shared from various sources.

Communicating with students. Many schools and universities are looking at more effective ways to communicate with students and others on their campuses when an incident occurs. Campus staffs are working with a student population that wants current information in a variety of formats. Through the use of their computer, laptop, iPod, or cell phones, students have become accustomed to obtaining information when and where they require it. Orientation professionals should research these methods of communication and determine, along with other campus administrators, what the best form of communication would be in the case of a crisis. By using a variety of delivery methods, a school is more likely to ensure that students receive the message (Kennedy, 2007).

Because orientation participants have not yet officially matriculated, communicating with them during an emergency can be challenging. To address this, institutions may require students to sign up for a campus e-mail address prior to registering for orientation or have parents and students register for text alerts during an orientation program session. During an orientation session at the University of Maryland, College Park in 2008, students, parents, and staff were notified via text message through the UMDAlerts system to stay indoors during a powerful storm. The notice provided up-to-date information on the storm's location and possible threats. Staff were able to monitor the situation and make appropriate decisions, and students and parents experienced how the alert system functioned.

Communicating with parents. Understandably, parents will worry about their children when they become aware of a crisis on campus, especially if they have not talked to their son/daughter during or immediately after the crisis. Occasionally, they make extreme requests, asking campus officials to locate their children and have them call home. While these requests are understandable, they cannot be addressed in the midst of a campus emergency. Staff should be prepared to provide general information about the institution's response to the crisis, while expressing concern about the welfare of individual students.

A crisis management plan should include strategies for responding to the potential onslaught of parental requests that might hit the campus during a crisis. Some suggestions include creating a campus phone bank such as the one that the Critical Incident Response Team created in the wake of the bonfire tragedy at Texas A&M University in 1999. Additionally, a room in the student center was designated as a meeting point for parents and students to receive information about the incident. Phone calls to each family member involved with a crisis (if possible) can also be made as they were when the Oklahoma State Men's Basketball Team's plane crashed in 2001. A parent and family affairs office may be another beneficial resource, serving as a coordinating point where parent questions can be routed in the event of crisis.

Communicating with media. Over the past 50 years, as advances in technology have expanded the reach of televised media and communications, campus tragedies have become more prominent, regardless of where they occur. During larger crises, campuses should expect some media coverage. What is unplanned for, at times, is the way the media works with the campus to get the information out to others. Many times, campus officials accept the notion that because they are in the middle of a crisis that the media will be their biggest supporter. This is not always the case.

Frequently, the media can be the vehicle that creates more problems for the campus. What they report and, quite often, what they do not report can cause panic, confusion, and anger among the local and campus community. Thus, campus officials need to ensure that they have a strong and solid plan of action for working with the media during these difficult times. What orientation professionals should strive for is a decrease in speculation and an increase in information gathering (Paterson et al., 2007). The more solid evidence that is in-hand, the less media outlets will be required to speculate and the less the situation will get out of control. Methods of communication with the media include: press statements, press conferences, visuals or videos, photos, teleconferences, e-mails, web sites, and telephone calls (Lawson, 2007). Orientation professionals are not often required to be the media spokesperson during a crisis; however, they may play a critical role in gathering information for the administrator who serves in that capacity.

Questioning of Decisions

As a part of serving in an administrative role on campus, it is inevitable that there will be times when decisions are questioned. However, having a plan in place will minimize questioning that may arise during a crisis. Such a plan should ensure that sound decisions are made before, during, and after a campus crisis and that appropriate campus personnel are involved. Once in the middle of the crisis, it is difficult to deal with individuals who question the decisions of administrators. A time of crisis is a time to act. As a result, it cannot be a time for public input. Administrative decision-makers will need to prepare to be steadfast in supporting their decisions during a crisis while remaining open to the notion that changes may have to be made. Conversely, if changes are required, these changes need to come from those charged with doing so and not because campus opinion differs.

Once a crisis has been resolved, those charged with managing the crisis should examine their response and its effectiveness. As part of this process, they may ask critical questions about their performance. For example, following the death of a student on campus, administrators might ask: Did the college or university reach out to the student's family and friends? Did the institution offer assistance to an affected department? Was the staff able to work through a difficult loss? Was there a sense of support and compassion among the staff? (Zdziarski et al., 2007). When appropriate, the larger campus community might also be invited to offer feedback on the response to the crisis and thoughts on how such events might be handled in the future.

Responding to the Psychology of Crises

In tragic incidents, people are "suddenly swept into an event over which they feel they have no control and which they think they may not survive ... they are left to repair their assumptions of the world and implement their capacities for adaptation" (Griffin, 2007, p. 150). No matter the severity of the incidence, the person may feel a lack of control and be unsure how to proceed or resume their normal activities, sometimes leading to depression or anxiety. It is the role of the counselor (e.g., orientation professional, campus counselor, administrator) to address the issue and provide coping mechanisms for this person. It is important to note that counselors should be well trained and credentialed and if the orientation professional is not that person, that the affected persons be referred to the correct resources. More often than not, the orientation professional will not be in this role, but basic counseling techniques such as Critical Incidence Stress Debriefing, a debriefing technique used to deal with those who sustained physical or psychological stress, can be used.

The National Institute of Mental Health (NIMH, 2002) provides basic guidelines for dealing with persons who have experienced a trauma. While focused towards violence victims, some of the same principles can be applied to all crises.

1. Most people recover from their traumatic events, but it is important not to minimize the importance of or ignore the recovery process. The goal is to assist them in recovery. This could mean referring them to the appropriate resources or being an informal counselor for their needs.
2. The basic needs of that person need to be met first (e.g., first aid, shelter, food) so that they can feel normalized before treatment or counseling can occur. This is more easily accomplished during orientation since many of these resources are readily available.
3. Interventions should be optional and open only *if* people want them, not as a mandatory part of recovery.
4. Crisis intervention programs need to be culturally sensitive. With an increasingly diverse student population on campuses, it is important to be appreciative of, responsive to, and respectful of differing cultural needs. For example, it has been shown that socioeconomic status may cause individuals to have lower self-perceived worth (Twenge & Campbell, 2002). Racial discrimination may be the perceived cause of a crisis and, therefore, should be treated as a valid concern by the counselor (Herman et al., 2007).
5. Emergency mental health should be a part of the crisis response plan of the overall institution.
6. Intervention is a "multidisciplinary, multiphasic and integrated program" (Griffin, 2007, p. 155), which includes planning, triage, training, assessment, and referral. This part will probably be handled by the counseling center, but follow-up can certainly be a role for the orientation professional to play.

Campus responses to psychological needs can be addressed at the individual level, in group meetings, or through vigils and remembrances (Griffin, 2007). Remembrances provide a way of the community to show respect for injured or deceased community members; help people to reflect on an event, person, or persons; and bring a community together.

Case Studies

The cases that follow describe the responses during crises affecting orientation programs. The first cases address responses to an emergent crisis while the third case addresses how the orientation program dealt with the aftermath of a campus tragedy. Questions follow both cases, prompting readers to consider how they might address similar crises on their own campuses.

Preparing for a Hurricane

Dealing with an impending natural disaster is never easy as there is always an element of unpredictability when dealing with Mother Nature. In 2004, the state of Florida was hit with multiple hurricanes. Most of them occurred during the academic year, but one hit the state in mid-August prior to the University of Central Florida's (UCF) fall term. Fortunately, the hurricane hit the campus a few days before the final series of orientation programs. However, there was a great deal of destruction both on the UCF campus and within the state of Florida. As orientation professionals prepared for orientation, they had to provide updated communication to the students that orientation was still occurring through e-mails, voicemails, web sites, and through the News & Information Department.

Due to the devastation of the hurricane, campus officials knew that many students would not be able to attend orientation and would only be able to make it for the start of classes. The orientation office put together a checklist of offices students would need to work with upon arrival to campus. As each student called, the office assistants explained what they needed to do and that the Orientation office should be the first point of contact upon arrival on campus. This was a university-wide effort with each office providing additional assistance to these students (e.g., advisors were available to assist with registration, late fees were waived).

More recently, UCF had a hurricane scare the week prior to classes for the fall 2008 term that threatened to disrupt fall orientation sessions for first-year and transfer students. On Monday afternoon of that week a decision was made by UCF to close the campus on Tuesday due to an impending hurricane. Upon receiving the official word that the University was closing, an e-mail was sent immediately to those students letting them know that the orientation session was cancelled and provided them with an alternate date. If they could not attend the alternate date, then further instructions were given. Besides notifying all of the students, plans were made for a larger than usual orientation program at the end of the week. All departments that work with orientation were contacted, and meetings were scheduled with staff in key offices to discuss logistics such as check-in, room capacities, and the computer system's ability to handle a large influx of students for registration at a particular time. Modifications to the orientation program were made and sent out as soon as possible.

Thoughtful questions for orientation professionals:

1. Based on the region of country where an institution is located, what types of natural disasters (e.g., blizzards or ice storms, tornadoes, floods, wild fires) may affect the campus?
2. Does the campus have an emergency plan if a natural disaster strikes?
3. How will program participants be notified if a natural disaster affects the campus before a program? During a program?

Responding to an Injured Student

In the evenings of the two-day first-year student orientation program, students spend an hour at the campus recreation centers—the Eppley Recreation Center (ERC) or the Outdoor Recreation Center (ORC), which includes a pool. Twenty-five orientation advisors, two student coordinators, and the ORC staff of trained lifeguards and medical personnel staff the program.

One evening in the summer of 2008, a participant in the first-year program was seriously injured at ORC. Approximately half way through the swim time, a student jumped off the diving board and hit the back of his head on the board. He was clearly injured and bleeding. The student coordinators immediately alerted the ERC and ORC staff members of the incident. Since the recreation center staff was trained to respond to medical emergencies, the orientation staff were not needed to assist the injured student. The student coordinators ensured that all other program participants exited the pool and escorted them back to the residence halls. Students who were inside the ERC (playing basketball, volleyball or climbing the rock wall) remained at those locations for the remainder of the period.

The student coordinators immediately notified the assistant director, who was on a campus visit out of state, concerning the situation. Contact was also made with the director of Orientation and the program coordinator to ensure that all parties in the office were made aware of the situation. The immediate health concerns of the participant were handed over to local emergency personnel, and the ERC staff took responsibility for contacting the student's parents.

The student coordinators and assistant director were, thus, free to handle the other needs of the injured student, including making arrangements with residence life and academic advising. Residence life staff were notified that the student would not be staying in the room overnight and that he would not be able to check out the following day. This required residence life to notify the staff handling checkout so that could make arrangements to store his luggage until his parents could collect it and waive charges associated with failure to return the room key. Residence life staff also talked with the injured student's assigned roommate to ensure that he was aware of the situation. Calls were also made to the college advising the student so that he could be advised and registered for classes without repeating the orientation program.

Thoughtful questions for orientation professionals:

1. What role will coordinators or other student staff members play during an emergency?
2. What types of communications and relationships does the staff have with orientation partners? Are the roles all partners assume in a crisis clear to the partners themselves? To the orientation staff?
3. Who needs to know about a crisis, and in what order do should those people be contacted?

Responding to a Campus Shooting

Acts of extreme violence, like shootings on college campuses, are shocking and unimaginable. On February 14, 2008 at Northern Illinois University (NIU), a former student opened fire during a lecture, killing five students and injuring 18 others.

The day before the campus shooting, Orientation & First-Year Experience (OFYE) had just conducted their first training session with the 2008 orientation leaders. One of the first things the office did on February 14 after details of the event were confirmed was to get in contact with the orientation leader staff. Once OFYE received confirmation the student staff was not directly impacted by the shooting, they were able to concentrate on helping NIU with its response.

A few weeks after the shooting, OFYE began to move forward with planning the orientation programs and orientation leader training. The location of the shooting, including two major lecture halls and other classroom space, was completely closed down. NIU had to move class meeting locations, and as a result, the program lost space for April orientation programs. Working closely with the advising offices, OFYE reformatted and cancelled two of the five scheduled orientation programs. In addition, the publication timeline for handbooks and other orientation items were pushed back.

Preparing for the first orientation leader training session following the shootings was extremely important. The professional staff knew that the student staff was not in the classroom where the shootings occurred but felt it was important to understand how the students were feeling about the campus shootings, especially since crisis reactions can be delayed or may resurface at later times. It was decided that the director of OFYE (who has a counseling background) and a counselor should be present. In the beginning of the session, the professional staff provided an opportunity for the student staff to talk about whatever they wanted. Several of the orientation leaders had classes with students who had been killed, but none had friendships with them. Also, several orientation leaders were in the surrounding area when the shootings occurred. The orientation leaders were concerned about how to handle questions from students and family members during the summer. The professional staff assured the students that while they may not know how to handle those questions now, they would certainly figure it out when summer arrived.

During summer training prior to the beginning of the first programs the NIU police department and Counseling and Student Development came in to speak with the staff. The director of Counseling and Student Development provided insight into how to handle questions related to the shootings but also suggested that most first-year students would ask the same questions and raise the same concerns that they had had in the past. The director also felt some students and family members may want to know what was going to happen to the classroom where the shootings occurred but would not be interested in the details of the event. Also, it was important for the orientation leaders to remember they were in control of the discussion. Therefore, the director suggested the orientation leaders bring up the campus shootings and discuss how campus was moving forward and move on to other topics.

The NIU police department gave the orientation leaders a broad overview of safety procedures and services provided on-campus. Safety and security are common concerns shared on most college campuses, so training in this area was no different. Similar to training in years past, the orientation staff discussed emergency preparedness with the orientation leaders. The content of this training was supplemented by the emergency protocol plan implemented by NIU prior to the shootings.

During the orientation program, the staff mentioned the campus shootings in the morning welcome. They did not focus on the event, but rather how the NIU community is strong and resilient in the face of tragedy. Throughout the orientation day, some students and family members asked questions regarding safety, security, and NIU's emergency response system. While some participants expressed interest in knowing plans for the classroom where the shootings occurred, the incident was rarely mentioned directly.

Dealing with the aftermath of the campus shooting was difficult both personally and professionally. It was certainly stressful to deal with the orientation program and training components and to try to process the events personally. However, with the support the NIU community provided, the program staff made it through the summer and year. An important lesson learned was to make sure to take care of one's self personally and to not be afraid to ask for help from colleagues.

Thoughtful questions for orientation professionals:

1. What plans are in place to communicate with student staff during an emergency? Because cell phones often stop working in an emergency, are alternate communication strategies being considered?
2. Have backup locations for orientation events been reserved?

Conclusion

While crises are rare and often minor, orientation professionals must plan for the worst while hoping for the best. Rarity and scope are hardly excuses for poor planning and preparation when dealing with large groups of students, family, and visitors on campuses. It is difficult to plan for every possible crisis, but it is possible to build a network of cooperating offices and their services, create a skeletal outline of a response plan, explore communication plans, and train staff members in basic crisis management techniques. As with all programs, assessment of these plans is key. Because major crises are rare, administrators may not have the opportunity to assess the effectiveness of their plan; however, they can study how other institutions respond to crises and make adjustments to their campus plans where appropriate. Administrators should also revisit crisis management plans yearly to ensure that all information is up to date and situation appropriate.

References

Archer, J. (1992). Campus in crisis: Coping with fear and panic related to serial murders. *Journal of Counseling and Development, 71*(1), 96-100.

Boin, A., & Lagadec, P. (2000). Preparing for the future: Critical challenges in crisis management. *Journal of Contingencies and Crisis Management, 8*(4), 185-191.

Gilliland, B. E., & James, R. K. (1993). *Crisis intervention strategies* (2nd ed.). Pacific Grove, CA: Brooks/Cole Publishing.

Griffin, W. (2007). Psychological first aid in the aftermath of crisis. In E. L. Zdziarski, N. W. Dunkel, & J. M. Rollo. (Eds.), *Campus crisis management: A comprehensive guide to planning, prevention, response and recovery* (pp. 145-181). San Francisco: Jossey-Bass.

Herman, K. C., Tucker, C. M., Ferdinand, L. A., Mirsu-Paun, A., Hasan, N. T., & Beato, C. (2007). Culturally sensitive health care and counseling psychology: An overview. *The Counseling Psychologist, 35*(5), 633-649.

Kennedy, M. (2007, May 1). Crisis on campus. *American School & University.* Retrieved November 21, 2007, from http://asumag.com/security/university_crisis_campus/index.html

Lawson, C. J. (2007). Crisis communication. In E. L. Zdziarski, N. W. Dunkel, & J. M. Rollo (Eds.), *Campus crisis management: A comprehensive guide to planning, prevention, response and recovery* (pp. 97-119). San Francisco: Jossey-Bass.

McConnell, A., & Drennan, L. (2006). Mission impossible? Planning and preparing for crisis. *Journal of Contingencies and Crisis Management, 14*(2), 59-70.

National Institute of Mental Health. (2002). *Mental health and mass violence: Evidence-based early psychological intervention for victims/survivors of mass violence. A workshop to reach consensus on best practices* (NIH Publication No. 02-5138). Washington, DC: U.S. Government Printing Office.

Paterson, B. G., Bird, L. E., Burks, S. M, Washington, C. K., Ellet, T., & Daykin, A. (2007). Human crises. In E. L. Zdziarski, N. W. Dunkel, & J. M. Rollo (Eds.), *Campus crisis management: A comprehensive guide to planning, prevention, response and recovery* (pp. 255-282). San Francisco: Jossey-Bass.

Perry, R. W., & Lindell, M. K. (2003). Preparedness for emergency response: Guidelines for the emergency planning process. *Disasters, 27*(4), 336-350.

Roan, S. (2007). Crisis on campus. *The Jed Foundation.* Retrieved May 1, 2009, from http://www.jedfoundation.org/press-room/news-archive/crisis-on-campus

Rollo, J. M., & Zdziarski, E. L. (2007). Developing a crisis management plan. In E. L. Zdziarski, N. W. Dunkel, & J. M. Rollo (Eds.), *Campus crisis management: A comprehensive guide to planning, prevention, response and recovery* (pp. 73-95). San Francisco: Jossey-Bass.

Schinke, S. P., Smith, T. E., Myers, R. K., & Altman, D. C. (1979). Crisis-intervention training with paraprofessionals. *Journal of Community Psychology, 7,* 343-347.

Sherwood, G. P., & McKelfresh, D. (2007). Crisis management teams. In E. L. Zdziarski, N. W. Dunkel, & J. M. Rollo. (Eds.), *Campus crisis management: A comprehensive guide to planning, prevention, response and recovery* (pp. 55-71). San Francisco: Jossey-Bass.

Stein, C. H., Vickio, C. J., Fogo, W. R., & Abraham, K. M. (2007) Making connections: A network approach to university disaster preparedness. *Journal of College Student Development, 48*(3), 331-343.

Twenge, J. M., & Campbell, W. K. (2002). Self-esteem and socioeconomic status: A meta-analytical review. *Personality and Social Psychology Review, 6*(1), 59-71.

Virginia Tech Review Panel. (2007). Report of the Virginia Tech Review Panel. Retrieved from http://www.governor.virginia.gov/TempContent/techpanelreport.cfm

Zdziarski, E. L., Rollo, J. M., & Dunkel, N. W. (2007) The crisis matrix. In E. L. Zdziarski, N. W. Dunkel, & J. M. Rollo (Eds.), *Campus crisis management: A comprehensive guide to planning, prevention, response and recovery* (pp. 35-51). San Francisco: Jossey-Bass.

PART III:

Serving the Needs of All Students in Orientation

Chapter 10

Orientation and First-Year Programs: A Profile of Participating Students

Maureen E. Wilson and Michael Dannells

The U.S. Department of Education (USDE) projected that total U.S. undergraduate enrollment in degree-granting postsecondary institutions would reach 16.4 million students by 2010. Between 2000 and 2007, enrollment increased 19% and is expected to reach 17.5 million in 2018. There are currently 4,339 public and private (both not-for-profit and for-profit) two- and four-year degree granting institutions (Planty et al., 2009). A growing diversity of students, both domestic and international, attends a wide array of institutions that vary in mission, size, type, control, and academic programs. The purpose of this chapter is to provide a profile of college students. We look at a range of student background (e.g., age, race) and experience (e.g., part-time enrollment, transfer students) characteristics and discuss their implications for orientation.

Student Background Characteristics

A wealth of data exists about college students. In attempting to create an accurate picture of undergraduates, particularly first-year students, we drew from a variety of primary sources, such as the Integrated Postsecondary Education Data System (IPEDS), a system of surveys conducted annually by the U. S. Department of Education's National Center for Education Statistics (NCES). All 6,800 postsecondary institutions (colleges, universities, and vocational and technical institutions) that participate in federal student financial aid programs are required to report data to IPEDS (Planty et al., 2009), and NCES generates a tremendous number of reports. For instance, the *Profile of Undergraduates in U.S. Postsecondary Education Institutions: 2003-2004* is a survey in which data were collected from 80,000 undergraduates, about 25,000 of whom were enrolled at community colleges (Horn & Nevill, 2006). Descriptive statistics on undergraduates were culled from this and other NCES and governmental agency reports. In addition, we referenced survey data collected by the Higher Education Research Institute (HERI) at the University of California, Los Angeles (Pryor et al., 2008; Pryor, Hurtado, Saenz, Santos, & Korn, 2007). *The American Freshman* survey is conducted annually by researchers in the Cooperative Institutional Research Program (CIRP) at HERI. The 2008 CIRP Freshman Survey (hereafter CIRP FS) included 240,580 first-time, full-time students enrolled in 340 baccalaureate colleges and universities. The data are adjusted statistically to reflect the 1.4 million first-year students who entered four-year colleges and universities in 2008. Due to the different populations studied, NCES and CIRP often yield strikingly different results and should remind readers of the importance of interpreting national norms in light of their similarities to and differences from students on their own campuses.

In the fall of 2008, 69% of the roughly 3.2 million 2008 high school graduates were enrolled in colleges or universities. College enrollment rates for these students were 72% for women and 66% for men. Of these first-year students, 93% were enrolled full-time, and about 60% attended four-year institutions (Bureau of Labor Statistics, 2009). Of all postsecondary students, 35% are enrolled in community colleges (Provasnik & Planty, 2008). A closer examination of college students' demographics provides a clearer profile of who goes to college.

Age

On average, undergraduates enrolled in four-year institutions are younger than their community college counterparts. In 2003-2004, the percentage of undergraduates 23 years old or younger at four-year institutions was 70% compared to 47% at community colleges (Horn & Nevill, 2006). The median age at four-year institutions was 21, and at community colleges, 24 (Provasnik & Planty, 2008). However, in the CIRP FS, the percentage of first-time, first-year students 19 and older has more than doubled over the last four decades from 14% in 1967 to 29% in 2008 (Pryor et al., 2007; Pryor et al., 2008). Between 1995 and 2006, there was a 33% enrollment increase of students under 25 compared to 13% who were 25 and older (Snyder, Dillow, & Hoffman, 2009). Yet, NCES has predicted a 19% increase in enrollment of students 25 and older between 2006 and 2017, compared to a 10% increase in those under 25, a reversal of prior trends (Snyder et al.).

Gender

Women have comprised the majority of undergraduate students since the early 1980s, and the gap continues to increase (KewalRamani, Gilbertson, Fox, & Provasnik, 2007). In 2003-2004, 59% of all community college students and 55% of students at four-year institutions were women (Horn & Nevill, 2006). Compared to the enrollment difference between White men and women (12%), this gender gap was greater for Blacks (29%)[1], American Indians (22%), and Hispanics (17%). It was smallest for Asian/Pacific Islanders (8%) (KewalRamani et al.). The gender gap is growing at all levels of education, and Mortenson (2008) has called it the "boy crisis in education" (p. A30).

Between 1997 and 2007, the number of women enrolled in college increased 29% compared to 22% for men. Women now comprise 57% of enrollment (Snyder et al., 2009). Increasing numbers of older women enrolling in college contribute to this gender gap; 39% of students were 25 years or older, and of those students, 62% were women. While women over age 25 comprised 24% of the total undergraduate population, the same age group of men comprised 15%.

Since the mid-1980s, women have earned more associate's, bachelor's, and master's degrees than men, and in 2006-2007, they earned more doctorates than men. From 1996-1997 to 2006-2007, the number of baccalaureate degrees earned by women rose 34% compared to a 25% increase for men. The share of degrees earned by women of color has tripled since the mid-1970s to 15% in 2003-2004. During the same period, the share of degrees earned by men of color rose from 5% to 9%. The share earned by White men has fallen from 49% to 33%. White women have earned about the same share of degrees since the 1980s (Snyder et al., 2009). King (2006) argued that there is no consensus on the causes for this expanding gender gap and concluded with a caution that while educators need to be cognizant of this gap and its implications, the real crisis "should not obscure the larger disparities that exist by income and race/ethnicity for students of both genders" (p. 21).

Race and Ethnicity

Overall, community colleges enroll a more racially diverse population than four-year institutions: White 60% vs. 69%, Black 15% vs. 11%, and Hispanic 14.4% vs. 10%. However, the percentages of Asians (5%), American Indians (1%), Pacific Islanders (1%), multiple races (2%), and others (1%) are virtually the same at the two institutional types (Horn & Nevill, 2006). The percentage of college students of color at degree-granting institutions has risen from 15% in 1976 to 32% in 2007. Asians or Pacific Islanders and Hispanics and have seen the greatest increases, from 4% to 11% and 2% to 7%, respectively. In 1976, the percentage of Black students was 9% and, after fluctuating during the early part of period, stood at 13% in 2007 (Snyder et al., 2009).

Income Level

A larger percentage of students classified as low-income (incomes at or below the 125th percentile of established poverty levels) are enrolled in community colleges than at four-year institutions, 26% vs. 20%, respectively. Community colleges also enroll more students who are independent of their parents for financial aid purposes than do four-year institutions, 61% vs. 35%. At community colleges, 29% of dependent students were from families whose income was less than $32,000 compared to 21% at four-year institutions. Just 19% of dependent community college students had family incomes of $92,000 or more compared to 29% of their four-year counterparts. The pattern for independent students is different. Of those with incomes of $25,000 or less, 46% were at community colleges versus 52% at four-year institutions. Independent students at community colleges were also more likely than those at four-year colleges to be working full-time and so likely had higher earnings (Horn & Nevill, 2006).

In 2007-2008, 66% of all undergraduates received financial aid; the average amount of aid awarded was $9,100. Fifty-three percent received grants, 38% took out student loans, 7% were awarded work-study jobs, 4% had parents who took out PLUS loans, and 2% got veterans' benefits (Wei et al., 2009).

When CIRP FS respondents were asked if they had any concern about their ability to finance their education, 53% indicated they had some concern but would probably have enough funds, and 11% claimed major concern that they would have enough funds to complete college (Pryor et al., 2008). Although the percentage indicating major concern in 2008 was up slightly (1.4%) from 2007, it was lower than every other year since 1970. However, more students reported that financial considerations such as cost of attendance and offer of financial aid played a large role in determining which college to attend. Many students planned to use multiple sources of funds to pay for college and decided to attend a different college based on financial circumstances, and this "may explain why although financial issues drive college choice for some students, we are not seeing larger changes in the percentages of students concerned about their ability to pay for college" (Pryor et al., 2008, p. 9).

Furthermore, higher educational attainment is associated with higher median earnings for those ages 25-34 who worked full-time for at least a full year. In 2007, young adults with a bachelor's degree earned, on average, 29% more than associate's degree holders and 55% more than those with a high school degree. The median earnings for those with four-year degrees were $45,000 compared to $35,000 with a two-year degree. These earning patterns were consistent for men and women, Whites, Blacks, Hispanics, and Asians (Planty et al., 2009).

First-Generation Students

An indicator of socioeconomic status (SES) is the highest level of formal education of students' parents. On average, parents' highest level of education is lower for students at community colleges than at four-year institutions. As shown in Table 10.1, the largest percentage of parents (41%) at two-year public colleges has a high school education or less. At four-year institutions, the largest percentage of parents has a bachelor's degree or higher (50% at publics and 52% at private not-for-profit institutions) (Horn & Nevill, 2006).

Table 10.1

Educational Attainment of Parents

	Two-year public	Four-year public	Four-year private not-for-profit
High school or less	41%	27%	28%
Some postsecondary education	27%	23%	20%
Bachelor's degree or higher	32%	50%	52%

Note. Adapted from *Profile of Undergraduates in U.S. Postsecondary Education Institutions: 2003-2004* by L. Horn and S. Nevill, 2006.

Since 1971, the proportion of first-generation students has declined steadily among first-time, full-time entering first-year college students at four-year institutions, reflecting increasing levels of education in the U.S. population (Saenz, Hurtado, Barrera, Wolf, & Yeung, 2007). However, Saenz et al. cautioned that differences between racial/ethnic groups are cause for concern. Since 1975,

> African Americans have shown the greatest decline in their representation of first-generation college students—a declining rate that is of concern because it is faster than the relative proportion of African American adults without a college education as well as the decline of first-generation students in other racial/ethnic groups. (para. 4)

In 2005, the proportions of first-generation students within racial/ethnic groups were: Hispanic, 38%; African American, 23%; Native American, 17%; Asian/Asian American, 19%; and White, 13%. Although "first-generation students tend to have lower educational aspirations than non-first-generation students" (para. 8), degree aspirations for both groups have been rising for the past three decades. This is encouraging because research provides evidence that "degree aspirations at college entry are critical indicators of eventual college success" (para. 8).

However, the college experience can be particularly difficult for first-generation students. "Not only do first-generation students confront all the anxieties, dislocations, and difficulties of any college student, their experiences often involve substantial cultural as well as social and academic transitions" (Pascarella, Pierson, Wolniak, & Terenzini, 2004, p. 250). They are also more likely to leave four-year institutions at the end of the first year of college and less likely to have earned a bachelor's degree after five years than students whose parents are college graduates (Pascarella et al.).

Sexual Orientation

It is notoriously difficult to accurately estimate the number of gay, lesbian, bisexual, and transgendered (GLBT) Americans. For the first time in its history, the 1990 Census allowed people to identify as unmarried partners. A massive campaign spearheaded by the National Gay and Lesbian Task Force likely contributed to a four-fold increase in same-sex cohabiting couples reporting in the 2000 Census; 549,391 households or nearly 1.2 million gay and lesbian adults did so (Bradford, Barrett, & Honnold, 2002). Furthermore, Gates (2006) suggested that the willingness of same-sex partners to identify themselves on government surveys will likely continue to increase as the stigma of homosexuality decreases.

Still, the GLBT community is undercounted. The Census does not ask specifically about sexual orientation. Single gays and lesbians, those not living with their partners, youth living with their parents, senior citizens living in a family member's household, those not comfortable outing themselves to a government agency, and bisexual and transgendered people are among those not specifically identified as GLBT in the Census. The Census did report same-sex partners living in 99% of all counties (Bradford et al., 2002). Based on analyses of the Centers for Disease Control and Prevention's National Survey of Family Growth, Gates (2006) estimated there are 8.8 million gay, lesbian, or bisexual adults in the US.

It is no simpler to count the number of college students who are GLBT, and data are not typically gathered in systematic ways. For example, NCES appears to collect no data regarding students' sexual orientation, and the CIRP FS does not include a demographic item for sexual orientation. Although participants are assured confidentiality, the CIRP survey is not anonymous, and so some students likely would not disclose that information even if it were asked.

Students with Disabilities

Students who report disabilities represent a growing constituency on campus. In 1989-1990, prior to the passage and implementation of the Americans with Disabilities Act of 1990, 7% of students reported having a disability (Horn & Khazzoom, 1994). Among all college students in the academic year 2003-2004, 11% reported they had a disability. Of those, the proportions of the disabilities they reported were: 25% orthopedic, 22% mental illness/depression, 17% health impairments/problems, 11% attention-deficit disorder, 8% specific learning disability, 5% hearing, 4% visual, 0.4% speech, and 8% other (Horn & Nevill, 2006). According to Silverman (2008), earlier diagnosis of and improved treatments for mental illnesses have helped more affected students complete high school and enroll in college. As a result, colleges and universities are likely to continue seeing an increase of these students on campus.

International Students

According to the Institute of International Education (IIE, 2008c), in the 2007-2008 academic year, a record-high 623,805 international college students studied in the US, an increase of 7% over the previous year. Enrollments of new international students rose by 10%. India, China, South Korea, and Japan were the top four countries of origin, comprising 45% of all international students enrolled in higher education in the US. International students comprised 4% of U.S. enrollments (IIE, 2008b). On some campuses, international students represent a significant proportion of the student body. For example, the IIE reported that 153 campuses hosted more than 1,000 international students; 63 had 10% or more international students. The 20 universities with the largest number of international students had enrollments ranging from a low of 3,910 (University of Wisconsin-Madison) to a high of 7,189 (University of Southern California) (IIE, 2008a).

Religion

In the CIRP FS, students indicated the following religious preferences: Christian, 72%; Jewish, 3%; Buddhist, 1%; Hindu, 1%; Islamic, 1%; other religion, 3%; none, 19% (Pryor et al., 2008). This last figure indicating no religious preference has been increasing steadily from 11% in 1986 (Pryor et al., 2007).

Bryant, Choi, and Yasuno (2003) found that "although students became less religiously active in the first year of college with respect to attending religious services, praying/meditating, and discussing religion, they became more committed to integrating spirituality into their lives" (p. 736). Based on their review of research, Pascarella and Terenzini (2005) argued that "[e]vidence is mounting to suggest that students' commitments to religious values during the college years may not so much increase or decrease as become reexamined, refined, and incorporated in subtle ways with other beliefs and philosophical dispositions" (pp. 284-285).

Families

The majority of college students are neither married nor parents, but that percentage is higher at four-year institutions (78%) than at community colleges (55%). A greater proportion of community college students than students at four-year institutions are married with no dependents (10% vs. 6%), married with dependents (20% vs. 10%), and single parents (15% vs. 6%) (Horn & Nevill, 2006). The CIRP FS data from 2001, the last time the item was used, showed only 0.4% of first-year students were married (Pryor et al., 2007). In addition to obligations some students have to partners and children, others may also be caring for aging parents.

Veterans

It is not known how many military veterans are currently enrolled in college, but in 2008, the Veterans Administration "helped pay for the education or training of 336,527 veterans and active-duty personnel, 106,092 reservists and National Guardsmen, and 106,092 survivors" (Department of Veterans Affairs, 2009, para. 9). On August 1, 2009, the Post-9/11 GI Bill went into effect, providing tuition, fees, books and supplies, and housing benefits to Iraq and Afghanistan war veterans. Department of Veterans Affairs officials estimated that 200,000 veterans would use these benefits to attend college in the fall 2009 semester (Wright, 2009).

In 2008, the Student Veterans of America (SVA) organized to address the issues of education benefits and resource development. According to SVA President Derek Blumke, "The majority of campuses throughout the country currently lack the infrastructure to adequately support returning veterans in their transition from service member to student" (SVA, 2008, para. 2). Of the 723 colleges and universities that responded to a survey to assess the availability of programs and services for veterans, 57% provided programs and services designed specifically for service members and veterans. Public four-year (74%) and two-year (66%) institutions were more likely to offer these than were private not-for-profit colleges and universities (36%). Veteran-specific orientation was the least commonly offered service; just 4% of respondents indicated that their campus targeted orientation to this student population (Cook & Kim, 2009).

While transition issues for veterans are already complicated, Grossman (2009) estimated that as many as 40% of student veterans may also be psychologically or physically disabled. Iraq and Afghanistan veterans are expected to have the highest survival rates compared to earlier military conflicts (Church, 2009). Advances in body armor and in-field emergency medical care have simultaneously promoted survival and resulted in higher injury-to-death ratios, leading to higher rates of disabled veterans (Church). An estimated 19% of Iraq and Afghanistan veterans suffer from traumatic brain injury, while an estimated 20% of all veterans will suffer from PTSD or major depression (Rand Center for Military Health Policy Research, 2008). Because their injuries were incurred after their secondary level of education, many veterans with disabilities will not have had previous exposure to disability services commonly available in primary and secondary education, which presents special transition issues for this population of students (Grossman).

Academic Preparedness

In surveys for the *Chronicle of Higher Education*, high school teachers and college professors were asked about their perceptions of students' preparation for college (Sanoff, 2006). Although both groups had reservations about students' preparation for college, high school teachers generally had more positive views than college faculty members, who said that "students are inadequate writers, have trouble understanding difficult materials, fall short in knowledge of science and math, have poor study habits, and lack motivation" (Sanoff, p. B9). One professor complained that "students don't know how to study, how to organize and retain the information, or how to apply it" (Sanoff, p. B9). The groups' assessments of students' writing abilities differed substantially: 36% of teachers believed students were very well prepared for college-level demands in writing compared to just 6% of professors. Only 10% of teachers thought they were not well prepared, while 44% of professors believed that.

In addition to concerns regarding students' academic preparedness, a trend toward academic disengagement continues. In the CIRP FS, 40% of students reported feeling frequently bored in class during their senior year in high school, and 61% were late to class frequently or occasionally during the last year. Only 36% reported studying or doing homework for six or more hours per week in the past year. Although they reported spending little time studying, 47% indicated they earned "A" averages in high school, a rise of 7% since 1998, compared to a low of 18% in 1968 (Pryor et al., 2007; Pryor et al., 2008). Said Astin, "The combination of academic disengagement and record grade inflation poses a real challenge for our higher education system, since students are entering college with less inclination to study but with higher academic expectations than ever" (qtd. in HERI, 2002, para. 26).

Once in college, estimates of the amount of time students spend studying vary. Students participating in the 2007 Your First College Year (YFCY) Survey (Liu, Sharkness, & Pryor, 2008) were asked to indicate how much time they spent studying/doing homework during a typical week; 39% did so five or fewer hours per week. Researchers from the National Survey of Student Engagement (NSSE, 2007) reported that "the number of hours full-time students spend studying per week has remained constant since 2001 at about 13-14 hours, only about half what many faculty say is necessary to do well in their classes" (p. 13). The common recommendation from faculty is to study at least two hours outside of class for every hour in class for general study classes and 3-4 hours for science courses (Kuh, 2003). Therefore, if students take 12-15 credit hours, they should be spending at least 24-30 hours per week studying and doing homework, if not more. In the YFCY study, just 7.1% of students studied/did homework more than 21 hours in a typical week.

Yet, students' studying behavior is at odds with expectations for their own academic performance. Of participants in the CIRP FS, 62% estimated that chances were very good that they would make at least a "B" average in college, a figure that has more than doubled from 27% when the question was first asked in 1971. Interestingly, the figure rose 6.1% in 2000, the year Millennial students, those students born between 1982 and 2002 (Howe & Strauss, 2000), began arriving on campuses. The Millennial generation has been described as confident, and that confidence seems to be reflected in that expectation of high grades.

Although students tend to study about twice as much in college as high school, many academics believe they still do not study enough, particularly if they intend to earn at least a "B" average, as most do. Furthermore, 74.9% of CIRP FS respondents intend to obtain a graduate or professional degree, and their undergraduate study habits are apt to influence if and where they do that. It appears that many students arrive at college having gotten high grades with little effort in high school and expect that will continue. "The wider and deeper college-going pool then brings these habits and expectations, not to mention a lack of preparation, with them to college" (Kuh, 2003, p. 28).

Student Experience Characteristics

In addition to learning about students' background characteristics, it is helpful to examine various choices that help shape students' college experiences. In this section, students are profiled in terms of their enrollment patterns and in their status as transfer, residential or commuter, online, and employed students.

Enrollment Patterns

For the 2003-2004 academic year, 49% of students were enrolled full-time, 35% were enrolled part-time, and 16% changed their enrollment status (Chen, 2007). From 2000 to 2007, full-time enrollment had larger relative gains (24%) than part-time enrollment (10%). This pattern holds at both two- and four-year institutions and is expected to continue (Planty et al., 2009). Compared to exclusively full-time students, students who enrolled part-time exclusively were more likely to be older, female, Hispanic, first-generation, financially independent, and from low-income families (for dependent students). They were also more likely to take remedial courses. They were less likely to have a regular high school diploma and had lower expectations for earning a graduate degree (Chen, 2007). According to Chen (2007), benefits to part-time enrollment include lower costs, increased access, and greater flexibility. However, part-time enrollment is often associated with behaviors that may deter degree completion, including enrollment interruption and excessive employment. Part-time and intermittent (stopout) students, taken together, are now the majority of college students. However, stopping out, or having non-continuous or interrupted enrollment, negatively affects both time to degree and degree attainment (DesJardins, Ahlburg, & McCall, 2006).

McCormick (2003) described additional enrollment patterns, including swirling and double dipping. Swirling involves back-and-forth enrollment at two or more institutions. Double-dipping involves simultaneous enrollment at two institutions. Peter and Forrest Cataldi (2005) concluded that the common practice of attending more than one postsecondary institution as an undergraduate is also negatively associated with time to degree and degree attainment. Among 2001 college graduates, 59% had attended more than one institution.

Transfer Students

According to the National Center for Educational Statistics (Wirt et al., 2003), "One-half of the undergraduates who start at a public, two-year institution with the intention of obtaining a bachelor's degree and about one fourth of those who start with an associate's degree goal transfer to a four-year institution within six years" (p. 44). About one quarter of those who begin at four-year schools transfer to another institution. Students who begin at public, as opposed to private, four-year institutions are more likely to transfer and less likely to complete their bachelor's degree. Obviously, transfer behavior is common; it can also be both beneficial and problematic. Vertical transfers (from two- to four-year schools) generally result in greater educational attainment, yet the time to degree completion is increased. Horizontal transfers (from four-year to four-year) may result in a better fit between the student and institution but will also likely result in greater time to degree completion and decreased likelihood of persistence to completion (Pascarella & Terenzini, 2005).

Residential and Commuter Students

In 2003-2004, 60% of undergraduate students lived off-campus and not with family, 25% lived with parents or other relatives, and 15% lived on campus. A larger percentage of undergraduates enrolled in private, not-for-profit institutions lived on campus (38%) than those attending public (12%) and private-for-profit institutions (2%) (Horn & Nevill, 2006). Of those participating in the CIRP FS, 80% planned to live in a college residence hall or other campus student housing (Pryor et al., 2008). Compared to commuter students, students who live on campus are more likely to persist and graduate. They are also more likely to participate in extracurricular activities and engage with other students and faculty (Pascarella & Terenzini, 2005).

Online Students

In the fall of 2006, almost 3.5 million students were taking at least one online course, a 10% increase over the previous year (as compared to the 1% increase in student enrollment during the same period). "Two-year associate's institutions have the highest growth rates and account for over one-half of all online enrollments for the past five years" (Allen & Seaman, 2007, p. 1). Demand for online learning is still growing, and "83% [of] institutions with online offerings expect their online enrollments to grow" (Allen & Seaman, p. 2). At 165,373 students, the online student population of the University of Phoenix has, by far, the largest enrollment of any institution of higher education in the country (Snyder et al., 2009).

Employed Students

Working while in college has become the norm (Pascarella & Terenzini, 2005). In 2007, about 46% of full-time students were employed, and they were working more hours than in the past. Roughly 22% worked 20-34 hours per week, and 9% worked 35 or more hours. Although the numbers of hours part-time students worked has not increased measurably since 1970, 81% were employed in 2007. However, the percentage of part-time students working 35 or more hours per week decreased to 46% from 60% in 1970. Employment rates for full-time students were higher for women (48%) than men (43%) and Whites and Hispanics (48% and 49%) than Blacks and Asians (36% and 29%) (Planty et al., 2009). According to the Bureau of Labor Statistics (2009), part-time students (76%) and students enrolled at two-year colleges (56%) participate in the labor force at higher rates than full-time (39%) and four-year college students (31%). Among the first-year students participating in the CIRP FS, 39% reported working 11 or more hours in a typical week during their last year in high school. Furthermore, 49% of students estimated that chances were very good that they would get a job to help pay for college expenses; only 8% planned to work full-time (Pryor et al., 2008).

Riggert, Boyle, Petrosko, Ash, and Rude-Parkins (2006) reported that nearly 80% of undergraduates are employed and more than half of students under age 24 at four-year colleges work during the academic year. In their review of the impact of employment on students' performance in college, they found inconsistent and contradictory findings. Salisbury, Padgett, and Pascarella (2009) found that the effects of work differed based on the nature of the employment and students' characteristics. Compared to non-workers, students who worked did not experience losses on educational outcomes. In some cases, working students experienced gains on several leadership development measures. "Overall students who work are not penalized in terms of their college experiences or gains on educational outcomes as compared to students who do not work—regardless of the job's location or the number of hours worked" (Salisbury et al., p. 1).

Salisbury et al. (2009) did, however, find some isolated negative effects for working students. For example, working 21 or more hours per week off campus had a significant negative influence on critical thinking. In another study, "students who worked more than 20 hours per week on or off campus had substantially lower grades than" students who did not work, worked 20 hours or less on campus, or worked 20 hours or less off campus (Pike, Kuh, & Massa-McKinley, 2008, p. 571). Pascarella and Terenzini (2005) concluded, "on- or off-campus work during college, particularly if it is only part-time, may not consistently or seriously inhibit student learning" (p. 149). Consistent with an earlier study, Salisbury et al. argued that "it seems reasonable to conclude that any negative consequences of work during college on cognitive growth may only become manifest when one is working more than about 20 hours per week" (p. 34).

However, Bozick (2007) found that "students from low-income families are more likely to work . . . and to live at home during the first year of college," and this can "impede their chances of continuing into the second year" (p. 1). Furthermore, "students who work more than 20 hours a week and who live at home are more likely to leave school during the first year than are those who work 20 hours a week or less and who reside on campus" (p. 1). Working necessarily reduces the discretionary time students have to devote to academics, but its impact is unclear.

Implications for Orientation

Understanding the characteristics of American college students leads to a number of implications for orientation. Students who integrate successfully into the academic and social environments of the campus are more likely to persist (Tinto, 1993), though some students may benefit from integration in one realm (academic or social) more than the other (Braxton, Hirschy, & McClendon, 2004). As they facilitate new students' transitions into college, orientation programs can play an important role in student retention (Council for the Advancement of Standards, 2009). A variety of factors addressed in the preceding sections can influence the ways in which students connect with the campus and persist at the institution.

Student Diversity

As noted throughout the chapter, there is tremendous diversity among today's students, and many of their background characteristics and college experiences will influence how they become engaged in campus life. Furthermore, the multiple dimensions of students' identities also interact to influence their outlook and experience. Harper and Quaye (2009) argued that,

When students enter with characteristics and backgrounds that suggest they need customized services and resources, we maintain that educators and administrators should be proactive in assessing those needs and creating the environmental conditions that will enable such students to thrive. (p. 12)

In writing about various groups of students, most authors in the Harper and Quaye collection point to orientation as one program that needs to be tailored to meet specific needs. Therefore, as student diversity increases, so does the need to attend to the issues it presents. Although some students enter college with much exposure to and interaction with diverse populations, many do not. However, there are positive indicators that students of the Millennial generation are more open to diversity and have a more expansive view of diversity, seeing it as more than a Black-White issue (Broido, 2004). In addition to being aware of national trends, it is critical for orientation professionals to know and understand the characteristics of students on their campus, ensuring that programming efforts help students interact successfully and substantively with diverse peers.

◊ *Age, gender, and race and ethnicity.* There is much interplay between this set of student characteristics. Rates of participation in higher education, retention, and graduation vary based on combinations of these characteristics. For instance, the enrollment of students 25 and older is predicted to increase, and older women are contributing to the growing gender gap (Snyder et al., 2009); there are also large disparities in degree completion by income and race/ethnicity for male and female students (King, 2006). It is important to evaluate orientation programs to be certain that both the content and structure of orientation are relevant and accessible to older students and racial and ethnic minorities of both genders.

◊ *Income level and first-generation students.* These factors are also closely correlated as more first-generation students come from low-income families than peers with college-educated parents. First-generation students are also more likely to be Black or Hispanic (Chen, 2005). As noted by Pascarella et al. (2004), first-generation students often face substantial social and academic transitions, as they have not been privy to tacit information from their families about how colleges work. Orientation offers an early opportunity to help ease these transitions, reinforce degree aspirations that are critical indicators of college success, and connect students with academic and social supports to promote their retention.

◊ *GLBT students.* In coming to college, GLBT students must decide whether to disclose this aspect of their identities and to whom. In their study of students coming out in college, Evans and Broido (1999) found that,

> The environment had a strong influence on whether and to what extent a person came out to others. Factors that encouraged individuals to come out included being around supportive people; perceiving the overall climate as supportive; and having lesbian, gay, and bisexual role models in the environment . . . . Factors that discouraged coming out included a lack of community in the residence hall, lack of support, and active hostility. (p. 663)

Orientation is one of the early opportunities GLBT students will have to assess the campus environment. Among factors that will contribute to a positive assessment of the climate are positive role models (e.g., student orientation leaders, staff, and faculty) who are openly GLBT, examples in discussions and programs that reflect their sexual orientation, and the inclusion of GLBT student services and resources in institutional web sites, orientation packets, and other materials.

◇ *Students with disabilities.* The USDE Office for Civil Rights (2007) provides information for students with disabilities transitioning to postsecondary education. Although students with disabilities are entitled to accommodations in college, they will not have an Individualized Education Program as they did in high school. Therefore, students must become more active agents in securing necessary accommodations. Orientation programs must also accommodate students with disabilities (e.g., sign language interpreters for students with hearing impairments, accessible venues for orientation events) and ensure that students know how to access necessary services. Staff members who work specifically with students with disabilities should be involved in planning for orientation, and student orientation leader training should help prepare them for assisting students with disabilities.

◇ *International students.* International students present a wide range of special needs. When they arrive on campus, many face challenges including homesickness, anxiety, language barriers, financial concerns, social norms, cultural expectations, diet, gender roles, academic demands, and discrimination (Anderson, Carmichael, Harper, & Huang, 2009). Anderson et al. recommended a three-stage orientation program for international students. First, a pre-orientation DVD with subtitles should be sent prior to a student's arrival to introduce the institution and its many available resources. The second stage would help domestic students learn about the challenges international students face and the benefits they provide to the campus. Finally, an ongoing orientation, perhaps as part of a semester-long course, would help students overcome culture shock, balance participation in the new culture with maintenance of their own cultural identities, and promote their academic and social growth.

◇ *Religion.* Because many students are apt to reexamine and refine their religious beliefs during college (Pascarella & Terenzini, 2005), orientation programs might address the possibility that new students' religious views will likely be challenged, and they will also be supported to examine their beliefs and values. Students should also be provided information on campus and community organizations to address their religious and spiritual needs.

Furthermore, "students who identify as members of minority religious groups can face a variety of barriers to their full participation in the campus culture and are at risk of feeling isolated or marginalized" (Mahaffey & Smith, 2009, p. 96). These barriers may include inadequate access to appropriate food (e.g., kosher meals, meatless dishes), strong presence of alcohol that violates religious beliefs, and lack of availability of places to worship. At minimum, orientation programs must recognize and accommodate various religious traditions.

◇ *Veterans.* Given the expected influx of veterans, more campuses might consider programs and services targeted specifically to help these students transition into college. Many veterans may need to access services for students with disabilities, and many may need assistance understanding and accessing benefits afforded through the Post-9/11 GI Bill. Orientation staff should be trained to understand veterans' needs and know where to refer them for additional support.

Student Enrollment Patterns and Experiences

Beyond students' background characteristics, their college experiences are shaped by the ways in which they participate in higher education. These enrollment patterns and experiences also have implications for orientation.

◇ *Transfer and mixed-enrollment students.* Transfer students and those who swirl or double-dip have special needs for information and academic advice at both their sending and receiving institutions. Issues of transfer credit, course substitution, course access, and different curricular requirements can be compounded by new and different terminology. Extra time and attention to advising these students is generally needed. Furthermore, some transfer students, because they have been to college, may operate under the shaky assumption that they already know what they need to know, and so may be less likely to participate actively in orientation programs.

◇ *Online students.* Completion rates in online courses are lower than in traditional course settings. Students must take more initiative and be more self-motivated in the online environment. The most critical barrier to widespread adoption of online education—the need for more disciplined study habits (Allen & Seaman, 2007)—has implications for orientation. Online students may need more guidance about study habits and academic advising that recognizes the special nature of taking one or more courses online. Because many online students are also geographically distant from campus, they are likely to need access to orientation online as well.

◇ *Commuter students, employed students, and students with families.* These students share at least one common trait—all are in situations that can reduce the amount of discretionary time they have to devote to academic pursuits. Commuter students are less likely than their on-campus peers to participate in extracurricular activities, engage with other students and faculty, and persist and graduate (Pascarella & Terenzini, 2005). Employed students should be alerted that working more than 20 hours per week may negatively affect their academic performance, and they should be offered strategies—including the possibility of on-campus employment—to mitigate those potentially negative impacts. Finally, orientation programs should be prepared to address the special needs of students for information about child care, spousal benefits, and how to help the family be supportive of the student's educational endeavors. Pike and Kuh (2005) recommended the development of innovative strategies to help nontraditional students and their families become engaged on campus. Because commuters, employed students, and students with families may rely on valuable social connections away from campus, academic integration may be more important to their persistence. Advice on ways to engage with faculty, academically related student organizations (e.g., the biology club), and their classroom peers may be beneficial.

◇ *Residential students.* In contrast to commuter students, residential students face a different type of transition. The move from living at home to living in a college residence hall is fraught with some of the greatest transitional challenges faced by new students. Learning to live with such challenges as a roommate (very possibly not of the student's choosing), noise, peers with different social and identity characteristics, and newfound personal independence are just a few of the issues that should be addressed in helping new students adjust to living on campus (Blimling, 1995). Orientation programs can alert both students and parents to expected challenges and provide strategies for dealing successfully with the transition.

Conclusion

A primary goal of orientation is to help students adapt to the academic demands of college. Given the mismatch between students' self-reported study habits and expectations for academic performance and subsequent graduate degrees, they should be aided in setting realistic expectations. In other words, in order to perform at a high level, students will need to invest substantial time in academic endeavors. Upper-class undergraduates who have performed well academically and engaged in campus activities can share strategies with new students about achieving this balance. It is important that these role models represent a diverse range of background characteristics and enrollment patterns. Orientation programs should make a special effort to encourage and enable involvement on campus in effective educational practices, such as learning communities, service-learning, and study abroad, since they are known to deepen student learning and lead to greater persistence and retention (NSSE, 2007).

Effective orientation programs should be built upon an understanding of the diverse characteristics and needs of students and should help students know what it will take to be a successful college student at their institutions. Staff should collaborate with experts across the campus to contribute to retention and graduation of students.

Notes

[1]In this chapter, we use both Black and African American as a racial identifier, retaining the language used in the original source.

References

Allen, I. E., & Seaman, J. (2007). *Online nation: Five years of growth in online learning*. Needham, MA: Sloan Consortium. Retrieved from http://www.sloan-c.org/publications/survey/pdf/online_nation.pdf

Anderson, G., Carmichael, K., Harper, S. J., & Huang, T. (2009). International students at four-year institutions: Developmental needs, issues, and strategies. In S. R. Harper & S. J. Quaye, (Eds.), *Student engagement in higher education: Theoretical perspectives and practical approaches for diverse populations* (pp. 17-37). New York, NY: Routledge.

Blimling, G. (1995). *The resident assistant: Working with college students in residence halls*. Dubuque, IA: Kendall/Hunt.

Bozick, R. (2007). The role of students' economic resources, employment, and living arrangements. *Sociology of Education, 80*, 261-284. Retrieved from http://www.asanet.org/cs/journals/soe

Bradford, J., Barrett, K., & Honnold, J. A. (2002). *The 2000 census and same-sex households: A user's guide*. New York: The National Gay and Lesbian Task Force Policy Institute, The Survey and Evaluation Research Laboratory, and The Fenway Institute. Retrieved from http://www.thetaskforce.org/downloads/reports/reports/2000Census.pdf

Braxton, J. M., Hirschy, A. S., & McClendon, S. A. (2004). *Reducing institutional rates of departure*. (ASHE-ERIC Higher Education Report, No. 30). San Francisco: Jossey-Bass. doi: 10.1002/aehe.3003

Broido, E. M. (2004). Understanding diversity in millennial students. In M. D. Coomes & R. DeBard (Eds.), *Serving the millennial generation* (New Directions for Student Services No. 106, pp. 73-86). San Francisco, CA: Jossey-Bass.

Bryant, A. N., Choi, J. Y., & Yasuno, M. (2003). Understanding the religious and spiritual dimensions of students' lives in the first year of college. *Journal of College Student Development, 44*, 723-745. doi: 10.1353/csd.2003.0063

Bureau of Labor Statistics. (2009, April 28). *College enrollment and work activity of 2008 high school graduates*. Washington, DC: U.S. Department of Labor. Retrieved from http://www.bls.gov/news.release/pdf/hsgec.pdf

Chen, X. (2005). *First-generation students in postsecondary education: A look at their college transcripts* (NCES 2005–171). Washington, DC: National Center for Education Statistics, U.S. Department of Education. Retrieved from http://nces.ed.gov/pubs2005/2005171.pdf

Chen, X. (2007). *Part-time undergraduates in postsecondary education: 2003–04* (NCES 2007-165). Washington, DC: National Center for Education Statistics, U.S. Department of Education. Retrieved from http://nces.ed.gov/pubs2007/2007165.pdf

Church, T. E. (2009). Returning veterans on campus with war injuries and the long road back home. *Journal of Postsecondary Education and Disability, 22*(1), 43-52. Retrieved from http://www.ahead.org/uploads/docs/jped/journals/JPED%2022_1%20Complete%20Issue.pdf

Cook, B. J., & Kim, Y. (2009). *From soldier to student: Easing the transition of service members on campus.* Washington, DC: American Council on Education. Retrieved from http://www.aascu.org/media/pdf/09_StudenttoSoldierFinalReport.pdf

Council for the Advancement of Standards. (2009). *CAS professional standards for higher education* (7th ed.). Washington, DC: Author.

Department of Veterans Affairs. (2009, January). *Facts about the Department of Veterans Affairs.* Retrieved July 1, 2009, from http://www1.va.gov/OPA/fact/docs/vafacts.pdf

DesJardins, S. L., Ahlburg, D. A., & McCall, B. P. (2006). The effects of interrupted enrollments on graduation from college: Racial, income, and ability differences. *Economics of Education Review, 25,* 575-590. doi:10.1016/j.econedurev.2005.06.002

Evans, N. J., & Broido, E. M. (1999). Coming out in college residence halls: Negotiation, meaning making, challenges, supports. *Journal of College Student Development, 40,* 658-668.

Gates, G. J. (2006, October 1). *Same-sex couples and the gay, lesbian, bisexual population: New estimates from the American Community Survey* (Paper gates_8). Los Angeles, CA: The Williams Institute. Retrieved from http://repositories.cdlib.org/uclalaw/williams/gates_8/

Grossman, P. D. (2009). Foreword with a challenge: Leading our campuses away from the perfect storm. *Journal of Postsecondary Education and Disability, 22*(1), 4-9. Retrieved from http://www.ahead.org/uploads/docs/jped/journals/JPED%2022_1%20Complete%20Issue.pdf

Harper, S. R., & Quaye, S. J. (Eds.). (2009). *Student engagement in higher education: Theoretical perspectives and practical approaches for diverse populations.* New York, NY: Routledge.

Higher Education Research Institute (HERI). (2002, January 31). *College freshmen more politically liberal than in the past, UCLA survey reveals* [Press release]. Retrieved from http://www.heri.ucla.edu/pr-display.php?prQry=19

Horn, L., & Khazzoom, A. (1994). *Profile of undergraduates in U.S. postsecondary education institutions: 1989-90* (NCES 93-091). Washington, DC: National Center for Education Statistics, U.S. Department of Education. Retrieved from http://nces.ed.gov/pubs93/93091.pdf

Horn, L., & Nevill, S. (2006). *Profile of undergraduates in U.S. postsecondary education institutions: 2003-04: With a special analysis of community college students* (NCES 2006-184). Washington, DC: National Center for Education Statistics, U.S. Department of Education. Retrieved from http://nces.ed.gov/pubs2006/2006184.pdf

Howe, N., & Strauss, W. (2000). *Millennials rising: The next great generation.* New York, NY: Vintage Books.

Institute of International Education (IIE). (2008a). *International students: Institutions with 1,000 or more international students.* Retrieved September 20, 2009, from http://opendoors.iienetwork.org/?p=131542

Institute of International Education (IIE). (2008b). *International student and U.S. higher education enrollment trends, Selected Years 1954/55 - 2007/08.* Retrieved September 20, 2009, from http://opendoors.iienetwork.org/?p=131533

Institute of International Education (IIE). (2008c, November 17). *International students on U.S. campuses at all-time high.* (Press release). Washington, DC: Author. Retrieved September 20, 2009, from http://opendoors.iienetwork.org/?p=131590

KewalRamani A., Gilbertson, L., Fox, M., & Provasnik, S. (2007) *Status and trends in the education of racial and ethnic minorities* (NCES 2007-039). Washington, DC: National Center for Education Statistics, U.S. Department of Education. Retrieved from http://nces.ed.gov/pubs2007/2007039.pdf

King, J. E. (2006). *Gender equity in higher education: 2006.* Washington, DC: American Council on Education.

Kuh, G. D. (2003). What we're learning about student engagement from NSSE. *Change, 35*(2), 24-32.

Liu, A., Sharkness, J., & Pryor, J. H. (2008). *Findings from the 2007 administration of your first college year (YFCY): National aggregates.* Los Angeles, CA: University of California, Higher Education Research Institute. Retrieved from http://www.gseis.ucla.edu/heri/PDFs/2005_YFCY_REPORT_FINAL.pdf

Mahaffey, C. J., & Smith, S. A. (2009). Creating welcoming campus environments for students from minority religious groups. In S. R. Harper & S. J. Quaye, (Eds.), *Student engagement in higher education: Theoretical perspectives and practical approaches for diverse populations* (pp. 81-98). New York, NY: Routledge.

McCormick, A. C. (2003). Swirling and double-dipping: New patterns of student attendance and their implications for higher education. In J. E. King, E. L. Anderson, & M. E. Corrigan (Eds.), *Changing student attendance patterns: Challenges for policy and practice* (New Directions for Higher Education No. 121, pp. 13-24). San Francisco, CA: Jossey-Bass.

Mortenson, T. G. (2008, June 6). Commentary: Where the boys were. *Chronicle of Higher Education*, p. A30.

National Survey of Student Engagement (NSSE). (2007). *Experiences that matter: Enhancing student learning and success* (Annual report 2007). Bloomington, IN: Center for Postsecondary Research, Indiana University. Retrieved from http://nsse.iub.edu/NSSE_2007_Annual_Report/docs/withhold/NSSE_2007_Annual_Report.pdf

Pascarella, E. T., Pierson, C. T., Wolniak, G. C., & Terenzini, P. T. (2004). First-generation college students: Additional evidence on college experiences and outcomes. *Journal of Higher Education, 75,* 249-284.

Pascarella, E. T., & Terenzini, P. T. (2005). *How college affects students: A third decade of research, Volume 2.* San Francisco, CA: Jossey-Bass.

Peter, K., & Forrest Cataldi, E. (2005). *The road less traveled? Students who enroll in multiple institutions* (NCES 2005-157). Washington, DC: National Center for Education Statistics, U.S. Department of Education. Retrieved from http://nces.ed.gov/pubs2005/2005157.pdf

Pike, G. R., & Kuh, G. D. (2005). First- and second-generation college students: A comparison of their engagement and intellectual development. *Journal of Higher Education, 76,* 276-300.

Pike, G. R., Kuh, G. D., & Massa-McKinley, R. (2008). First-year students' employment, engagement, and academic achievement: Untangling the relationship between work and grades. *NASPA Journal, 45,* 560-582. Retrieved from http://naspa.org/pubs/journals/default.cfm

Planty, M., Hussar, W., Snyder, T., Kena, G., KewalRamani, A., Kemp, J., . . . Dinkes, R. (2009). *The condition of education 2009* (NCES 2009-081). Washington, DC: National Center for Education Statistics, U.S. Department of Education. Retrieved from http://nces.ed.gov/pubs2009/2009081.pdf

Provasnik, S., & Planty, M. (2008). *Community colleges: Special supplement to the condition of education 2008* (NCES 2008-033). Washington, DC: National Center for Education Statistics, U.S. Department of Education. Retrieved from http://nces.ed.gov/pubs2008/2008033.pdf

Pryor, J. H., Hurtado, S., DeAngelo, L., Sharkness, J., Romero, L. C., Korn, W. S., & Tran, S. (2008). *The American freshman: National norms for fall 2008*. Los Angeles, CA: Higher Education Research Institute.

Pryor, J. H., Hurtado, S., Saenz, V. B., Santos, J. L., & Korn, W. S. (2007). *The American freshman: Forty year trends*. Los Angeles, CA: University of California, Higher Education Research Institute.

Rand Center for Military Health Policy Research. (2008). *Invisible wounds: Mental health and cognitive care needs of America's returning veterans*. Retrieved from http://www.rand.org/pubs/research_briefs/2008/RAND_RB9336.pdf

Riggert, S., Boyle, M., Petrosko, J., Ash, D., & Rude-Parkins, C. (2006). Student employment and higher education: Empiricism and contradiction. *Review of Educational Research, 76*, 63-92. doi: 10.3102/00346543076001063

Saenz, V. B., Hurtado, S., Barrera, D., Wolf, D., & Yeung, F. (2007, May). *First in my family: A profile of first-generation college students at four-year institutions since 1971* (HERI Research Brief). Los Angeles, CA: University of California, Higher Education Research Institute. Retrieved from http://www.gseis.ucla.edu/heri/PDFs/pubs/briefs/FirstGenResearchBrief.pdf

Salisbury, M. H., Padgett, R. D., & Pascarella, E. T. (2009, June). *The effects of work on the educational experiences and liberal arts outcomes of first-year college students*. Paper presented at the annual forum of the Association for Institutional Research, Atlanta, GA. Retrieved from http://www.education.uiowa.edu/crue/publications/documents/Salisbury-Padgett-Pascarella-WorkPaper.pdf

Sanoff, A. P. (2006, March 10). What professors and teachers think: A perception gap over students' preparation. *Chronicle of Higher Education*, p. B9.

Silverman, M. M. (2008, April 18). Campus security begins with caring. *Chronicle of Higher Education*, p. A51.

Snyder, T. D., Dillow, S. A., & Hoffman, C. M. (2009). *Digest of education statistics 2008* (NCES 2009-020). Washington, DC: National Center for Education Statistics, U.S. Department of Education. Retrieved from http://nces.ed.gov/pubs2009/2009020.pdf

Student Veterans of America. (2008, January 18). *Student veterans establish national coalition*. Retrieved from http://www.studentveterans.org/media.html

Tinto, V. (1993). *Leaving college: Rethinking the causes and cures of student attrition* (2nd ed.). Chicago, IL: University of Chicago Press.

U.S. Department of Education, Office for Civil Rights. (2007). *Students with disabilities preparing for postsecondary education: Know your rights and responsibilities*. Washington, DC: Author. Retrieved September 20, 2009, from http://www.ed.gov/about/offices/list/ocr/transition.html#reproduction

Wei, C. C., Berkner, L., He, S., Lew, S., Cominole, M., & Siegel, P. (2009). *2007-08 national postsecondary student aid study (NPSAS:08): Student financial aid estimates for 2007-08: First look* (NCES 2009-166). Washington, DC: National Center for Education Statistics, U.S. Department of Education. Retrieved from http://nces.ed.gov/pubs2009/2009166.pdf

Wirt, J., Choy, S., Provasnik, S., Rooney, P., Sen, A., & Tobin, R. (2003). *The condition of education 2003* (NCES 2003–067). Washington, DC: National Center for Education Statistics, U.S. Department of Education. Retrieved from http://nces.ed.gov/pubs2003/2003067.pdf

Wright, A. (2009, July 31). Expanded GI Bill funds readied for distribution. *Chronicle of Higher Education*. Retrieved from http://chronicle.com

Chapter 11

Creating a Developmental Framework for New Student Orientation to Address the Needs of Diverse Populations

Archie P. Cubarrubia and Jennifer C. Schoen

A successful transition during the first year of college is critical to student success (Pascarella & Terenzini, 2005; Robinson, Burns, & Gaw, 1996), especially for students from low-income and racial and ethnic minority groups, who persist and graduate at lower rates than their majority counterparts (NCES, 2008). As an increasingly diverse group of students enters higher education, the challenge for higher education administrators is to ensure that all students—regardless of their cultural, racial, ethnic, or socioeconomic background—are integrated successfully into the academic and social communities of the institution (Chang, Altbach, & Lomotey, 2005; Kerr, 1993; Tinto, 1993). Institutional interventions such as new student orientation and first-year programs assist students in their transition to college and foster their integration into the campus community during the first year (Pascarella, Terenzini, & Wolfle, 1986; Robinson et al.; Zakely, 2003). However, the body of literature on the impact of college experiences on student development and success is mainly theoretical (Pascarella & Terenzini), and the extent to which these developmental theories are applied in the implementation of student services, particularly those theories that address minority student groups, is unknown. Despite the generally accepted and understood value of using student development theory in practice (Evans, Forney, Guido-DiBrito, 1998; McEwen, 2003; Strange & King, 1990) and despite the proliferation of these theories since the 1980s (King & Howard-Hamilton, 2000), there is little research that indicates the extent to which student affairs functional units regularly apply student development theory in the design and implementation of their programs. Although the standards and guidelines for orientation programs promulgated by the Council for the Advancement of Standards in Higher Education (CAS) notes that the orientation program "must incorporate student learning and student development in its mission" (Dean, 2006, p. 267), the extent to which this standard is applied is also unknown. We believe that intentionally using student development theory to develop and deliver new student programs is critical to ensure that the needs of diverse student populations are addressed.

This chapter suggests a framework for delivering first-year experiences that address diverse students' developmental needs. First, an overview of changing student demographics in higher education is presented. Second, several challenges facing diverse student populations are addressed. Third, a theoretical basis for creating a developmental framework is presented. Finally, considerations for planning and implementing orientation based on the developmental needs of diverse student populations are discussed.

Changing Demographics in Higher Education

Consistent with changes in the U.S. population and as a result of key federal and state legislation allowing increased access to college, there are more—and increasingly diverse—students entering postsecondary education. For example, 32% of students enrolled in postsecondary degree-granting institutions in 2007 were students of color (Planty et al., 2009). At public four-year institutions, students who are racial or ethnic minorities comprised 28% of enrolled students, while at public two-year institutions, students who are racial or ethnic minorities comprised 38% of enrolled students (Planty et al.). In addition, almost three quarters of all students enrolled in postsecondary education display at least one characteristic that classifies them as "nontraditional" (Choy, 2002). These characteristics include delayed enrollment, part-time attendance, full-time employment while enrolled, financial independence, responsibility for dependents other than a spouse, single parent status, and a lack of a high school diploma. Finally, postsecondary enrollment patterns since the 1970s reflect an increasingly mobile student body. For example, Peter and Forrest Cataldi (2005) found that 59% of first-time bachelor's degree recipients attended at least two institutions. Similarly, Adelman (2006) found that 57% of high school seniors in 1992 who subsequently earned more than 10 credits at a postsecondary institution attended at least two institutions.

The impact increasing enrollments and diversification of the student body have on higher education institutions is clear. Between the mid-1970s to the mid-2000s, the number of postsecondary degree-granting institutions increased more than 40%, the greatest increase of which was among two- and four-year for-profit institutions (NCES, 2008). Accordingly, the past 30 years have also seen shifts in academic and social offerings, services, and amenities across campuses.

Challenges Facing Diverse Student Populations

Diverse student populations in higher education face a number of challenges. Although these challenges may apply to majority student populations as well, they are particularly salient for minority student populations. These challenges include decreased access to and affordability of postsecondary education; inadequate preparation for postsecondary education; and limited networks of support. New student programs must address these challenges to ensure the successful transition of students—particularly those from diverse populations.

Limited Accessibility to and Affordability of Postsecondary Education

Despite gains in postsecondary enrollment across all ethnic and racial minority groups over the past 30 years, certain populations continue to experience limited access to postsecondary education (Haycock, 2006). The Secretary of Education's Commission on the Future of Higher Education observed, for example, that "too few Americans prepare for, participate in, and complete higher education—especially those underserved and nontraditional groups who make up an ever-greater proportion of the population" (U.S. Department of Education, 2006, p. 8). In addition, those students who do enroll in postsecondary education often find that the cost of attendance can be a barrier to retention and success. The Commission found that access to and success in higher education is "unduly limited by the complex interplay of inadequate preparation, lack of information about college opportunities, and persistent financial barriers" (p. 8).

Although the interrelated challenges of accessibility and affordability can impact many postsecondary students, they are particularly salient to students from low-income families. In 2006, it was estimated that more than 38 million people—13% of the entire U.S. population—were defined as living below the poverty threshold (Webster & Bishaw, 2007). Of those low-income students who are academically qualified to attend college, fewer than half enroll in a four-year institution within two years of graduating high school compared with 80% of students who come from higher-income families (Carnevale & Desrochers, 2003). More recent data show that family income continues to be a barrier to immediate college enrollment. Enrollment rates were consistently higher for students from high-income families than for students from low-income families in each year between 1972 and 2006 (NCES, 2008). The Advisory Committee on Student Financial Assistance (ACSFA, 2002) estimates that nearly two million college-ready high school graduates from low- and middle-income families are not able to attend college because of financial barriers. Of those low-income students who do enroll in postsecondary education, only half receive their bachelor's degrees within six years, compared with more than three quarters of students from high-income families (Berkner, He, & Forrest Cataldi, 2002).

Clearly, issues of college accessibility and affordability can have an impact on students' success, not just during the first year but throughout their academic careers. Even for those students who are admitted to an institution and enroll, financial concerns can hinder a smooth transition into the campus community.

Inadequate Preparation for Postsecondary Education

Similarly, another challenge that students from diverse populations face is inadequate preparation for the academic and social demands of postsecondary education. Widely varying levels of academic rigor in high schools can have an impact on students' preparation for college-level work. Of the 70% of public high school attendees who graduate, only 32% are qualified to attend a four-year college (Greene & Forster, 2003). This challenge is particularly relevant to students from low-income and racial minority families. For example, only 8% of students from low-income families have access to a rigorous secondary school curriculum that prepares them for college, compared with 28% of students from higher-income families (Greene & Forster). Even for those low-income students with college aspirations, inadequate preparation can hinder college attendance. The literature indicates that most low-income teenagers say they plan to attend college, but few actually receive adequate information on what it takes to enroll and succeed in college (Matthews, 2009). The situation is more dire for racial minority students. Of the 51% of Black students who graduate from public high schools, only 20% are considered college-ready. Similarly, only 16% of Hispanic students who graduate from public high schools are college-ready (Greene & Forster). For those racial minority students who do enroll in postsecondary education, inadequate preparation can lead to poor success and attainment rates. Bachelor's attainment rates for students aged 25-29 reveal disparities across racial groups, with 34% of White students receiving their bachelor's degree by age 29, compared with 18% of Black students and 11% of Hispanic students (Haycock, 2006).

A key consideration in the inadequate preparation of students for postsecondary education is a fundamental misalignment between the K-12 curriculum and college expectations. For example, a survey of high school teachers and college faculty conducted by *The Chronicle of Higher Education* (Sanoff, 2006) found that 44% of college faculty held the view that incoming students were not prepared for college-level writing, compared with 90% of high school teachers who considered them prepared. The frequency of remediation at the college level provides a disturbing indicator of students' lack of preparation for postsecondary education; nearly half of all students take at least one remedial course in college (Adelman, 2004).

Limited Networks of Support

Finally, limited networks of support at home and on campus can lead to disengagement from the campus community, particularly for first-generation, racial, and sexual minority student groups. For many minority students, college-going may not be perceived as a priority or necessity by family and friends. For those students who are the first in their family to enroll in postsecondary education, a perceived lack of support can have an impact on the transition to the campus community. In 2000, 34% of students entering four-year colleges and 53% of students entering two-year colleges were first-generation college students (Choy, 2002). Literature suggests that these students are often at a disadvantage, lacking knowledge about attending college, support from family income, expectations of attaining a degree, and specific career plans (McCarron & Inkelas, 2006; Terenzini, 1995). In addition, many first-generation students, particularly those from working-class backgrounds, experience an "identity crisis" during their transition to college in their first year. They feel compelled to leave their cultural heritage behind and adopt new identities as college students (Duffy, 2007). This new identity, unknown to family and friends, can alienate students from their support systems at home. Many of these students feel ostracized for pursuing postsecondary education, while at the same time obligated to maintain ties to their families in their roles as breadwinners (Ortiz, 2000). Therefore, students whose parents do not have a college degree often have a more difficult transition to college.

Similarly, youth from foster care backgrounds often experience challenges resulting from a limited support network. More than 500,000 children and youth, the majority of whom are racial minorities, are in foster care in the United States (U.S. Department of Health and Human Services, 2007). Of the college-aged youth in foster care, a majority have little to no support for pursuing postsecondary education. Only 7–13% of students who have spent time in foster care attend college, and only 2-12% of those students obtain their bachelor's degree (Pecora et al., 2005). Students coming to college from foster care often require more attention than other first-generation college students because of their independent status. They often arrive at college in survival mode and are focused on their basic needs for safe and stable year-round housing, food, transportation, money, and healthcare (Bassett & Emerson, 2008). Too many youth and their caregivers lack basic information about what college entails and the resources that exist at the college level that can address their life circumstances and unique support needs (Basset & Emerson).

A lack of adequate support networks on campus can also impact lesbian, gay, bisexual, transgender, and questioning (LGBTQ) students' transition into an institution. According to Evans and Broido (1999), the importance of a supportive college environment is particularly relevant to this population given that college is often the environment for the coming out process (as cited in Longerbeam, Inkelas, Johnson, & Lee, 2007). However, the campus climate is often inhospitable for these students, and they spend a great deal of energy hiding a crucial component of their identities from their peers, faculty, and staff for fear of harassment. In a 2005 study conducted by the National Gay and Lesbian Task Force (Rankin), for example, more than a third of LGBTQ undergraduates experienced harassment. Twenty percent of LGBTQ students, faculty, and staff feared for their physical safety, and nearly 60% of the undergraduates in the survey concealed their sexual orientation or gender identity to avoid intimidation. Clearly, for LGBTQ students, a perception of a lack of a safe and supportive network can impact their transition into the campus community.

A lack of support networks can have a negative impact on student transition and success. This challenge is perhaps the least tangible among the myriad issues that new students face during their first year. However, this challenge is one that orientation and first-year programs can have the most impact addressing.

Using Student Development Theory to Address the Needs of Diverse Student Populations

Given the importance of student development theory in practice (Evans et al., 1998; King & Howard-Hamilton, 2000), a developmental approach should be used to address the challenges that diverse student populations face in their transition to college. For example, the successful transition and integration of first-year students to college, particularly traditional-aged students, hinges on the accomplishment of certain developmental tasks, among the most important of which are the negotiation of an individual's identity and the subsequent process of enculturation to the institution (Casas & Pytluk, 1995; Cubarrubia, 2003). Berry (1993) defines enculturation as "the socialization process by which individuals acquire...the host of cultural and psychological qualities that are necessary to function as a member of one's group" (p. 272). Because the first year of college is developmentally significant (Robinson et al., 1996), higher education administrators have an opportunity to actively engage in students' enculturation and engender integration into the college community from students' first year.

The challenges for practitioners in addressing the demands on students' identity development are as diverse as the groups to which they belong. Each population establishes its own cultural identity, i.e., shared values, beliefs, knowledge, and traditions (Cubarrubia, 2003), with unique needs and demands that are placed on students. Individual students can choose to identify with many different cultures depending on their individual identity development and how they manage conflicts among these identities or assimilate their differences. The goal for higher education administrators is to help students develop bicultural efficacy, "an individual's expectations that he or she can manage the stress and conflict of living in two cultures at the same time without suffering negative psychological consequences or compromising his/her personal and cultural identity" (Coleman, 1992, p. 7). By providing students with first-year experiences that help facilitate their bicultural efficacy, higher education administrators help ensure students' smooth transition into the academic and social contexts of the institution—their enculturation into the campus community.

To facilitate students' enculturation into the institution, we propose a framework for developing and implementing new student orientation programs that recognizes the developmental needs of all students and facilitates their integration into the campus community. We offer this framework not as a prescriptive approach but rather as a series of considerations that should be explored when planning, implementing, and assessing new student orientation programs.

Several developmental theories serve as the foundation for this framework. Chickering and Reisser's (1993) vectors of student development, based on Erikson's (1959) stages of identity development, identified critical developmental milestones in college-aged students. Similar theories of identity development addressing specific cultural groups based on ethnicity (Phinney, 1992), race (Cross, 1991; Helms & Cook, 1999; Pope, 2000), sexual orientation (Cass, 1979; Chojnacki & Gelberg, 1995; D'Augelli, 1991; 1994), and religious development (Love & Talbot, 1999) provide insight on approaches to developing and delivering interventions that may impact that cultural group more effectively. Tinto's (1993) model of student attrition cites developmental milestones as potential variables in determining student persistence. Jones and McEwen's (2000) model of multiple identity development provides context for how different facets of students' identities interact with situations and with each other. Finally, Schlossberg's Transition Theory (Schlossberg, Waters, & Goodman, 1995) provides a context to view student development issues occurring during the first year of college. A few of these theories are briefly discussed here.

Chickering and Reisser's (1993) vectors of student development are based on Erikson's (1959) model of identity formation and describe the developmental experiences of college students. Each vector identifies a set of physical, emotional, psychological, and social developmental tasks that students typically accomplish while they are in college. Establishing identity is the key consideration in this framework, as it describes the process by which individuals integrate various life experiences with their own sense of self, their personality, motivation, and skills. In essence, once students know who they are (i.e., they become comfortable with their own values, beliefs, and motivations), they are better able to understand and embody their social and cultural roles in the institutional community, particularly regarding race, gender, and sexual orientation. The process of integration is ongoing and dependent on an individual's values and experiences. Indeed, "the discovery and refinement of one's unique way of being" (p. 35) is central to Chickering and Reisser's process of individuation.

The development of minority identity follows a similar dynamic in that "minority cultural identities are not fixed or monolithic but multivocal, and even contradictory" (McCarthy, 1994, p. 82). In developing strategies for counseling racial minorities, Atkinson, Morten, and Sue (1993) outlined the following five stages of racial identity development: (a) conformity, (b) dissonance, (c) resistance and immersion, (d) introspection, and (e) synergistic articulation and awareness. These stages describe the process by which racial minority individuals negotiate the demands of identity formation while living in a majority environment. A similar progression of questioning and acceptance is present in the stages of sexual identity development (Cass, 1979; Chojnacki & Gelberg, 1995; D'Augelli, 1991; 1994). The final stage in both racial and sexual identity development models represents the point at which individuals develop an identity that reflects elements from both dominant and minority cultural groups. For many institutional programs, the goal is to help students achieve "cultural savvy" by helping them articulate and express their individual cultural identities and by facilitating an understanding of life experiences in a multicultural society. Indeed, "inhibiting the expression of cultural identity in [our communities] denies learning opportunities that not only promote the development of complex meaning-making but also strengthens students' sense of self and [helps them] acquire competencies needed to thrive in a diverse world community" (Ortiz, 2000, p. 67).

Because social identities rarely exist in a vacuum, individuals have multiple dimensions of identity that influence their attitudes and behaviors in any given context. The intersection of students' membership in various identity groups exemplifies the integrative and contextual interaction of multiple identities proposed by Jones and McEwen (2000). In this model, "the importance of considering the influences of dimensions such as race, culture, social class, and sexual orientation" (p. 410) is significant in understanding the effects of multiple dimensions of identity. That multiple identities, even conflicting ones (such as sexual identity, gender identity, and religious identity) can simultaneously coexist and even influence each other, is possible in this model. Indeed, "more than one identity dimension can be engaged by the individual at any one time" (p. 410). The relative salience of each dimension of identity is contextual; in some instances, a particular dimension may take precedence over another. Individuals must continuously negotiate these elements based on changing contexts and life experiences.

A successful transition to college engages an individual's identity with institutional culture in Tinto's (1987) interactional model of student attrition. In this model, the interplay between student characteristics and institutional experiences determines student persistence. Successful student retention rests on the congruence between the following major factors: (a) an individual's expectations prior to arriving at college and his or her experiences while there and (b) the institution's academic and social orientation. If there is a "fit" for both the student and the institution, commitment to the institution and subsequent persistence is more likely.

Similarly, Schlossberg's (1995) transition theory is relevant to a discussion of student transition into the college environment. Although originally conceived as an adult development theory, Schlossberg's theory is applicable to traditional-aged student populations as well (Evans et al.,

1998). The transition theory considers events in an individual's experiences that result in significant changes in roles, relationships, routines, and assumptions and identifies factors that influence an individual's ability to cope with the transition. These factors include situation, self, support, and strategies. In a postsecondary setting, a student's transition experience is influenced by these factors. As such, higher education administrators have an opportunity to provide appropriate interventions to ensure that the student's transition is as smooth as possible.

Considering Tinto's interactional model of attrition and Schlossberg's transition theory along with research on identity development of minority students, a powerful framework emerges for developing and implementing new student orientation programs that address the needs of diverse student populations. These developmental theories are lenses through which the challenges faced by students from diverse backgrounds may be addressed.

Considerations in Creating a Developmental Framework for Orientation Programs

To facilitate students' successful transition into the campus community, orientation, retention, and transition professionals must address the developmental needs of students from diverse backgrounds in their programs. We suggest creating a framework for planning and implementing programs using student development theory for minority student populations which considers the unique challenges and experiences each student brings to campus. This framework should intentionally embed developmental theories for specific student populations (as appropriate to the institution) in all aspects of program development and delivery: staff recruitment, staff training, marketing, and outreach. Although we do not advocate a one-size-fits-all approach as institutional mission and student populations differ widely from campus to campus, we provide a set of six questions to consider when creating first-year experiences that address the developmental needs of diverse student groups.

Assessment and Planning

Assessment is critical to the success of new student orientation programs designed to address the needs of diverse student populations. Assessment ensures that programs meet the needs of internal and external constituents (Love & Estanek, 2004; Upcraft & Schuh, 1996). Effective planning uses the assessment process to consider the changing demographics of the campus, explore current research on student development theory, and measure effectiveness from previous years' iterations of the program. In many cases, new student programs rely too heavily on tradition and do not demonstrate the flexibility to address changing student demographics and the needs of those populations. To ensure that orientation and first-year programs remain relevant, orientation professionals must regularly assess the institutional landscape and identify student populations whose unique needs are not currently being addressed by existing programs. In planning, orientation and transition professionals should explore the following questions:

1. *What do I know about my student population?* Since each incoming class is unique, we advocate for planning that involves an annual landscape analysis and corresponding needs assessment of the institution's current and expected student population. Such an analysis may provide a helpful overview of how adequately and effectively current services address the needs of specific student groups. Such an analysis will also allow orientation professionals to identify gaps in the services needed by students, particularly those from low-income

and minority populations. Partnerships with admissions staff, enrollment managers, and institutional researchers are critical to facilitate the collection and analysis of student demographic information. In addition, focus groups with current first-year students from diverse backgrounds may provide feedback on the effectiveness of existing programs in meeting their unique developmental needs.

2. *What does current research say about my student population?* To address fully the needs of diverse student groups, it is important to consider current research on student development in planning orientation and first-year programs. Orientation professionals must increase their professional expertise and functional knowledge of critical issues facing diverse student populations to better facilitate the creation of learning environments for these populations. Accordingly, time and effort for research and analysis must be built into the program planning process. Partnerships with faculty, library services, and colleagues in other student services areas, such as multicultural services or offices for specific cultural groups, can facilitate increased professional capacity for analyzing and applying relevant research.

3. *What is the balance between creating programs for some students and creating programs for all students?* The goal of addressing specific underrepresented populations during orientation is not to give each student group a unique or segregated orientation experience; rather, it is to recognize that each group needs specific information and connections, presented in a specific way, to make the most of their first-year experience. For example, orientation professionals should explore the impact of existing program facets (e.g., fees, format, length, schedule of educational sessions, social activities) on the development of students from diverse populations. Careful planning around the method and timing of developmental interventions during students' transitions in their first year allows orientation programs to facilitate the development of student identity, minimize student stigmatization, and provide opportunities to interact with other students from both similar and different backgrounds. Students from diverse backgrounds, including those from majority groups, benefit from this thoughtful planning and incorporation of developmental theory. For some programs, interest sessions targeted for specific student groups may be appropriate. For others, a reiteration of the institution's nondiscrimination policy throughout the summer orientation session may suffice. An in-depth discussion or series of discussions and presentations started during the summer orientation session and continued during the first-year seminar may be necessary for other groups. Although approaches differ, the opportunity for students to interact with peers from similar and different backgrounds is critical to their successful transition into the campus community.

Implementation

The implementation of new student orientation programs for diverse groups requires that all aspects of the program are viewed from the mindset of students who may be facing significant challenges in their transition to the campus community. Given the realities of program constraints, orientation professionals may need to leverage existing programs in order to respond to students' needs. Orientation, retention, and transition professionals must clearly articulate the value of orientation to the entire campus community and use existing human and financial resources available in other offices on campus to address first-year student issues—especially those issues that have a critical impact on diverse student populations. The goals of the orientation program must also be tied to the mission of the institution and clarify why all members of the campus community must deliver services to first-year students using a developmental framework during the transitional first year of college. Additional questions to ask during the implementation phase include:

4. *How does my program address challenges related to accessibility and affordability?* Although increasing access to college is not typically addressed during orientation programs (unless the program is offered in conjunction with the institution's recruitment activities), it is critical to recognize that accessibility and affordability pose a challenge to a number of students, particularly those from low-income and racial minority backgrounds. For example, some first-year students may have overcome significant challenges to be admitted and enrolled in the institution. Similarly, some students who attend orientation programs may be facing significant financial challenges, including taking on substantial student loan debt or foregoing a paycheck in order to attend the program, particularly in the summer. A key consideration is recognizing that these circumstances are the reality for many students, and orientation programs must either explicitly or implicitly acknowledge these challenges when establishing program fees. If feasible, financial contingencies, in the form of scholarships or fee waivers, help ensure that students from low-income backgrounds are able to participate in these programs. If an institution recognizes the importance of support systems—such as familial support—to the success of its students, the institution should also consider waiving fees for parent/guardian programs for some students.

   In addition, all students benefit from receiving information related to funding their college education. First-generation and low-income students often face financial barriers to persistence and success in college. Introducing financial aid counselors as approachable, active partners with students and their families is a first step toward demystifying the aid process. Information during orientation should also include programs on scholarships and work-study opportunities, timing of financial aid disbursements, penalties for withdrawing from classes, budgeting, deadlines that have an impact on aid, and helpful resources for completing the FAFSA each year.

5. *How does my program address challenges related to inadequate preparation?* Because varying levels of academic rigor in high school can affect students' preparation for college-level work, orientation and first-year programs need to address challenges related to inadequate preparation. Interest sessions on study skills and navigating the college classroom may be appropriate for some programs. For others, in-depth discussions with academic advisors on coursework, placement, and career aspirations may be necessary. Inadequate preparation may increase anxiety related to the college transition. Programs can ease these concerns by directly addressing students' perceptions of academic and social expectations. Again, approaches may differ when communicating the expectations and standards of institutional culture. However, a critical consideration is to ensure that programs do not assume that all students entering college have the requisite knowledge, skills, and cultural savvy to navigate the academic and social landscapes of the institution.

6. *How does my program address students' needs for adequate support networks?* Building an adequate support network for students, particularly those from low-income, racial minority, and first-generation backgrounds, begins with programming workshops and events for family members during orientation, helping parents/guardians increase their knowledge of the campus community, and giving families the tools to help their students. Families participating in orientation build the social capital necessary to provide student support from what is often the student's most trusted resource. It is critical that orientation materials contain inclusive language to indicate that parents, foster parents, guardians, and nontraditional families are welcome. This necessitates ensuring brochures, web sites, and other marketing

materials are consistent in messages sent to family members about the kinds of students welcomed at the institution. As appropriate, bilingual materials may make a significant difference in the level of student engagement in the program because the materials give families a better understanding of the importance of participating in orientation and the need to prepare students for the transition to college. For entering students and families who have young children, providing childcare at little to no cost during family orientation also signals the campus community's support for students who may need additional resources to build their network of support.

Creating an on-campus support network also means providing students opportunities to develop their own network of support within the institution. Academic advisors, financial aid counselors, and other student services personnel play a significant role in the student's support network, and their collaboration is crucial to orientation. Ensuring that institution staff understand students' needs for adequate support will facilitate their successful transition into the campus community. Staff must have a visible role in orientation so students will see them as approachable resources who are critical to their success.

Finally, peers are a critical part of building support networks for new students. Peers provide advice that may sometimes be more relevant to students than information presented by professional staff. Student staff, in appearance and substance, need to represent the demographics of the campus community and the incoming class. Strategies for increasing student staff applications from diverse groups include advertising in places where more diverse groups of students are found, such as multicultural centers, LGBTQ centers, commuter lounges, and ethnic studies departments. In addition, recruiting students who may work with or have participated in GEAR UP (Gaining Early Awareness and Readiness for Undergraduate Programs) and TRIO programs may also add to the economic diversity of student staff. These and other federally supported programs help first-generation and low-income students in preparing for, applying to, and persisting in college.

Conclusion

This chapter provides a framework for planning and implementing orientation programs to account for the needs of diverse student populations. The use of current student development theory and research and continuous assessment to improve first-year program success for all students are the centerpieces of this framework. However, none of the questions in the framework will be answered effectively if student voices are not included in the process, and if we as professionals do not broaden our perspectives of the student experience.

As the diversification of the postsecondary student population in the United States continues, higher education institutions must increasingly address the needs of student populations that face unique challenges in their transition into the campus community. As the primary vehicle for disseminating information about institutional culture and context, orientation and first-year programs must increasingly consider the developmental needs of diverse student groups in their programmatic interventions. To ensure that all students, regardless of their cultural, racial, ethnic, or socioeconomic background, are integrated successfully into the academic and social communities of the institution, orientation professionals must use a framework that takes into consideration the critical developmental needs of these students and that allows them to address the unique challenges they face during their first year.

References

Adelman, C. (2004). *Principal indicators of student academic histories in postsecondary education, 1972-2000*. Washington, DC: U.S. Department of Education.

Adelman, C. (2006). *The toolbox revisited: Paths to degree completion from high school through college*. Washington, DC: U.S. Department of Education.

Advisory Committee on Student Financial Assistance (ACSFA). (2002). *Empty promises: The myth of college access in America*. Washington, DC: Author.

Atkinson, D. R., Morten, G., & Sue, D. W. (1993). *Counseling American minorities: A cross-cultural perspective*. Dubuque, IA: Brown & Benchmark.

Bassett, L., & Emerson, J. (2008). *Supporting success: Improving higher education outcomes for students from foster care*. Seattle, WA: Casey Family Programs.

Berkner, L., He, S., & Forrest Cataldi, E. (2002). *Descriptive summary of 1995-96 beginning postsecondary students: Six years later* (NCES 2003-151). Washington, DC: U.S. Department of Education, National Center for Education Statistics.

Berry, J. W. (1993). Ethnic identity in pluralistic societies. In M. E. Bernal & G. P. Knight (Eds.), *Ethnic identity: Formation and transmission among Hispanics and other minorities* (pp. 271-296). Albany, NY: State University of New York Press.

Carnevale, A. P., & Desrochers, D. M. (2003). *Standards for what? The economic roots of K-16 reform*. Princeton, NJ: Educational Testing Service.

Casas, J. M., & Pytluk, S. D. (1995). Hispanic identity development: Implications for research and practice. In J. G. Ponterotto, J. M. Casas, L. A. Suzuki, & C. M. Alexander (Eds.), *Handbook of multicultural counseling* (pp. 155-180). Thousand Oaks, CA: Sage Publications.

Cass, V. C. (1979). Homosexual identity formation: A theoretical model. *Journal of Homosexuality, 4*, 219–235.

Chang, M. J., Altbach, P. G., & Lomotey, K. (2005). Race in higher education: Making meaning of an elusive moving target. In P. G. Altbach, R. O. Berdahl, & P. J. Gumport (Eds.), *American higher education in the twenty-first century: Social, political, and economic challenges* (2nd ed., pp. 517-536). Baltimore: The Johns Hopkins University Press.

Chickering, A. W., & Reisser, L. (1993). *Education and identity* (2nd ed.). San Francisco: Jossey-Bass.

Chojnacki, J. T., & Gelberg, S. (1995). The facilitation of a gay/lesbian/bisexual support-therapy group by heterosexual counselors. *Journal of Counseling and Development, 73*(3), 352–54.

Choy, S. (2002). *Nontraditional undergraduates* (NCES 2002-012). Washington, DC: U.S. Department of Education, National Center for Education Statistics.

Coleman, H. L. K. (1992). *Bicultural efficacy and college adjustment*. Presented at the annual meeting of the American Educational Research Association, San Francisco, CA.

Cross, W. E. (1991). *Shades of black: Diversity in African American identity*. Philadelphia: Temple University Press.

Cubarrubia, A. P. (2003). *What's your story: Cultural identity development and the first-year student*. Paper presented at the National Orientation Directors Association Annual Conference, Seattle, WA.

D'Augelli, A. R. (1991). Gay men in college: Identity processes and adaptations. *Journal of College Student Development, 32*, 140-146.

D'Augelli, A. R. (1994). Identity development and sexual orientation: Toward a model of lesbian, gay and bisexual development. In E. J. Trickett, R. J. Watts, & D. Birman (Eds.), *Human diversity: Perspectives on people in context* (pp. 312-333). San Francisco: Jossey-Bass.

Dean, L. A. (Ed.) (2006). *CAS professional standards for higher education* (6th ed.). Washington, DC: Council for the Advancement of Standards in Higher Education.

Duffy, J. O. (2007). Invisibly at risk: Low-income students in a middle- and upper-class world. *About Campus, 12*(2), 18-25.

Erikson, E. H. (1959). *Identity and the life cycle.* New York, NY: International Universities Press.

Evans, N. J., Forney, D. S., & Guido-DiBrito, F. (1998). *Student development in college: Theory, research, and practice.* San Francisco: Jossey-Bass.

Greene, J., & Forster, G. (2003). *Public high school graduation and college readiness rates in the United States.* New York, NY: Center for Civic Innovation at the Manhattan Institute.

Haycock, K. (2006). *Promise abandoned: How policy choices and institutional practices restrict college opportunities.* Washington, DC: Education Trust.

Helms, J. E., & Cook, D. A. (1999). *Using race and culture in counseling and psychotherapy: Theory and process.* Needham Heights, MA: Allyn and Bacon.

Jones, S. R., & McEwen, M. K. (2000). A conceptual model of multiple dimensions of identity. *Journal of College Student Development, 41*(4), 405-414.

Kerr, C. (1993). *Troubled times for American higher education: The 1990s and beyond.* Albany, NY: State University of New York Press.

King, P. M., & Howard-Hamilton, M. F. (2000). Using student development theory to inform institutional research. In J. W. Pickering & G. R Hanson (Eds.), *Collaboration between student affairs and institutional researchers to improve institutional effectiveness* (New Directions for Institutional Research No. 108, pp. 19-36). San Francisco: Jossey-Bass.

Longerbeam, S. D., Inkelas, K. K., Johnson, D. R., & Lee, Z. S. (2007). Lesbian, gay, and bisexual college student experiences: An exploratory study. *Journal of College Student Development, 48*(2), 215-230.

Love, P. G., & Estanek, S. M. (2004). *Rethinking student affairs practice.* San Francisco: Jossey-Bass.

Love, P. G., & Talbot, D. (1999). Defining spiritual development: A missing consideration for student affairs. *NASPA Journal, 37*(1), 361-375.

Matthews, D. (2009). *A stronger nation through higher education: How and why Americans must meet a "big goal" for college attainment.* Indianapolis, IN: Lumina Foundation for Education.

McCarron, G. P., & Inkelas, K. K. (2006). The gap between educational aspirations and attainment for first-generation college students and the role of parental involvement. *Journal of College Student Development, 47*(5), 543-549.

McCarthy, C. (1994). Multicultural discourses and curriculum reform: A critical perspective. *Educational Theory, 44*(1), 81-98.

McEwen, M. K. (2003). The nature and uses of theory. In S. R., Komives, D. B. Woodard, Jr., & Associates (Eds.), *Student services: A handbook for the profession* (4th ed., pp. 153-178). San Francisco: Jossey-Bass.

National Center for Education Statistics. (2008). *Digest of education statistics 2008* (NCES 2009-020), Table 265. Washington, DC: U.S. Department of Education.

Ortiz, A. M. (2000). Expressing cultural identity in the learning community: Opportunities and challenges. In M. B. Baxter Magolda (Ed.), *Teaching to promote intellectual and personal maturity: Incorporating students' worldviews and identities into the learning process* (New Directions for Teaching and Learning No. 82, pp. 67-79). San Francisco: Jossey-Bass.

Pascarella, E. T., & Terenzini, P. T. (2005). *How college affects students: A third decade of research.* San Francisco: Jossey-Bass.

Pascarella, E. T., Terenzini, P. T., & Wolfle, L. (1986). Orientation to college and freshman year persistence/withdrawal decisions. *Journal of Higher Education, 57,* 155-175.

Pecora, P., Kessler, R., O'Brien, K., Downs, C., English, D., et al. (2005). *Improving family foster care: Findings from the Northwest Foster Care Alumni Study*. Seattle: Casey Family Programs.

Peter, K., & Forrest Cataldi, E. (2005). *The road less traveled? Students who enroll in multiple institutions* (NCES No. 2005-157). Washington, DC: U.S. Department of Education, National Center for Education Statistics.

Phinney, J. S. (1992). The multigroup ethnic identity measure: A new scale for use with diverse groups. *Journal of Adolescent Research, 7,* 156-176.

Planty, M., Hussar, W., Snyder, T., Kena, G., KewalRamani, A., Kemp, J. . . Dinkes, R. (2009). *The condition of education 2009* (NCES 2009-081). Washington, DC: U.S. Department of Education, National Center for Education Statistics.

Pope, R. L. (2000). The relationship between psychosocial development and racial identity of college students of color. *Journal of College Student Development, 41,* 302-312.

Rankin, S. R. (2005). Campus climates for sexual minorities. In R. L Sanlo (Ed.), *Gender identity and sexual orientation: Research, policy, and personal perspectives* (New Directions for Student Services No. 111, pp. 17-24). San Francisco: Jossey-Bass.

Robinson, D. A. G., Burns, C. F., & Gaw, K. F. (1996). Orientation programs: A foundation for student learning and success. In S. C. Ender, F. B. Newton, & R. B. Caple (Eds.), *Contributing to student learning: The role of student affairs* (New Directions for Student Services No. 75, pp. 55-68). San Francisco: Jossey-Bass.

Sanoff, A.P. (2006, March 10). What professors and teachers think: A perception gap over students' preparation. *The Chronicle of Higher Education*, p. B9.

Schlossberg, N. K., Waters, E. B., & Goodman, J. (1995). *Counseling adults in transition* (2nd ed.). New York: Springer.

Strange, C. C., & King, P. M. (1990). The professional practice of student development. In D. G. Creamer & Associates (Eds.), *College student development: Theory and practice for the 1990s*. Alexandria, VA: American College Personnel Association.

Terenzini, P. T. (1995). Academic and out-of-class influences on students' intellectual orientations. *Review of Higher Education, 19*(1), 23-44.

Tinto, V. (1987). *Leaving college: Rethinking the causes and cures of student attrition*. Chicago: University of Chicago Press.

Tinto, V. (1993). *Leaving college: Rethinking the causes and cures of student attrition* (2nd ed.). Chicago: University of Chicago Press.

U.S. Department of Education. (2006). *A test of leadership: Charting the future of U.S. higher education*. A report of the commission appointed by Secretary of Education Margaret Spellings. Washington, DC: Author.

U.S. Department of Health and Human Services. (2007). *AFCARS Report: Preliminary FY 2005 Estimates of September 2006*. Retrieved July 2009, from http://www.acf.hhs.gov/programs/cb/stats_research/afcars/tar/report13.htm

Upcraft, M. L., & Schuh, J. H. (1996). *Assessment in student affairs: A guide for practitioners*. San Francisco: Jossey-Bass.

Webster, B. H., & Bishaw, A. (2007) *Income, earnings, and poverty data from the 2006 American Community Survey*. Retrieved July 2009, from http://www.census.gov/prod/2007pubs/acs-08.pdf

Zakely, J. (2003). Orientation as a catalyst for student success: Effective retention through academic and social integration. In J. A. Ward-Roof & C. Hatch (Eds.). *Designing successful transitions: A guide for orientating students to college* (Monograph No. 13, 2nd ed., pp. 55-66). Columbia, SC: University of South Carolina, National Resource Center for The First-Year Experience and Students in Transition.

Chapter 12

Designing Orientation and Transition Programs for Transfer Students

Shandol C. Hoover

hanging enrollment patterns reflect an increased trend in the number of students attending multiple institutions (Jacobs, Lauren, Miller, & Nadler, 2004). According to the National Center for Education Statistics (2007), 60% of all students who graduate from a four-year institution began their collegiate career at a different institution. Of students beginning in the fall of 1995, approximately 40% attended at least two institutions over a six-year period, and at one point in time, 11% were co-enrolled in more then one college (Jacobs et al.). Further, at some institutions, new transfer students outnumbered the number of entering first-year students. In light of the growing transfer student numbers and a push from policy makers to assist students in attaining four-year degrees in a timely manner, it is critical for educators to examine the unique needs of this population and design intentional initiatives to aid in their transition and matriculation (Eggleston & Laanan, 2001; Goldsberry, McKenzie, & Miller, 2004; Kodama, 2002; Townsend, 2008; Zamani, 2001). This chapter describes the transfer student experience and highlights initiatives designed to facilitate seamless transitions and foster sustained student success.

Defining the Transfer Student Profile

In the higher education literature, transfer is defined as "the movement of a student from one postsecondary institution to another" (Cuseo, 1998, p. 1), while the term "native" is used to describe students who have attended the same institution for their entire undergraduate career (Kodama, 2002). It is important to note that although this definition provides a foundation, the definition of "transfer" can vary greatly from campus to campus. For example, some institutions identify a student previously enrolled in any course for at least one college credit after graduating from high school as a transfer, while another institution might identify a transfer student as any student having completed at least 12 college credits at another institution since high school (Kodama). As such, it is important to be cognizant of differing institutional definitions before generalizing information and experiences.

Defining a specific transfer profile is challenging as the transfer experience is varied with respect to the number of earned credits, types of educational experiences, and length of time between educational experiences (Kodoma, 2002). The decision to transfer can be prompted by a variety of factors related to access, finances, institutional proximity to family and friends, academics, and other personal reasons (Li, 2010; Townsend, 2008). The literature identifies the following transfer paths: (a) vertical transfers, moving from two-year institutions to four-year institutions; (b) horizontal/lateral transfers, moving between similar type institutions (two-year to two-year or four-year to four-year); and (c) reverse transfers, moving from four-year institutions to two-year institutions (Cuseo, 1998; Ward-Roof, Kashner, & Hodge, 2003). The term "swirling" identifies a fourth pattern that refers to students moving between multiple institutions (Borden, 2004; de los Santos & Wright, 1990; McCormick & Carroll, 1997). Although much of the research regarding transfer students focuses on vertical transfers, there is an emerging body of literature that explores the dynamics of four-year to four-year transfer experiences (Li).

As a whole, the transfer student population is rich in diversity. A review of the literature suggests that many transfer students also identity as first-generation students or nontraditional students with respect to age, family responsibilities, and commitments related to part-time or full-time work (Dennis, Calvillo, & Gonzalez, 2008; Horn & Nevill, 2006; Lehning, 2000). The diversity within the transfer population is not surprising given the community college populations from which they frequently come (Horn & Nevill; Ward-Roof et al.). Race, gender, age, ethnicity, and cultural background may impact a transfer students' adjustment to campus (Eggleston & Laanan, 2001; Wawrzynski, & Sedlacek, 2003); thus, it is important for institutions to define and identify the institutional transfer student profile. The creation of this profile can assist educators in designing intentional, holistic programs to address the needs of this diverse population (Hrabowski, 2010).

Understanding the Transfer Student Experience

Transfer students experience a variety of social, psychological, and academic adjustments as they acclimate to a new college environment (Laanan, 2001). Based upon qualitative studies conducted at a large, public research institution located in the Midwest, Townsend (2008) identifies the transfer transition as occurring in two stages, the first being the transfer process and the second being the experience after enrolling at the new institution. During the transfer process, Townsend suggests that among the most salient challenges students face is understanding the transfer credit evaluation process. Although articulation agreements can provide initial insight on applicability of previous credits, in some instances, agreements are challenging to access (Townsend). Further, few articulation agreements specify credit equivalencies for four-year to four-year transfer students (Enzi, Boehner, & McKeon, 2005; Li, 2010). When designing initiatives to assist transfer students, it is clear that one of the primary concerns to address early on is helping students understand how many credits are applicable towards electives, general education requirements, and academic major requirements (Townsend).

Beyond the acceptance notification, transfer students must then adjust to new academic and social environments, as well as, learn procedures for completing university business (Townsend, 2008). Although transfer students are familiar with aspects of these transition issues at their former institutions, it is important to recognize students must acclimate to a new institutional culture (Townsend). In addition, notification of admissions for transfer students is out of sync with the university's processes for currently enrolled students. Often notification of admission occurs after current students have registered for courses and important deadlines for housing, parking, and financial aid have passed. As a result, transfer students often describe the transition experience as confusing, frustrating, and stressful as they work to build their first schedule of classes and attempt to complete university business (Cuseo, 1998; Kodama, 2002; Laanan, 2001).

The stress associated with transitioning to a new institution may also manifest itself in a transfer student's academic performance. The literature articulates a phenomenon known as "transfer shock" to describe a temporary decline in grade point average during the initial transition period to the new institution (Hills, 1965; Laanan, 2001; Townsend, 2008). Studies conducted at national, state, and institutional levels and across a range of demographic variables show support for this phenomenon during the first semester on campus (Townsend & Wilson, 2006). The lower grade point average might be reflective of challenges related to adjusting to more rigorous academic demands, acclimating to a larger campus environment, navigating a new institutional culture, and managing faculty expectations (Dennis et al., 2008; Townsend & Wilson). It is important to note that most research finds transfer students progress past the initial drop in GPA, steadily improve academic work, and persist toward degree completion (Dennis et al.).

On average, transfer students are less likely to graduate in four years compared to native students (NCES, 2003). Students attending a single institution completed a four-year degree in 51 months, while students attending two or more institutions completed in 59 months, and students attending three or more institutions completed the degree in 67 months (NCES). With respect to vertical transfers, students transferring from a two-year institution to a public, four-year institution attained a degree in a year and one-half longer than students beginning at public, four-year institutions and roughly two years longer compared to students beginning at private, four-year institutions (NCES). The extra time toward degree could result from a variety of factors such as switching academic majors or needing to repeat coursework due to non-transferable credits (Enzi et al., 2005; Li, 2010).

It is well established that engaging in cocurricular activities and interacting with faculty and peers outside of class-required activities are positively associated with student persistence (Astin 1984). Kuh (2009) suggests that engagement in high-impact activities such as study abroad, student/faculty research projects, capstone courses, and internships can help students with at-risk characteristics persists towards degree attainment. Unfortunately, although transfer students participate in required class-related activities to the same degree as native students, research suggests that compared to native students, transfer students are less involved in student organizations, have fewer informal interactions with peers and faculty outside of class, and are less likely to engage in research with faculty. Within the transfer student population at four-year institutions, horizontal transfer students are more likely to engage in high-impact activities than vertical transfer students (Terris, 2009). Often, the decreased level of involvement is attributed to outside commitments such as family and work responsibilities or lack of interest; however, educators should consider strategies to make such opportunities more accessible to transfer students such as adjusting the timing of events and remarketing events towards transfers (Townsend & Wilson, 2006).

Enhancing Transfer Student Success

Fostering transfer student success involves validating students' prior college experience, assisting transfer students through the transfer process, orienting students to the new institutional culture, and integrating students into the academic and social fabric of the campus community (Townsend & Wilson, 2006). The following section describes programs and services that can assist transfer students toward degree completion in a timely, supported and efficient manner.

Determining the Institutional Transfer Student Profile

As mentioned previously, the complexity and variation of transfer students' experiences, is a prompt for educators to review institutional demographics and establish an institution-specific transfer student profile before designing transfer student programming (Goldsberry et al., 2004).

Data obtained through the admission process or through departments responsible for institutional studies and assessment can inform the campus community about the incoming transfer cohort with respect to age, ethnicity, race, educational background, first-generation status, and other important identifying factors. Focus groups and individual interviews serve a dual purpose of providing important qualitative information as well as exemplifying that the institution values listening to transfer student voices (Townsend, 2008). Reviewing such data can provide insight into important trends related to academic major aspirations, previous educational experiences, campus engagement, estimated time to graduation, and the overall transition experience. Understanding the specific transfer student profile provides a framework for educators to design intentional success initiatives and assists in facilitating conversations with stakeholders about the importance of engaging transfer students in the university community (Goldsberry et al.).

Designing Orientation Programs for Transfer Students

Although there is not a one-size-fits-all transfer student orientation model, there are important considerations for creating effective orientation programming. In addition to helping transfer students navigate the new institutional cultural (Eggleston & Laanan, 2001), an orientation program should validate transfer students' prior experiences. In addition, the orientation program should address students' immediate needs and concerns such as transfer credit evaluations, academic advising, housing, financial aid, and identifying campus resources (Goldsberry et al., 2004). Transfer orientation models usually include one, or some combination of, the following: a summer transition program, presemester program, or a first-semester orientation seminar. In addition, peer mentoring is a component commonly found in most models (Cuseo, 2001). Online orientation programs can be an appropriate complement to traditional orientation programs if the programs are intentionally designed and incorporate purposeful tasks that help students learn about the institutional culture and the expectations of being a citizen of the campus community.

Timing of orientation programs is an important consideration. With an increase in articulation agreements established between community colleges and four-year institutions, the number of transfer students with sophomore and junior standing is growing. As a result, students may have few lower-division courses to complete and may be ready to progress to upper-division courses required for the major. These circumstances have an impact on the academic advising and course registration process for upper-level transfer students. If course registration is an aspect of transfer student orientation, it is important to consider facilitating the transfer student orientation program during a time in which both lower-division and upper-division courses remain available (Cuseo, 2001).

James Madison University (JMU), a public institution located in Harrisonburg, Virginia, annually enrolls approximately 16,619 undergraduate degree-seeking students, of whom approximately 651 are transfer students (JMU, 2010). Orientation programs for incoming JMU transfer students occur prior to programs for incoming first-year students. This is particularly beneficial for students needing to fulfill lower-division courses, as transfer students are afforded first availability of selected courses before first-year students. However, the timing still poses a challenge for students ready to enter major courses, which typically have limited availability as current students have already registered for courses (T. McCoy-Ntiamoah, personal communication, March 8, 2010).

The University of Central Florida (UCF) located in Orlando, Florida, has an undergraduate population of 47,000 and annually enrolls approximately 7,000 transfer students at the Orlando campus. UCF sees orientation as a key element in the retention of new students; thus, it requires all new transfer students to participate in orientation. Orientation programming begins during the spring semester prior to fall matriculation, allowing incoming transfer students to register for fall courses at the same time as other currently enrolled students with a comparable number of completed academic credits. In total, the UCF Orlando campus facilitates approximately 16 programs inviting 450-500 students throughout the entire year (J. Ritchie, personal communication, October 13, 2009).

Further, to offer UCF transfer students greater flexibility in completing the mandatory orientation requirement, students have the option of either participating in a day-long on-campus program or completing part of the program online and coming to campus for academic advising and course registration only (approximately four hours). Approximately 1,000 students chose to participate in the online program. Students review online modules facilitated via the UCF online course system and must attain a 100% on quizzes addressing the material. Mirroring the on-campus orientation presentations, online orientation modules include an overview of academic policies, academic integrity, career services, financial aid, student involvement opportunities, health services, university libraries, counseling and wellness, academic college specific information, and other important information related to campus departments, policies, and services. Initial assessments conducted by the UCF First Year Experience Office suggest that there is greater material retention and comprehension among the students who completed the online orientation compared to the students who attended the on-campus program (J. Ritchie, personal communication, October 13, 2009).

The University of Minnesota, Twin Cities, enrolls approximately 33,000 undergraduate students and admits approximately 900 transfer students for the spring term and 1,800 transfer students for the fall term. Attending orientation is a requirement for all new transfer students. Prior to 2004, transfer orientation was an adapted version of the first-year orientation schedule; the morning consisted of workshops and presentations related to campus services, information, and resources while the afternoon was focused on academic advising and course registration. Assessment data from evaluations and focus groups indicated the program was not congruent with incoming transfer students' concerns at that particular point in time. Apprehensive about afternoon sessions related to academic advising and course registration, the transfer students struggled to retain information presented in the morning workshops. As such, a campus-wide committee worked to create a new orientation model that allows students the flexibility of attending a full-day on-campus program with academic advising and course registration in the morning followed by afternoon workshops or a half-day on-campus program with advance participation in an online orientation. The flexible program model recognizes transfer students' diverse experiences and empowers students to select the program that is the best fit for their needs (K. Granholm, personal communication, October 12, 2009).

Parent and Family Orientation Programming

Knowing that involved parent and family members can augment student success (Cutright, 2008), creating intentional programming for parents and families of transfer students is an emerging focus in the orientation field. Although there is much diversity within the transfer parent and family population and it is challenging to design a one-size-fits-all program, there are important messages and information that serve parents and family members of transfer students. Orientation programming for parents and families of transfers should communicate opportunities for appropriate involvement and offer strategies and information for parents and families to support transfer students toward graduation.

Noting that transfer students are very diverse and may include a variety of family members in their support systems, all parent and family communications and presentations should use inclusive language. In terms of content, it is important to acknowledge the previous experiences parents/

family members offer while highlighting what may be unique or different about academic and social environments at the new institution. Most notably, it is important to communicate that the overall institutional culture might be different and that conducting university business related to paying bills, registering for courses, scheduling academic advising appointments, accessing student information, and other related tasks likely differ from previous experiences. Sharing insights on transfer shock with parent and family members at orientation serves to normalize this phenomenon as well as helps parents and family members consider strategies for supporting students through the new academic challenges. Recognizing that transfer students often have a short time to degree completion, it is appropriate to incorporate staff from Career Services to suggest how parents and families can assist students in preparing for careers after graduation. Depending upon the institutional transfer profile, orientation professionals might partner with family service and/or nontraditional student colleagues to discuss services related to supporting students with children or other family obligations. On-campus employment opportunities, parking, transportation, and off-campus living might also be important orientation partners.

The University of California-Davis (UC Davis), located in Davis, California, enrolls approximately 24,655 undergraduates. In 2009, the incoming class consisted of 4,413 new students admitted directly out of high school and 2,237 transfer students (UC Davis Communications, 2009). Given the large number of transfer students at the institution, a Transfer Reentry Veterans (TRV) Student Center was established to provide helpful online resources that assist transfer students with meeting important deadlines and connecting to campus services. UC Davis also offers an intentionally designed Transfer Family Orientation program. The program runs parallel to Transfer Student Orientation, with separate sessions that provide insight into ways family members can assist students towards graduation. Program highlights include opportunities for family members to engage with Family Hosts, current UC Davis transfer students, to learn about the transfer student experience first hand. The Counseling and Psychological Services office speaks to specific transfer family transition issues, while other sessions provide insight on UC Davis processes and procedures related to managing student accounts and loans, course registration, health services and insurance, campus safety protocols and procedures, and other related services. Family members also have the opportunity to stay in a residence hall during orientation, thus, providing a low-cost option for housing and exposing them to the benefits of on-campus living (UC Davis, New Student Services, 2010).

Role of Peer Transfer Student Leaders

Recruiting, hiring, selecting, and training student staff to facilitate orientation-related programs is critical to the success of transition initiatives. Work by Townsend and Wilson (2006) suggests that incoming transfer students find insights from current transfer students especially helpful. Orientation professionals should make a concerted effort to hire current transfer students to serve as orientation leaders. In addition to assisting new students, empowering transfer students to serve as student leaders provides a meaningful engagement opportunity for transfer students.

DePaul University, a private Catholic University, situated in Chicago, Illinois, enrolls approximately 16,000 undergraduate students on two campuses. The entering class includes approximately 2,700 first-year students and 2,000 transfer students. Operating on a quarter system, DePaul facilitates 23, one-day transfer student orientation programs referred to as Transition DePaul. To help implement the program, the Office of Academic Enrichment selects a diverse staff of approximately 10 to 15 current transfer students to serve as Transition Leaders. Participant feedback and evaluations suggest that new transfers place high value on the opportunity to engage with current transfer student leaders. Among the challenging aspects of the DePaul transfer experience is the transition to the quarter system as most incoming transfer students bring experiences from a semester system. The Transition Leaders are able to articulate specific strategies for not only transitioning to the new academic and social environment but also for adjusting to the new institutional cultural in general (C. Ruff, personnel communication, March 8, 2010).

In addition to enhancing the transition of new students, the Transition Leader experience serves as a dynamic leadership opportunity for current transfer students. Recognizing that transfer students often maintain a challenging schedule that might impact their ability to engage in campus activities and organizations, the position hours are intentionally scheduled to provide flexibility for leaders who enroll in summer school, engage in internships, and maintain other full-time work responsibilities. The training not only helps students articulate information related to campus services such as academic advising, adult student affairs, commuter needs, and other campus resources but also strives to help students develop skills related to group facilitation, public speaking, and working as a member of a diverse team. The training curriculum is grounded in an overall socially responsible leadership framework, one of DePaul's core student development goals. As such, the Transition Leader position serves as an avenue to welcome new transfer students and engage current transfer students in a meaningful way (C. Ruff, personnel communication, March 8, 2010).

Located in Chapel Hill, North Carolina, the University of North Carolina at Chapel Hill enrolls approximately 18,000 undergraduate students and typically enrolls 800-900 new transfer students each fall. Transfer students are admitted in April and are eligible to register for classes upon paying the enrollment fee. In addition to facilitating a one-day optional orientation program offered in June and again in August, the Office of New Student & Carolina Parent Programs coordinates a T-Link mentoring program to help new transfer students become acclimated to the University. T-Links mentors, comprised of current transfer students, serve as resources for easing the academic and social transition of new transfer students. Approximately 30-40 students are selected to serve as T-Link mentors. Each mentor is assigned roughly 30 new students based upon hometown regions, prior institutional type, and academic major. Throughout the spring and summer, T-Link mentors communicate with assigned students via e-mail to answer questions related to living and learning at Carolina, help new transfers develop a social network, and provide referrals to appropriate campus resources. T-Link mentors are also paired with Orientation Leaders during the optional Transfer Student Orientation program to ensure new students are presented an opportunity to engage with current transfer students and learn first-hand, about the Carolina transfer student experience. The formal aspect of the program concludes with T-Link mentors hosting new transfer students at Fall Week of Welcome programs during the first week of school (J. Hewitt, personnel communication, October 8, 2009).

Creating Transfer Specific Publications

Just as new student checklists and publications are helpful for first-time college students, publications and web resources specifically designed for transfer students can be instrumental in helping transfers students navigate their new university. JMU mails a publication entitled *Transfer One Book* to all admitted transfer students. The guide provides information on transfer credit evaluation, housing, academic curriculum components, graduation requirements, transfer specific resources, and checklists related to the transfer student transition process. As such, the guide not only assists students through the admissions decision but also helps transfer students navigate the transition to the new institutional culture in an organized and informed way (JMU Orientation Office, 2010).

Transfer Student Seminars

Noting the positive outcomes associated with first-year seminars such as retention, academic performance, and overall student success, Cuseo (2001) urges four-year institutions to offer transfer seminars, suggesting that such courses might help transfer students adjust to the new institutional cultural and refine academic major goals and aspirations. Transfer seminars vary greatly in structure ranging from a loosely structured workshop series to a more formal credit bearing course. Flaga (2006) suggests that where possible, institutions offer transfer seminars that are specific to academic college or major. This structure might assist students in further refining academic major plans as well as connecting with faculty, staff, and students with similar academic interests.

Virginia Polytechnic Institute and State University (Virginia Tech) located in Blacksburg, Virginia, enrolls approximately 22,987 undergraduates. Each year, roughly 1,000 transfer students enroll at Virginia Tech, 50% of whom transfer from a Virginia community college. All new undergraduate transfer students may participate in a Transfer Student Seminar Series (TS3), a free, four-week series that is specifically designed to provide continuous support to transfer students. Students may elect to attend one or more of the free seminars. Topics typically include campus resources, time management, working with professors, and participating in research (J. Thompson, personal communication, May 15, 2008).

The University of North Carolina Charlotte (UNCC), located in the Charlotte, North Carolina, metropolitan area enrolls approximately 18,000 undergraduate students. Admitting students in the fall, spring, and summer terms, UNCC enrolls approximately 3,187 new first-year students and 2,340 new transfer students. UNCC offers a three-credit seminar, UCOL1011, that is designed to help students become more engaged in the intellectual and cocurricular campus community as well as enhance problem-solving and communication skills. Intentional experiential course assignments not only allow students to learn about important campus services but also to establish connections with faculty and staff in the campus community. In addition to helping students through the transition to the new institutional culture, the course allows students to progress towards the completion of a general education requirement (S. Calega, personal communication, March 4, 2010).

As transfer seminars become more plentiful, seminar textbooks are also evolving. Two commonly used texts include: *Transitions: A Guide for the Transfer Student* (Weir, 2008) and the *Transfer Student Companion* (Grites & Rondeau, 2009). These texts provide insight on topics related to transition issues specific to transfer students including transfer shock, goal setting in the new academic environment, career planning, time management, and planning for the first year after graduation.

Establishing Transfer Centers/Offices

Transfer centers serve to help connect transfer students to important campus services (Zamini, 2001). Although many transfer centers exist as an office, several institutions host virtual transfer centers (With & McGuire, 2009). Often, transfer centers are aligned with the pre-admissions aspect of the transition and connect students to the admissions process, orientation, financial aid, credit evaluation, and academic advising. The goal of such centers is to serve students through the first semester so that students are more comfortable and confident navigating the campus. Other transfer centers expand services to connect students to career planning, academic skill enhancement, and student involvement opportunities (With & McGuire).

Northern Illinois University (NIU) is a teaching and research institution with a student enrollment of approximately 24,424 total graduate and undergraduate students located in Dekalb, Illinois. NIU enrolls approximately 2,000 transfer students in the fall, of whom 75% identify as

Illinois public community college transfers. NIU also enrolls approximately 1,000 transfer students in the spring (NIU, 2010a). The NIU transfer center, closely connected with Undergraduate Admissions, serves prospective students, community college staff, and NIU community members by communicating information related to articulation, dual admissions, limited admission majors, and other related admissions questions. The center also offers social media and networking opportunities for students to ask transfer center staff questions as well as communicate upcoming transfer admission-related events. The center functions to serve students through admissions and towards the next steps in the transition process such as orientation (NIU, 2010b).

The University of North Texas (UNT), located in Denton, Texas, enrolls approximately 34,698 undergraduate students with an admissions profile of approximately 3,335 new students enrolling from high school and 4,012 new transfer students (With & McGuire, 2009). The UNT Transfer Center is comprehensive, serving prospective students, new students, and current students. Most notably, the center hosts Transfer Student Orientation and Transfer Ambassadors, a mentor program that connects new students to current transfer students, faculty, and staff. Recognizing the academic excellence and involvement of transfer students, the center is home to Tau Sigma, an honorary association for transfers. To foster an inclusive living community, the center works with two residence hall wings that are dedicated as transfer student communities as well as oversees lockers for commuting transfer students. Transfer Talkbacks are monthly workshops that allow transfers the opportunity to share insights regarding their transfer experience and discuss pressing issues and concerns with fellow students and staff. The Center also hosts online web resources to connect prospective students, new students and current transfer students to important campus services and programs (UNT, 2009). In addition to providing intentional programs and services for transfer students, it is interesting to note that UNT is home to the Association of the Study of Transfer Students (ASTS), which strives to promote transfer student success, expand transfer student related research, and facilitate partnerships between two-year and four-year institutions. ASTS hosts the National Institute for the Study of Transfer Students each winter.

Articulation Agreements

Occurring on the state, institutional, and programmatic level, articulation agreements are often cited as a critical element for fostering a successful transfer experience (Wellman, 2002). Articulation agreements are "cooperative relationships [between institutions] that can be legal, governed by state entities, or voluntary" (Ward-Roof et al., 2003, p. 105). Typically, articulation agreements determine how the courses a student completed at a specific two-year institution will transfer to a specific four-year institution. The degree to which these agreements are clearly outlined and accessible online can significantly ease a student's transition of credits from one institution to another (Townsend & Wilson, 2006).

Articulation databases make it easier for students to determine how courses will transfer to other institutions. Developing agreements out of increased population growth and the number of students entering college, Texas, California, and Florida are among the states with advanced articulation agreements. As policymakers are pressing toward greater access and efficient transfer transition processes, more articulation agreements are being developed and refined. The American Association of Collegiate Registrars and Admissions Officers (AACRAO), a nonprofit association serving admissions and registrar staff, maintains a comprehensive list of state transfer articulation program web sites. The AACRAO list provides insight on the legislation related to the state articulation program as well as a web link to the articulation database (AACRAO, 2010).

The Course Applicability System (CAS) is a proprietary database developed by redLantern, LLC and used by some institutions to facilitate an easier connection between transfer articulation systems and automated degree audit systems. Also referred to as U.Select, the system is free for students to view course equivalencies, review program requirements, enter and store coursework, and request transfer evaluations from participating institutions. Institutions pay a fee to participate in the database (redLantern, LLC, 2010). The primary difference between statewide articulation databases and U.Select is that the latter helps students determine how courses will transfer to an institution in a different state, whereas the former typically provides information on course articulation between institutions within one state. Although two-year to four-year articulation agreements are quickly evolving and becoming more accessible, Li (2010) calls for greater attention on four-year to four-year articulation programs. Often, four-year to four-year transfer students must wait for admissions staff or faculty from academic departments to complete a transfer course evaluation to determine how many credits are applicable towards curriculum and degree requirements. The course review process can be time consuming and depending upon the outcome, students might be required to repeat courses, which can delay academic progress. Statewide core curricula and common course numbering systems facilitate a more efficient transfer credit review of not only two-year to four-year students but also four-year to four-year transfer students (Li.). It is important to note that although articulation programs and other related transfer credit policies can facilitate a seamless transfer of credits, intentional orientation programming is critical to assisting students with the transition to the new institutional culture (Townsend & Wilson, 2006).

Conclusion

Projected population growth and legislative efforts to increase college access by strengthening collaborative relationships between two- and four-year institutions are prompts for educators to examine the transfer student population. Transfer students add to alumni bases, shape both the on- and off-campus culture, and bring rich diversity to the campus community. When designing orientation and transition programming for transfer students, it is important to first understand the institutional profile of the population and to then incorporate both academic and cocurricular programming that validates students' prior experience and prepares students to be successful in the new campus community. The flexibility of online orientation programs, evolution of transfer centers, expansion of online articulation databases, development of transfer student parent and family orientation programs, and an emerging body of literature regarding the transfer student experience are evidence that progress is being made to ease transfer students' transitions, but educators must continue to assess transfer student needs and remain committed to assisting this population.

References

American Association of Collegiate Registrars and Admissions Professionals (AACRAO). (2010). *Transfer and state articulation websites.* Retrieved March 8, 2010, from http://www.aacrao. org/pro_development/transfer.cfm

Astin, A. W. (1984). Student involvement: A developmental theory for higher education. *Journal of College Student Development*, 25, 297-308.

Borden, V. (2004). Accommodating student swirl. *Change, 36*(2), 10-17.

Cuseo, J. (1998). *The transfer transition: A summary of key issues, target areas, and tactics for reform.* (Report No. JC990017). Washington, DC: Department of Education. (ERIC Document Reproduction Services No. ED425771)

Cuseo, J. (2001). *The transfer transition: Student advancement from 2-year to 4-year institutions* (Report No. JC02199). Washington, DC: U.S. Department of Education. (ERIC Document Reproduction Services No. ED462130)

Cutright, M. (2008). From helicopter parent to valued partner: Shaping the parental relationship for student success. In B.O. Barefoot (Ed.), *The first year and beyond: Rethinking the challenge of collegiate transition.* (New Directions for Higher Education No. 144). San Francisco: Jossey-Bass.

de los Santos, A., Jr., & Wright, I. (1990). Maricopa's swirling students: Earning one-third of Arizona State's bachelor's degrees. *Community, Technical, and Junior College Journal, 60*(6,), 32-34.

Dennis, J. M., Calvillo E., & Gonzalez, A. (2008). The role of psychosocial variables in understanding the achievement and retention of transfer students at an ethnically diverse urban university. *Journal of College Student Development, 49*(6), 535-550.

Eggleston, L. E., & Laanan, F. S. (2001). Making the transition to the senior institution. In F. S. Laanan (Ed.), *Transfer students: Trends and issues.* (New Directions for Community Colleges No. 114, pp. 87-97). San Francisco, CA: Jossey-Bass.

Enzi, M. B., Boehner, J. A., & McKeon, H. P. (2005). *Transfer students: Postsecondary institutions could promote more consistent consideration of coursework by not basing determinations on accreditation.* Washington, DC: U.S. Government Accountability Office.

Flaga, C. (2006). The process of transition for community college transfer students. *Community College Journal of Research & Practice, 30*(1), 3-19.

Goldsberry, K. L., McKenzie, B. L., & Miller, D. (2004). Designing effective transition programs for transfer students. In M. J. Fabich (Ed.), *Orientation planning manual 2004* (pp. 39-42). Flint, MI: National Orientation Directors Association.

Grites T. & Rondeau, S. (2009). *Transfer student companion.* Boston, MA: Houghton Mifflin Harcourt.

Hills, J. R. (1965). Transfer shock: The academic performance of the junior college transfer. *The Journal of Experimental Education, 33*(2), 201-215.

Horn, L., & Nevill, S. (2006). *Profile of undergraduates in U.S. postsecondary education Institutions: 2003-04: With a special analysis of community college students* (NCES 2006-184). Washington, DC: National Center for Education Statistics, U.S. Department of Education.

Hrabowski, F. (2010, January 28). *Keynote address.* National Institute for the Study of Transfer Students Conference, Addison, TX.

Jacobs, B.C., Lauren, B., Miller, M. T., & Nadler, D. P. (Eds.). (2004). *The college transfer student in America: The forgotten student.* Washington, DC: AACRAO.

James Madison University. (2010). *About JMU: Just the facts.* Retrieved March 8, 2010, from http://www.jmu.edu/jmuweb/aboutJMU/factsheet.shtml

James Madison University Orientation Office. (2010). *The transfer one book.* Retrieved March 8, 2010, from http://www.jmu.edu/orientation/transfer/fall.shtml

Kodama, C. M. (2002). Marginality of transfer commuter students. *NASPA Journal, 39*(3), 233-250.

Kuh, G. D. (2009). What student affairs professionals need to know about student engagement. *Journal of College Student Development, 50*(6), 683-706.

Laanan, F. S. (2001). Transfer student adjustment. In F. S. Laanan (Ed.), *Transfer students: Trends and issues* (New Directions for Community Colleges No. 114, pp. 87-97). San

Lehning, E. M. (2000). The influence of student development in articulation agreements. *Journal of College Orientation and Transition, 7*(2), 33-40.

Li, D. (2010). They need help: Transfer students from four-year to four-year institutions. *The Review of Higher Education, 33*(2), 207-238.

McCormick, A. C., & Carroll, C. D. (1997). *Transfer behavior among beginning postsecondary students, 1989-94.* Washington, DC: National Center for Education Statistics Report, U.S. Department of Education.

National Center for Education Statistics. (2003). *The condition of education 2003* (NCES 2003-067), Indicator 21. Washington, DC: U.S. Department of Education. Retrieved February 7, 2010, from http://nces.ed.gov/fastfacts/display.asp?id=40

National Center for Education Statistics. (2007). *The condition of education.* Washington, DC: U.S. Department of Education.

Northern Illinois University. (2010a). *Fast facts.* Retrieved March 8, 2010, from http://www.niu.edu/about/fastfacts.shtml

Northern Illinois University. (2010b). *Undergraduate admissions: Transfer admissions.* Retrieved March 8, 2010, from http://www.niu.edu/admissions/transfer/transfercenter/index.shtml

redLantern, LLC. (2010). *About u.select.* Retrieved, March 8, 2010, from http://clients.redlanternu.com/home/display/USL/About+u.select

Terris, B. (2009, November 8). Transfer students are less likely to take part in 'high impact' activities. *Chronicle of Higher Education.* Retrieved February 7, 2010, from http://chronicle.com/article/Transfer-Students-Are-Less-/49070/

Townsend, B. K. (2008). "Feeling like a freshman again": The transfer student transition. In B. O. Barefoot (Ed.), *The first year and beyond: Rethinking the challenge of collegiate transition* (New Directions for Higher Education No. 144). San Francisco: Jossey-Bass.

Townsend, B. K., & Wilson, K. B. (2006). A hand hold for a little bit: Factors facilitating the success of community college transfer students. *Journal of College Student Development, 47,* 439-456.

University of California Davis, Communications. (2009). *UC Davis Facts.* Retrieved March 7, 2010, from http://facts.ucdavis.edu/

University of California Davis, New Student Services. (2010). *Transfer family orientation.* Retrieved March 7, 2010, from http://orientation.ucdavis.edu/transfers/programtransferparents.asp

University of North Texas. (2009). *Transfer center.* Retrieved March 8, 2010, from http://transfercenter.unt.edu/index.html

Ward-Roof, J. A., Kashner, P., & Hodge, V. (2003). Orienting transfer students. In J. A. Ward-Roof & C. Hatch (Eds.), *Designing successful transitions: A guide for orienting students to college* (Monograph No. 13, 2nd ed., pp. 97-107). Columbia, SC: National Resource Center for The First-Year Experience and Students in Transition.

Wawrzynski, M. R., & Sedlacek, W. E. (2003). Race and gender differences in the transfer student experience. *Journal of College Student Development, 44,* 489-499.

Weir, S. B. (2008). *Transitions: A guide for the transfer student.* Boston, MA: Thompson Wadsworth.

Wellman, J. (2002). *State policy and community college–baccalaureate transfer* (National Center Report No. 02-06). San Jose, CA: National Center for Public Policy and Higher Education and the Institute for Higher Education Policy.

With, E., & McGuire, M. (2009, May 27). *Best practices for transfer: Transfer centers.* NISOD International Conference on Teaching and Leadership Excellence, Austin, TX.

Zamani, E. M. (2001). Institutional responses to barriers to the transfer process. In F. S. Laanan (Ed.), *Transfer students: Trends and issues* (New Directions for Community Colleges No. 114, pp. 15-24). San Francisco: Jossey-Bass.

Chapter 13

Nontraditional Is the New Traditional: Understanding Today's College Student

Michael J. Knox and Brittany D. Henderson

Higher education professionals have for years noted an upward trend in the number of non-traditional students on most college and university campuses (Rosenbaum, Deil-Amen, & Person, 2006; Seftor & Turner, 2002; Spitzer, 2000). This increased enrollment of nontraditional students has changed the profile of higher education students; no longer is the 35-year-old, married-with-children student seeking his/her first bachelor's degree unique. In today's college environment, these students are plentiful in number, and on certain campuses, community colleges and market-funded private colleges in particular, they have even replaced "traditional" students to become the "new traditional" student (Headden, 2009).

Moreover, for the first time in our modern society, adults outnumber youth (Merriam, Caffarella, & Baumgartner, 2007). This coupled with the recent economic downturn, increased tuition benefits for military veterans, and the inevitable decrease of people aged 18 to 22 in our population as the Baby Boomer generation ages (Headden, 2009) means it is unlikely that any of our college campuses will be untouched by this trend. Alarmingly, while college enrollment among nontraditional students has increased, many of these students fail to complete degrees or certificates that will better prepare them for the workplace (Rosenbaum et al., 2006). Additionally, nontraditional students drop out of college at a much higher rate than their traditional counterparts, with a graduation rate of only 10.8% (Headden).

As the nontraditional student population has grown, our understanding of their characteristics has changed. No longer are nontraditional students classified merely by their age, but also by the degree to which they can be described by a particular set of characteristics, which may include marital status, the number of hours the student works per week, the student's ethnic and cultural background, a learning or physical disability, the educational background of the student's parents, the distance a student commutes to campus, or whether some or all of her/his coursework is completed online. Indeed, nontraditional learners can now be categorized by the number of characteristics each student exhibits (Horn, 1996; Macari, Maples, & D'Andrea, 2005-2006; Spellman, 2007). In the end, this method of defining the nontraditional learner tends to be more inclusive and, as a result, allows orientation professionals and other practitioners to better meet the needs of this growing student population.

Despite the increases in the number of nontraditional students attending postsecondary institutions, policies, procedures, and programs have continued to emulate the traditional four-year college model. Resources are often poured into programs for first-year students or seniors, while nontraditionals have needs that are not well-served by programs designed for traditional populations.

Moreover, some states, such as Texas, have even implemented policies that penalize students who do not maintain progress towards a four-year degree plan (TX. Const., amend. 54.068(a) and (c)). While these plans may provide motivation for traditional students to stay on track, they may create unintended difficulties for nontraditionals. Orientation and retention professionals should design programs with the differing needs of these students in mind. After all, persistence to graduation begins for many students in their orientation to the campus.

The purpose of this chapter is to describe the nontraditional student population; to identify the motivations and needs of the nontraditional student population; and to make recommendations for practices that serve this population via campus orientation, retention, and transition programs.

By the Numbers: Nontraditional Student Population Trends

The past two decades have seen dramatic changes in the makeup of all student populations, with many of these trends strongly in place by the end of the 1990s. For example, by 1995, only about 20% of college students were full-time, residential students under the age of 22 (Spitzer, 2000). From 1984 to 1994, the minority population, including Asian, Hispanic, African American, and Native American students, increased 61%, while the White population increased just 5.1% over the same time period. By the mid-1990s, 40% of the undergraduate student population was already over 25 years old, and 43% were attending college on a part-time basis. By 1997, the median student age among all college students was between 22 and 24, with approximately 29% over the age of 30 (Seftor & Turner, 2002).

In addition to the ethnic/cultural diversity and the increase in the median age of the college student, a commonality found throughout the current nontraditional student population is that of managing multiple priorities, which compete with their educational goals. The number of part-time students is increasing, and studies also show an increase in the number of students with dependents other than a spouse and in students who work full-time (Marques, 2007; NCES, 2002).

Another notable trend in the overall college student population is the increasing role community colleges and proprietary institutions play in educating nontraditional students. In 1970, community colleges accounted for approximately 27% of the total college-going population in the country, that percentage increased to 37% by 1980 and maintained about the same ratio through the 1990s (Seftor & Turner, 2002). Over the years, a large number of the students enrolled at community colleges have been nontraditional. Alongside the growth of the community college population, the number of nontraditional students enrolled in private for-profit institutions has also increased dramatically (Nunley, 2007). Rosenbaum et al. (2006) state since these types of institutions serve the nontraditional student population in such large numbers, there is much to learn about how these institutions engage students who come to college campuses because, in many cases, students are ill-prepared for navigating the complex systems our institutions have created and are inexperienced in making informed choices on their own.

Nontraditional Student Motivations for Attending College

The competing priorities that define the nontraditional student population can also provide clues to identify student motivations for enrolling in a postsecondary institution. Work or career-related issues, life transitions, and past experiences are often strong motivators for nontraditional students to pursue an education. Understanding these motivations can help orientation, transition, and retention professionals design programs that best respond to the needs of this ever-growing student population.

Since the mid-1960s, job-related motivations have been consistently identified as a reason for nontraditional students to enter postsecondary education (Merriam et al., 2007). Many nontraditional students find that returning to school and earning a degree can teach them new skills necessary for professional advancement. Nontraditional students tend to perceive a financial benefit to earning a college degree, as well. For example, research shows that in 1979, a college graduate's first job paid an average of 35% more than a high school graduate and in 1999, that difference was 80% (Rothstein, 2000). These job-related motivations and financial benefits, when supported by university services, can be powerful enough to impact the persistence of these students. Because work and career-related issues are often a significant motivating factor for nontraditional students, orientation programs should highlight career services offered by the institution in order to maximize the use of these services by the nontraditional student population.

Additionally, past experiences can often motivate students to pursue higher education. Breese and O'Toole (1995) conducted a qualitative study examining the issues and events that led women at an urban, commuter campus to enroll in postsecondary education. They found that for the majority of these women, ranging in age from 28 to 64, past life experiences played a significant role in determining their degree programs and involvement in campus activities. For instance, one participant noted that her role as a caregiver for most of her life greatly influenced her choice to enter the nursing field. Another noted that she chose social work since she had similar experiences and was able to relate to the battered women she anticipated would be her future clients. Additionally, Headden (2009) reported more than 40% of the students enrolled in an online gerontology program at Portland Community College were over 50 years old. Headden suggested the program attracted people not only because of the growing number of jobs in this field but also because students could relate their coursework to the experiences they had in their own lives. Wlodkowski (2008) concurred, stating "[w]hen adults begin courses or new learning activities, we can provide experiences from which they can derive higher self-efficacy and, consequently, greater self-confidence as learners" (p. 188). Based on this research, orientation professionals can better meet the needs of the nontraditional populations by inviting current nontraditional students to share their stories and motivations. Additional considerations are to include nontraditional students as orientation leaders, on information panels, or as small group leaders who can share their stories and provide encouragement.

It is important to remember that for many nontraditional student learners, their past experiences and their desire to enter/re-enter the workforce with skills needed by employers can weigh heavily on the decisions they make to integrate their new role as a student into their identities. Despite the research that has been conducted since 1965 to determine the underlying motivations of nontraditional students' pursuit of higher education, it is also important to note that for today's nontraditional students these motivations are "many, complex, and subject to change" (Merriam et al., 2007, p. 65). Given this information, practitioners must continue to assess the motivations of the nontraditional student to ensure that they are designing programs that can appeal to a wide variety of students and address a myriad of student needs. Assessment of these motivations can be achieved in a number of ways. The Noel-Levitz Adult Student Priorities Survey (2009) monitors student satisfaction and offers a glimpse into motivations for attending school by asking students to indicate how important certain factors were in their decision to enroll (e.g., cost, financial aid, academic reputation, size of institution, future employment opportunities, recommendations from family/friends/employer, campus location, availability of evening/weekend classes, and personalized attention prior to enrollment). Collecting and analyzing this information would help orientation professionals design programs to meet the needs of the nontraditional population. At the same time, sharing this information with colleagues across campus may encourage them to consider the needs of these incoming students in their program design and service delivery.

Understanding Nontraditional Student Needs

Much of what we know about what leads to success in college is based on research done on mostly White, full-time, residential students (Pascarella & Terenzini, 1998). Even current research on nontraditional student development is rooted in traditional models of student development theory (Macari et al., 2005-2006). Given the vast change in demographics in our college-going population and that what we know is based on a completely different student body, it is important to reconsider what is effective in orientation programs, particularly if the campus serves large numbers of commuter or nontraditional students. Although past research may not include all facets of the nontraditional population, current research has consistently painted a picture of the differing needs and characteristics of nontraditional students (Berg, 2005; Macari et al.). Armed with this research, orientation professionals should take into account factors such as family responsibilities, work conflicts with class and extracurricular activities, prior college experience, and goal orientation when designing and implementing programs and services.

As noted earlier, nontraditional students are often motivated to return to school due to work-related or professional reasons. Not only does vocation serve as a motivator for the student, but it also signals something about what these students may need. Nontraditional students tend to view themselves as "employees who learn rather than students who work" (Headden, 2009, p. 5). As such, they may need classes offered at night, on weekends, and during vacations, as well as programs that allow them to complete their degrees as quickly as possible. Consequently, if students are to benefit from them, programs and services designed to support their academic success must acknowledge this reality. Orientation programs are no exception. Orientation professionals should consider these needs when making decisions about the nontraditional student orientation schedule (i.e., offering shorter programs in the evening or weekends). In addition, supplementing in-person interactions with an online component that could be completed by the student at a time that works best with his/her schedule is important to consider.

Research indicates that nontraditional students tend to be more astute in the classroom and very focused on a specific career objective (Spitzer, 2000). They have high expectations of the classroom environment and are often more vocal and interactive (Headden, 2009). However, they are also more likely to feel out of place in the classroom, leading to feelings of inadequacy and marginality. These feelings can be more prevalent in those students who need developmental coursework before they can be successful in college-level courses. As Wlodkowski (2008) notes,

> Some learners may not have a negative attitude toward their instructor or the subject, but they may judge that they lack the capability to successfully learn the task at hand . . .This learner is likely to give up easily when he encounters frustration or failure during the learning process. (p. 187)

These students need assistance in developing the belief that they can be successful academically (Macari et al., 2005-2006). Orientation professionals can help meet this need by including appointments with key personnel (i.e., academic advisors, student finance advisors, peer mentors) during the orientation process to build confidence and prepare these students for the challenges ahead (Hatch, 2003; Rosenbaum et al., 2006).

Although nontraditional student learners may be motivated and earn high grades for their work in the classroom, orientation professionals and other student affairs practitioners must work to eliminate institutional barriers that will keep the student from engaging more fully in the college environment, and thus, from attaining academic, personal, and professional development. Nontraditional students may also be in need of intervention services to help support student development and personal growth throughout the college experience (Macari et al., 2005-2006). The research conducted by Macari et al. suggests that because students with nontraditional characteristics often have priorities and responsibilities outside of the classroom, they have little time to devote to college-sponsored cultural events or to engage in personal, academic, or career counseling. Moreover, nontraditional students are unlikely to seek these resources out on their own. To this end, the research by Rosenbaum et al. (2006) demonstrates that proactive procedures, such as mandatory advising, reduce the chance of mistakes by the student and increase the chances of success in college. Orientation professionals should be aware of these trends when designing programs and services for nontraditional students.

Eliminating Barriers to Nontraditional Student Success: Recommendations for Practice

According to Spellman (2007), nontraditional students may face a number of situational, institutional, or dispositional barriers to continuous enrollment and achievement of educational, personal, and career goals. Lack of academic preparation, financial needs, cultural and language differences, and any number of personal issues (e.g., health conditions, substance abuse, criminal history, or personal relationships) can impede student progress. While the college campus cannot remove all these barriers, particularly those of a situational or dispositional nature, orientation and retention professionals can ensure that programs do not pose any additional institutional barriers to student success and can lead the campus in eliminating those procedures and policies that unduly inhibit the success of nontraditional students. As discussed throughout the first part of this chapter, professionals should learn from those who serve large populations of nontraditional students; adjust the timing and format of programs; include current nontraditional students in programs to offer incoming students pictures of success; assess their population to best understand motivations for returning to college; and build expectations into the process, such as mandatory academic advising, to remove barriers and best support the success of nontraditional students.

In addition, because orientation and retention professionals are often the first point of contact for nontraditional students, the attitudes, knowledge, and resources presented to these students by orientation professionals and paraprofessionals (i.e., student volunteers) are often key in developing the students' perception of the institution and its ability to meet their specific needs. It is, therefore, paramount that orientation professionals and all staff associated with the orientation programs are knowledgeable not only of the needs of the nontraditional student but also of the resources the campus has to meet those needs. The following suggestions address the common barriers to success for nontraditional students in the college environment. Many of the strategies demand collaboration across the campus. Berg (2005) suggests that collaboration and coordination are critical in order to serve the needs of these students.

Orientation Program Delivery

Work schedules and family responsibilities prevent some students from attending classes in daytime hours or attending full-time (Spellman, 2007). Just as classes must now be offered at times and in formats convenient to these students, so must orientation programs be offered at times and in formats that meet the needs of the nontraditional student population. Orientation programs should be mandatory so they are seen as important. Offering programs in the evenings and on weekends can make orientation programs more accessible. In addition, adding an online orientation component, which can be offered alone or in conjunction with campus-based programs, may also increase access to this important resource.

Additionally, assessing the length of time students must be present and focusing on the services that pertain to their greatest needs (as discussed below) can increase the likelihood that nontraditional students benefit from attending orientation programs. Hatch (2003) noted that "the length of the program is less important than schedule order. . . the opening of the program needs to communicate clearly a positive and inclusive climate for learning" (p. 114) in order to set the stage for later learning events.

Essential Services for Nontraditional Students

Nontraditional students need access to key services on campus as they have competing priorities and are less likely than their traditional counterparts to seek out these resources on their own. Orientation programs should outline how nontraditional students can successfully use resources and highlight the ease and success rates for those who do. Research suggests that professionals must do even more to increase access to these services for our nontraditional student population. Rosenbaum et al. (2006) found that there are times that traditional college procedures impede nontraditional students' progress inadvertently. Some colleges require students to have skill sets that may be typical for traditional students (e.g., soft skills and job search skills), but not necessarily for nontraditional students. Ultimately, orientation and retention programs that help students negotiate the complex campus environment and incorporate introductions to the essential services can lead their campuses in removing these obstacles.

Financial aid. Inadequate financial resources pose serious challenges to many nontraditional students, and many potential students have cited rising education costs as a significant hurdle impeding enrollment (Nunley, 2007; Spellman, 2007). In 2004, Senator Hillary Rodham Clinton proposed legislation to help improve graduation rates among nontraditional students, including increasing access to Pell Grants, increasing the percentage of education expenses that could be counted toward the Lifetime Learning tax credit, rewarding schools that offer flexible class schedules and childcare services, and raising the level of funding for innovative remedial programs and student support service programs (Lane, 2004). Elements of her original proposal were enacted in 2005 via the Deficit Reduction Act, and the U.S. Senate made Pell grants available year round when they approved the Higher Education Amendments of 2007.

Despite the efforts of the U.S. government, many students who apply for aid complain about the difficulty of the forms and the lack of assistance they receive. Still others are not aware of all of their options or mistakenly believe that they are not eligible based on their work status or the cost of tuition at their institution (Rosenbaum et al., 2006). While financial aid services are key prior to enrollment, students need continuing access to these resources and assistance in deciphering changes made in the legislation if they are to persist to graduation. Offering a session during the orientation program that introduces students to financial aid personnel and educates them about the aid available throughout their educational career would be valuable to many nontraditional students, particularly those from disadvantaged backgrounds and/or those who are first-generation college students. Orientation professionals should also collaborate with financial aid offices to ensure that financial aid staff members are available to consult with individuals about specific financial aid questions that cannot be answered in presentations, and the orientation schedule should allow time for students to meet with them in person.

Career services. Since professional goals may be a strong motivator for many nontraditional students entering college, orientation programs should consider implementing career-related sessions in a number of ways. Spellman (2007) suggests that partnerships with the local business community facilitate student learning by situating it in real-world experience, which increases the chance of employment post-graduation. Therefore, inviting local business partners to take part in orientation program activities may draw more participation from the nontraditional student population.

Furthermore, Macari et al. (2005-2006) recommended offering free personal and career assessments to nontraditional students. Along with these assessments, orientation programs should include a focus on connecting nontraditional students with all career services offered on the campus, ranging from part-time jobs to internship experiences to career advising, in order to greatly improve their chances of future success. In addition, orientation programs can jointly partner with career services personnel and local employers to provide sessions that increase student knowledge about proper conduct and appearance in the workforce and to reinforce the importance of communication, cooperation, and punctuality (Rosenbaum et al., 2006).

Counseling resources. Nontraditional students often find managing multiple roles to be a source of stress (Spellman, 2007), which negatively correlates with academic success (Zajacova, Lynch, & Espenshade, 2005). Moreover, policy experts from the American Council on Education (ACE) suggest that counseling is essential (Headden, 2009). Furthermore, this group indicates that counseling is especially important for nontraditional male students, who are less likely to open up, more likely to feel self-conscious about age, and more likely to feel as if their enrollment in school impedes their immediate ability to provide for a family.

Pre-existing psychological or medical conditions, combined with the stress of managing multiple roles, may also create barriers for nontraditional students. Hudson, Towey, and Shinar (2008) conducted a study on depression and racial/ethnic variations with a diverse nontraditional student sample. Based on their results, they suggested counseling centers develop more explicit outreach programs to target nontraditional students.

Orientation professionals can help facilitate this outreach by designing programs during the transition process that: (a) address stress and how it relates to academics, (b) address multiple roles and how families can serve as a support network for the student, and (c) introduce students to counseling personnel and resources available on campus. Orientation professionals can also invite counseling center staff to participate in the training of orientation staff, so that all involved can begin to identify and address the special needs and cultural adjustments facing these students (Hudson et al., 2008).

Academic success and study skills. Assessing students' time-management skills, comfort level with technology, and learning styles can be an invaluable step in assuring student success, particularly for those students taking courses in a nontraditional delivery style (Berg, 2005). Study skills classes or seminars can help to change students' perceptions about their ability to succeed, particularly for those who are returning to academia after many years in the workplace or caring for family members (Macari et al., 2005-2006).

Further, studies show that academic self-efficacy is a significant predictor of college success, particularly in the first year of study (Zajacova et al., 2005). It is reasonable to assume that nontraditional students may have lower academic self-efficacy if they have not been enrolled in college courses in a number of years. Orientation programs can be designed to boost self-efficacy and/ or connect students to services to fill in gaps in their academic study skills. Many campuses have academic support services that specialize in teaching these skills. Orientation professionals should work collaboratively with these offices (where they exist) to help them tailor their message to non-traditional students, who sometimes may feel these programs are designed with only traditionally aged students in mind. In instances where campuses may not have this office, professionals should seek support from on- and off-campus resources to include programming on these topics.

Social skills. Nontraditional students appear to be less likely than traditional students to participate in extracurricular activities (Macari et al., 2005-2006). However, research shows that social events and service projects help to build a sense of community and support among nontraditional students, as well as provide experiences that are critical when searching for a job after graduation (Headden, 2009). Offering free admission to cultural events for students and their families, providing more multicultural activities tied to academic requirements, weaving student development activities into the curriculum, and engaging faculty as part of the student development process (Macari et al., 2005-2006) can give nontraditional students an opportunity to connect with the university community, while simultaneously helping these students clarify purpose and develop tolerance of others. To begin to meet these needs during orientation, professionals should assess their social programming events and consider how these programs may be re-vamped to attract a nontraditional student population. Considerations for program change could include timing, participants, perceived purpose, and expectations for attendance.

Many student activities on campus can also aid in the development of the soft skills employers are looking for in college graduates. Again, the ability to connect orientation and transition programming to the career goals and motivations of the new traditional student can help lay the foundation for student engagement and success: "Besides helping students to catch up academically, colleges can also help many students catch up socially, providing them with direct guidance about how to dress, speak, and interact in job interviews and in the professional workplace" (Rosenbaum et al., 2006, p. 201).

Information and technology literacy. Given the increasing numbers of underprepared students entering college campuses, it would be beneficial to include librarians and information technologists as part of the orientation process to support student learning in these areas (Berg, 2005). Non-traditional students may sometimes lack technological skills or confidence in their technological ability compared to their traditional-aged peers (Cordes, 2009). The increasing use of technology to facilitate distance education, communication with faculty and peers, collaboration on academic projects, and engagement in academic discussions suggests that information and technology literacy is a critical need for all students. Many, but not all, nontraditional students come to college with a lack of exposure to technology and a subsequent low self-esteem as it relates to managing technology during their college career. To combat this phenomenon, orientation professionals should partner with librarians, information technology (IT) staff, and faculty to address available technology, training tools, and other related resources during orientation programs. Otherwise, technology may remain a barrier to nontraditional students' success. Besides including the librarian and IT staff in the orientation process, orienting students to campus computing policies regarding network and wireless services can help prevent future frustrations (Cordes). Additionally, integrating opportunities to experience technology in orientation programs can provide students time to practice important skills, such as navigating online learning platforms and campus e-mail systems with support from campus faculty, staff and students who are more familiar with the systems.

Disability services. According to the United States Census Bureau (2000), approximately one out of five adults age 21 to 64 in United States has a qualifying disability under the Americans with Disabilities Act. Rather than seeing these conditions as disqualifiers, the higher education community should welcome students with disabilities and provide services through a centralized office. Nontraditional students may be unaware of these services or may be accustomed to self-accommodation in the workforce or their daily lives. Even when students are aware of these services, they often express reluctance in asking for accommodations (Denhart, 2008). Academic work may provide unique challenges for nontraditional students with disabilities, and appropriate academic accommodations may further reduce barriers students encounter. Inviting disability services providers to orientation can help facilitate a connection for many nontraditional students who may not otherwise seek out assistance. Providing lists of community resources may also assist students who suspect they have a disability but have yet to receive a diagnosis, particularly for older students who may never have had access to disability services in their secondary education. In addition, orientation professionals should also invite disability service providers to train orientation staff and collaborate on ways to ensure the program delivery and content offers a welcoming environment for students with disabilities

Veterans' services. Estimates indicate as many as a third of veterans returning from Operation Enduring Freedom and Operation Iraqi Freedom will have a mental disorder, the most common of which are depression, traumatic brain injury, and post-traumatic stress disorder (Zoroya, 2009). With the passage of the new G.I. Bill in 2008, this special population of nontraditional students is a quickly growing demographic across higher education (Jones, 2009; LaPlante, 2009; Schuster, 2009; Schwartz, 2009).

Transitioning from a military to a civilian/academic culture can be a challenge to veteran students, who are used to a highly structured environment. Many find the college environment to be chaotic, freewheeling, and lax; they often find themselves feeling isolated, stressed, and awkward (Brown, 2009; Colimore, 2009; Heavin, 2009; LaPlante, 2009; Schuster, 2009; Schwartz, 2009). Programs designed to meet the needs of this population have been developed throughout the nation. For example, Heavin described a learning and transition strategies course implemented in the fall of 2008 at the University of Missouri that focuses on teaching veterans much-needed academic skills and helps them learn how to navigate campus and government resources available to them. The course also gives students a chance to network with other veterans and identifies ways they can feel connected to the campus community.

Along with courses such as this one, many campuses have veterans' affairs offices or have designated offices or individuals who work with this population. Orientation professionals should identify these staff and faculty and include them in their orientation planning and communications plans as well as assist veterans in connecting with their services. For smaller campuses, local veterans' affairs offices may be of assistance if campuses are unable to designate individuals or offices for this purpose. However, because these offices are also dealing with high volumes of applications for G.I. Bill and other veterans' benefits, orientation professionals on campuses with little or no existing resources should lead the charge in responding to the needs of veterans in the transition process.

In addition, when large numbers of veterans enroll on campus, an orientation program designed specifically for veterans may be one way to begin providing resources for these students. Regardless of the format of the program, topics should include accessing counseling and tutoring resources on campus, navigating government resources, academic planning advice, and understanding financial aid requirements (Colimire, 2009; Heavin, 2009; LaPlante, 2009; Schuster, 2009).

Orientation professionals should also seek opportunities to learn about military culture and combat experience and add it to diversity training elements in orientation leader training sessions. Knowing that due to their past experiences some of these students may not want to sit in front of the class or walk in crowded areas can assist professionals with designing programs that are inclusive and supportive. Understanding the anxiety some veterans may feel the first time the Iraq war is discussed in a classroom setting can help all members of the campus community begin to facilitate productive discussions on campus without devaluing the students' military service (Schwartz, 2009; Zoroya, 2009).

Mentoring. Many nontraditional students have established relationships outside of college and do not proactively seek out friends on campus (Macari et al., 2005-2006). Yet, these students may benefit from informal connections with peers, faculty, and staff, especially when these are centered on academic experiences. Implementing a mentoring program and/or offering support groups for first-year or transfer nontraditional students could encourage students to use the services introduced in orientation programs (Breese & O'Toole, 1995; Macari et al., 2005-2006; Spellman, 2007). Faculty members, continuing students, or both could serve as mentors to nontraditional students and help anchor them in the academic environment and campus community. One example of a successful mentor program exists at the University of Akron where peer mentors play an important role in the transition and retention of nontraditional students. These mentors must be at least 25 years of age and be nontraditional students themselves. The mentors uniquely understand the stresses their peers are facing and offer support to incoming nontraditional students in a way that other students cannot (Headden, 2009). Orientation professionals should consider including mentor opportunities when they design programs and services to encourage nontraditional students to connect to campus.

Conclusion

This chapter began by describing nontraditional students as an emerging majority or a *new* traditional student, based on demographic trends and characteristic changes that have occurred in the college-going population over the last few decades. While students have become more ethnically diverse, older, and more likely part-time, the most effective way to describe nontraditional students is by the number of competing priorities in their lives. To help nontraditional students manage competing priorities, orientation professionals must assess the needs and motivations of the incoming population, take time to learn from those who serve larger populations of nontraditional students, adjust for the timing and format of programs, include current nontraditional students in programs, and build mandatory elements into the process to best support the success of nontraditional students. In addition, it is paramount that orientation professionals and all staff associated with the orientation programs are knowledgeable not only of the needs of the nontraditional student but also of the resources the campus has to meet those needs. Although the basic elements of orientation remain the same (e.g., a welcome to the campus, academic advising, introduction to resources, interaction with peers) the format, participants, speakers, and information provided should be considered when creating a program that will meet the needs of nontraditional students.

This chapter presented programmatic suggestions that should be considered when taking the needs of nontraditional students into account. However, the authors also recognize that each campus and student body is unique and should be treated as such. Readers should take data about their own students into consideration when deciding whether and how to implement these suggestions.

The faces of the college student population have changed dramatically in recent years. Increasingly, nontraditional students make up larger portions, if not the majority, of the students on many college campuses today. Orientation professionals are uniquely situated to see these changing trends as they emerge and to bring campus partners together to respond to them. Orientation professionals should leverage their role as collaborators to educate different campus units on the changing nature of the student population and to help them reshape their services and messages to better serve these new traditional students.

References

Berg, S. (2005). Two sides of the same coin: Reaching non-traditional students. *The Community College Enterprise, 11*(2), 7-20.

Breese, J. R., & O'Toole, R. (1995). Role exit theory: Applications to adult women college students. *The Career Development Quarterly, 44*(1), 12-26.

Brown, E. (2009, September 29). From combat to classroom: Soldiers making transition to students face challenges. *The Washington Post.* Retrieved October 9, 2009, from ProQuest database.

Colimore, E. (2009, September 15). New Jersey acts to help veterans adjust to college. *McClatchy-Tribune Business News.* Retrieved October 9, 2009, from ProQuest database.

Cordes, S. (2009). Adult learners: How IT can support "new" students. *Educause Quarterly, 32*(1). Retrieved June 30, 2009, from http://www.educause.edu/EDUCAUSE+Quarterly/EDU-CAUSEQuarterlyMagazineVolum/AdultLearnersHowITCanSupportNe/163869

Denhart, H. (2008). Deconstructing barriers: Perceptions of students labeled with learning disabilities in higher education. *Journal of Learning Disabilities, 41*(6), 483-98.

Hatch, C. (2003). Orienting nontraditional students to college: Creating opportunities, supporting success. In J.A. Ward-Roof & C. Hatch (Eds.), *Designing Successful Transitions: A Guide for Orienting Students to College* (Monograph No. 13, 2nd ed., pp. 109-123). University of South Carolina, National Resource Center for The First-Year Experience & Students in Transition.

Headden, S. M. (2009, Fall). Adult ed grows up: Higher education seeks to better serve increasing numbers of nontraditional learners. *Lumina Foundation Focus,* 3-17, 19-21.

Heavin, J. (2009, September 16). Veterans get leg up from new class: Transition to school is difficult for some. *McClatchy-Tribune Business News.* Retrieved October 9, 2009, from ProQuest database.

Horn, L. J. (1996). *Nontraditional undergraduates: Trends in enrollment from 1986 to 1992 and persistence and attainment among 1989-90 beginning postsecondary students.* Washington, DC: National Center for Education Statistics, U.S. Department of Education. (ERIC Document Reproduction No. ED402857)

Hudson, R., Towey, J., & Shinar, O. (2008). Depression and ethnic variations within a diverse nontraditional college sample. *College Student Journal, 42*(1), 103-115.

Jones, C. (2009, September 9). G.I. Bill allows vets to attend private schools. *McClathcy-Tribune Business News.* Retrieved October 9, 2009, from ProQuest database.

LaPlante, M. D. (2009, September 4). Veterans influx could change college culture. *The Salt Lake Tribune.* Retrieved October 9, 2009, from ProQuest database.

Lane, K. (2004). Sen. Clinton unveils plan to help nontraditional students. *Black Issues in Higher Education, 21*(1), 6.

Macari, D. P., Maples M. F., & D'Andrea, L. (2005-2006). A comparative study of psychosocial development in nontraditional and traditional college students. *Journal of College Student Retention, 7*(3-4), 283-302.

Marques, J., (2007). Five things we should know about part-time students. *Recruitment and Retention in Higher Education, 21*(10), 8.

Merriam, S. B., Caffarella, R. S., & Baumgartner, L. M. (2007). *Learning in adulthood: A comprehensive guide* (3rd ed.). San Francisco: Jossey-Bass.

National Center for Educations Statistics (NCES). (2002). *Profile of undergraduates in U.S. postsecondary institutions: 1999–2000.* Washington, DC: U.S. Department of Education.

Noel-Levitz. (2009). *Adult Student Priorities Survey.* Iowa City, IA: Author.

Nunley, C. R. (2007, October 26). Community colleges may be losing their edge in educating adults. *The Chronicle of Higher Education*, p. B18. Retrieved October 9, 2009, from ProQuest database.

Pascarella, E. T., & Terenzini, P. T. (1998). Studying college students in the 21st century: Meeting new challenges. *The Review of Higher Education, 21*(2), 151-165.

Rosenbaum, J. E., Deil-Amen, R., & Person, A. E. (2006). *After admission: From college access to college success.* New York: The Russell Sage Foundation.

Rothstein, R. (2000, November 1). *Lessons: Supply, demand, wages and myth.* New York: New York Times.

Schuster, K. (2009, September 16). Hundreds of veterans enroll in Long Island colleges. *McClatchy-Tribune Business News.* Retrieved October 9, 2009, from ProQuest database.

Schwartz, J. (2009, October 4). As more veterans enroll, local universities adjust. *Austin American Statesman.* Retrieved October 9, 2009, from ProQuest database.

Seftor, N. S., & Turner, S. E. (2002). Back to school: Federal student aid policy and adult college enrollment. *The Journal of Human Resources, 37,* 336-352.

Spellman, N. (2007). Enrollment and retention barriers adult students encounter. *The Community College Enterprise, 13*(1), 63-80.

Spitzer, T. M. (2000). Predictors of college success: A comparison of traditional and nontraditional age students. *NASPA Journal, 38*(1), 1-17.

U.S. Census Bureau. (2000). *American FactFinder: Allegany County, NY.* Retrieved July 1, 2009, from http://factfinder.census.gov/servlet/QTTable?_bm=y&-geo_id=D&-qr_name=DEC_2000_SF3_U_DP2&-ds_name=D&-_lang=en&-redoLog=false

Wlodkowski, R. J. (2008). *Enhancing adult motivation to learn* (3rd ed.). San Francisco: Jossey-Bass.

Zajacova, A., Lynch, S. M., & Espenshade, T. J., (2005). Self-efficacy, stress, and academic success in college. *Research in Higher Education, 46*(6), 677-706.

Zoroya, G. (2009, October 5). More colleges develop classes on how to treat war vets: Mental health problems spur curriculums. *USA Today.* Retrieved October 9, 2009, from ProQuest database.

PART IV:

Institutionalizing and Sustaining Orientation Programs

Chapter 14

Building the Case for Collaboration in Orientation Programs: Campus Culture, Politics, and Power

Beth M. Lingren Clark and Matthew J. Weigand

As Mullendore (1998) reminds us, "Orientation programs can have a tremendous impact on both academic and social integration into the institution and thereby provide the foundation for improvement in student retention" (p. 5). Given the importance of orientation to future student success, the case for college-wide collaboration among disparate units that contribute to the program and among competing institutional priorities is clear. Effective orientation and first-year programs are not isolated, single-unit programs; instead, they are institution-wide endeavors requiring an investment of time and energy from myriad campus constituents. In fact, "active involvement by faculty, staff, administrators, and students is a prime factor in creating a community environment where entering students want to belong, perform, and contribute" (Smith & Brackin, 2003, p. 40).

While the benefits are significant, there are also real challenges associated with this interdependence. The various campus departments and external constituents may have competing needs and goals related to their involvement in transition programming, and orientation professionals must work with these entities to develop a shared vision and implementation strategy. In order to nurture relationships and maximize collaborative efforts, orientation professionals must have a deep understanding of organizational culture, as well as the influence of politics and power on their work. The ways in which these factors are recognized and negotiated may impact our ability to gain institutional support, increase collaboration, and ultimately, implement successful programs. This chapter summarizes the importance of collaboration; discusses the literature on organizational culture, politics, and power and the influence they have on our campuses and programs; highlights examples of effective collaboration in orientation programs; and offers strategies for enhancing campus partnerships.

The Importance of Collaboration

While collaboration is essential for the work of orientation and other transition programs, its importance is not limited to these areas. In fact, developing positive relationships for collaboration is central to *all* student affairs work. In their joint statement, *Principles of Good Practice for Student Affairs*, ACPA and NASPA (1997) assert that good practice "initiates educational partnerships and develops structures that support collaboration [which] involves all aspects of the community in the development and implementation of institutional goals and reminds participants of their common commitment to students and their learning" (p. 5). More recently, Woodard and Komives (2003) suggested that collaborative work will be even more important in the future, as complex issues such as first-year student retention require cooperation among various campus service and academic units.

Sandeen (2000) further posits that the effectiveness of student affairs professionals is heavily dependent upon the degree to which they have cultivated mutually beneficial relationships within the campus and community. Those who are most effective are active within the campus and community and involve others in policies, programs, staffing, and evaluation. Conversely, Sandeen frankly states that "the best way to fail is for student affairs leaders to isolate themselves, thinking that they can do their jobs without involving others" (p. 378).

The benefits of collaborative campus relationships are numerous and may include improved understanding and support of initiatives by stakeholders, a greater sense of community on campus, and better problem solving (Sandeen, 2000). When trusting relationships exist among those involved in a program, there is also a greater likelihood that difficult decisions, policy changes, and new initiatives will be accepted and supported (Sandeen). Moreover, relationships developed across campus units "demonstrate a healthy institutional approach to learning by fostering inclusiveness" (ACPA & NASPA, 1997, p. 5), thereby contributing to the sense of community (Sandeen). Finally, collaboration brings together the multiple perspectives and unique contributions of diverse constituents, leading to stronger, more campus-wide interventions; higher quality cocurricular programs; and ultimately, better educational opportunities for students (ACPA & NASPA; Sandeen; Woodard & Komives, 2003).

In order to forge these robust relationships for effective collaboration, it is helpful to understand the institutional context and factors that may influence those relationships and/or their development. While an in-depth review of organizational theory is beyond the scope of this chapter, an overview of key tenets—including campus culture, politics, and power—as they relate to designing, implementing, and improving orientation programs, is warranted.

Understanding Campus Culture

The culture of our campuses serves as an important backdrop for the work of orientation and transition professionals, and understanding its impact is critical for success. According to Farmer (1990), "failure to understand the way in which an organization's culture will interact with various contemplated change strategies... may mean the failure of the strategies themselves" (p. 8). On the other hand, work that intentionally takes into account cultural characteristics may "facilitate the development of trust, can help develop institutional 'buy-in,' and reflect the proper scope for innovative and transformational change efforts" (Farmer, p. 8).

Kuh and Hall (1993) define culture as

the collective, mutually shaping patterns of institutional history, mission, physical settings, norms, traditions, values, practices, beliefs, and assumptions, all of which guide the behavior of individuals and groups in an institution of higher education, and which provide frames of reference for interpreting the meanings of events and actions on and off campus. (p. 2)

Understandably, the definition of culture is campus-specific and must be actively created by the campus community. When attempting to define campus culture with regard to orientation programming, program planners may ask the following questions:

1. What basic assumptions exist among the campus constituents?
2. What do campus constituents value in the orientation process?
3. What organizational cultural values and beliefs are perpetuated through the institutional traditions?
4. How are problems solved within the process?
5. How is change or adversity in programming managed?

The ability to answer these questions can lead to increased cultural understanding, which is critical to successful program implementation.

Schein (1992) suggests, "These dynamic processes of culture creation and management are the essence of leadership and make one realize that leadership and culture are two sides of the same coin" (p. 1). To this end, Schein outlines three levels of culture, which orientation professionals can use as both a framework for defining campus culture and as a guide for leadership within that culture. The first level involves identifying the visible organizational structures and processes called artifacts (e.g., the structure of academic advising in each college, as well as expectations and specific requirements involved with the advisement process). Investing time reaching out to the academic units and engaging them in conversations in an effort to increase understanding of their specific structures and processes will allow program planners to look at the orientation program through the lens of faculty and academic affairs administrators and identify their role with orientation. Examining these structures and processes provides more objectivity, a greater understanding, and acknowledgment of the challenges other units face while offering an opportunity to meet in the middle and reach a common ground where requests for orientation programming are concerned. This should also assist in creating a more meaningful orientation experience for the new students.

The second level of culture deals with espoused values by identifying the organizational strategies, goals, and philosophies that drive the campus organization and are usually supported by the individuals in the organization (Schein, 1992). More specifically, this level of culture may explain how orientation programming fits into the institutional mission, as well as the extent to which operational philosophies focus on student success and retention through interdepartmental cooperation. When developing orientation programs, there are often differences of opinion on how to approach a process or change content. After discussing possible alternatives, the orientation director may offer a solution that the larger group agrees to adopt. If this solution is successful, then the larger group has a shared perception of accomplishment. Schein refers to this as the beginning of the cognitive transformation process. If the success continues, then the group moves from a shared value to a shared assumption. If the solution is not successful, then the process will be challenged and questioned. Being aware of this transformational process enhances the ability of orientation professionals to manage challenges and use a shared decision-making process more effectively.

The third and final level of culture involves identifying the unconscious, taken-for-granted beliefs, perceptions, thoughts, and feelings, or the basic underlying assumptions (Schein, 1992). These underlying assumptions guide the behavior of individuals in a department or group. There are many strategies that orientation professionals can implement to bring the assumptions into the open and involve departments in the decision-making process. One strategy involves establishing an Orientation Advisory Committee, inviting key departmental constituents including academic advisors, admissions, financial aid, housing, ID card office, international programs, and the honors program to discuss orientation goals, challenges, and decisions. Identifying key constituents is an important part of the process. While some departments may not be on the formal organizing committee (i.e., campus police or parking), it may be important to meet with them individually to share program goals and plans and to gain their perspective on how they can best support orientation programs. Such meetings emphasize the importance of the working relationship; provide an opportunity to learn individual thoughts, feelings, and perceptions while involving them in the decision-making process; and prevent miscommunications and faulty assumptions, thereby building trust. As Farmer (1990) notes, "Trust is also enhanced when there is a history of making decisions in a way that reflects a clear and sensitive understanding of the culture of a campus" (p. 10).

Analyzing the three levels of campus culture by answering the basic questions provided above can assist practitioners in understanding the institutional context and identifying strategies to assist with orientation program development and implementation. Leading the orientation planning process by investing the time with key constituents and developing effective partnerships can provide clarity in decision making and drive program changes and improvements.

Campus Politics and Power

In addition to examining the institutional context from a cultural perspective, it is also important for orientation and transition professionals to view their campus through a political lens. As they strive to build collaborative partnerships to support student transition programs, understanding the role politics and power play on college and university campuses and in orientation programming becomes essential.

Moore (2000) argues that the political dimensions of institutional life are omnipresent and that politics is a necessary and ubiquitous process by which decisions are made. Similarly, Bess and Dee (2008) posit that colleges and universities are combinations of rational organizations, which rely upon hierarchical authority to accomplish goals, and polities, where political behaviors are used to advance goals. Although it may invoke negative sentiments for some, politics is not necessarily a negative. Rather, it is "part of the process of democratic conflict resolution in a community that involves persons and units with different goals and interests" (Bess & Dee, p. 545).

In essence, politics refers to the use of influence to shape institutional direction and policy, as well as the allocation of resources (Moore, 2000). Politics is most likely to come into play under conditions of uncertainty and dissensus (Bess & Dee, 2008); for example, when clear lines of authority do not exist or when institutional priorities are ambiguous or in conflict. Thus, politics is a common reality for those directing orientation and transition programs that rely on several campus units with a variety of reporting structures and with a range of priorities. For example, an orientation director may report to student affairs, while the academic advisors with whom he or she works closely may report to academic affairs. As such, different priorities or work practices may become apparent when these partners come together to make decisions about the orientation program, such as the best procedures to register students for first-semester courses. With several options available and no clear "best" method, and without a single supervisor to offer guidance, politics will likely be involved in the decision-making process.

The political model recognizes differing levels of power within a college or university (Kuh, 2003) and "assumes that the power of the various participants will determine the outcome" (Moore, 2000, p. 181). Thus, successful student affairs administrators possess the political skills necessary to understand who the stakeholders are, the factors that determine their stand on an issue, and how much relative power they hold (Dickerson, 2001; Moore).

Power may be defined as the ability or potential to influence others in such a way that they will do something that they would not otherwise do (Bess & Dee, 2008; Moore, 2000). It shapes and modifies the desires and beliefs of others in ways that are contrary to, or not directly in line with, their interests (Bess & Dee). For example, an orientation director may exert power to get campus stakeholders to participate in an additional orientation session due to larger-than-expected enrollment, when the stakeholders' original intentions were to use that time to work on other projects important to their respective offices.

Authority is a specific type of power that exists through a formal hierarchical relationship (Bess & Dee, 2008). An orientation coordinator exercises his or her authority—or legitimized, positional power—when he or she directs staff members to perform tasks or to act in ways they would not otherwise do. For example, while orientation leaders may be inclined to take the shortest route when escorting incoming students from one campus location to another, their supervisor may direct them to take a more circuitous route in order to provide the new students with a more comprehensive tour and with more experience navigating the campus.

However, this chain-of-command view of power is limited; "the challenging, changing, and dynamic nature of higher education makes this traditional view of leadership ineffective and obsolete" (Schroeder, 1999, p. 139). Moreover, because orientation and first-year programs professionals rely on so many other campus constituents who do not report to them, the remainder of this discussion focuses on power that is not a result of hierarchical reporting relationships.

Such power may be revealed through political situations—that is, through conflicts of interest for which there is no clear priority or authority (Bess & Dee, 2008). When conflict arises as a result of competition for limited resources or different views on important issues, alternative policies or solutions may be proposed and often lobbying and debating among stakeholders take place (Kuh, 2003). Decisions in these cases are usually determined through consensus-building, majority vote, or by a formal pronouncement from institutional leaders. Power may also be revealed in more subtle ways. One exercise of power is the ability to control what is—and what is not—brought up for discussion. For example, as chair of the campus-wide orientation planning committee, the director may choose whether or not to initiate conversation regarding alternative orientation models or programs (e.g., summer programs, welcome week programs, tradition camps, outdoor/wilderness experiences). The director is exerting power by controlling the agenda. These types of power and uses of power are prevalent for orientation professionals, and in fact all higher education professionals, as "wishes for power, the exercise of power, and the results of using power pervade higher education" (Bess & Dee, p. 540).

The strategic contingencies theory of power is particularly relevant for orientation and transition professionals, as they often depend on other (horizontally positioned) campus units, that are, in turn, dependent on them. Briefly, this theory suggests that units or subunits that are relied upon for critical information, services, or resources hold organizational power (Bess & Dee, 2008). In particular, units that control scarce resources, that help others predict and deal with the uncertain future, and whose work is central to the organizational mission and difficult or impossible to replace will have greater power. Understanding the campus culture assists in the decision-making process when politics are involved. If there is trust and buy-in with the program, then all can approach the political situation as a unified group identifying alternatives to solve the conflict.

Much like understanding campus culture, the importance of understanding politics and power lies in the ability of orientation and transition professionals to build collaborative relationships and influence others to affect change, ultimately improving the quality of transition and retention programs. As Dickerson (2001) noted, student affairs professionals at all levels believe that change—including new program development and improvement to current programs—is a political process, and importantly, that practitioners at all levels can be influential in the politics of change at an institution. Kuh (2003) calls collaboration and partnerships—marked by trust and good will—key to such organizational improvement and suggests that limited understanding of power and politics can perpetuate misunderstandings. Dickerson further argued that managing the politics associated with change and ensuring the planned change responds to identifiable organizational needs reduces negative resistance.

Understanding politics and power is also "particularly useful for identifying those who are most likely to be influential in the process" of program development or improvement "and for maximizing the potential benefits of conflict management and collaborative policy making" (Kuh, 2003, p. 275). In other words, it is critical to include colleagues who will be affected by the outcome in the decision-making process. If not, commitment and enthusiasm may be lacking, feelings of alienation may arise, and difficulty implementing the decision or program changes may result. At the same time, it is also important to understand that constituents are not equally invested in all decisions. If the issue is not important to particular participants, they are not likely to invest their limited time and energy in the decision-making process. Thus, examining the institutional context from a political view helps orientation professionals maximize efforts to build partnerships and develop collaborative relationships. Further, understanding campus culture, politics, and power helps orientation professionals make the most of those collaborative relationships to provide the best programming to incoming students.

Models for Effective Practice

There are countless examples of effective collaboration in orientation programs at every type and size of institution. Two such dynamic programs are described here. These programs have developed, evolved, and improved through planned change and transformation as a result of continual assessment and evaluation of program effectiveness and participant satisfaction. They have also succeeded in part because of their leaders' understanding and competently managing the culture, politics, and power relationships that provide the institutional context for the programs, allowing for effective collaboration and program transformation (Keup, Walker, Astin, & Lindholm, 2001; Kuh, 2003). Their champions appreciate that trust and open communication are conditions that contribute to productive change (Keup et al.) and that "meaningful involvement and participation [by campus stakeholders] are needed when diagnosing what is going on, figuring out what to do, and actually doing it" (Schein, 1992, p. 392). They understand program planning as a social activity involving the "negotiation of interests within relationships of power" (Cervero & Wilson, 1994, p. 185).

While many examples of effective collaboration exist, the following two highlight deliberative efforts to infuse an understanding of campus culture, politics, and power into work with valued constituents. This proactive approach to building relationships for the good of orientation and transition programs may reduce the number and severity of conflicts and issues that arise in planning and implementing first-year programs. Examples of conflicts may include: miscommunications, decisions made by an individual unit without considering the entire process, misinterpretation of policies or procedures, inconsistencies in messages to the student, and little to no buy-in from key campus stakeholders such as academic advisors. The two examples are provided to demonstrate how involving people early, communicating often, and planning processes collaboratively within the context of campus political and power structures can prevent or minimize adversity and conflict.

University of Minnesota

At the University of Minnesota-Twin Cities campus, many strategies are used to understand campus culture, increase collaboration, and balance politics and power. The staff members in the

Orientation & First-Year Programs (OFYP) office spend a tremendous amount of time and energy obtaining institutional buy-in. Contributing to this campus-wide buy-in is the clear connection of orientation programming, welcome week programming, and other first-year initiatives to the overall institutional mission. Additionally, the University has strategic priorities and student learning and development outcomes, to which all OFYP programming is also linked. Clearly identifying how the programs and initiatives contribute to institutional priorities is essential in obtaining campus resources and support. Moreover, multiple committees are established where program goals are set, challenges are identified, solutions are offered, and decisions are made. There are times when OFYP staff members will ultimately have to make the decision, but it is not done without consulting these committees. This extensive committee work is supplemented by meeting frequently with key departmental partners individually.

Constant communication among campus constituents is also an important strategy for collaboration. Asking constituents to help set the agenda for meetings and provide input on decisions and following up with them after decisions have been made are important elements for effective communication. The constituents value this communication and involvement in the process and feel empowered to contribute to the success of the programs. Understanding what the institution values, how traditions influence programming, and how behavior and attitudes are formed, allow program planners to manage change for greater program success.

Northern Illinois University

The First-Year Connections program at Northern Illinois University (NIU) consists of an extended orientation course and mentoring program, as well as faculty and staff training sessions designed to help first-year students make a successful transition to college life (Kuchynka, Rode, & Reeves, 1998; Peska & Young, 2007). The program is a collaborative effort of NIU's academic and student affairs divisions; and it involves faculty, staff, and students from across campus (Kuchynka et al.; Peska & Young). The program started in the mid-1980s as a single pilot course offered by an academic counselor, and over the next two decades grew to more than 90 sections serving more than 1,800 first-year students (Kuchynka et al.; Peska & Young). Early partners in the program's evolution included an academic dean (who negotiated financial support for faculty and staff training workshops) and institutional researchers (who compiled data showing higher retention rates and grade point averages for course participants than nonparticipants). Support grew to include others in university administration; well-respected, tenured faculty; a campus-wide committee that oversaw the undergraduate academic environment; and student affairs staff, among others (Refer to Kuchynka et al. for a more extensive description of the program's development.).

The administrators leading the development and growth of this extended orientation course emphasized the importance of understanding issues of politics and power in the planning process. "The course could not have matured and developed without nurturing campus relationships among faculty and student affairs staff. Moreover, understanding the curricular process, the influences of decision-making power, and the political structure of campus committees played a critical role" (Kuchynka et al., 1998, p. 11). Specifically, champions of the course recognized that the university curriculum committee held the exclusive power to officially develop the university-wide course. As such, they garnered support from key faculty and academic administrators and participated in extensive collaborative work to develop and discuss course objectives, content, and instructor qualifications, among other matters, ultimately resulting in official approval of the course. Their planning involved "negotiating, mediating, and shaping the needs and values of the campus community to collectively create the desired program and hence successful outcomes" (Kuchynka et al., p. 8).

Conclusions and Recommendations

The need for orientation professionals to establish collaborative relationships with a variety of campus constituents, in order to develop, implement, and improve transition programs is clear. Comprehensive programs require more than single-office or single-division support; they require a campus-wide commitment to welcoming new students and helping them succeed in college. Understanding the institutional context, including the campus culture, politics, and power, will help educators build and maintain these partnerships more effectively and efficiently. Fried (1999) supports this contention, writing that "the most powerful educational interventions connect us rather than divide us" (p. 18).

Knowing the importance of collaboration, however, is not enough. Orientation professionals would be well-served to learn continuously about and practice the skills necessary to develop these effective partnerships. Cawthon and Ward-Roof (1999) found that orientation professionals ranked human relations skills among the top skills necessary for effective practice in the field. These include the ability and willingness (a) to establish cooperative relationships, (b) coordinate diverse groups involved in the implementation of a university-wide program, (c) listen to and work with those wanting input into the orientation program, and (d) negotiate and exercise diplomacy. Several scholars have offered tips and suggestions for establishing effective collaborative relationships against the backdrop of campus culture, as well as dealing with campus politics and power (c.f., Fried, 1999; Kuh, 2003; Moore, 2000; Sandeen, 2000; Schroeder, 1999). Following is a synthesis of those ideas as they relate to orientation and transition programs.

1. *Spend time actively cultivating, managing, and supporting relationships.* While relationship building may not appear on an orientation professional's job description, it is absolutely vital to accomplish the goals and objectives associated with the position. This may include hosting orientation kick-off events with all those involved in the program; scheduling individual or group meetings with stakeholders in order to gather feedback about the program; or attending informal lunch or coffee meetings to stay connected with colleagues and to stay abreast of potential issues, trends, and ideas. It may also include participating in committees or other work that might not otherwise be a priority, in order to increase visibility and position oneself to influence decisions. As Moore (2000) suggests, political activity "is not our work, but it affects our work" (p. 189).

2. *Understand program priorities and the priorities of various stakeholders, anticipate conflict over those priorities, and be prepared to handle conflict constructively* (Moore, 2000). Conflict is inevitable (and often healthy) in relatively decentralized organizations where multiple priorities exist. Orientation professionals should be prepared to learn about stakeholders who have differing priorities and reporting structures in order to predict and be prepared for conflict. Such knowledge also increases the capacity for empathetic understanding. Taking into account the campus culture and subcultures, politics, and power will allow orientation professionals to propose reasonable and realistic solutions that may benefit all stakeholders. Such resolutions may not always match up with program priorities, so orientation professionals should be prepared to debate when important principles are at stake. They must also be prepared to compromise when it contributes to the common good.

3. *Learn to speak a common language.* Fried (1999) suggests that the gap between subcultures on campus, particularly those between academic and student affairs can be significant. Each group thinks about their work, describes the outcomes of that work, and measures accountability differently. However, "student learning should be of profound interest to [all] groups" (Fried, p. 13). Creating a common language to talk about issues that all stakeholders care

about, in a way that all can understand, is essential to effective collaboration. Student affairs administrators and faculty may have very different ideas about the purpose, content, and delivery methods of orientation programs; however, both are keenly interested in student success. Creating a common language to discuss orientation—with the ultimate goal being to maximize the chances for student success—may allow for deeper conversations among disparate constituents, ultimately resulting in stronger programs.

4. *Value multiple perspectives.* Chairing orientation planning meetings, inviting others to share ideas and feedback, and otherwise striving for collaboration are effective only when these diverse perspectives are actually valued. Stakeholders quickly learn the difference between an orientation director who goes through the motions of inviting others to be at the table and an orientation director who listens, supports, challenges, and incorporates others' ideas into transition programs. Further, while it is sometimes easier to partner and seek relationships with others who generally hold similar views or approaches, participation by those with divergent views may be more effective. Not only is it likely to produce original ideas and critiques, it may also help both sides understand the real constraints and consequences involved in a political situation and "have a tempering effect" (Moore, 2000, p. 191). Finally, effectively meeting the needs of the dramatically changing student body requires thinking and planning in ways that value and affirm multiple perspectives—those of the diverse incoming students and those of the various campus constituents. Now, more than ever, higher education professionals must construct communities that embrace diversity—of background, culture, thought, and worldview—and develop programs, policies, strategies, and interventions that enhance this diversity (Pope, Miklitsch, & Weigand, 2005).

5. *Be the type of professional and person with whom others want to partner.* Establishing effective relationships requires being trustworthy and honest, being competent and following through on promises, maintaining confidentiality, and maintaining integrity (Moore, 2000; Sandeen, 2000). Further, directing successful orientation programs with demonstrated results in a way that also advances the goals of other units or in a way that other units come to rely upon makes orientation professionals valuable to (and thus more powerful on) the campus.

By incorporating these strategies into everyday practice, orientation professionals will improve current collaborative relationships and lay the foundation for broader and deeper collaborations to come. These relationships also ensure the continued success of orientation programs. Intentionally studying the context in which these mutually beneficial relationships exist—that is, the campus culture and the power and politics involved—will provide practitioners with the knowledge necessary to maximize these partnerships to improve transition programs and ultimately contribute to student success.

References

American College Personnel Association (ACPA), & National Association of Student Personnel Administrators (NASPA). (1997). *Principles of good practice for student affairs.* Washington, DC: Authors.

Bess, J. L., & Dee, J. R. (2008). *Understanding college and university organization: Theories for effective policy and practice* (Vol. 2). Sterling, VA: Stylus.

Cawthon, T. W., & Ward-Roof, J. A. (1999). A survey on the skills necessary for effective orientation professionals. *The Journal of College Orientation and Transition, 6(2),* 15-19.

Cervero, R. M., & Wilson, A. L. (1994). *Planning responsibly for adult education.* San Francisco: Jossey-Bass.

Dickerson, J. C. (2001). Perceptions of organizational change by different levels of student affairs administrators. *The Journal of College Orientation and Transition, 9(1),* 13-23.

Farmer, D. W. (1990). Strategies for change. In D. W. Steeples (Ed.), *Managing change in higher education* (New Directions for Higher Education No. 71, pp. 7-18). San Francisco: Jossey-Bass.

Fried, J. (1999). Steps to creative campus collaboration. *The Journal of College Orientation and Transition, 7(1),* 11-19.

Keup, J., Walker, A., Astin, H. S., & Lindholm, J. A. (2001). *Organizational culture and institutional transformation.* Washington, DC: ERIC Clearinghouse on Higher Education.

Kuchynka, S. J., Rode, D. L., & Reeves, K. (1998). The dynamics of creating a freshman year program: A decade of reflection. *The Journal of College Orientation and Transition, 5(2),* 7-13.

Kuh, G. D. (2003). Organizational theory. In S. R. Komives & D. B. Woodard, Jr. (Eds.), *Student services: A handbook for the profession* (4th ed., pp. 269-296). San Francisco: Jossey-Bass.

Kuh, G. D., & Hall, J. (1993). *Cultural perspectives in student affairs.* Lanham, MD: University Press of America & American College Personnel Association.

Moore, P. L. (2000). The political dimensions of decision making. In M. J. Barr & M. K. Desler (Eds.), *The handbook of student affairs administration* (2nd ed., pp. 178-196). San Francisco: Jossey-Bass.

Mullendore, R. H. (1998). Orientation as a component of institutional retention efforts. In R. H. Mullendore (Ed.), *NODA orientation planning manual.* Bloomington, IN: National Orientation Directors Association.

Peska, S. F., & Young, K. N. (2007). *First-year connections 2007 annual report.* Retrieved June 22, 2008, from http://www.orientation.niu.edu/orientation/firstyear_conn/2007%20Annual%20Report.pdf

Pope, R. L., Miklitsch, T. A., & Weigand, M. J. (2005). First-year students: Embracing their diversity, enhancing our practice. In R. S. Feldman (Ed.), *Improving the first year of college: Research and practice* (pp. 51-71). Mahwah, NJ: Lawrence Erlbaum Associates.

Sandeen, C. A. (2000). Developing effective campus and community relationships. In M. J. Barr & M. K. Desler (Eds.), *The handbook of student affairs administration* (2nd ed., pp. 377-392). San Francisco: Jossey-Bass.

Schein, E. H. (1992). *Organizational culture and leadership* (2nd ed.). San Francisco: Jossey-Bass.

Schroeder, C. C. (1999). Forging educational partnerships that advance student learning. In G. S. Blimling & E. J. Whitt (Eds.), *Good practice in student affairs: Principles to foster student learning* (pp. 133-156). San Francisco: Jossey-Bass.

Smith, R. F., & Brackin, R. K. (2003). Components of a comprehensive orientation program. In J. A. Ward-Roof & C. Hatch (Eds.), *Designing successful transitions: A guide for orienting students to college* (Monograph No. 13, 2nd ed., pp. 39-53). Columbia, SC: University of South Carolina, National Resource Center for The First-Year Experience and Students in Transition.

Woodard, D. B., Jr., & Komives, S. R. (2003). Shaping the future. In S. R. Komives & D. B. Woodard, Jr. (Eds.), *Student services: A handbook for the profession* (4th ed., pp. 637-655). San Francisco: Jossey-Bass.

Chapter 15

Assessment and Evaluation in Orientation

Robert Schwartz and Dennis Wiese

Higher education has come under increasing scrutiny at the local, state, and federal levels. As costs for tuition and fees, books, room and board, and even entertainment have gone up, more and more students, parents, legislators, and agencies have asked for greater accountability. Why does it cost so much? What are students and parents getting for their money? Who benefits from these programs and activities? These are now common questions heard on most campuses and even more so from off campus. The challenge is to answer these questions effectively and in a timely manner. Assessment and evaluation, as discussed below, offer a variety of good answers to these tough questions.

Orientation and related programs that help students to transition to campus life and persist to graduation would seem to be necessary on any campus. However, a sound assessment and evaluation of such programs can help to demonstrate their vital contributions to student and institutional success for both internal and external audiences. Orientation directors and their staffs should view assessment and evaluation as a natural and important part of their jobs. By gathering responses from students and parents who participate in orientation as well as information from student leaders and professional staff in orientation and other participating offices, orientation professionals have the opportunity to assess existing programming and evaluate their efforts overall. New ideas, innovations, and the effective delivery of services to students are the results of a sound assessment and evaluation effort.

What Is Assessment and Evaluation?

The difference between assessment and evaluation can be confusing; however, a simple example from daily life helps clear this up. A person who gets up in the morning and looks in the mirror is making an assessment (i.e., How do I look? Is what I am wearing appropriate? Do these shoes match my outfit?) However, evaluation typically involves a decision based on the assessment. For example, the person who looks in the mirror might see that his tie does not match his shirt and, based on that assessment, decide not to wear it.

Healy (2000) argued that evaluation is intended to give an administrator the information needed to make decisions. Upcraft and Schuh (1996) described evaluation as any effort to use evidence to improve effectiveness. Thus, evaluation is a process of using enough information and evidence to implement change and make decisions. A useful working definition of evaluation for an orientation program includes a review of any and all available information gathered through a process of assessment and then using that information to reach a conclusion (evaluation) or to justify a modification to the program.

Astin (1996) stated that assessment is the gathering of information. More specifically, it is the means of gathering the needed evidence for the evaluation process. Erwin (1996) described assessment more comprehensively and included defining, measuring, and analyzing in the information-gathering process. Upcraft and Schuh (1996) also provide a wide-ranging definition of assessment and concluded that assessment includes not only evidence collection but also analysis and interpretation. A useful working definition of assessment for an orientation program is the continuous practice of collecting, analyzing, interpreting, and disseminating information about the program.

Evaluation has the word "value" built into it (Bhola, 1989). Evaluations often come at the end of a process and attempt to place a value on the activity and motivate a decision as to the worth of a program or action. Assessment is often an ongoing process, typically reviewed on a regular basis, to provide a measure of performance. For the orientation professional, the assessment process is the means by which one learns about the performance of the planned program; whereas, evaluation is the means of determining the quality and worthiness of a set of activities.

The Assessment and Evaluation of Orientation Programs

In a practical sense, the answer to, "Why assess and evaluate orientation programs?" can be summarized into the following categories: (a) habit, (b) requirement/expectation, (c) conformity, (d) politics, (e) accreditation, (f) planning, and (g) improvement and development (Schuh & Upcraft, 2001). The rewards of a rigorous assessment, evaluation, and reporting practices apply regardless of the impetus of their actions.

The practical benefits of assessment within orientation are greatest in two areas— politics and programmatic improvement and development. The methods associated with achieving success in each are not dissimilar; however, each requires specific attention. The political nature of assessment is well documented (Schuh & Upcraft, 1998; 2000; 2001). In 2000, Schuh and Upcraft cautioned student affairs professionals to be politically astute before diving into an assessment process—one must realize and accept that all assessment is political. Similarly, assessment can and should facilitate quality improvements and program development. The focus on quality allows for improvement through an examination of current practice and future planning (Schuh & Upcraft, 2001).

The current culture of assessment is an outgrowth of the intersection of external competition and accountability (Schuh & Upcraft, 2001; Upcraft & Schuh, 1996; Walvoord, 2004). These authors argue against the perpetuation of the status quo and poorly executed assessment practices (Walvoord). The benefits of assessment for orientation directors are to be found in meeting the demands of competition and accountability and the ability to answer several common questions. First, are the goals of the program aligned with those of the institution and the administrative unit where orientation is housed (Pike, 2000)? Second, is the program achieving the intended outcomes, provided those outcomes have been clearly identified (Barham & Scott, 2006)? Third, is the program effective and efficient (Healy, 2000)? Finally, are decisions grounded in program assessment and evaluation (Healy)?

For the orientation professional, the ability to answer the questions of external and internal constituents with rigorous assessment and evaluation data is essential, providing a strong foundation for a better orientation program. By addressing those four essential questions, orientation directors can ensure their position within the administrative unit and the institution, manage political pressures, and justify resource requests and/or current allocations. By addressing these issues, others can be assured that the orientation program is meeting—or exceeding—the needs and expectations of the orientation participants as well as those inside and outside the institution who demand accountability.

The need for assessment and evaluation is recognized, and in many cases demanded, by accrediting bodies and professional associations. The Council for the Advancement of Standards (CAS) as well as the National Orientation Directors Association (NODA) argue that assessment and evaluation are integral elements of a high-quality orientation program (CAS, 2008; Wiese, 2004). Many of the accrediting agencies, such as the Southern Association for Colleges and Schools (SACS), now require that institutions assess and demonstrate the use of outcomes measures as a part of the accreditation process (SACS, 2008). Outcomes, as will be discussed later, should be tied directly to assessment and evaluation and vice versa. Outcomes demand assessment and evaluation, and assessment and evaluation need outcomes as guides. When conducting assessment and evaluation, translating measures into an outcomes evaluation should be a smooth transition.

Quantitative, Qualitative, and Mixed-Method Assessment

Modern orientation programs provide opportunities to use a variety of assessment techniques. Yet, the selection of the most appropriate assessment method can be challenging. While orientation professionals may be able to collect large amounts of data, the use of that data and the overall needs of the program must be the driving factors in selecting the optimal assessment technique.

The Council for the Advancement of Standards (2008) concluded that orientation programs should employ both qualitative and quantitative methods in assessment plans. Creswell (2003) defined quantitative methods as involving numerical data, variables, analytical tests, hypotheses, and experimental and nonexperimental data collection practices. These methods yield data that can be counted and manipulated statistically. Qualitative data, on the other hand, usually seeks to capture participants' experiences from their own perspectives. To do so, it is often important to record the participants own words or perceptions through open-ended questions, in transcripts from interviews or focus groups, through observations, or even photographs (Creswell, 2003). Such data can then be analyzed to reveal themes or patterns of responses.

Historically, quantitative methods such as statistical testing and general "number crunching" were thought more objective and thus better suited to decision making (Creswell, 2003; Schuh & Upcraft, 1998; 2000; Upcraft & Schuh, 1996). However, qualitative methods such as interviews, focus groups, and the like have gained in popularity and value. Integrating the two methods can provide orientation professionals with a richer understanding of program performance and a more nuanced set of data to guide decision making.

While qualitative methods use words, quantitative methods require numerical data collection. Most often, these numbers are collected from items in a survey administered at the end of an orientation experience. These surveys are often composed of satisfaction questions related to the length of the program, the usefulness of the activities, and so on (Wiese, 2004). Some surveys may also inquire about the amount of time required to complete certain tasks or the number of students served by a particular program element. The finite and limited nature of quantitative data collection allows for quick statistical analysis and the use of descriptive and inferential analysis techniques, all of which provide an expedient means of assessment.

Instead of numbers, qualitative techniques use words or images derived from broad and general open-ended questions, observations, and similar methods (Creswell, 2008; Upcraft & Schuh, 1996). Instead of asking respondents to assess their satisfaction using a forced-choice tool such as a Likert scale, open-ended surveys or interviews allow students to share their experiences by inviting them to respond to statements such as, "Tell me about your orientation experience."

Just as the analysis of the quantitative data follow standardized statistical techniques, the analysis of the qualitative data uses rigorous techniques (Creswell, 2008). The qualitative approach requires the use of more resources per assessment participant (Upcraft & Schuh, 1996) in data collection and analysis. For example, qualitative analysis can be more labor-intensive because each response must be examined individually rather than collectively as in the statistical analysis (Upcraft & Schuh). There is no "mean" or average answer in qualitative data collection. Results that represent the comprehensive and holistic experience of a small number of respondents may not be generalizable to the whole (Creswell, 2008).

To thoroughly assess a campus-wide orientation program, the most vigorous approach would be to combine both quantitative and qualitative methods. This approach is referred to as mixed-method approach, and it maximizes the benefits of the individual techniques while minimizing the limitations and drawbacks (Creswell, 2003). Such approaches have proven especially effective following the implementation of significant changes or modifications to the orientation experience. The use of a mixed-method approach provides a measure of what participants think while allowing them to elaborate on their opinions. In such instances, a mixed-method assessment approach may provide a more accurate picture of an orientation program's success than employing only one approach, as the use of a single technique may exclude essential information (Creswell, 2003).

The choice among quantitative, qualitative, and mixed methods may be difficult to make. Many factors influence the decision (e.g., time, money, resources, campus culture, personnel, and preferences). The most important deciding factor should be the problems or needs for which the data are being collected (Creswell, 2003). For example, quantitative assessment can be appealing because it tends to be expedient, allowing for the collection and analysis of a large number of responses in a short time. However, it does not provide an in-depth perspective. A valid and reliable survey provides a narrowly focused and specific snapshot pertaining only to the preconceived questions designed by the assessment team.

A well-constructed qualitative interview or focus group is limited in the number of participants, but each allows for a more in-depth probe of specific information and deeper, richer understanding of participants' experiences (Creswell, 2008). In a face-to-face qualitative setting, additional information beyond the spoken responses is often collected, and participants' non-verbal responses are observed (e.g., tone and facial expressions). These behaviors can spur unscripted follow-up questions if needed. Areas of inexperience or uncertainty are best served by the use of both quantitative and qualitative measures through a mixed-method approach; thus orientation professionals are able to examine both the what and the why related to the program or orientation element in question. Regardless of the technique, orientation professionals are best served by placing the problem or need at the forefront of the decision-making process, thus increasing the likelihood of selecting the most suitable assessment technique.

Establishing an Orientation Assessment Program

Orientation professionals are often called on to supply feedback and assessment information to many constituents (Wiese, 2004). Such a program need not rest solely with the orientation office; in many cases, there are other professionals on campus who can help with this process, such as in a student affairs research office or the institutional research office (Upcraft & Schuh, 1996). Upcraft and Schuh also found that graduate students and faculty members in sociology, psychology, educational research, or any number of other related areas may have the time and skills to be helpful.

Irrespective of the primary job function of the identified individuals, there are distinct benefits to recruiting these individuals to assist with the design and implementation of the assessment and evaluation plan. They can provide invaluable expertise and may also increase the credibility of the findings as they bring both their own campus reputation and professional rigor to the assessment process (Posavac & Carey, 2007; Schuh & Upcraft, 2001; Upcraft & Schuh).

Developing an Assessment Plan

High-quality assessment begins with a defined question or problem (Creswell, 2008; Posavac & Carey, 2007; Schuh & Upcraft, 2001; Upcraft & Schuh, 1996). The Council for the Advancement of Standards (2008) has advocated that orientation programs be guided by a set of primary goals and objectives, and that these goals and objectives be in compliance with the mission statement of the host institution. Since most institutions are engaged in some form of regular assessment, whether for accreditation, fulfillment of a legislative mandate, or a prescribed internal evaluation, orientation program coordinators should align their assessment initiatives with larger institutional goals (Schuh & Upcraft, 2001). The coordination of the orientation assessment plan with the larger assessment needs of the institution also increases the likelihood that any assessment findings and conclusions will impact future decision making.

Practical steps can and should follow the establishment of an orientation assessment plan within the larger context. Leaders of orientation programs must identify who, what, when, where, and how the data will answer the previously defined questions and how that data will be collected (Wiese, 2004). In addition to these general questions, assessment plans are impacted by specific institution issues (e.g., What contribution does orientation make in meeting or exceeding institutional goals? Does the orientation program help with first- to second-year retention rates? Are there fewer academic or disciplinary difficulties with students who participated in orientation than those who did not? Are parents/family members who attend an orientation program more satisfied with their student's education? Are parents/family members less concerned about their student's safety than those who did not attend?) These questions and many others are critical to most institutions, and without an ongoing assessment and evaluation process, it will be difficult to provide good answers to them.

Developing and Using an Outcomes-Based Assessment

An outcome is the desired end result of a program or activity related to orientation. It is what students and, to a lesser degree, parents and family members of those students need to know, think, or be able to do as a result of their participation in orientation. Depending on the scope of the orientation program, several outcomes can be identified (e.g., New students will be familiar with and knowledgeable about college/university traditions, culture, and history.).

The next step after identifying and defining an outcome is to ensure that it is measurable. In the case of the outcome "New students will be familiar with and knowledgeable about college/university traditions, culture, and history," achievement can be measured by collecting student feedback through a survey, creating a competition to have students name as many college traditions as possible to see what they remember, or conducting interviews with randomly selected students to ask them about their knowledge of specific traditions and events.

Beyond specific program outcomes, there may also be some interest in looking at orientation activities as related to broader institutional outcomes (i.e., matriculation, retention, or attrition). Several research studies (Astin, 1970; 1993; Noel & Levitz, 2007) found that students who were connected to an institution through a high-quality orientation program and involved through organizations and activities were less likely to leave the institution. Such arguments supported by extensive data are critical points to be made on behalf of an orientation program, especially in terms of maintaining or expanding resources for orientation (e.g., expanding staff, arguing for more in-depth programming).

Astin's (1996) Input, Environment, and Outcomes (I-E-O) model provides a useful framework for conceptualizing the assessment plan. Inputs are those characteristics and attributes brought to an institution by the student. These variables may be anything from SAT or ACT scores to high school grades to race and gender and parental influences. Environment is the climate and culture that students experience once they are on the campus. The orientation program itself is often the first contact students have with the institutional environment, which is why it is so critical to new students' adjustment to campus. Finally, the third leg of the model is outcomes, or the results of these interactions between inputs and environments. Outcomes are intentional and should reflect the goals and mission of the institution. Specific outcomes that result from a strong orientation program can include (a) retention of students; (b) greater involvement within the institution; (c) stronger attachment to the institution and to other students, faculty, and staff; and (d) an alumni commitment. By thinking in terms of the I-E-O model, connections between programs and activities and links to a broader view of how an orientation program fits into the institutional mission will emerge.

Creating an Assessment Survey

Clearly, it is important to know how the students who participate in orientation feel about the program and what they learn. In most cases, some sort of survey is the most efficient and effective means of gathering information from a large number of people. A good survey is well-constructed; includes questions that are easy to understand and respond to; and takes minutes, not hours, to complete. An excellent resource for understanding how to construct a good survey or to evaluate an existing survey is Suskie's (1996) *Questionnaire Survey Research: What Works*. This monograph offers excellent suggestions and guidelines on everything from planning the survey to analysis of the data and reporting the results.

Instead of creating a new survey, it may be possible to borrow a survey from another institution, especially if it is a survey that has been successfully piloted and has had reliability and validity measures calculated. Academic journals or presentations from conferences such as National Orientation Directors Association, National Association of Student Personnel Administrators, American College Personnel Association, and others can also be good resources to find existing surveys. Obviously, survey items will need to be rewritten for different campuses, and some questions may need to be added or deleted. Again, consulting Suskie (1996) on how to revise an existing survey will be helpful in this process.

Another option is to use a commercial instrument, such as the National Survey of Student Engagement (NSSE), the Cooperative Institutional Research Program's (CIRP) Freshman Survey and Your First College Year Survey, and the Noel-Levitz Student Satisfaction Survey, among others. One drawback is that commercial instruments must typically be purchased and scored by the company that owns them. However, the benefits are significant: Commercial surveys are readily available, provide a national norm for comparison to other institutions, and are typically reliable in terms of accuracy.

A survey may also be a useful tool for understanding why students choose not to participate in orientation and for determining how they differ from participants in terms of entry characteristics and selected outcomes. Getting students who did not participate in orientation to complete a survey may be a challenge as they may not feel compelled to respond. Nevertheless, their responses are important.

Survey construction. The appearance of a survey can make a difference in the quality of the data collected. A good survey should be professional in appearance and easy to navigate. It must be carefully edited and then reviewed for mistakes. Once a survey instrument has been created, piloting the survey with students or colleagues will ensure that it is clear and easy to follow in terms of directions. Pilot survey participants can offer feedback on whether the questions are clear and easy to answer. Piloting the survey will also give the survey administrator an idea of how long it takes to complete.

"Talking" as Assessment - Qualitative Approaches

While much of the discussion so far has focused on quantitative approaches such as surveys, there is much to be said for using qualitative measures. Specifically, interviews or focus groups are an excellent means of collecting very valuable information about students' experiences. Individual interviews with students who participate in orientation activities can be extremely enlightening. However, the amount of time involved in sitting with an individual student can be very time-consuming. A more effective approach may be to use focus groups. A focus group gathers 8 to 10 students together at one time and leads them through a structured interview process. The focus group requires advance preparation and planning, but excellent guides, such as Krueger and Casey's (2000) *Focus Groups: A Guide to Applied Research*, are available to assist with this.

Focus groups allow students to share and express their responses to an orientation activity or the entire program in a structured setting. It is useful to have one person facilitate the discussion from prepared questions and another person take notes and keep track of responses, including non-verbal cues. It can also be useful for both facilitators to be prepared to alternate asking questions and taking notes. Video and/or audio recording can be useful in capturing the data as well.

Focus groups are a very useful way to gather reactions, responses, and more complete information from students. Because responses between participants in a focus group can spark reactions across the group, a great deal of information can be generated quickly. A response from one student will often generate several other responses from others. For example, in response to the question, "Did your parents make you come to orientation?" a student might say, "Oh, yeah, and I really didn't want to," which causes others to share their initial reactions as well.

Data from focus groups or interviews can be transcribed and then grouped into categories or themes. Transcription can be time consuming and even expensive. While these may be drawbacks to qualitative research, reading the actual words from a focus group or a set of interviews can be very illuminating and powerful.

Once results from a survey(s), interviews, or focus groups are collected and analyzed, they can be compared to previous data collected about the program or used to establish a baseline of data for the future. From data collection and analysis, the process moves from assessment to evaluation. As noted earlier, evaluation relates to the value of the program. Are there goals for the program, and do they fit with the mission of the institution? Does the program meet its goals? Is the program long enough or is it too long? What areas that aim to assist students in their transition to the institution are not being addressed, if any? Additional means of conducting an evaluation may come from other staff, faculty, or students at the institution, so sharing the results of the process may be very helpful.

Following the Student Cohort

A key element of the assessment and evaluation process is to keep track of the students who participated in orientation activities and have progressed in their college career. While orientation programs and other transition to college activities may end after a few weeks or an academic term, the assessment and evaluation process does not. It is important to ask the question: Do students who participate in orientation and its related programs and activities stay in school longer? Are their grades better than students who do not participate? Are they more likely to take advantage of and use institutional resources than students who do not participate? These are key elements that a good orientation and transition to college program should be addressing. These goals are critical not just to the orientation program but to the entire institution. If orientation and related programs can be shown to make a difference in retention and academic success, additional resources and support will be much more readily available. It is important to follow the cohort of students who participated in orientation (and to some extent, those who did not) through the first year of college, at a minimum, to see who stays, who does well, and who really benefits from orientation.

Sharing the Success and Correcting the Problems

The full potential of assessment is not met if the data are not used to drive future decisions. Schuh and Upcraft (1998) argued strongly for the importance of reporting and the use of assessment studies, saying, "A study that goes unread will not bring about change" (p. 8). The Council for the Advancement of Standards (2008) furthers the point, emphasizing that "assessment data must be used in revising and improving programs and services and in recognizing staff performance" (p. 238).

The high-profile nature of orientation programs means that most, if not all, other student services programs are interested in the success of their efforts. More and more, academic programs are realizing the importance of a good orientation program as well. The effective reporting of assessment that results from the orientation process helps to ensure that orientation programs are meeting the needs of the students they serve as well as the interests of the institution. By making the assessment and evaluation data available to a wide range of individuals, all interested parties can see how valuable the orientation program is and how much it benefits the college or university. Orientation directors should be able to celebrate their successes but also be willing to work on areas that may need improvement based on the results of the assessment and evaluation process.

Discussing and sharing assessment data among the orientation staff and with other institutional programs can help to generate greater support for orientation activities and programs. Good assessment and evaluation efforts allow the orientation program to reach out to supervisors and campus partners in a "let's solve this issue together" approach that can be very appealing and productive. For example, if the data indicate that more time is needed for orientation activities, it is likely that others will be willing to work on extending the program if it is clear from the assessment and evaluation process that those changes are necessary.

The challenges faced by orientation directors are numerous. Assessment allows directors to identify and meet current and future challenges with both short- and long-term strategies. By having a plan based on an ongoing assessment and evaluation process, orientation directors are able to indicate both attentiveness to their responsibilities and demonstrate an understanding of the ongoing and changing needs of their constituents.

As many orientation directors know, the profession as a whole can benefit from effective assessment and evaluation practices. By reporting findings from assessment and evaluations at regional and annual conferences, professionals can expand their knowledge and learn from each other's good work. Reporting on data collected at one institution often facilitates broad regional and even national changes to programs, thus benefiting many others beyond the boundaries of the reporting institution.

Reporting to Stakeholders

Having a solid and comprehensive assessment and evaluation process embedded in an orientation program is a very effective way to address the many constituencies (e.g., parents, administrators/supervisors, legislators, and accrediting agencies) who may want to review the program. Having such information readily available is impressive, as it demonstrates competence and a thorough knowledge of the program. It also allows orientation professionals to quickly demonstrate how efficiently the program is working, what areas need attention, and the efforts being made to address problems.

Conclusion and Implications

As noted earlier, once the basics of assessment and evaluation are put in place, for example, by using a survey at the end of each orientation program, it becomes a part of the orientation program. It is important to understand that assessment and evaluation are not one-time events. Assessment and evaluation should be conducted every year and be a continuous process. The assessment process may be enhanced by doing a survey at the beginning of the program and repeating the same survey at the end of the program. The pre- and post-survey method is very powerful way to demonstrate how much students have learned through orientation.

Another important step to consider is doing an assessment with the orientation staff, including student orientation leaders. Student orientation leaders have invested heavily in working with orientation and often observe a great deal in terms of their interactions with students and parents. They are a valuable resource for assessment and evaluation purposes. Again, a survey can be used for this purpose. However, using focus groups with orientation leaders at the end of the program may be very helpful in gathering information. Sometimes it can be helpful to do a survey first and then use the results in a focus group to extend the data collection by talking about the survey results.

By conducting a regular process of assessment and evaluation, a very valuable set of data and information about the orientation program will be generated. Having a steady stream of information about the program allows those who work with orientation programs and related areas to answer any inquiries about the value and benefits of the program. It also allows orientation staff to be able to quickly and confidently describe how and why an orientation program or individual activities within orientation are important to the institution. Planning for the future of the orientation program cannot be successful without good assessment and evaluation. Through the use of effective assessment and evaluation, the value of an orientation program will be clear and evident to both the orientation professional and to stakeholders in and outside the institution.

References

Astin, A. W. (1970). *Preventing students from dropping out*. San Francisco: Jossey-Bass.

Astin, A. W. (1993). *What matters in college: Four critical years revisited*. San Francisco: Jossey-Bass.

Astin, A. W. (1996). *Assessment for excellence: The philosophy and practice of assessment and evaluation in higher education*. Phoenix, AZ: ACE/The Oryx Press.

Barham, J. D., & Scott, J. H. (2006). Increasing accountability in student affairs through a new comprehensive assessment model. *The College Student Affairs Journal, 25,* 209-219.

Bhola, H. S. (1989). Evaluating "literacy for development" projects, programs and campaigns. Evaluation planning, design and implementation, and utilization of evaluation results. *UIE Handbooks and Reference Books 3.* Hamburg, Germany: Unesco Institute for Education.

Council for the Advancement of Standards in Higher Education. (2008). *The book of professional standards in higher education.* Washington, DC: Author.

Creswell, J. W. (2003). *Research design: Qualitative, quantitative, and mixed methods approaches.* Thousand Oaks, CA: Sage Publications.

Creswell, J. W. (2008). *Educational research: Planning, conducting, and evaluating quantitative and qualitative research* (3rd ed.). Upper Saddle River, NJ: Pearson.

Erwin, T. D. (1996). Assessment, evaluation, and research. In S. R. Komives & D. K. Woodard, Jr. (Eds.), *Student services: A handbook for the profession.* San Francisco: Jossey-Bass.

Healy, M. A. (2000). Knowing what works: Program evaluation. In D. L. Lindell & J. P. Lund (Eds.), *Powerful programming for student learning: Approaches that make a difference* (New Directions for Student Services No. 90, pp. 56-65). San Francisco: Jossey-Bass.

Krueger, R., & Casey, M. A. (2000) *Focus groups: A practical guide for applied research.* Thousand Oaks, CA: Sage Publications.

Noel, L., & Levitz, R. (2007). *National research report: Student retention practices at four year institutions.* Retrieved from http://www. noellevitz.com/

Pike, G. R. (2000, March/April). Rethinking the role of assessment. *About Campus, 5*(1), 11-19.

Posavac, E. J., & Carey, R. G. (2007). *Program evaluation: Methods and case studies* (7th ed). Upper Saddle River, NJ: Pearson.

Southern Association of Colleges and Schools (SACS). (2008). *Principles of accreditation.* Retrieved July 27, 2009, from http://www.sacscoc.org/pdf/2008PrinciplesofAccreditation.pdf

Schuh, J. H., & Upcraft, M. L. (1998, November/December). Facts and myths about assessment in student affairs. *About Campus, 3*(5), 2-8.

Schuh, J. H., & Upcraft, M. L. (2000, September/October). Assessment politics. *About Campus, 5*(4), 14-21.

Schuh, J. H., & Upcraft, M. L. (2001). *Assessment practice in student affairs: An application manual.* San Francisco: Jossey-Bass.

Suskie, L. (1996). *Questionnaire survey research: What works* (2nd ed.). Tallahassee, FL: Association for Institutional Research.

Upcraft, M. L., & Schuh, J. H. (1996). *Assessment in student affairs: A guide for practitioners.* San Francisco: Jossey-Bass.

Walvoord, B. E. (2004). *Assessment clear and simple: A practical guide for institutions, departments, and general education.* San Francisco: Jossey-Bass.

Wiese, D. (2004). The assessment of orientation programs: A practical approach. In M. J. Fabich (Ed.), *National Orientation Directors Association planning manual* (pp. 57-62). Pullman, WA: National Orientation Directors Association.

Additional Resources

Banta, T. (2002). *Building a scholarship of assessment.* San Francisco: Jossey-Bass.

Conley, D. T. (2008). *College knowledge: What it really takes for students to succeed and what we can do to get them ready.* San Francisco: Jossey-Bass.

Howard, R. (Ed.). (2007). *Using mixed methods in institutional research*. Tallahassee, FL: Association for Institutional Research.

Upcraft, M. L., & Schuh, J. H. (2002, March/April). Assessment vs. tt Why we should care about the difference. *About Campus, 7*(1),16-20.

Chapter 16

Reflections on the History and Future of Orientation, Transition, and Retention Programs

Jeanine A. Ward-Roof and Kathy L. Guthrie

Throughout the past 20 years, there have been a number of articles written and many research studies conducted on orientation, transition, and retention, and the contributors to this monograph have collaboratively offered readers a wealth of insights about these resources. The final chapter moves away from the literature to focus on what we have learned through practice and provides readers with anecdotal thoughts on changes in the field. Experienced professionals were asked to respond to a series of questions sent via e-mail, which asked them to reflect on trends in the field; predictions about the future; the role of orientation, transition, and retention professionals; and advice for today's professionals.[1] The combined experience in the field of student affairs of the nine professionals who responded totaled close to 300 years, and together they have held positions in orientation, admissions, alumni relations, residence life, enrollment management, and instruction. Their responses were analyzed and organized thematically. The chapter opens with a brief examination of the history of the field before turning to a discussion of current and future trends.

History

Higher education in the United States has transitioned from a model once heavily dominated by English education to one Thelin (2003) described as the "American Way," with a strong focus on undergraduate education. Roles have changed from the early years of education when many of the duties currently performed by student affairs professionals were the province of faculty (Horowitz, 1987; Lucas, 1994). During this transition, one might assume there has always been some sort of campus induction or orientation programming to help students (specifically undergraduate students) understand the institutional expectations and environment. Strumpf, Sharer, and Wawrzynski (2003) identify the earliest such effort at Harvard University in 1888, while Drake (1966) reports the origin at Boston University during the same year. The literature focusing on the impact and expectations of orientation programs was not established for quite some time, but early works can be found in a review of the literature by Drake. More contemporary research provides a comprehensive view of how orientation programs have changed during the history of higher education (Johnson, 1998). Because the history has been covered elsewhere in the monograph, highlights are summarized in Table 16.1.

Table 16.1

Milestones in the History of the Orientation, Transition, and Retention Field

Year(s)	Activity
1888	Earliest documentation of orientation-type activity at Harvard (Strumpf et al., 2003) and Boston University (Drake, 1966)
1920-1940	Freshmen courses and freshmen weeks were the primary method for orientating first-year students (Drake; Johnson, 1998).
1948	First meeting of orientation directors to discuss issues germane to their roles on campus. This event was the precursor for NODA (Fabich, 2008).
1950s	More structure emerged in orientation-type programs, freshmen weeks became less popular, and interest in first-year courses increased (Drake).
1960s	Pre-college programs began to emerge and small groups and peer mentors were introduced to assist with transitional issues (Drake; Johnson).
1970s	Diversity among the student populations increased (Barefoot & Gardner, 1993).
1976-1977	NODA's first Board of Directors was established, and NODA was chartered as a professional organization (Fabich).
1980s	Orientation became an established common practice on college and university campuses (Johnson). Student retention became an important part of orientation as accountability increased among campuses across the nation (Mann, 1998; Grantham, 1999).
1982 - 1986	In 1982, John Gardner hosted 175 people at the University of South Carolina to discuss freshmen seminars. The National Center for The Study of the Freshmen Year Experience (currently the National Resource Center for The First-Year Experience and Students in Transition) was founded in 1986 (National Resource Center, n.d.).
1990s-2000s	Increase in hybrid orientation programs focused on orientation, transition, and retention issues. Students attending programs were more consumer-minded, and programs had a strong focus on inclusion of parents and family members. Greater variety of programming enabled students to choose more than one type of interaction.

Reflections on Evolution of Program and Profession

The NODA *Databank* (2008; Strumpf, 2000; Strumpf & Sharer, 1993; 1996; Strumpf et al., 2003) is a useful resource for examining the evolution of this field. Two trends, in particular, are of note: (a) academic preparation of orientation professionals and (b) an expansion of job functions. Although the total number of respondents is low, the authors are confident that these responses are reflective of the larger orientation, transition, and retention field. It is also important to note that because the participants for each *Databank* administration are different, it is difficult to comment on trends. Nevertheless, these data highlight some interesting possibilities for how the field may be evolving. Most professionals in the field hold a master's degree, though it appears that those holding doctoral degrees may be decreasing (Table 16.2). While the majority of those responding to the *Databank* have orientation as their primary job function, there has been a slight increase in those who handle additional responsibilities (Table 16.3). Based on conference presentations, networking with professionals, and changes on our own campuses, we conclude that orientation has expanded beyond traditional offerings to include outdoor initiatives, camps, college- or major-centered first-year courses, transfer services, and parent programming. It may be reasonable to expect that this expansion will become increasingly apparent in the number of professionals asked to take on more than the orientation program.

Table 16.2

Academic Preparation of Orientation Professionals

	Databank Collection Period			
Highest Degree Earned	**1993-1995**	**1995-1997**	**2000**	**2008**
Bachelor's	14%	14%	16%	11%
Master's	87%	73%	76%	77%
Doctoral	14%	11%	9%	3%

Table 16.3

Orientation as Primary Job Function

	Databank Collection Period		
	1993-1995	**1995-1997**	**2000**
Orientation is primary job function	87%	83%	79%
Manage orientation in addition to other functions	13%	16%	20%

To gain a more comprehensive understanding of how the orientation, transition and retention profession has changed over the years, we consulted professionals who have spent time in the field. These professionals provided reflections on numerous changes they have experienced throughout their careers. From the responses, four major themes emerged, including (a) the use of technology, (b) the expansion of programs' role to reach wider audiences, (c) the addition of an academic component to programming, and (d) the shift in funding.

The use of technology has increased and evolved, as has the delivery of educational programs and services. In fact, technology has permeated and changed almost every aspect of orientation, transition, and retention programming including how we connect with today's students. From the proliferation of cell phones during programs providing students with constant and direct contact with parents/families/friends to including additional types of electronic media during programs, technology has evolved the entire field and will continue to do so. Although the traditional program models are still prevalent on many campuses, there is an increasing student population who are served by online programs. Additionally, electronic media such as web-based interactions and listservs have helped professionals deliver more timely resources. This approach to information dissemination ensures that resources are available when students need them—sometimes weeks or months after a brief, on-campus orientation program. Chapter 8 offers a broader discussion about the influence of technology in orientation, transition, and retention.

Orientation programs have also evolved to serve a wider audience including parents and a more diverse student body. The overall influence and involvement of parents in orientation, transition, and retention programs has increased dramatically with parent and family programs growing in length and depth. Because parents may be more ready to absorb vast amounts of information, different expectations for content and delivery are placed on parent orientation programs than on student programs. There is also a greater need to spend more time clearly defining the relationship between the parent and college/university. Chapter 6 addresses how parental involvement is important for student success. Working with a more diverse student body creates a rich learning environment; however, programming appropriately for these diverse groups' needs is challenging. As such, there is an increased presence of more focused orientation, transition, and retention programs for identified cohorts such as students of color, nontraditional or returning adult students, international students, honors students, and intercollegiate athletes.

Another aspect of the evolving role of programs is the emergence of more long-term student success initiatives. Ultimately, many programs are now designed to help students transition through their life cycle from prospective students to alumni. In some instances, such programs have transformed orientation from a stand-alone program to one component of an intentionally designed collection of programs and services for new students. This has led to an overall increase in the credibility of orientation programs as a whole. Another aspect of this role expansion is developing assessment tools to track cohorts and to contribute to retention research.

The third major theme emerging from professionals' responses is the increase of academic components in orientation, transition, and retention programs. Faculty have become more involved in broader first-year programming enabling the development of a more comprehensive approach, which includes first year seminars, convocations, workshops and experiential based courses.

Funding for orientation has shifted from institutional budget allocations to fee-based models. A positive outcome of this shift is that staff can better predict revenue; however, programs may also lose any vestiges of institutional support (e.g., salary lines) and be expected to cover their entire operating cost during tight budget times. Orientation, transition, and retention programs have also become more influenced by external forces such as parents and legislators. Some state governments even regulate costs and mandate specific program components. Due to some of these legislative mandates, even the orientation leader role has become much more complex.

Because of the evolution in technology, content, and populations served, there has also been a significant change in how orientation, transition, and retention professionals view themselves. In the past, many professionals in this field were seen as generalists, but now due to the complexities of campus life, their roles are much more specialized. Along with this change, staff members also have become more research-oriented and committed to developing future professionals.

Changes in the Student Population

While there have been significant changes in the profession of orientation, transition, and retention, there have also been significant changes in the student populations being served. Professionals provided reflections on the significant changes in students over the years. Three major themes emerged including students' unrealistic expectations of programs and services, an increased need for socialization and counseling support, and a more diverse student population attending college.

Students' expectations about the programs and services being offered have changed dramatically. There has been an increase in second- and third-generation college students attending college. Both parents and students possess higher levels of expectations for campus resources and service, which are often unrealistic. Along with unrealistic expectations, a sense of consumerism often arises. In prior years a college education was viewed as a privilege, but increasing numbers of college students believe they are entitled to receive an education, especially as the price they pay for that education increases.

Another theme to emerge in relation to changes in the student population includes an increased need for socialization and counseling support. While overall students' academic preparedness and quality have increased, their coping skills are often lacking. Students come to campus with more college credits and are able to achieve high grades in their courses; however, they have difficulty coping with relationship issues, negative interactions, policies, and procedures. Additionally, as technology continues to offer all people more access to information, students arrive on campus with a greater sophistication, but poorly developed social and interpersonal skills and less independence and autonomy. As a result, students are less able to navigate organizations and systems. In addition to the increased need for socialization, there has also been an increase in students with significant mental health challenges arriving on campuses. Many of these students' use of psychotropic drugs require corresponding treatment plans. During orientation, many professionals are challenged with how to address issues of care and support while communicating the limits of campus resources in these areas.

Finally, the diversity of students continues to change. Although each campus is unique and often includes more homogenous populations, the overall diversity of college students across North America has increased. At the same time, students appreciate and expect differences in their peers especially in race, gender, sexual orientation, and religion more than ever before. Students are also more oriented toward social justice issues, more tolerant, and more service-oriented, and they expect to see these values mirrored in college programming.

Predictions for the Future of Orientation, Transition, and Retention Programs

When asked about their predictions for the future of orientation, transition, and retention programs, professional responses echoed three themes: inclusiveness, technology, and accountability.

Those surveyed believe the future of orientation, transition, and retention programs will include a more comprehensive focus that sets a serious academic tone with opportunities to initiate and nurture working relationships with academic advisors and faculty members. In addition, on campuses with higher numbers of international students, professionals will need to program more intentionally to help native and international students form more meaningful relationships. They also suggested it was highly likely programs would need to include more ongoing career components, especially when students are expected to select majors prior to or early in their college tenure. In addition, the professionals stated staff will be asked to develop more opportunities for students to engage during programs, and it was suggested that this might be particularly true where programs serve small groups of students. Lastly, the professionals stated that current programs will develop into processes that shepherd students through their college careers. These programs will be hybrid in nature including in-person, online, physical, and other resources and services.

The second theme that emerged was that of technology. Respondents believed that programs will include more online opportunities to connect students to campus support services staff at non-traditional times. In addition, technology will continue to play a prominent role in the programs offered; developing online services and using such resources as online communities, social networking sites, blogs, and downloadable files as a means to reach out to students and host information in places where they frequently spend time. Professionals will be challenged to maintain the human interaction aspects of programs using these media and determine when and if the interactions can be managed online or in person. In addition, students will continue to arrive on campus using and expecting the latest technology while staff may struggle to stay current and find resources to purchase and support the technology needed to meet those expectations.

Lastly, the theme of increased accountability for the field emerged. Several respondents stated orientation, transition, and retention programs will be measured by their direct benefit to retention; this will be particularly important when first-generation students are welcomed to campus. As accountability levels continue to increase, several individuals predicted a potential for greater proliferation of orientation-like programs being offered well before students complete their high school experience. They indicated these types of programs will be designed to help students commit to the institution. Due to the current and likely future budget climate, there is a potential for the loss of summer programs or mandates to shorten program length. These changes could result in a departure from student development-based content, forcing staff to think differently about how to meet the needs of incoming students.

Advice for Orientation, Transition, and Retention Professionals

When asked to offer advice for other professionals in the field, the respondents touched on a number of areas including campus partnerships, program development, and personal professional development.

1. *Finding a voice and establishing a place at the table when administration gathers to discuss retention.* It is particularly important that others begin to understand how vital orientation, transition, and retention programs are to fulfilling the institutional mission, but it is difficult to communicate that message when orientation professionals are not a part of the conversation. In order to make sure they are included, professionals in the field need to develop working relationships/partnerships with members of academic departments, finance personnel, and all aspects of campus. They can use these relationships as a way to help others on campus understand how the key elements associated with effective, comprehensive orientation, transition, and retention programs relate to student success. Soliciting

involvement from individuals across campus or at least meeting with them to discuss how orientation and transition programs may relate to programs and services in their units are critical first steps in building these relationships.

2. *Creating and implementing well-rounded, inclusive programming that meets the needs of the campus community and incoming students.* It is critical that orientation programs maintain a balance between the social and academic aspects of college life. Moreover, orientation professionals should take time to learn the traditions and culture of the campus so that they can accurately reflect those foundations in programming. Helping new students learn about these aspects of campus life enables them to understand the origins of the campus community. While orientation and transition programs may sometimes become a catchall for a wide range of good ideas to help students make a successful transition, the orientation program cannot cover everything. Here again, relationships with units on campus that serve first-and second-year programs can help ensure that critical transition services are delivered in a timely and meaningful way to all students.

3. *Engaging students and challenging them in an atmosphere that is supportive but not always comfortable.* As student development educators, we are charged with being role models and demonstrating that congruence and leadership, values-integration, and personal integrity are about acknowledging and accepting one's blemishes and those of others.

4. *Using emerging technologies in innovative ways to connect students, faculty, and staff to learn and network.* For the most part, orientation, transition, and retention programs are opportunities to help students and their families understand the expectations, offerings, and culture of an institution. Using technology can help professionals offer information in real time and at appropriate intervals throughout a student's college career. Orientation professionals should take time to determine what needs to be offered in person and what can be offered online or through other media.

5. *Remaining engaged in orientation, transition, and retention work throughout the career.* Many professionals spend their careers coordinating programs and thoroughly enjoy the work and outreach they are able to do on a daily basis. Others have aspirations to advance in their careers, yet want to stay connected with orientation, transition, and retention programs. Opportunities to supervise these programs, present during orientation events, serve on the planning committee, or facilitate training exist on every campus. The best programs are populated with staff and faculty who are kind, enthusiastic, and emphatic, who reach outward and look inward, and who share a wealth of information with their colleagues. Successful orientation, transition, and retention programs require professionals who provide daily oversight and guidance as well as a network of campus consultants and champions who offer resources and support at critical moments.

Conclusion

This chapter offered some observations on the history, evolution, and future of the orientation, transition, and retention field. We must use this information as a foundation for moving forward, embracing the changes that lead us to implement stronger programs and services. As professionals, we need to figure out how to continue meeting students where they are developmentally while supporting their growth. All of the programming and services that are developed should support the fundamental needs of students and their families throughout the college experience. Former NODA vice president Diane Austin reflected on how we might achieve this:

The renowned cellist, Yo Yo Ma is quoted as having said, " I've tried to play a 'perfect' concert... and knew the music inside and out. While sitting there at the concert, playing the notes correctly, I started to wonder, 'Why am I here? I'm doing everything as planned. So what's at stake? Nothing. Not only is the audience bored, but I myself am bored. Perfection is not very communicative. However, when you subordinate your technique to the musical message you get really involved. Then you can take risks. It doesn't matter if you fail. What does matter is that you tried."

In the same way, when a program transcends its component parts, students can be transformed. As professionals who design and deliver programs, we need to learn the scores, and understand the beats and rhythms and tonalities of our handicraft; and then we need to put the sheet music aside, and focus on the moment and what we are creating with, and for, our audiences. It is at that moment that programs realize their mission.

As Austin eloquently stated, despite the type of institution, people involved, or students and families served, the ultimate goal of any orientation, transition, and retention professional is to know his or her institution and students and, therefore, develop programs and services that meet the needs of each while easing the transition of those involved. This is accomplished in similar and yet different ways at each institution. It is the role of the orientation, transition, and retention specialist to partner with others on campus and in the community to determine the best methods for this to occur at his or her institution.

Those who contributed their insights to shape this chapter continue to express excitement about the challenges and opportunities that exist for those in the orientation, transition, and retention field. Although we cannot be certain what the future will offer, we do know change, fast-paced environments, overwhelming amounts of information and campuses full of potential partners will be a part of our lives. We are going to help incoming students and their family members make successful transitions to their new roles, use the latest technologies to facilitate that work, and collaborate with those around us. Professionals who master strategies for accomplishing these tasks will be successful regardless of the challenges they face.

Notes

[1]We want to thank each of the professionals who offered their views on changes in the field that have affected our work and on how our work is likely to change in the future. They are listed below in alphabetical order along with their current affiliation and information on leadership roles they have held in this field.

Charlie Andrews
Director of Academic Advising at Florida International University; Former NODA President

Diane Austin
Vice President of Student Affairs at Lasell College; Former NODA Vice President

Dick Brackin
Retired Academic Advisor and Director of Orientation at Ohio University, Former NODA Director of Regions

Dave Hansen
Retired Special Assistant to the Vice President for Student Services at the University of Nevada, Reno; Former NODA President

Pam Horne
Assistant Vice President for Enrollment Management and Dean of Admission at Purdue University; Past NODA Vice President

Jim Martin
President, Lee Campus of Edison State College; Former NODA Annual Conference Facilitator

Ray Passkiewicz
Director of Kent Regional 4C; Former NODA Executive Secretary Treasurer

Jack Rhodes
Associate Vice Provost for Enrollment Management at Indiana University; Former NODA Director of Membership Services

Jim Zakley
Director of the Center for Advisement and Student Achievement at Colorado State University; Former NODA President

References

Barefoot, B. O., & Gardner, J. N. (1993). The freshmen orientation seminar: Extending the benefits of traditional orientation. In M. L. Upcraft, R. H. Mullendore, B. O. Barefoot, & D. S. Fidler (Eds.), *Designing successful transitions: A guide for orienting students to college* (Monograph No. 13, 1st ed.). Columbia, SC: University of South Carolina, National Resource Center for The Freshmen Year Experience.

Drake, R. W., Jr. (1966). *Review of the literature for freshmen orientation practices in the U. S.* (Report No. CG 004 110). Colorado State University, Fort Collins, CO: American College Personnel Association. (ED 030 920).

Fabich, M. J. (2008). *National Orientation Directors Association new member handbook.* Retrieved April 12, 2008, from http://nodaweb.org/files/MemberHandbook2008.pdf

Grantham, M. (1999). *Accountability in higher education: Are there "fatal errors" embedded in current U.S. policies affecting higher education?* Retrieved April 12, 2008, from http://danr.ucop.edu/eeeaea/Accountability_in_Higher_Education_Summary.htm

Horowitz, H. L. (1987). *Campus life: Undergraduate cultures from the end of the eighteenth century to the present.* Chicago: University of Chicago Press.

Johnson, M. J. (1998). First year orientation programs at four-year public institutions: A brief history. *The Journal of College Orientation and Transition, 5*(2), 25-31.

Lucas, C. J. (1994). *American higher education: A history.* New York: St. Martin's Griffin.

Mann, B. A. (1998). Retention principles for New Student Orientation programs. *The Journal of College Orientation and Transition, 6*(1), 15-20.

National Resource Center for The First Year Experience and Students in Transition. (n.d.). *History.* Retrieved April 12, 2009, from http://www.sc.edu/fye/center/history.html

Strumpf, G. (2000). *National Orientation Directors Association databank 2000*. College Park, MD: National Orientation Directors Association.

Strumpf, G., & Sharer, G. (1993). *National Orientation Directors Association databank 1993-1995*. College Park, MD: National Orientation Directors Association.

Strumpf, G., & Sharer, G. (1996). *National Orientation Directors Association databank 1995-1997*. Ann Arbor, MI: National Orientation Directors Association.

Strumpf, G., Sharer, G., & Wawrzynski, M. (2003). 20 years of trends and issues in orientation programs. In J. A. Ward-Roof & C. Hatch (Eds.), *Designing successful transitions: A guide for orienting students to college* (Monograph No. 13, 2nd ed., pp. 31-38). Columbia, SC: University of South Carolina, National Resource Center for The First-Year Experience and Students in Transition.

Thelin, J. R. (2003). Historical overview of American higher education. In S. R. Komives, D. B. Woodard, Jr., & Associates. *Student services: A handbook for the profession* (pp. 3-22). San Francisco: Jossey-Bass.

About the Contributors

Charlie Andrews is currently the director of the Academic Advising Center at Florida International University (FIU) in Miami, FL. He has been working in higher education since 1994 and has held various positions in academic advising, orientation, student activities, and Greek life at a number of institutions including Bowling Green State University (BGSU), Heidelberg College, and FIU. He earned a bachelor of science degree in mathematics education from FIU and a master of arts degree in college student personnel from BGSU. Andrews has presented at several regional and national conferences and has served as an external consultant for new student orientation programs. He has been an active member of the National Orientation Directors Association (NODA) since 1996. During his time as a NODA member, he has been involved with several committees and strategic planning efforts. He has served in several leadership positions within NODA, including a term as president from 2004-2007.

J.J. Brown currently serves as the associate vice chancellor and dean of students at Appalachian State University in Boone, North Carolina. Brown joined the student development team at Appalachian State University in June 2010 after working at The University of Tennessee (UT), Knoxville for 17 years, where he began his career. At UT, Brown served as the director of student orientation and leadership development for eight years. He then worked nine years as an associate dean of students. During this time, he also was elected to a three-year term (2001-2004) on the National Orientation Directors Association (NODA) Board representing Region VI. Brown has his bachelor's degree in speech communication and master's degree in college student personnel from The University of Tennessee, Knoxville.

Tony W. Cawthon currently serves as department chair of Leadership, Counselor Education, Human and Organizational Development at Clemson University. Prior to his faculty career at Clemson University, Cawthon worked as a student affairs administrator for more than 15 years at Clemson University, Mississippi State University, and The University of Tennessee, Knoxville. During his time as a practitioner, he worked in university housing. He has written extensively in the areas of student affairs and higher education and has presented nationally and internationally on numerous student and higher education issues. Specifically, his publications and presentations have been in the areas of career/professional development, new professionals, student and faculty issues, and student affairs administrative issues. He has written numerous book chapters and articles in scholarly and practitioner journals such as the *NASPA Journal*, the *College Student Affairs Journal*, the *Journal of College and University Student Housing*, and the *Journal of College*

Orientation and Transition. He is the co-editor of *Using the Entertainment Media to Facilitate Student Learning: Movies, Music, Television, and Popular Press Books in Student Affairs Classrooms and Practice* (New Directions for Student Services series). Cawthon is also currently active in a number of professional associations and is a senior scholar with ACPA. Cawthon serves on the editorial board as a reviewer for *Journal of the Professoriate* and *Journal of College Student Retention: Research, Theory, and Practice.* He currently serves as the director of knowledge enhancement of the executive board of the Association of College and University Housing Officers International (ACUHO-I). He previously served as program chair for ACUHO-I and the Southern Association for College Student Affairs.

Archie P. Cubarrubia is an education statistician at the National Center for Education Statistics (NCES) in the Institute of Education Sciences at the U.S. Department of Education. He serves as the survey director for the student financial aid component of the Integrated Postsecondary Education Data System (IPEDS) and as the designated federal official for the U.S. Department of Education's Advisory Committee on Measures of Student Success. Before joining NCES, he coordinated program oversight and monitoring activities in the Office of Postsecondary Education at the Department and developed risk-based performance assessment models for postsecondary grant programs. He also served as senior analyst for the Office of the Under Secretary and was part of the team responsible for implementing the Department's higher education transformation agenda to increase the accessibility, affordability, and accountability of America's colleges and universities. Specifically, he was responsible for the Department's activities around promoting higher education accountability and transparency in transfer of credit, accreditation, and student learning outcomes. In addition, Cubarrubia served as senior analyst for former Secretary of Education Margaret Spellings' Commission on the Future of Higher Education. Prior to joining the U.S. Department of Education, he coordinated first-year student success programs at the University of Rhode Island, Northern Arizona University, and Boston University.

Cathy J. Cuevas has worked with new students in the areas of admissions, recruitment, orientation, and retention since 1995. She earned her bachelor's and master's degrees from Florida State University. She served as director of new student orientation at Tallahassee Community College (TCC) from 1999-2007 and led a complete redesign of the program, including the creation of the college's first online orientation program. She has been a member of NODA for 10 years, serving as a NODA board member from 2004-2007 and as co-host for SROW (Southern Regional Orientation Workshop) in 2007. Cuevas has presented at numerous national/international conferences, including NODA, the League of Innovations Conference, and the National Institute for Staff and Organizational Development. She has also served as a panelist for two audio conferences, "Trends and Best Practices in Orientation" and "Orientation Plugged In: How to Create an Online Orientation Program." Cuevas co-authored a chapter on two-year orientation programs in NODA's *Orientation Planning Manual.* Most recently, Cuevas has worked with Tallahassee Community College's Title III Grant, working to improve student retention and graduation rates.

Michael Dannells is the former director of admissions at Eastern Oregon University. He also served as a faculty member in the Department of Higher Education and Student Affairs at Bowling Green State University. He was the director of residence life and new student programs at Northern Arizona University. He holds a Ph.D. in college student development from the University of Iowa, and his undergraduate degree is in business management from Bradley University.

Kathy L. Guthrie is an assistant professor in the Department of Educational Leadership and Policy Studies at Florida State University. In addition to teaching courses in higher education and student affairs, she is the coordinator of the undergraduate certificate in leadership studies. Guthrie completed her doctoral work at the University of Illinois at Urbana-Champaign, earning a Ph.D. in educational organization and leadership. She earned her bachelor's degree from North Central College and a master's degree in education from Illinois State University. Guthrie was a student affairs practitioner for 10 years in the areas of leadership, civic engagement, student unions, and student activities. Her research interests and areas of expertise focus on development of leadership skills and responsible citizenship in undergraduate students. Her current research focus is the impact of leadership and civic education programs, distance education, and reflective teaching and learning.

Brittany D. Henderson currently serves as the senior student services coordinator at DeVry University's Federal Way, Washington campus. In 2003, she was a winner of the graduate student case study at the National Orientation Directors Association (NODA) Annual Conference and served as NODA Regional Coordinator from 2007-2010. Her work at DeVry University has earned her numerous accolades, including three Campus MVP awards, the DeVry Seattle Associated Student Body Outstanding Staff award, the DeVry Legacy of Service award, and two Ron Taylor awards. Henderson received her bachelor's degree from the University of Puget Sound and master's degree from Seattle University. She is looking forward to starting her doctoral degree in the fall of 2011.

Cynthia L. Hernandez serves as the special assistant to the vice president for student affairs at Texas A&M University. She has more than 14 years of experience in higher education and student affairs. Her passion for first-year student programming began during her undergraduate years while serving as an orientation leader and continued during her time as a graduate assistant and as the assistant coordinator in the Office of Student Life Orientation at Texas A&M University. A three-year stint as the orientation coordinator at Northern Arizona University was followed by a return to Texas A&M, where she progressed from coordinator of New Student Programs to interim assistant director of the department, before accepting a position as special assistant to the vice president for student affairs. In this role, she remains committed to first-year student issues by co-chairing the university-wide Task Force for the First Year Experience and serving on the Orientation Oversight Committee. Throughout her career, she has remained an active contributor to National Orientation Directors Association (NODA), earning the organization's Outstanding Orientation Professional Award in 2004 and was recently elected to serve the 17th president of the association. Prior to her selection as president, she served as Region IV Coordinator, editor of the quarterly newsletter, and vice president for internal relations and membership. Hernandez holds a bachelor's degree in animal science and a master's degree in student affairs administration in higher education from Texas A&M University. She is currently pursuing her doctorate in educational administration. In addition to the NODA Outstanding Orientation Professional Award, she has received The Association of Former Students' Randy Matson '67 Professional Staff Award. She is a member of the National Association of Student Personnel Administrators (NASPA) and the Association for Student Conduct Administration (ASCA).

Shandol C. Hoover is the associate director of New Student & Carolina Parent Programs at the University of North Carolina at Chapel Hill. She has worked with new student programs at The Pennsylvania State University and Purdue University and also worked in the areas of residence life, academic advising, and admissions. Hoover is the NODA Transfer Student Network co-chair and has also served as a NODA Region VIII Board of Directors' member and co-chair of the NODA Graduate Student Network. An ACPA Annuit Coeptis Emerging Professional recipient, Hoover received her bachelor's degree from Purdue University and a master's degree from the University of Maryland, College Park.

Bonita C. Jacobs is the executive director of the National Institute for the Study of Transfer Students and an associate professor of higher education at the University of North Texas, a research university of more than 36,000 students. She holds an undergraduate degree in Spanish and a master's degree in counseling from Stephen F. Austin State University with additional studies in Morelia and Monterrey, Mexico, and a Ph.D. in educational administration from Texas A&M University. She was dean of students and interim vice chancellor for student development at Western Carolina University prior to assuming the position of vice president for student development at the University of North Texas, a position she held for 11 years. Jacobs is a former editor of *The Journal of College Orientation and Transition* and is the recipient of the Outstanding Contributions to the Orientation Profession Award and The President's Award, both from NODA, and the Ted. K. Miller Achievement of Excellence Award from the Council for the Advancement of Standards. She received the John Jones Award from NASPA Region III and was a faculty member for ACPA's Donna M. Bourassa Mid-Level Management Institute. She is the recipient of the Texas Higher Education Coordinating Board Star Award and a NASPA Gold Excellence Award recipient for her work with the UNT Student Money Management Center. Jacobs is a past president of TACUSPA and an outgoing member of the advisory board for the National Resource Center for The First-Year Experience and Students in Transition. She is a member of the Executive Board for APLU Council on Student Affairs. Her publications include *The College Transfer Student in America: The Forgotten Student* and *Starting From Scratch* (a first-year experience textbook) and numerous chapters, journal articles, and reviews. She has received more than three million dollars in grant funding and is a frequent speaker and consultant on transfer student issues.

Michael J. Knox is currently the assistant vice president for student affairs and director of orientation at the University of Texas (UT) at Arlington. He has been involved in orientation programming and development for more than 15 years at various institutions, including Texas A&M University, The University of Kentucky, Bellarmine University, and UT Arlington. He served two years on the Board of Directors for NODA, is a member of NASPA and ASCA, and is active in his state student affairs professional associations. Knox has a bachelor's degree from Texas A&M University, a master's degree from the University of Pennsylvania, and is currently completing his dissertation towards his Ph.D. degree at the University of Louisville. His dissertation plans are to investigate the transfer student experience compared to the faculty perceptions of student experience and preparation.

Jennifer A. Latino is an educator and practitioner whose career has centered on support for first-year students through a variety of roles at a diverse array of institutions including a private women's college, a community college, and large research universities. Through positions in new student orientation, student leadership development, residence life, and the first-year seminar, Latino has developed a thorough understanding of the needs and challenges that face students in transition. Her research interests include identifying and implementing best practices in the first-year seminar, the unique needs of at-risk populations, and exploring how students from diverse backgrounds perceive their college experiences. Latino supports first-year students through her work with the nationally recognized University 101 program at the University of South Carolina. She assists in the direction of the first-year seminar including faculty development for more than 150 instructors, coordination of the peer and graduate leader programs, assessment of learning outcomes and course success, coordination of the annual University 101 Scholarship and Outstanding Freshman Advocate awards processes, and direction of the annual First-Year Reading Experience. Latino is an author and the editor of *Transitions*, the common textbook for the UNIV 101 course, an author of *Connections: An Insider's Guide to College Success*, and is a regularly invited presenter for institutes and conferences sponsored by the National Resource Center for The First-Year Experience and Students in Transition. Latino serves as an instructor for UNIV 101, The Student in the University, as well as adjunct faculty to the College of Education as an instructor for the EDLP 520 course, The Teacher As Manager. She has a bachelor of science degree from the University of North Carolina at Pembroke, a master of science in higher education from North Carolina State University, and a doctorate of education in higher education from Florida State University.

Beth M. Lingren Clark is the director for Orientation & First-Year Programs at the University of Minnesota. She is responsible for providing direction and support to those who manage the processes for orientation, Welcome Week, and other first-year initiatives to ensure that students have a seamless transition to university life and are personally and academically successful. She has worked on creating a common campus culture for assessment while developing an intentional assessment plan for her office in an effort to identify transitional themes and issues to alter program content and messaging to impact retention. Lingren Clark is committed to using data to validate the work being done to impact the student experience. She received her bachelor's degree from South Dakota State University, her master's from Western Illinois University, and her Ph.D. from Southern Illinois University – Carbondale. She has served in various capacities with National Orientation Directors Association (NODA), including the NODA Board of Directors from 2002-2005, as conference cohost in 2004, and as vice president (2005-2008). In 2002, she was the recipient of the NODA Outstanding Research Award for her dissertation work on the experience of first-year students at a four-year, public institution.

Ryan Lombardi is the associate vice president for student affairs and dean of students at Ohio University, where he has served since May 2008. Prior to his current role, he was associate and assistant dean of students at Duke University from 2001-2008. He has also worked in residence life and orientation at Colorado College. In his current role, Lombardi is responsible for providing leadership to the student experience at Ohio University and does so through supervisory responsibility of multiple departments including the dean of students office, campus involvement center (Greek life, community service, student organizations, health promotion, leadership, campus programs, performing arts series), student health services, counseling & psychological services, campus recreation, university judiciaries, career services, and parent outreach programs. Lombardi is completing a doctorate in higher education administration at North Carolina State University and has a master's degree in higher education from the University of Kansas and a bachelor's degree in music education from West Chester University. He is an active member of NASPA and currently serves as the national co-chair of the Parent & Family Relations Knowledge Community.

Craig E. Mack has a variety of professional experiences ranging from a large, private university to a small, public community college. He currently serves as the associate dean of students at MassBay Community College. During the course of his professional career, Mack has been responsible for several student affairs areas including orientation, off-campus services, student conduct, compliance, wellness, community service, and student development. Mack earned his bachelor's degree from Bowling Green State University and his master's from University of South Carolina. He is currently pursuing his doctorate in educational leadership at Johnson and Wales University. Mack has been involved in a number of professional associations and volunteer agencies over the past two decades. In addition, he has served as the executive director for the Allston-Brighton Food Pantry in Brighton, MA, and most recently as the president of the National Orientation Directors Association (NODA).

April Mann is the director of New Student & Carolina Parent Programs at the University of North Carolina at Chapel Hill where she oversees all aspects of orientation, the Carolina Summer Reading Program, first-year and transfer student initiatives, and parent/family programs and communications. Prior to her position at UNC, Mann served as the associate director of Orientation & Commuter Student Services at Florida International University in Miami, FL. She also served as assistant dean of students at Arkansas State University. At both Florida International and Arkansas State Universities, Mann taught first-seminar courses. In 2008, Mann was elected to a three-year term on the executive board for the National Orientation Directors Association (NODA) as the director of annual conferences. She holds a bachelor's degree in history and English from Mississippi State University, a master's degree in student personnel services from the University of South Carolina, and is completing her doctorate in higher education administration at Florida International University.

Blaire Moody Rideout is an academic advisor for Ross School of Business at the University of Michigan Ann Arbor. In addition to advising students, Moody Rideout coordinates the Preferred Admission first-year workshop series and mentorship program and directs MREACH (Michigan Ross School of Business Enriching Academics in Collaboration with High Schools), an outreach program for underrepresented students in Southeast Michigan. Prior to her work in advising, she served as the recruitment coordinator for the Visitors Center and Outreach Initiatives in the Office of Undergraduate Admissions at the University of Michigan Ann Arbor. Moody Rideout received her master's degree in higher education and student affairs administration from the University of South Carolina where she served as a graduate assistant for the National Resource Center for The First-Year Experience and Students in Transition and as a graduate teaching assistant for University 101. Her bachelor's degree is in psychology from Ohio Wesleyan University.

Laura A. Page is the coordinator for parent relations at the University of Missouri (UM), and formerly the director of parents' programs at the University of South Carolina. She earned a master's degree in counseling and student-affairs administration from Clemson University and a bachelor's degree in sociology from Western Carolina University. Her broad experience in higher education and student affairs includes Greek life, orientation, undergraduate admissions, and development.

Most recently, she established a centralized parent relations office at UM, collaborating with colleagues campus-wide to expand the services offered to all parents of undergraduate students. Page is involved with parent relations on both a regional and national level. She serves as a regional representative for the Parent and Family Relations Knowledge Community and on the national leadership team with responsibility over member engagement and blog moderation. Numerous presentations at the NASPA annual conference by Page and her colleagues have centered around the topic of positive parental engagement on college campuses.

Joe Ritchie is currently in his 10th year at the University of Central Florida, serving as the executive director of the First Year Experience. He oversees orientation programming for all undergraduate students and their family members, welcome week activities, a first-year connection program called LINK, and coordinates the first-year experience course, Strategies for Success in College. Over the past four years he has increased enrollment by more than 250 students, instituted a peer mentor program, and worked on a university-wide information fluency project that was implemented within the course. He received both his bachelor's and master's degrees from Indiana University of Pennsylvania and worked there for seven years in the Advising and Testing Center office. He has been involved with NODA since 1992 and has served as a state coordinator, regional conference host, editor for the New Member Handbook, the Annual Conference Facilitator, a member of several NODAC planning committees, and as a faculty member for the Orientation Professionals Institute. Personally, he is a member of Phi Mu Alpha Sinfonia music fraternity and serves as an advisor and province governor for numerous chapters within Florida.

Denise L. Rode, director of orientation & first-year experience, has directed Northern Illinois University's new student and family orientation programs since 1987. As part of her responsibilities, she also oversees an extended orientation course enrolling more than 1,800 first-year and transfer students each fall. She has led the Foundations of Excellence in the First Year of College self-study and improvement initiative on her campus. Rode has been honored with a Presidential Supportive Professional Award for Excellence on her campus and was designated a semi-finalist for the Outstanding First-Year Student Advocate Award, cosponsored by the National Resource Center for The First-Year Experience and Students in Transition and Houghton Mifflin Publishing. She was named the National Orientation Directors Association's (NODA) Outstanding Orientation Professional in 2002, received the award for Outstanding Contributions to the Orientation Profession in 2007, and was honored with the Outstanding Editor award in 2009. Rhode's scholarly interests include the application of student development/learning theory to the field of orientation and transition and preparing new professionals for service in higher education. An avid writer and editor, Rode has authored or coauthored 26 journal articles, textbooks, and several manuals and monograph chapters. She is a frequent presenter at NODA, NASPA, and First-Year Experience conferences. Beyond the campus, Rhode is editor of *The Journal of College Orientation and Transition* for NODA and teaches graduate student affairs courses at DePaul University in Chicago. Rode is a three-time alumna of NIU, earning a bachelor's degree in English and journalism, a master's degree in counselor education, and a doctorate of education with an emphasis in college student development. Her most significant current learning experience is parenting a successful college student.

Norma Rodenburg currently works as the student affairs officer in the Office of the Dean of Students at the University of Alberta. Prior to this, she worked for the University of Alberta Students' Union as the transition programs manager for four years and as the senior manager of student services for another four years. Rodenburg has been an active member of NODA since 2002. She was a member of the Board of Directors representing Region 1 from 2005-2008, hosted the first Region 1 conference in Canada, and has presented at numerous annual and regional conferences. Rodenburg is also an active member with the Canadian Association of College and University Student Services (CACUSS) and the Student Affairs and Services Association (SASA). Her most recent achievement is completing her master of arts degree in leadership from Royal Roads University. Her research focused on how to develop the leadership capacity of student group executive members at the University of Alberta. She is now working on implementing the recommendations of her study.

Jennifer C. Schoen is the student outreach and pre-college programs coordinator in the Office of Minority Affairs and Diversity at the University of Washington (UW). In her position, she coordinates the University's Champions Program for Alumni and Youth in Foster Care and serves more than 400 College Success Foundation Scholars (CSF) as the scholar coordinator, helping high school CSF scholars with the admissions process and advising the UW scholars through college graduation. Schoen has been working in higher education for the past 23 years and has 12 years of experience in admissions work, including the past nine years at the University of Washington. She earned her bachelor's degree from Muhlenberg College and her master's in higher education and student affairs administration from the University of Vermont. During her career Schoen has held positions in orientation and first-year programs, career development, student activities, and leadership development. She has served on the Board of Directors for the National Orientation Directors' Association and is a member of NACAC, NASPA and HECA. Her upcoming publication, *The Zinjenzo Guide to a Great College Application*, is written specifically for high school seniors. Through her web site, www.Zinjenzo.com, Schoen hopes to guide many students and parents through the college admissions process.

Robert Schwartz is a faculty member in the higher education program at Florida State University. He teaches a wide range of courses in higher education to both masters and doctoral students. He has published in the *Journal of College Student Development, Journal of Higher Education, Review of Higher Education, The Journal of Negro Education,* and the *College Student Journal.* He is a member of NASPA, AERA, AIR, and HES. He completed his doctoral work at Indiana University in higher education with minors in American studies and women's studies. His research interests include women and minorities in higher education, history of higher education, and research on student concerns. He received the 2008 Faculty Seminole Award, presented to a faculty member who is "responsible for major contributions to the university through service to students."

Tracy L. Skipper is assistant director for publications for the National Resource Center for The First-Year Experience and Students in Transition at the University of South Carolina. Prior to her work at the Center, she served as director of residence life and judicial affairs at Shorter College in Rome, Georgia, where her duties included teaching in the college's first-year seminar program and serving as an academic advisor for first-year students. She also served as director of student activities and residence life at Wesleyan College. Skipper has taught both first-year English and University 101 at South Carolina. She edited (with Roxanne Argo) *Involvement in Campus Activities and the Retention of First-Year College Students* (2003) and wrote *Student Development in the First College Year: A Primer for College Educators* (2005). In 2010, Skipper was appointed to a three-year term on the directorate board for the ACPA Commission on Admissions, Orientation,

and the First-Year Experience. She holds a bachelor's degree in psychology from the University of South Carolina, a master's degree in higher education from Florida State University, and a master's in American literature and doctorate in rhetoric and composition from the University of South Carolina. She has presented on the application of student development theory to curricular and cocurricular contexts and on the design and evaluation of writing assignments. Her research interests include the application of cognitive-structural development to composition pedagogy and the use of writing in first-year seminars.

Dian Squire is currently the assistant director of orientation at the University of Maryland, College Park. His main duties include the planning and implementation of new student orientation programs for approximately 12,000 students and family members annually. Additionally, he teaches new student seminars and leadership courses. Squire is the Region VIII coordinator for the National Orientation Directors Association and as such sits on the Board of Directors. He has received awards such as Outstanding Regional Coordinator and Outstanding Professional for Region VIII. He is a directorate board member for the ACPA Commission for Admissions, Orientation and First Year Experience. Squire received his bachelor of science degree from Florida State University in English education and his master of arts degree in educational policy and administration from the University of Maryland, College Park.

Christine Timmerman earned an associate's degree from Kansas City Kansas Community College and a bachelor's degree in business administration and a master's in education from Kansas State University. She has worked in the areas of orientation, career planning, counseling, and new student programs at Illinois Benedictine College, The University of Texas at San Antonio, and Lone Star College-CyFair. Timmerman has been involved in NODA for 20 years and has served as vice president, a member of the Board of Directors, a committee member for three regional and national conference committees, and a presenter at multiple conferences. She was the coordinator and a faculty member for the inaugural NODA Orientation Professionals Institute and coordinated the program for 10 years. Timmerman co-authored a chapter on orientation leader training and on two-year college orientation programs for two separate NODA orientation planning manuals. She was honored as an Outstanding First-Year Student Advocate by the National Resource Center for The First-Year Experience and Students in Transition and Houghton-Mifflin Publishing, received one of the first inaugural employee recognition awards at Illinois Benedictine College, the Outstanding Professional Staff Member award at The University of Texas at San Antonio, the Unsung Hero and Star Morale awards at Lone Star College-CyFair, and both the Outstanding Service Award and the President's Award from NODA.

Jeanine A. Ward-Roof serves as the dean of students at Florida State University where she is responsible for Greek life, new student and family programs, disability resources, student rights and responsibilities, victim advocate programs, withdrawal services and crisis management. Prior to her role at Florida State, she worked at Clemson University for 16 years with a variety of areas including orientation, parent and first year programs. She has been in a number of leadership roles in the National Orientation Directors Association (NODA), including president, and is the Region III secretary/treasurer for NASPA. Ward-Roof is also a lead facilitator for LeaderShape and most recently worked with an Institute in Doha, Qatar. She has published and presented on a number of topics including orientation, parents, transfer students, change, and international experiences. Most recently, she wrote two chapters with colleagues: "Designing a Study Abroad Experience:

Academic and Student Affairs Collaboration" which appeared in *Internationalization of Student Affairs and Services* and "Capitalizing on Parent and Family Partnerships Through Programming" in *Managing Parent Partnerships: Maximizing Influence, Minimizing Interference, and Focusing on Student Success*. She also wrote "Parent Orientation: Begin with the End in Mind" in *Partnering with the Parents of Today's College Students*, a NASPA publication. She received her bachelor's degree in communication from Ohio University, master's degree in college student personnel from Bowling Green State University, and doctor of philosophy degree in educational leadership from Clemson University. She has received a number of awards during her career including the Florida State University Jeffrey A. Gabor Superior Achievement Award and the Outstanding Research, President's, and New Professional Awards from NODA.

Matthew J. Weigand is director of New Student Programs at the University at Buffalo (SUNY), overseeing orientation programs, first-year seminars, and parent and family programs. He has presented and published on such topics as first-year student success, multicultural competence and diversity, and transfer student services. He is actively involved in professional associations such as ACPA, NASPA, and particularly NODA, where he has served on the Board of Directors, on national and regional conference planning committees, and in several other roles. He received his bachelor's, master's, and doctoral degrees from the University at Buffalo, where he currently serves as an adjunct assistant professor in the Department of Educational Leadership & Policy.

Dorothy Weigel is an editor for publications for the National Resource Center for The First-Year Experience and Students in Transition at the University of South Carolina. Prior to her work at the Center, she served as the director of residence education at Messiah College in Grantham, PA. While at Messiah, she was also a residence director and adjunct career counselor. She holds a bachelor's degree in English from King College, a master's degree in student development from Appalachian State University, and doctorate in higher education administration from the University of South Carolina. Weigel received several fellowships through the College of Education at the University of South Carolina, including the James A. Stoddard and Paul P. Fidler fellowships. She has presented at several national conferences on topics such as student development theory and transition. Her research interests include the first-year transition experiences for third-culture students.

Dennis Wiese earned an associate's degree in computer science and pre-engineering from Lincoln Land Community College in Springfield, Illinois. He achieved both his bachelor's and master's in history from Illinois State University. While working full-time as the director of First Year Programs at Clemson University, Wiese earned his Ph.D. in educational leadership. In 2006, Wiese was appointed as a visiting professor for educational leadership at Clemson after working at the university in administration for six years. Wiese brought 13 years of orientation and first-year program experience when he joined the University of North Carolina at Charlotte as the assistant dean of students for New Student Programs. In 2009, he was promoted to lead and develop the Office of New Students and Family Services as the associate dean of students and director of the Office. In this position, he works extensively with new students and their families through both summer orientation programs and academic year initiatives including the Common Reading Program. He teaches both a first-year seminar and a course on leadership development. Wiese remains scholastically active as an associate editor for the *Journal of College Orientation and Transition* and maintains a research and publication agenda in the areas of student spirituality, attributes of academically high-achieving students, and application of student development theory in higher education.

Maureen E. Wilson is associate professor and chair of the Department of Higher Education and Student Affairs at Bowling Green State University. She worked previously at Mississippi State University, University of South Carolina, and the College of William and Mary. She holds a bachelor's degree from Aquinas College in Michigan, a master's degree from Michigan State University, and Ph.D. from Ohio State University. She currently serves on the governing board of ACPA—College Student Educators International and was named an ACPA Diamond Honoree. Wilson also received the NASPA Region IV-East Outstanding Contribution to Student Affairs through Teaching Award. Her current scholarship is focused on professional practice and socialization. The second edition of the *ASHE Reader on College Student Development Theory*, for which she serves as co-editor, is forthcoming.

Victor K. Wilson has a long and distinguished history of service to a variety of organizations and institutions. He began his college career at the University of Georgia (UGA) where he earned a bachelor's degree in social work and his master's degree in student personnel in higher education. Wilson has worked at Northern Arizona University and Agnes Scott College in addition to holding positions at UGA that included director of orientation, assistant director of admissions, assistant to the president, and associate vice president for student affairs. In June of 2004, he was appointed to his present position and joined the College of Charleston as executive vice president for student affairs. He has contributed leadership to several national organizations including the National Orientation Directors Association (NODA) and the American College Personnel Association (ACPA). Wilson has also contributed to the field through numerous presentations such as Imperatives for Further Learning: Discussions Between White and Black Men, Right or Wrong: The Power of Positive Ethics, and The Ever Changing Face of the African-American Male. Among his publications, he has authored *A Lesson in Black and White: Top Ten Tips for Black Students at Predominately White Institutions, Incorporating Crisis Planning and Management Into Orientation Programs, Staff Development,* and *Fostering Interracial Friendships on Campus: Taking it Up a Level.* Wilson's service and leadership activities extend outside the campus to the surrounding community. His efforts have been recognized with awards/honors such as the President's Award for Outstanding Service and Contributions to the National Orientation Directors Association, Outstanding Master's Graduate Award from UGA's Student Affairs Administration Program, and the naming of the Alumni Room after him at the UGA Sigma Phi Epsilon Fraternity House, which was dedicated in his honor in October 2001.

Abbey Wolfman is associate director of Orientation & First-Year Experience at Northern Illinois University. She is a 2001 graduate of the University of Minnesota where she served as New Student Weekend coordinator. Wolfman earned her master's degree in college student personnel at Western Illinois University and gained experience as a graduate assistant for the WIU orientation program. Her varied background includes working as a residence life coordinator, sorority house director, athletic advisor, and coordinator of student centers at institutions as diverse as Elmhurst College, the University of Mississippi, Montclair State University (New Jersey), and the University of Minnesota. Wolfman is a member of the National Association of Student Personnel Administrators (NASPA) and the National Orientation Directors Association (NODA), which she serves as a regional coordinator. She was the recipient of the 2007 Region V Outstanding New Professional Award. She also is the faculty advisor for both Sigma Nu social fraternity and Delta Gamma social sorority.